POLICE   STORIES

France during the first half of the nineteenth century. Map Collection, Sterling Memorial Library, Yale University.

POLICE STORIES

Building the French State, 1815–1851

John Merriman

OXFORD
UNIVERSITY PRESS

2006

Oxford University Press, Inc., publishes works that further
Oxford University's objective of excellence
in research, scholarship, and education.

Oxford   New York
Auckland   Cape Town   Dar es Salaam   Hong Kong   Karachi
Kuala Lumpur   Madrid   Melbourne   Mexico City   Nairobi
New Delhi   Shanghai   Taipei   Toronto

With offices in
Argentina   Austria   Brazil   Chile   Czech Republic   France   Greece
Guatemala   Hungary   Italy   Japan   Poland   Portugal   Singapore
South Korea   Switzerland   Thailand   Turkey   Ukraine   Vietnam

Published by Oxford University Press, Inc.
198 Madison Avenue, New York, New York 10016

www.oup.com

Oxford is a registered trademark of Oxford University Press

Library of Congress Cataloging-in-Publication Data
Merriman, John M.
Police stories: building the French state, 1815–1851 / John Merriman.
   p. cm.
Includes bibliographical references and index.
ISBN-13 978-0-19-507253-2
ISBN 0-19-507253-7
1. Police—France—History—19th century. 2. Law enforcement—France—
History—19th century. 3. France—Politics and government—
19th century. I. Title.
HV8203.M46   2005
363.2'0944'09034—dc22   2005040656

9 8 7 6 5 4 3 2 1

Printed in the United States of America
on acid-free paper

For Peter Gay

ACKNOWLEDGMENTS

Undertaking a study like this has allowed me the pleasure of exploring some seventy departmental archives, each of which, as in the others in previous projects, has served as a happy starting point to further explore cities, towns, and villages. Such is the joy of archival research and of the enormous, wonderful regional variation that is France.

I have benefited greatly from reading the works of other historians who have studied aspects of policing in early modern and modern France. Clive Emsley's work on the police has been particularly inspiring, and I learned much from reading the studies of Steve Kaplan and Alan Williams on the police of eighteenth-century Paris; Robert Schwartz on the *maréchaussée* of the *généralité* of Caen during the eighteenth century; Howard Brown on the Directory and Napoleonic periods; Patricia O'Brien on the police in Paris during the first half of the nineteenth century; Marie Vogel's *thèse* on the police of Grenoble during the Third Republic; and the work of Pierre-Yves Saunier and Alexandre Nugues-Bourchat on Lyon.

I owe a considerable debt of gratitude to Ted Margadant (as on several occasions before) and David Troyansky, two good friends and talented historians. Both were extremely generous with their time, offering helpful suggestions on a text that was overly long and occasionally rambling. Jay Winter, Peter McPhee, Bob Schwartz, Howard Brown, and Carol Merriman all offered suggestions here and there. Margit Kaye of Yale's wonderful Map Collection in Sterling Memorial Library provided a fine map that William Sacco at AM&T Media Services at Yale accommodated to publishing requirements. At Oxford University Press, Nancy Lane, my editor on other projects, first expressed interest in this book. Susan Ferber has been a wonderful editor with whom to work.

Much love and many thanks to Carol, Laura, and Christopher Merriman. At the University of Michigan, Chuck Tilly taught me to keep my eye on the big changes and the dynamics that helped produce them, while relishing the telling experiences of ordinary people.

This book is dedicated to Peter Gay, my close friend, longtime colleague at Yale University, and historian of unparalleled range, style, and generosity.

I have had the pleasure of spending a good part of the past eighteen years in the village of Balazuc in Ardèche in France, which has become home. In the archives in Privas a few years back, I came across a certain Joseph or Jean-Baptiste Bosq, a peddler, who was known as Jean (or John) the American and who makes an appearance in chapter 5. Thus it appears that I had something of a predecessor in Ardèche. The other Jean was arrested in Aubenas in 1827 because his passport (required for internal travel in France, at least for the poor) was not in order—he only had part of a passport and that had been stamped in Grenoble for a trip to Tournon in Ardèche, but he was rather off the route he had put forward to the authorities. I love meeting such people in the archives, and this book is about folks like that peddler and the policeman who arrested him.

Balazuc, December 22, 2004

CONTENTS

POLICE   STORIES

INTRODUCTION

The growth of the modern state and the police evolved hand in hand. During the first half of the nineteenth century, the police increased the reach of the centralized state in France's growing urban world. For most people, the "police" meant the *commissaires de police* (CPs), who are the principal focus of this study.[1] In July 1815, a month after the battle at Waterloo, the new subprefect of Châtellerault accurately described the commissaire de police as "the first instrument of the law, the man most directly tied to the measures that executive authority requires in a town so important by virtue of its population, commerce, and location."[2] In 1831, a rural schoolteacher and publican placed a pipe in the mouth of a bust of the CP of Nontron (Dordogne). The fact that there was a bust of a policeman is itself telling.[3] Note the remarkable stationary of the CP of the town of Rians in the Mediterranean *département* of the Var in 1834. It offers the highly dramatic but perhaps misleading image of the all-seeing eye, the gaze of the police in the service of the state (see Fig. 1).

The *gendarmerie*, the uniformed military force responsible to the ministry of war, could be summoned by civil authorities to back up CPs and assist troops as necessary. But they were principally rural police, the successors established in 1791 (by the law of February 16, 1791) of the *maréchaussée* of the Ancien Régime. Disagreements and rivalries between the CPs and gendarmes were not uncommon. Many towns had garrisons, large or small, but the use of soldiers to maintain order was generally limited to the repression of crowd action, such as grain riots and of course mass demonstrations and insurrections, including those in Paris and Lyon (the silk worker uprisings of 1831 and 1834), and in the Second Republic (the June Days, the insurrection of May 1849 in Paris, and the resistance to the coup d'état of December 2, 1851).[4] National guard units enjoyed only a brief revival in provincial cities in the aftermath of the Revolution of 1830, and again after that of 1848, after which many units were subsequently dissolved by the government of Louis Napoleon Bonaparte because they were considered politically unreliable.[5] For most people throughout the

3

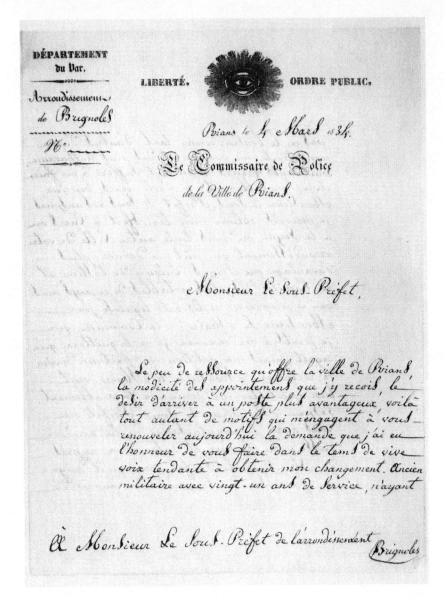

DÉPARTEMENT
du Var.
───
Arrondissement
de Brignoles
───
96°
───

LIBERTÉ.   ORDRE PUBLIC.

Rians le 4 e Mars 1834.

Le Commissaire de Police
de la Ville de Rians.

Monsieur le Sous-Préfet,

Le peu de ressource qu'offre la ville de Rians,
la modicité des appointemens que j'y reçois, le
désir d'arriver à un poste plus avantageux, voilà
tout autant de motifs qui m'engagent à vous
renouveler aujourd'hui la demande que j'ai eu
l'honneur de vous faire dans le tems de vive
voix tendante à obtenir mon changement. Ancien
militaire avec vingt-un ans de service, n'ayant

À Monsieur Le Sous-Préfet de l'arrondissement
Brignoles

FIGURE I.   Stationery of the commissaire de police, town of Rians, 1834. Courtesy of
the Archives Départementales du Var, 6M 8/1.

period in France's urban world, the face of the police belonged to the CP (see
Fig. 2).

Yet we know very little about the French CPs during the first half of the
nineteenth century, including the Restoration (1814–30), the July Monarchy
(1830–48), and the Second Republic (1848–51), important turning points in
the history of the French police. The preoccupation of historians with Paris,
and perhaps also the unsavory reputation of the police of that great city, has

dominated views of the institution. Historian Clive Emsley has aptly posed the question:

> Who were the police? For men who played a significant role in the preservation of the state and in collecting the material subsequently so thoroughly quarried by historians, remarkably little is known about the individuals who served as provincial commissaries de police. Nor has much work at all been done on how they viewed their responsibilities and the people with whom they dealt in their daily routines, nor on their relationships with their superiors. Ubiquitous the French police may have been—or that is certainly the impression which their superiors wished to give, and which many historians have accepted; but they remain largely faceless.[6]

The term *police* in French extends its meaning to the sense of policing as "control," affirming important continuities from the eighteenth century.[7] Delamare's *Traité de la police* in 1729 classified eleven areas in which the police intervened,

l'Audience d'un Commissaire de Police

Figure 2. The office of a commissaire de police, before whom stands a client. Courtesy of the Bibliothèque nationale de France.

suggesting that the very notion of police "seems extendable to infinity."[8] Steven Kaplan writes that "the extent of functions properly speaking of the 'police' is stupefying. . . . One need only recall the definition of the vocation of police given by Commissaire Lemaire: 'The science of governing men.'"[9] Writing of the *métier* he loved, Bertrand Cazeaux, CP in Tours, reflected in 1832 on the vast range of police authority: "The police concern themselves with each instant; their actions, extending to infinity, should be prompt, but often secret or hidden, are almost inevitably constituted by the daunting process of putting together fragments (of information). Policing is above all an administration of details."[10]

The system of policing that emerged from the French Revolution and the Empire (with telling antecedents in the Ancien Régime) expanded in provincial France during the period. Although major centers of industry like burgeoning St. Étienne, Lille-Tourcoing-Roubaix, and Paris were the exceptions in France during the first half of the nineteenth century, manufacturing was slowly but surely transforming other cities and towns, particularly their peripheries.[11] The number of CPs assigned to cities and sizable towns increased with their growth, and policemen were appointed to many small towns.

France was and remains a nation of diverse regions. At the time of the Revolution in 1789, French was spoken as a first language by only about half the population, and by the mid-nineteenth century little had changed. Minority languages and patois remained the preferred language of millions of people, even if most of them had reason to consider themselves French. Moreover, bilingualism remained common well into the twentieth century in many regions, including Provence, Languedoc, Brittany, Alsace, Lorraine, and Auvergne, as well as in parts of old Gascony and French Flanders. The police, who were increasingly not from the towns where they were assigned nor even necessarily from the same region, played a role in extending the reach not only of the state but also of a national culture that cut across regions. As they came to know the neighborhoods and small towns for which they were responsible, the CPs enforced the laws of and were increasingly identified with the French state. Even given important regional variations based in history, culture, and language, differences in policing between, for example, cities and towns in the Nord and those in the Charentes or Languedoc might still be noteworthy, but by the end of the period under consideration they would be less.

The Ancien Régime provided important antecedents for the development of the police during the first half of the nineteenth century. The CPs in eighteenth-century Paris demonstrated a spirit of *corporation,* purchasing their offices and in some important ways policing themselves.[12] The police there acquired "more men, more money, new equipment . . . and a new efficiency" during the reigns of Louis XV and Louis XVI. During the 1770s and 1780s, the lieutenants généraux stressed "duty, professional integrity and public service," as policing "became more centralized and more systematic."[13] Contemporary views of the police in Paris ranged from those viewing the house of the CP as "'the civil temple' evoked by the apologists for the police," or, with the rank of a magistrate, "an Olympian personage," to contemporary images attributing low status and venality if not outright corruption to the commissaires de police.[14]

The Revolution also established important foundations for the modern French police. The Declaration of the Rights of Man and Citizen (August 26, 1789) specified that "the guarantee of the rights of man and of citizen requires a *force publique*." The municipal law of December 14, 1789, and article three of Title XI of the Decree of August 16–24, 1790, established or defined police powers and obligations in the municipal and judicial domains, refined with considerably more precision in the *Code des délits et des peines* of 3 Brumaire, year 4. The police were "to maintain order and public tranquility, liberty, property, and individual security" (article sixteen), combining vigilance and respect for the law. These laws reflect apparent continuities with the Ancien Régime, with one significant difference: The police were now specifically charged with protecting the rights of the individual and of property.[15] The political policing of the Directory and particularly Napoleon's Empire reflected increasingly centralized techniques of policing.[16] Following Waterloo, the Restoration found in the centralized apparatus inherited from the Revolution and Empire a most useful way of watching its own enemies.[17]

The professionalization of the French police should be seen in the context of some notable occupations that would become part of modern life, including doctors, notaries, engineers, prefects, and magistrates.[18] As in these other professions, the professionalization of the CPs during the period 1815–51 brought standardized training and assessment of professional competency within the context of a hierarchical structure of authority and a sense of collective identity.[19]

By 1850, notes about service to "the profession" of the police were considerably more common, and regular reports mentioned whether or not the CP in question merited or sought "advancement" up the professional ladder. For example, the case for naming François Caubet, CP in Tulle (Corrèze), to the rank of *commissaire central* in Toulouse included "his attachment to the duties of his *profession* [emphasis added], his probity and abilities [which] can be very useful to the government." Moreover, to repeat, CPs were less likely to be from the same town or city in which they served; that more of them were appointed to posts far from their place of origin may also be taken as a sign of professionalization. So can new categories required for local reports on the CPs, asking for their level of education and the foreign languages they could speak. Early in 1851, the assessment of Claude Michel, CP in Villefranche (Haute-Garonne), noted that the former soldier and ex-gendarme had "sufficient education and abilities for the position he holds" and that he spoke German, although he did not desire—or merit—advancement. The steady flow of often extremely detailed reports assessing the performance of CPs to the ministry of the interior reflects the bureaucratization of a crucial institution.[20] By the end of the Second Republic, the oath of office taken by CPs before the mayor was referred to as a "professional oath." References by the CPs to their "careers" became far more frequent.[21]

During the Restoration and July Monarchy, the CPs began to develop a professional identity, before the reforms of 1854, which established the principle of a civilian police force, and the appearance a year later of the *Journal des commissaires de police* and policemen in Paris with their numbers on their collars, and before the Third Republic, when standards for recruitment and even competitive examinations were instituted.[22]

The question of professionalism itself is closely tied to the increased centralized control of the police by the French state, one of the central points of this study. If one of the original goals in the creation of a new police in 1789–90 had been to decentralize policing, the ultimate authority of the central government was recognized from the very beginning of the new regime, even if local interests still played a role in policing.[23] Control over the police continued to be an essential part of the struggle between the state and French municipalities, a contest that helped define the emergence of modern France.[24] Before the French police could achieve something of a balance between national/state imperatives and local needs and direction during the Third Republic, the French state first assumed preponderant control of the apparatus itself. The ministry of the interior appointed the CPs on the recommendation of the prefects and could transfer or fire them. The periodic reports submitted by the prefect that assessed the performance of CPs were sent to the ministry of the interior.[25]

Although most directly under the supervision of the minister of the prefects and ultimately the minister of the interior during the period we are considering, the CPs remained for the entire period in question subject to two other separate and at times competing authorities. As judicial authorities, they served warrants (*mandats*) issued by prosecuting attorneys (*procureurs généraux*) and were to otherwise help the *police judiciaire* as ordered. And as municipal employees, they were subject to the orders of the mayors of the towns in which they were employed.[26]

However, the ultimate responsibility or allegiance of the commissaires was not to the mayor, nor even to the ministry of justice, but to the prefect. Yet provincial municipalities were forced to pay the salaries of the CPs, despite the fact that the state would retain ultimate authority over policing. French towns with more than 5,000 inhabitants had a customs barrier (*octroi*), at which goods brought into town were taxed. Municipalities paid the salaries of CPs out of this revenue, which provided the bulk of municipal resources. The contradiction between local financing and ultimate government control did not limit the centralization and professionalization of the CPs, even if local police inevitably were influenced by local traditions and solidarities that could weigh more heavily on the police than they did on prefects, magistrates, army officers, and gendarmes. The original thrust of the law of 1789 toward decentralization was reversed, above all in 1800 by the law of 28 pluviôse, year 8. This granted control of the municipal police to mayors but gave prefects the power to dismiss mayors and deputy mayors, who were named by the state. The decree of 5 Brumaire, year 9, left the CPs dependent on the ministry of police; when that institution disappeared in 1818, this dependence passed to the office of the ministry of the interior. Prefects effectively appointed and oversaw the commissaires and could fire them at any moment. They could override the mayors, even if the latter oversaw the daily routines of policing French cities and towns.[27]

In principle, the professionalization of the police should also include political neutrality. Yet policing and politics were inextricably linked. A CP posted in Lons-le-Saulnier (Jura) in 1831 reflected the contradiction between in principle being neutral while representing the government that hired him. In his view, the CPs were to be "the citizens who are the most attached to the government, and who are the most vigilant (in its interests) and the most devoted to the state. They are sentinels placed in each locality who watch over everything; nothing is indifferent to them, because like the Gallic rooster (they remain) ever alert at the expense of their sleep to assure the security, tranquility, and happiness of their fellow men."[28] The police have been accurately described as "the advanced sentinel of (those in) power . . . intimately part of the political system."[29] A police official in 1814 asked rhetorically, "Without the ministry of police, how would one know the movement of society, its needs, its deviations, the state of opinion, the errors and the factions which agitate minds?"[30] Each regime looked to the police to provide precisely this kind of information. CPs often found themselves engaged in political policing, following the orders of centralized state authority.[31] A manual for police in the early 1850s stated unequivocally that the most important duty of a commissaire was to discover the "enemies of the government."[32] Political police reports were to be marked confidential and sent directly to the prefect in sealed envelopes. Other, less important reports were to be sent every five days or so, with a report at the end of each month, which was to include a list of contraventions and the result of each judgment. In a revolutionary nation in the "rebellious century," each successive regime's fear of insurrection considerably influenced the work of the police.

Thus the police had the reputation of being anything but neutral. This was particularly true during several crucial periods: in the first years of the Restoration; following the assassination of the Duc de Berri in 1820; as liberal opposition accelerated in what turned out to be the Bourbon's last two years in power; during the first several years of the July Monarchy, which brought the rise of organized republicanism that would characterize and ultimately help bring the downfall of the Orleanist monarchy; and during 1849–51, when the Montagnards of the Left fell victim to Louis Napoleon Bonaparte's *chasse aux rouges.*

During the Restoration, liberals in the capital had reason to have lost all confidence in the police. They criticized the close ties of the prefect of police, Guy Delavau, who had been named in the surge of Ultra appointments in 1821 (the Ultras on the extreme right accepted no compromise with the Revolution), to reactionary clericalism (it was said that *inspecteurs* had to attend Mass and obtain a *billet de confession*), and what seemed to be police obsession with political surveillance, complete with a veritable battalion of police spies (*mouchards*).[33]

The police were widely perceived as representing and enforcing the interests of those in power.[34] Although liberal denunciations of attacks against individual liberties during the last years of the Restoration had helped bring about that regime's collapse during the *Trois glorieuses* of July 1830, the new Orleanist monarchy reestablished political policing with barely more than a pause, if that. In political policing, things went on as before.[35] "What they do for Justice, they do also for the government," Balzac wrote of the police, "in political matters they are as cruel and as partial as the late Inquisition."[36] Thus, Stendhal's Lucien Leuwen is greeted in Caen, where he has been sent to work against the candidacy of the liberal Charles de Rémusat: "Down with the spy, down with the commissaire de police! Look at him! Look at him! There is this little pipsqueak of a policeman, sent from Paris to spy for the prefect."[37] During the July Monarchy, some 25,000 political dossiers accumulated, along with about 60,000 individual *bulletins* in alphabetical order of those who had been condemned for violations of various laws. By the time the *hôtel de ville* burned in May 1871, the number of registers that had accumulated since 1790 had reached about 10 million.[38] Many contemporaries denounced the CPs for their obsession with political repression and, increasingly, in particular the surveillance and containment of workers.

No figure contributed more to the unfortunate reputation of the police, at least in Paris, during the Restoration and July Monarchy than François Vidocq, the "escaped convict" who had been a criminal and then a mouchard and who ran the *Sûreté de police* from 1812 until 1827 (when Delavau fired him), employing many former convicts. The publication of Vidocq's memoirs the following year only increased public fascination with the police.[39] The police suffered the damning reproach, "One becomes a policeman when one can't do anything else."[40]

In 1835, the *Nouveau Dictionnaire de Police* reminded the police that while "watching over the safety of honest and law-abiding people, even toward offenders, they must discard anger and brutality, and set against any aggravation the calm which should always accompany the rule of law."[41] Yet the police in Paris and Lyon were particularly unpopular, widely accused of venality, violence, and arbitrary arrests, resented by ordinary people.[42] Thus in France's two largest cities, potentially any incident could spring out of control. [43]

Small wonder, then, that in the February Revolution of 1848, Parisian crowds turned quickly against the police, particularly the municipal guards, unleashing pent-up hostility. Calls were heard for a "purely civil" police, neutral and preventive, citing the model of policing in London.[44] During the Second Republic, political policing again became increasingly predominant. Yet again, a change in regime brought an obsession in the ministry of the interior with political policing.[45] At such times, the routines of daily policing in any provincial town could be overwhelmed by orders from Paris transmitted through the prefecture, not the *mairie*. The intermittent politically inspired purges of the police could intervene with total devastation to end a policeman's career. Yet political policing was just one of the duties of the CPs, a preoccupation that waxed and waned depending on political circumstances.[46] For the most part, the police in provincial cities had other preoccupations, as we shall see.

As police authority became more centralized, to what extent did the police systematically try to control the lives of ordinary French men and women, some of whom we will meet? Michel Foucault's influence has been strongly felt in work on policing in modern France. Foucault quotes one description of the authority of the police of Paris in 1720: "Police power must oversee everything that happens."[47] Consider again the watchful eye on the stationery of the town in the Rians, symbol of omnipresence (Figure I). Foucault has the police helping capitalism impose its own order by expanding the regulation of social life. By this view, the police helped "discipline and punish" ordinary people, "discipline effectively being 'a political anatomy of detail.'" Order is achieved by discipline, not by confrontation with the "forces of order," however much the latter were prepared to intervene violently. Thus, the eye becomes to Foucault an appropriate image for police surveillance, "permanent, exhaustive, omnipresent," and then classifying:

> The distance between "above" (authority) and below (society) is thus reduced by the principle of the microscope extended to politics, by the view from above. If it is true that he observes, the policeman, whose function it is to survey, should above all take notes and write up reports. His observation is blind and empty: it is a look that surveys the banal as the extraordinary. He is attentive to all below. . . . Just as the police finds itself between the state—with its centralized administrative apparatus—and society, it slides between investigation and inspection.[48]

In this sense, surveillance "should be considered a faceless gaze (*regard*) that transforms the entire social body into a field of vision (*perception*); thousands of eyes placed everywhere, everywhere attentive and always alert, a long hierarchical network."[49] By this view, the line to the modern video surveillance camera can be readily drawn.

Foucault's influence can, for example, be easily seen in Arlette Farge's description of eighteenth-century Paris. The street, the "only refuge" for the poor who had "no where else to go," seemed threatening to the wealthy by virtue of its unpredictability, replete with "the steamy sensuality of life, its instantaneous excitability, its emotional tide of impressions and sensations . . . (from which) surged energy, raw and mordant vitality." In such an account, the police, serving the interests of the elite, attempted to change habits of sociability, the goal being to "separate spaces," to divide and conquer in the volcanic Paris of the Ancien Régime. The police appear as part of a plan to "construct a productive and pacified space." This interpretation reflects the obsessive fear of the police that an incident, any incident, could spin out of control. Paris had by one count 8,500 riots during the eighteenth century.[50] In this scenario, the CP becomes something like a guard in Jeremy Bentham's Panopticon prison (or hospital, hospice, or school), representing "the architecture of surveillance," though without walls, which would make unnecessary vigilant, aggressive policing.[51]

To be sure, elite fears of crime helped justify increasing police intervention into the lives of ordinary people. Girod de l'Ain's reflections in the *Bulletin de Paris* on August 17, 1830, had demonstrated amazingly little awareness of the public mood or even memory of the very recent events that had brought the Orleanists to power. In his description, the revolutionary crowd was nothing more than a mob: "It is probable that most of the people who participate in these riots are cheats and vagabonds motivated only by the possibility of plunder and theft. Perhaps among them are some who are paid by the enemies of the government to incite the population to trouble public tranquility."[52]

Many people of means took begging as the first step toward criminality, reflected by the definition provided in the *Instruction sur le service journalier de la garde municipale de Paris* (1847), approved by Delessert, which defined the urban poor as "most often thieves."[53] We see much of this view in Louis Chevalier's classic study of Paris during the first half of the nineteenth century, brilliant and convincing on elite views of the poor, in which insurrection and indeed revolution are seen as extensions of purse snatching. Watching potential revolutionaries becomes another dimension of protecting bourgeois property. Honoré Frégier, who served as an official during the July Monarchy, associated poverty with crimes committed by the "dangerous classes," holding that the intervention of the state in social life was absolutely necessary to stem the spread of disease through contagion.[54] Thus to Frégier, the humble CP had a crucial role in preserving society from moral and physical corruption: "The commissaire de police . . . is a censor of working-class areas . . . invested with a kind of patronage that comes from his position, much more than from the law itself."[55] In dealing with the wandering, begging poor, the provincial CPs, following the lead of the governments they served, developed and followed a set of basic practices intended to limit geographic mobility. Yet French CPs were too experienced, too shrewd, to consider the mass of ordinary people to be, in the words of Clive Emsley, historian of the police, "an undifferentiated agglomeration."[56] Moreover, the police faced important constraints, including the "lack of material resources, occasional popular resistance when the police seemed to be defying the local sense of how things had always been done, and legal procedures themselves."[57]

The "policing" of France is a vast subject, of which the police themselves are just one component. We will meet some of the people whom they encountered in a variety of settings that range from the customs barriers of their towns and shabby rooming houses (*garnis*) to markets, cafés, cabarets, and theaters. The role of the police in the regulation of ordinary travelers rich and poor, market entertainers and merchants, as well as mediation in brawls and domestic disputes, the investigation of thefts, and the control of crowds bring us into the varied world of nineteenth-century French provincial cities and towns. And in the case of begging and prostitution, among other ways that poor people survived, we shall see that the police took a markedly different approach to outsiders than they did to those who lived in the cities and towns for which they were responsible.

We will enter the world of the police and the people they encountered in the cities and towns in which they were assigned. The chapters that follow discuss the institutional structures of the police (chapter 1); career patterns (chapter 2); the reality of political purges and dismissals for incompetence, in the context of the professionalization of the *métier* (chapter 3); the policing of social protest and political dissent (chapter 4); the policing of outsiders (chapter 5); the policing of daily life (chapter 6); and finally the largely one-sided struggle tensions between municipalities and the state over control of the police in the context of the victory of state centralization (chapter 7).

Many of the rich dossiers of the CPs may still be found in Paris and in *archives dé-partementales* (one of the benefits for historians of the centralization of the French state).[58] I have tried in this study to pay close attention to the rich, telling language in these reports that permit the analysis and evocation of the experience of these privileged observers during a time of great change.[59]

I often leave it to the commissaires speak for themselves, as they described their routines of daily life, their hopes, fears, and careers, and the people they encountered. They would have insisted on this. I have a story to tell because they had fascinating stories to relate. Police records and reports allow us to follow a distinctive social type in provincial French towns, the CP, whose mentality, daily activities, and career ambitions tell us much about continuities and changes in French society and politics in the nineteenth century.

Yet police reports must be read and considered with care. Writing of the First Empire, Richard Cobb warns, "Evidence from police sources reveals much more about the attitudes and assumptions of the repressive authorities than it does about popular attitudes and motivations and popular movements as such. . . . A police that informs will slant its information to the authorities to be informed, it has to be careful about the choice of its information, and will generally seek to please; a police that rules can create its own information, it can even create events." Cobb cautions against "the French disease, which is to read into every assumption and every interpretation of the French police and of the French authorities a depth of calculation and guile that may never have existed."[60] Like Cobb, I am also more interested in the routines of daily life and the richness and variety of French urban life than the spectacular moments of political contention, for example, before and following the Revolutions of 1830 and 1848. Yet I insist that fundamental coherence may be found in the story of the police during this exciting period of change. The dossiers and reports of the CPs of provincial France provide us with a rare opportunity, not to be missed, to stroll through the complex, varied, and changing urban world of French cities during the first half of the nineteenth century.

1

THE SYSTEM

The commissaires de police of the nineteenth century followed to some extent in the footsteps of their predecessors in Paris during the Ancien Régime. Policing in France had been most organized in Paris since 1667 under the direction of the lieutenant-général of police.[1] Arguably the creation of the post of lieutenant-général in 1667, against the backdrop of the Fronde and waves of tax riots, began the long process of centralization that eventually characterized policing in France during the first half of the nineteenth century. During the eighteenth century, forty-eight commissaires, policeman whose origins can be traced to the Middle Ages, watched over the city, including the *gardes françaises* and the Swiss Guards. The CPs purchased their offices, but took office only after the corps found them acceptable and the *procureur du roi* at the Châtelet had completed an investigation of their character and behavior.[2] They were investigative magistrates for the Châtelet, and in provincial towns the CPs performed the judicial functions of *bailliage* or *présidial* judges. Richard Cobb notes that if the revolution of July 1789 may have been due in part to Paris being underpoliced, "There would never be another occasion in French history when it could be said that Paris was under-policed."[3]

Yet no uniform system of urban policing really had existed in eighteenth-century France. The *parlements* controlled the police in the larger provincial towns, where policing remained primarily the responsibility of the local municipal authorities.[4] Lyon had only 200 guards, not many for a city of such size, Grasse only six. The 4,000 cavaliers of the *maréchaussée,* who first began its patrols in the sixteenth century, were responsible for rural policing, although they worked with urban authorities as well.[5]

Several of the *cahiers de doléances* in 1789 had called for an improvement in better policing.[6] The revolutionaries set out to sweep away the police system of the Ancien Régime, which had become identified with arbitrariness, inefficiency, venality, and corruption. The Revolution brought the end of the lieutenant-général de police in Paris, replaced on July 15, 1789, by a provisional committee of twenty members. The police of Paris were placed under the authority of the municipality, where they would remain until the beginning of the year 3.[7] The law of May 21–June 27, 1790, again divided the capital into forty-eight sections, each under the surveillance of a CP, who would be elected in each section for two years.[8] Yet despite these changes, overall the Revolution strengthened the centralizing system of police that had developed during the Ancien Régime, making further sense of Alexis de Tocqueville's insistence on the determining role of the centralization of state authority by absolute monarchs. At the same time, the police arguably became less tolerant, more bureaucratic.[9]

The law of September 21–29, 1791, authorized the establishment of CPs "in the towns of the kingdom where their presence is judged necessary, in the opinion of the departmental administration." Elected by active (that is, property-owning) citizens, they were charged with executing "the laws of municipal and correctional police, and they can make arrests in criminal matters."[10] The law authorized municipalities "with the approval of departmental authorities to assign to them the functions that are compatible with power delegated to municipalties."[11] During the last stages of the Terror in 1794, the Comité de sûreté générale assumed the right to name and fire commissaires. The following year, municipalities obtained this right, one that they held through the Directory. The hierarchy of authority that developed during the Revolution and Empire left the CP subject to several separate authorities. Departmental authorities were empowered to set the amount of the salaries of commissaires, which were to be paid by the commune in which they functioned. This stood in contrast with gendarmes, who were paid by the state because they were technically military personnel. Thus this early legislation emphasized the municipal functions of the black-suited CPs.

The 1791 legislation had first established the competence of CPs within the judiciary. The *Code d'instruction criminelle* instructed them to send *procès-verbaux* of crimes and misdemeanors to the *procureurs*.[12] Moreover, article 8 of the criminal code authorized them to search for the authors of crimes, misdemeanors, and contraventions; to gather proof; and deliver those they had arrested and proof to the courts. Affirming the continuities between regimes, a circular in 1817 reiterated the judicial responsibilities and status of the commissaires, who had to understand his role vis-à-vis the various tribunals. CPs had the powers to arrest, interrogate, and release suspects for misdeeds that were punishable by a fine up to three days of wages or three days in jail. Thus, increasingly they came to see themselves as magistrates. In a case in Lyon in 1831, the CPs "were outraged by the fact that during a session at the tribunal they were attributed the same status as gendarmes, thus depriving them of their title of magistrate."[13]

On 12 nivôse, year 4 (January 2, 1796), the Directory created a ministry of police (ministère de la police générale). Its goal was political: "To establish a rigorous surveillance that will discontent the factions and foil the plots against liberty." The wily Joseph Fouché was appointed in July 1799 to the post he would hold for a decade, "the machiavellian master of an all-powerful imperial police with a tentacular network of spies and informants."[14]

The establishment of the prefecture of police in Paris in 1800 reflected the primacy of the capital as the central focus for policing. The prefect of police sent the names of those nominated to serve as CPs to the ministry of police.[15] However, the constitution of year 8 left it to the first consul—that is, Bonaparte—to appoint the police, although in practice in consultation with Fouché. The imprint of the centralizing thrust of policing in France would remain strong, closely linked to the determination of each subsequent regime not to go the way of those that had preceded it. The ministry of police was abolished in 1818 (under pressure from liberals), but police générale continued within the ministry of the interior.[16]

Napoleon included the reorganization of the police as one of the "several blocks of granite" that would form the base of his regime.[17] The law of 28 pluviôse, year 8 (February 17, 1800), established prefectoral supervision of local policing, made the appointment of a CP obligatory in towns with more than 5,000 inhabitants—that is, about the size of a modest market town in a country in which beginning in 1841 any nucleated settlement of 2,000 people was considered to be urban. Another commissaire was in principle to be added for each additional 10,000 inhabitants. It established an urban hierarchy based on population that determined which towns had to have CPs and how many. This law thus established the precedent for determining the salaries of CPs, again following a hierarchy of the size of the towns in which they would serve. The result was to create a career ladder within the police. The decree of 17 Floréal, year 8 (May 7, 1800), established the uniform of the commissaires, which was to included a tricolor sash emblematic of his authority (the tricolor disappeared with the advent of the Restoration, during which the color was often blue, but returned in 1830).[18]

In 1800 the first prefects were sent from Paris to the départements. These *hommes du gouvernement* became the cornerstone of the centralized Napoleonic state, which sets French history apart from most of its European rivals and neighbors. Here, too, a career ladder existed, with varying salaries, a ladder analogous to the considerably smaller ladder of the CPs, who would serve under their authority.[19] But there was one very important difference: The state paid the salaries of the prefectoral corps, whereas the municipalities were responsible for paying the salaries of the CPs assigned to their town. Instructions from the commissaire général de police on June 8, 1811, reminded the mayors that they should only receive from the CP reports concerning municipal policing, "except in matters in which they compete with you."[20] Thus, a distinction had emerged between municipal policing under the direction of the mayor—that is, making sure that municipal regulations, for example, sweeping in front of buildings, not blocking streets with wagons, properly disposing of garbage, and so on—judicial police, answering to the senior local magistrate; and "administrative" policing, including political policing, under the direction of the prefect. Urban policing tasks provided justification for forcing the towns to pay for the police there employed.

As a result of the Revolution and the Empire, the reach of the state unquestionably increased in provincial France. The number of gendarmes, who were under military authority, had increased by four times, reaching 18,000 men in

1815. Almost all towns with more than 5,000 inhabitants now had a CP, and larger towns and of course cities more than that. Such police presence thus gave, in Clive Emsley's words, "the French people a greater awareness of the state, particularly the state's demands and its claims to impose and to maintain its definition of order."[21]

The Restoration left in place the administrative organization of the police shaped by Bonaparte. Prefects (often on the recommendation of the subprefects but sometimes on that of mayors) provided a list of three names, with the first choice usually approved in Paris. CPs were named by the king through the ministry of general police until 1818, and, on the abolition of that ministry that year, by the minister of the interior (with the exception of those in Paris, where they were appointed by the prefect of police).

The Revolution accentuated the construction of an urban hierarchy in France, one based on population but also strongly influenced by urban function (such as market towns and administrative centers).[22] Yet by establishing arbitrary demographic criteria, the law of 1800 left several departmental capitals (chef-lieux) without a CP because their populations fell below the minimum of 5,000 inhabitants. Several departmental capitals still did not have CPs, including Privas, at least until 1823. In Montbrison, the chef-lieu of the Loire (until 1856, when St. Étienne became the departmental capital), the municipal council in 1820 at first refused to allocate funds to pay for a CP. Because Montbrison's population fell short of 5,000, the council was within its (limited) rights.[23]

Yet during the 1815–51 period, the system of urban policing expanded considerably: Larger towns acquired more CPs (although not necessarily as many as legislation in principle required), and commissaires were named to small towns that previously had not had one. At the same time, however, some towns during the Restoration implored the ministry of the interior to reduce the number of their CPs to save funds.[24]

During the Restoration and July Monarchy, some towns with fewer than 5,000 inhabitants had CPs appointed to them in special circumstances, as we shall soon see, provided the municipal council was willing or could to forced to allocate funds to pay for a CP.[25] Thus, the arbitrary demographic threshold of 5,000 established in 1800 had to be adjusted because of other considerations, including the location of a town or its social composition. In such cases, the interests of the state and the perceived interests of such small-sized municipalities did not necessarily correspond. Marennes (Charente-Inférieure) had only 2,400 inhabitants at the time of the promotion of its agent to the rank of CP in 1820. Travelers going to the Ile d'Oléron passed through, and so did a large number of beggars.[26] When Bourgoin (Isère) lost its CP in 1831 because he was called into military service and several municipal council members suggested that the town could get along without one, thus saving some money, the mayor joined the subprefect in arguing that a CP was needed because Bourgoin was "too exposed to numerous and frequent comings and goings" to do without a CP.[27] Likewise, a CP, with the meager salary of 400 francs, was appointed to Lambesc (Bouches-du-Rhône), a town with 4,000 inhabitants located on the well-traveled road from Aix to

Avignon. When the prefect of the Creuse expressed his opinion in 1814 that Aubusson should have a CP, he argued that although its population was only 4,000 inhabitants, it seemed like a teeming agglomeration in the rural Creuse, with markets and fairs and "a great many workers" producing the famous Aubusson tapestries. When Aubusson welcomed its first CP two years later, the municipal council could allocate only 400 francs in salary. The first *titulaire,* transferred from the Nord, could only survive by taking another job, and he left many of the tasks of policing to the mayor and his deputy. The post was then eliminated. However, five years later, as Aubusson's population inched toward 5,000, the ministry appointed another commissaire.[28] Cosne (Nièvre) requested the appointment of a CP in 1815, to replace the deputy mayor who had been saddled with the task for a year. Cosne was the distribution center for most of the wood sent downstream to Paris, and the town attracted workers whose transience caused authorities anxiety.[29]

Thus the location of towns counted for much. Rumor had La Charité, another Loire River town, losing its CP, although it had 6,000 residents (despite the fact that the mayor had cleverly managed to have the town's population counted at fewer than 5,000, so that it did not have an octroi, making him a local hero). But La Charité retained its policeman by virtue of its location as the meeting point of four major routes and site of a major grain market. Furthermore, it had the only bridge that crossed the Loire between Nevers and Gien.[30]

Some municipal councils did not want to allocate funds to pay for a commissaire de police. Nowhere was resistance more marked than in Corsican towns. Bonifacio, on the island's southern tip, cried out for policing. In 1836, the subprefect, supporting the nomination of a CP, invoked Bonifacio's proximity to Sardinia, a short but extremely treacherous journey across the straits "where take refuge most of our criminals and from where come convicts who escape from various Sardinian prisons," and the constant commerce between the two islands. He instructed Bonifacio's mayor to convoke the municipal council to approve the necessary funds. Two months later, the council still had not met, leaving the subprefect to wonder whimsically if they had all fallen victim to illness. After more prodding, they met, but expressed its unwillingness to pay for a CP. In 1851, the prefect asked for government funds to supplement the council's modest allocation of 500 francs so that a CP could be appointed to watch for bandits trying to reach Sardinia.[31] By 1852, CPs could be found on Corsica in Ajaccio, Bastia, Calvi, Ile-Rousse, and Sartène.

Frontier towns had special claims on a CP, even if they had fewer than 5,000 inhabitants. Near the eastern frontier, many travelers passed through St. Louis (Haut-Rhin) on the way to or from Switzerland or the German states. The ministry paid the CP's salary until the post was suppressed in 1819.[32] In 1821, the government decided to create a post in Briançon, high in the Alps near the Piedmontese border, still standing as the town with the highest altitude in Europe. Briançon's budget was miniscule, and the ministry of the interior came through with the necessary funds.[33]

Some spa towns like Bourbonne-les Bains, with barely 3,000 inhabitants during the Restoration, also received CPs because their populations swelled considerably in season, attracting foreigners of means and also pickpockets, hustlers, and frauds. Likewise, the summer population of Bagnères in the Hautes-Pyrénées reached more than 15,000 people, including a good many Spanish refugees.[34] In 1842 Vichy, despite falling short of 5,000 inhabitants, received a CP, assigned to monitor the thermal season.[35]

During the first two years of the July Monarchy, at least twenty-eight towns with far fewer than 5,000 inhabitants received a commissariat.[36] In Ardèche, the largely Protestant town of Vallon Pont-d'arc, which was a center for democratic-socialist support, did not have a CP until 1850, when the municipal council requested that an appointment be made.[37] However, it was the rapid growth of cities and particularly the concentration of the working class in and around an urban nucleus that generated the most adamant calls for CPs. Officers undertaking military reconnaissances frequently expressed their surprise at the transformation of small towns like Elbeuf, "whose population increases every day, with superb factories popping up everywhere."[38] The ministry of the interior demanded the establishment of a commissariat in Fourchambault (Nièvre), which had about 5,000 inhabitants, including about 800 workers, some employed in two large metallurgical factories; furthermore, the town's location on a major departmental road attracted the feared "floating population."[39] With the development of France's railway network during the July Monarchy, new railroad towns—such as Laroche-Migennes (Yonne) and St. Germain-des-Fossés (Allier)—popped up or expanded at important junctures, bringing first transient workers and then voyagers. Indeed the origins of the *commissaires spéciaux* who assumed important roles in political policing during the Second Republic (and in subsequent regimes) may be found in official concern of the dangers believed inherent in the "nomadic" workers employed to build France's railroads, for example in Tours and Poitiers.[40] By 1849, St. Étienne had four CPs, and ten other towns in the Loire, the "cradle of the Industrial Revolution in France," had them as well.[41]

In this way, the overgrown villages surrounding the capital began to receive organized policing as the arrival of newcomers from the provinces turned them into towns. The factories of Corbeil, in the suburbs of Paris, attracted workers, leading the municipal council to ask for a CP in 1817. Although its population was below 5,000, Corbeil's location just beyond the capital attracted "the worse subjects of the capital, or those who make Corbeil and Essonnes stopover points on the way to Paris." Corbeil and Essonnes split the cost of a CP.[42]

During the period, the state extended police authority into the suburbs of many cities, the periphery of urban life increasingly considered threatening by urban elites and administrators.[43] The suburban communes on the edge of Nantes were so poor that they would not vote funds to pay for a commissaire. The most able CP in 1826 was assigned responsibility for the peripheral, sometimes turbulent hamlet of Ville-en-bois, which lay with its seemingly innumerable *auberges* and *guinguettes,* in the commune of Chantenay.[44] Doulon, St. Sébastien, Rezé, and Chantony were off-limits to convicts subject to surveillance of the *haute police* because they were relatively wide-open spaces, *le far-west français*. Châteauneuf approved a modest contribution to help pay for one of the CPs of Nantes to extend his territory, but St. Sébastien and Doulon did not have sufficient resources, and Rezé twice refused the prefect's request that they allocate funds to extend a commissaire's authority into their commune.[45]

The département of the Haute-Garonne provides an example of the multiplication of posts of CP during the period. In 1815, only four towns in Haute-Garonne had CPs: Toulouse, St. Gaudens, Villemur, and Revel. Villefranche was added in 1825, although the commissariat ended in 1831, returning in the Second Republic. By 1850, another ten towns had CPs: Besièges, Muret, Autrerive, Montesquieu-Volvesine, Boulogne, Montréjean, Bagnères-de-Luchon, Grenade, Foz, and Carman. In all, fifteen towns, including Toulouse, St. Gaudens, Villemur, Revel, and Villefranche, now had CPs, eleven more than in 1815. In the Var in that same year, nine towns already had CPs (including two in Toulon), because of the strategic importance of the département.[46] During the two-year period beginning in October 1830, the July Monarchy named CPs to at least twenty-eight small towns in twenty-one different départements; these ranged in population from 3,223 (Raon-L'Étape in the Vosges) to 1,422 (Aire in the Landes).[47]

Conditions of Work

CPs were divided into six classes, each drawing a commensurate annual salary. The classes corresponded to the size of the cities and towns to which they were assigned. Paris led the way, the ultimate goal for every ambitious CP, whether he patrolled in obscurity in distant St. Gaudens in the Pyrénées or in isolated Mende in the Lozère, an honorable post of some prestige like Poitiers or Orléans, or had reached the big-time of Toulouse, Nantes, or Strasbourg.[48]

During the Restoration and July Monarchy, salaries ranged from the pathetic 300 francs paid early in the Restoration to the CP in Neufchâteau (Vosges) to 600 francs in St. Gaudens (Haute-Garonne) to the 1,800 francs paid the CPs of Toulouse and Montmartre during the Restoration, 2,400 francs in Lyon and Bordeaux, to the 3,000 to 6,000 francs enjoyed by the police of Paris. In Lyon, at least one CP in 1833 employed a domestic servant (although the wages of the latter were notoriously low, and many families of modest means had servants). With such salaries, most CPs scrimped along in hope of a promotion that would bring them some more money. By way of comparison, the bare minimum salary for a primary school teacher was 600 francs after the Guizot Law of 1833, of which only 200 francs was guaranteed—paid by the municipal council—with the rest in principle to be paid by the parents of pupils who were not classified as "indigents."[49] Constraints on the salaries of CPs reflect the contradiction inherent in a system whose employees worked for the centralized state but relied on local funding.

Some CPs also earned small sums for special duties, such as assisting tax officials and bailiffs, but these amounts, as in the case of Nantes, for example, rarely amounted to more than twenty francs a year. A CP in Nevers during the July Monarchy earned small sums for *exhumations* in the cemetery.[50] A few CPs were, like schoolteachers, lodged in the town hall or some other municipal building, but this arrangement was unusual. Most had to pay their own lodging expenses.[51] Occasionally CPs boldly asked for supplementary sums, citing, for example, the fact that they received no extra funds to compensate them for their work under the direction of judicial authorities (for example, delivering warrants). On receiving such a request in 1826 from CP Louis Vendeville, the municipal council of Coulommiers recognized that his salary was inadequate. Although the council and the subprefect thought well of him, he was regretfully informed that "the revenue of the town does not allow an increase in expenses."[52] From the booming port of Toulon in 1834, Cartier complained that in three years of police work he had arrested so many culprits that sometimes he had to testify at three court sessions a week and asked in vain for reimbursement of some of his expenses.[53] In Grenoble early in the Restoration, CPs received three francs every so often from the justice of the peace in the hope of encouraging "zeal."[54] In this regard, Versailles offered by far the best situation. In addition to 1,700 francs in salary and another 700 francs for his office expenses, Jean-François Blanchard received 1,650 francs in Versailles for helping protect the king. But there was only one Versailles. Moreover, Blanchard had an unusually good deal, as the kings had not lived in the château since the October Days of 1789.[55] However, it became increasingly rare for a CP to take home a special bonus for certain duties.

Occasionally CPs did receive small sums for certain accomplishments. François Hernot received a raise of 200 francs a year from the municipal council of Thionville for his actions to end popular protest during the hard times of 1817. Following the death of Schaueffle, who had served in Colmar, his widow received the exceptional sum of 500 francs from the state so she could pay the family debts and 300 francs to pay for the education of two of his daughters, a most unusual largesse that suggests his role in surveillance at the time of the military plots of 1820. And in Nantes in 1832, amid plots in the West to restore the Bourbons to the throne, the mayor asked for and received additional funds for each CP, 300 francs for the "most deserving."[56] A CP in Tours, recently assigned the post of patrolling St. Symphorien, a turbulent suburb across the Loire, penned a long, self-serving account in 1844, relating his trials and tribulations. The prefect's scrawled commentary (or that of one of his underlings) on the first page summed it up with cutting precision. The lengthy letter could be summed up as a "request for additional funds or a bonus of 200 francs, and from what funds?"[57]

A few CPs were in the very unusual situation of having supplementary income. Théophile Pons in Arles was helped by a fortuitous inheritance and Jean-Marie Verrye, named Pontivy's first CP in 1835, also had family money. Jean Caumont, CP in Lectoure (Gers) during the last three years of the Restoration, could afford to accept a post paying just 600 francs annually because a military pension swelled his annual income to 1,200 francs.[58] L.-F. Claverie, CP in

Toulouse during the Second Republic, was one of the fortunate few who married into money; his wife owned a property worth 20,000 francs.[59]

Some CPs managed to maintain other sources of income because their spouses ran small businesses. The wife of Brédif, CP in Châtellerault, operated a small private school, supplementing her husband's salary of 600 francs early in the Restoration. In St. Gaudens early in the Restoration, CP Thévenot continued to work as a surgeon, a position then with relatively low status. One of his successors, Joseph Adoue, tried to open a small workshop producing potassium, but was fired in 1823 before he could get the business going. The CP of Lavoulte (Ardèche) also served as the paid secretary of the town hall.[60]

However, some occupations were by their very nature deemed incompatible with police work, including serving as a notary, or operating a café or cabaret, or holding a commercial license (*brevet de commerce*). Thus, the CP named to Montbrison in 1817 had to give up his small store, because he would be in the rather awkward position of having to police his own business.[61] The interdiction of other remunerative activities was in itself a step in the history of professionalization.

The vast majority of CPs were married, family men who struggled to make ends meet.[62] CP requests for more money ring with a desperation only surpassed by their letters dramatically expressing their situation should they lose their jobs ("I would be reduced to shame and I would die of hunger and misery").[63] In 1843, the minister of the interior complained that a great number of CPs simply left their posts without authorization to go to Paris to ask the ministry of the interior for advancement or some other favor.[64] Jean-Marie de Gallemont in Poitiers, a former émigré and soldier wounded in 1792, was described in 1822 as being so poor that he was ill at ease in aristocratic Poitiers, despite the "de" he proudly carried with him.[65] The minister of the interior complained in 1837 that so many CPs in unimportant places were asking for promotion that the ministry required much more accurate information on their capacity to assess such requests.[66] On Corsica, Gaétan Rebora claimed to have brought more than 1,200 cases before the justice of the peace during the two years he had served as CP in Ile-Rousse, with 906 having resulted in some sort of penalty for those accused. The subprefect asked the municipal council to raise his salary. But the municipal council refused to do so. Rebora wrote with some bitterness about his "career"—an important reference in itself: "It is so unrewarding, in that it offers no chance for advancement, at least with a government whose arbitrariness dominates all the services and all considerations." The Revolution of 1848 brought Rebora hope. It alone "can save me from the oblivion in which I have been left for so many years," a typical complaint about the arbitrariness of the administration during the July Monarchy.[67]

Some prefects, as well as the CPs themselves, insisted that better policing could only be achieved by making the post more attractive through the augmentation of salaries. However, prefects and sometimes mayors as well were hamstrung by municipal councils that could or would not allocate more money and by the low pay scale set at the national level.

The low salary for CPs in small towns limited the number of capable applicants. Dussouchet-Renclos accepted appointment to Senlis in 1829 and then visited his new post incognito. Discovering that the miserable salary that awaited him was not to be supplemented by additional funds voted by the municipal council, he left town as quietly as he had arrived, never taking up the position.[68] With a small applicant pool for the post, more than a few CPs who would have been fired held on to their jobs. In Brioude (Haute-Loire), Faure's work brought official complaints. But who would come to Brioude for 800 francs a year? Not until Faure failed to prevent a public disturbance did he lose his job. His replacement, Barthélemy Gelly, must have been of some means; it was noted that his wife owned some silver, and he was lodged "very decently." But he, too, could not or at least did not want to live on 800 francs on what he considered a bump in the road between Clermont-Ferrand and Le Puy and resigned in 1829.[69]

Particularly difficult posts could make low salaries seem simply unbearable. After Joseph Peraldi was removed from his position in Ajaccio for having ignored his job and stood accused of raking in illegal sums, the prefect claimed that he had searched the entire population of Corsica's two largest towns in an attempt to find a replacement. "It is hardly likely," he complained, "that a Frenchman would agree to go to Corsica for such a modest salary." Louis Ruffin, appointed to Bastia, Corsica's other town of any size, in 1817, resigned three years later after the ministry of the interior rejected his request for additional monies. Ruffin provided an impressive list of the duties he had fulfilled. He had assisted health authorities in monitoring those arriving in port; helped customs officials; watched out for smugglers, "intriguers," and other "bad subjects"; carried out the tasks of municipal policing; and followed the orders of magistrates. He had exchanged relative comfort and the proximity of his family in distant Senlis, a world away, to police "a people naturally independent, difficult, and vindictive." His last trip home had been a nightmare; violent winds had turned a trip of two days into a miserable odyssey of twenty-five days, followed by an obligatory period of quarantine in Antibes. He earned only 1,200 francs a year but not the respect of the Corsicans. The prefect, while thinking that Ruffin exaggerated his duties at the port, believed the salary was too small. By the end of the Restoration, the salary for the CP of Ajaccio had reached 1,800 francs, which made it easier to find candidates for a difficult task among "this people so difficult to handle." In 1829, after serving five years as CP in Ajaccio and Bastia, Michel Meissonnier wrote, "The fever of this place took a terrible toll on me," comparing this time to the eleven military campaigns in which he had participated during the Napoleonic wars. On August 1, 1830, he disembarked after a visit to the mainland to learn that street fighting had broken out in Paris, a revolution that cost him his job three months later.[70]

CPs took no vacations. Prefects authorized leaves of absence (which had to be approved by the minister of the interior) for CPs to attend to family business for short period of times, but usually only granted them to those who had served a long time in the same place. The beleaguered Santelli in Bastia wrote in July 1832 that he needed to get away and wanted to spend time resting in a hamlet several kilometers away to rest, returning periodically to his post. The prefect rejected his plan for something of a paid vacation.[71]

CPs received a sum from the municipal council for office expenses. The amount, too, predictably depended on the size of the town in which they were employed, ranging from 800 francs allocated in Bordeaux to 600 francs in Toulouse to 200 francs in St. Gaudens. Some municipal councils cut back on the sum allocated for office expenses, such as in Bagnères (Hautes-Pyrénées) in 1829 where the municipality tried to eliminate such expenses entirely, before agreeing to maintain a smaller allocation on the budget.[72] Most police offices were in or near the town hall. In cities divided into *arrondissements,* some CPs had smaller offices—some also serving as their homes—in the district for which they were responsible.

In 1817 Toulouse had five CPs, nine inspectors, and four *sergents-de-ville* responsible for policing. The central police office stood at the Place du Capitole at the hôtel de ville. Despite the fact that the mayor believed that each CP should have an office in the *quartier* to which he was assigned, with an official seal and a lamp indicating their residence, police of all ranks came and went. A giant police register listing all crimes and misdemeanors stood ready to keep track of "all the events that could concern public security." An inspector was there at all times, assisted by one of the sergents-de-ville. The commissaires at the main office at the Place du Capitole handed out orders to the inspectors and agents, who monitored the markets, departure and arrival of boats, hotels and rooming houses, theaters, and public gatherings of any kind, as well as undertook night patrols. One CP was assigned to the mayor's office, and the other four each took responsibility for an arrondissement. All five would meet at the mairie at three in the afternoon to report on the previous twenty-four hours.[73]

Toulouse had a special kind of corps of *surveillants* during the Restoration. It consisted of merchants and artisans who had long had responsibility for watching over the quartier in which they lived. The *dixainiers* were a particularly *toulousain* institution that dated back centuries. Each of these *hommes de confiance* was to alert the CP when the latter's services were required in the quartier. The dixainiers provided information requested by the mayor or departmental authorities, assessed taxes, arranged as necessary for the lodging of troops, broke up brawls, and reported disorders. Traditionally every ten families provided one dixainier, and every hundred families a *centanier,* an officer of the corps. Each dixainier had surveillance of a *mulon,* a group of about twenty houses. In 1817, 400 dixainiers could be found at least on the books in Toulouse, unpaid and without any distinctive sign of any authority, but exempt from service in the national guard and from having to lodge troops. The decline of the dixainiers reflected the growing role of the police as a professional corps.[74]

We enter Toulouse's tiny central police office in 1819, a small, noisy room about eighteen by twelve feet. Half of it was taken up by the desks of the five policemen, "sometimes surrounded by thirty plaintiffs or witnesses who howl or argue in the office, as in a market, without any consideration for the *magistrats de police* who are in front of them." One day a CP had before him a couple who accused a married man and father of having corrupted their young daughter, who stood at their side. Next to them was an older woman who claimed that her niece, who accompanied her, had been impregnated by a married man. The CP concluded that the charge was false, because the niece had not previously come forward and perhaps because he believed the accused *père de famille,* who denied the accusation and claimed that the young woman had told him that she had "known several other men before him and would name them." Also demanding the CP's attention was a woman who had come with her three children to complain that her husband was squandering the twenty-five *sous* that he earned per day as an apprentice miller. Close by, another of his colleagues was listening to the impassioned story of a young married woman who had wanted to "end a relationship she had with a young man," at which point the latter had made off with the contents of her wardrobe. The accused man had brought with him several witnesses who denied the woman's claims. Elsewhere in the by then very uncomfortable room another colleague had before him five or six people, each of whom had a variety of tales of mistreatment to relate.[75]

Gradually during the period under consideration, police offices were stocked with the tools of the trade. This helped CPs follow the impetus of the state to develop routinized procedures. When in 1829 Gabriel Baille took the oath of his office as commissaire in Paris, he found in his new office the four volume *Dictionnaire de police moderne* (1829) compiled by Julien Alletz, a former typographer and CP; eight boxes of copies of laws, ordinances, and regulations along with three notebooks of recent additions to the law; a register of the *livrets* held by workers, domestics, and coachmen; twenty brochures on a variety of topics; the *Annales de l'industrie nationale;* a *Tableau des boulangers*; two small volumes of police ordinances on transportation; and the *Instructions du procureur au Roi* for 1817; in addition to office materials, such as pens, paper, and seals.[76] When the general secretary of the prefecture in the Rhône went to the hôtel de ville to carry out an inventory of the two-room police office in 1822, he found enormous registers of people arrested since year 6, registers listing everyone who had been incarcerated, however briefly, in the *maison d'arrête* and the prison of St. Joseph; a register of ex-convicts under surveillance, as well as others placed under surveillance in other police cases since 1811; a collection of legislative laws from 1789 until the creation of the *Bulletin des lois,* and copies of the latter until 1813 (when the government ceased sending it for free); lists of hotel registers and foreigners who had arrived since August 1815; two boxes of blank passports, fourteen boxes of passports, that had been deposited but never retrieved, three cartons of passports left in exchange for *cartes de sûreté,* and a register of passports stamped by the ministry of police and the Division générale de la police since August 1, 1815; various lists of indigent passports and cartes de sûreté handed out; and an enormous register of correspondence.[77] The appearance of instruction manuals for the use of CPs was a sign of increased professionalization. So was the increased use of police stationary, as in 1824 in Niort, with the heading "commissaire de police and official of administrative and judicial police of the town of Niort."[78]

In Rouen, the prefect recommended Alletz's dictionary to the mayors of the towns of his department. It provided models of reports, which he hoped would enhance police uniformity. The mayor of Rouen took the hint, ordering several copies.[79] Alletz's helpful dictionary was not the last such effort. In 1844, Houzé, a

CP in Lille, produced a "Manuel de police pour la ville de Lille" (amended and augmented thirteen years later).[80] Like that of Alletz, it was organized alphabetically: *abattoir public, abreuvoirs, accotemens des chaussées et chemins,* and so on. Citing relevant legislation, *accouchement, art d'* informed policemen that declarations of birth should be made by midwives, doctors, *officiers de santé,* and all other persons who assisted a birth within the delay specified by article 55 of the civil code, noting penalties for failure to do so as given by article 346. For the case of *aliénés* (the mentally disturbed), relevant laws and a royal decree in 1839 were noted, along with instructions that the prefect had given in 1838 (which gave this particular dictionary a local context, although such instructions often merely duplicated or reflected those coming from Paris). As for "ferocious animals," those leading them "should follow major routes without deviating from them." A CP would then move on to *attroupement,* participation in which violated various laws promulgated in 1789, 1791, and the early 1830s. *Aubergistes,* along with *caffetiers, traiteurs,* and *restaurateurs,* could not serve "people who are drunk," with reference to a municipal ordinance dating from 1821. Bakers merited the longest series of laws, articles, and ordinances, relating to "the baking of bread of various quality," "types of bread," "merchants," "prohibited substances and those employed in their production." Ducks, pigs, chickens, and other poultry were not supposed to "circulate on the public way," by virtue of a municipal ordinance of 1839. Peddlers could not knock on doors without prior authorization of residents, nor buy gold, silver, jewelry, or clothes from "suspicious or unknown people or those for whom no one can vouch." Houzé's dictionary cited relevant legislation and decrees constraining the performances of "traveling actors," regulating the ringing of church bells, noting that mayors could ban public religious ceremonies. Houses were to be numbered five inches above the door in the color that each quartier had adopted. Police were to know that horses could not gallop in town and that those moving to Lille had to appear within three days at the town hall to change residences officially. Regulations establishing conditions for Belgian workers (including exchanging their passports at the town hall for provisional stay cards) also lent a local tone to the dictionary, as did regulations concerning the fortifications and empty zones beyond them ("it is forbidden to gather there in order to fight") and navigation on the canals.

Insiders and Outsiders

The issue of whether someone should be named to serve as CP in his own town was hotly disputed. On one hand, there was much to be said for knowing the lay of the land. The question of language, too, was essential. In many towns, particularly those on the hexagon's periphery, someone from the locality would offer the advantage of speaking, depending on the locality, Gascon, Provençal, Languedocien patois, Savoyard, the Alsatian German dialect, and Catalan, to say nothing of Breton or Basque, neither of which is even remotely related to French. For example, the CP of Wissembourg in the Bas-Rhin on the frontier with the Palatinate obviously needed to speak and write German to communicate with town residents and correspond with German authorities. In many towns of the Midi, versions of Languedocien (Occitan) would need to be mastered and across the Rhône, Provençal. In and around the fortified town of Berques, near Dunkerque, the municipal council spoke French, but the *bas peuple* communicated in Flemish; this was still true of other pockets in the northwestern part of the Nord, and even near St. Omer in the Pas-de-Calais, where Flemish had influenced the local patois.[81] In Corsica, CPs would be lost if they could not understand the Corsican dialect. The military officer carrying out a survey in and around Montbrison (Loire) in 1836 made a point of the fact that he had heard only patois, translating sentences from patois into French. Moreover, unusual local habits of pronunciation could confuse anyone. In Tarbes (Hautes-Pyrénées) and its region, inhabitants who spoke French did so with a local twist, pronouncing all letters, like many places in the Midi, thus, *loupe* for *loup,* but, more unusual, ignoring the "f" in *faire,* which became *haire, fabricant* emerging from the local tongue as *habricant.* For any new CP from the outside, it would at least take some getting used to.[82]

In Ste. Marie-aux-Mines, CP Pêchetaux resigned because he did not know the German dialect, which he would have had no opportunity to learn as an inspector of weights and measure in his native Normandy, but which he might have picked up while serving as CP in Belfort, then in the Haut-Rhin.[83] In Toulouse, Auguste Lallemand certainly understood the patois of Languedoc, but he did not understand Gascon very well, which led him to some embarrassing mistakes: On one occasion in 1819, he provided a certificate to a woman that stated that she had died in indigence, although she was standing before him asking for a certificate attesting to her husband's death.[84] In the Lot, the prefect opposed in 1816 the appointment of a former captain in the gendarmerie and tax employee because "an outsider in town, he does not know the local idiom."[85] In St. Brieuc, Charles Kerliviou, a Breton who had fought as a royal volunteer in 1815, seemed a natural for appointment in 1827 because he spoke Breton and knew the *moeurs* of Brittany.[86] CPs in Perpignan who did not speak Catalan not only had a difficult time in *quartiers populaires* carrying out their duties but were resented and mocked.[87]

In Vannes, Philippe Karmel, a Breton from Auray, spoke German well, though how this helped him in his work as CP in Brittany is hard to imagine, but a glowing report in 1829 praised his command of the language, perhaps confusing German with Breton! In fact, Karmel's good German was no accident, for he had served in Berlin during the Napoleonic Wars and then worked in the police in the short-lived département of the Bouches d'Elbe.[88]

In 1844, the minister of the interior himself noted that it was important to know if a CP spoke a foreign language.[89] Indeed in 1849 in the Loire, the "Notes on the commissaires de police sent to the Minister of the Interior" included a category for "foreign languages spoken" for assessments of the performance of CPs.[90] In February 1851, the category "knowledge of foreign languages" was added to the report sheets on commissaires in service in the Haute-Garonne. Toulouse in 1851 had CPs who spoke English, Spanish, Greek, and Italian; one knew Latin, although probably did not have much occasion to speak it. There a year earlier Marie-Prosper Crouzet was noted as speaking "Indian," but that particular fact had been crossed out in his file.[91]

Many if not most mayors preferred that a CP from the region and even from town be hired (see chapter 7). In Troyes, Hyacinthe Blasson became CP in 1820, a post he held until 1831. Although he had been born in Strasbourg, he got the post in part because his family had lived in Troyes more than fifty years.[92]

Yet in sharp contrast, prefects increasingly opposed hiring police from the town in which they were to work. This in itself also reflected the increased professionalization of the police, part of the construction of an identity as a corps independent of local identity and influence but attached to the state it represented. As the prefect of the Manche put it, "Policing a town is rarely done well by someone from the region. More or less subject to local considerations, he cannot always resist these influences. From this stems abuses of all sorts that an outsider has no reason to tolerate."[93] In Marseille, the commissaire central complained in March 1849 that unlike most other towns, the CPs only infrequently mentioned political matters in their reports. He blamed this in part on the fact that most of them were originally from Marseille, too influenced by local events and by the municipal council to be objective. The prefect noted with some bitterness that even CPs who were from the interior of the *pays* fall into *le farniente*—laziness—which he condescendingly called the "the illness of the region."[94]

In Périgueux, CP Andrey in the early 1830s learned that everything appeared to be done in a certain way, the way it had always been there, and not necessarily as the law seemed to dictate. He first argued with the mayor, a wealthy landowner who did not know or care much about the laws of France. Andrey's predecessor, a former gendarme, had been barely able to sign his name. The secretary of the mayor had always penned all police correspondence, and resented the new CP. In Andrey's opinion, only someone from Périgueux could cope with "a tenacious antipathy for any outsider" that he faced in a town of "chatterboxes and liars . . . yes, we need not a commissaire de police from the region, but someone born in Périgueux. Prevent some poor devil such as me from being so trapped!" With his wife and children ill, he desperately wanted to be posted back to a town in the Ain, his own distant *pays*.[95] In Toulouse during the Restoration, a CP insisted that his colleagues were in effect "the spies of the government" because they had been brought from the outside. Certainly those brought to serve in Toulouse were *malvus* locally, everything being done to reduce them to mere clerks.[96] And so the debate went on.

Local ties, especially those of family, could indeed compromise the objectivity of a policeman. One of the advantages noted by the subprefect of St. Étienne in urging the appointment of Joseph Sihol in 1820 was that he was not from the burgeoning manufacturing town but rather from the nearby Ardèche, close enough to understand the region but not too close to be compromised by familiarity.[97] In Rodez, whose commissaire had just resigned in 1817, the prefect of the Aveyron argued that the new CP should be brought in from the outside, thus not necessarily subject to the "patronage, favors, the considerations of family and neighborhood, and the fear of making enemies." Rodez was still a country town, despite its prefecture, where "the strangest infractions have become accepted and shock no one. In the middle of the afternoon pigs wander through the streets, knocking down amazed passersby." A CP should speak Auvergnat patois, to be sure. Thus, it was difficult to find suitable candidates who were not from there. If someone from a rival town were brought in, that might itself prove to be a problem (for example, from Aurillac, or St. Flour, whose inhabitants retained strongly unfavorable opinions about Rodez, the departmental capital). The new commissaire was to be Guillaume Tournemire, a "bourgeois" from Millau, a former gendarme who could speak Auvergnat patois and was willing to work for 800 francs a year.[98]

The mayor of Nantes was among those who complained about the ruling of the Orleanist Chamber of Deputies that the CPs were principally functionaries of the state. This inclusion in the category of functionaries was in itself an important step toward the professionalization of the police. The municipalities were forced to accept and pay, but not select commissaires who demonstrated nothing less than "their disdain and their negligence for those details of policing that alone could concern and assure public peace and health." Two more "outsiders" had just arrived as commissaires. It would take them weeks if not months for them to get to know Nantes, its expanding faubourgs, including the rough quarters of the ship workers. They also spent considerable time providing the detailed information frequently requested by the ministries in Paris. Meanwhile, the streets of Nantes remained dirty, wagons blocked the streets, and bakers systematically cheated on the weight of the bread they sold. He wanted commissaires who were from Nantes and already knew the city and its port well.[99]

Thus, when a post opened up in Poitiers in 1835 when one CP was named to be a justice of the peace in the Vendée, a man from town with experience in commerce applied (for the second time) for the position. He knew Poitou well. A former notary from Poitiers also applied, but the position went to Davanne, an *inspecteur des subsistances* from the Ardennes. His appointment signaled that choosing candidates from outside a town increasingly became at least part of growing police professionalism, in principle above the pressure of family, friends, and neighbors.[100] Yet over time, the issue of whether a CP should be from the city or town in which he served itself surfaced less frequently, this, too, further evidence that that state and its principal representative, the prefects, had won. Moreover, the predilection for outsiders in itself reflected increased professionalization.

Agents

In large towns, *agents* (in some towns they were called *appariteurs, gardes-de-ville,* or *inspecteurs*) took their place within the institutional structure of the police. Hired by mayors to assist the CPs, the agents were paid very little, in some cases only 150 francs a year. Like the CPs, many had a military background (as inevitably had many males in the wake of the Napoleonic era). In 1831, the six agents of St. Étienne included two former soldiers, two former gendarmes, and a seventy-year-old retired CP.[101] Most agents held other jobs as well. Like CPs, some agents received small sums for specific duties, such as one of Poitiers's agents during the Restoration who earned an extra 100 francs for monitoring the butchers of the town.[102] In Bastia, where the mayor gave agents the job of policing prostitution and begging, they appear to have received absolutely no salary. This leads inevitably to the question of why they did such work, suggesting that perhaps they made money by looking the other way in certain situations. They also earned no respect in Bastia, but they did provide useful information, leading the CP in 1836 to request that they be paid something.[103]

The number of agents employed by each city and town varied according to the size, resources, and inclinations of the municipality. In 1835, Nantes had fourteen agents, or gardes-de-ville as they were called there, a typical number for a city of its size. Six of them were to appear at the mairie at eight in the morning to receive their orders for the day. They were assigned to markets, fairs, streets, promenades, the theater, and public baths. Eight more were assigned to the eight CPs, each required to reside in the arrondissement to which he was assigned. Agents accompanied the CPs on their rounds between one and three in the afternoon, after which they could take an hour to eat, before returning to the mairie to receive their orders for the evening and night. Regulations warned that they could be guilty of "indecent conduct" if they frequented cafés and brothels, except in the course of their duties. They were also to avoid "risky marriages." Indeed, amazingly enough, in Nantes agents could marry only with the permission of the mayor![104]

Some towns with fewer than 5,000 inhabitants had to make do with only an agent. The small Nivernais town of Prémery combined the duties of an agent and rural guard in one miserably paid man, 150 francs a year! Château-Chinon, the nearest subprefecture, had only an agent during much of the Restoration, paying him an annual salary of 300 francs, far from enough on which to live.[105] Such beleaguered agents naturally drew criticism. The agent in Bourg St. Andéol (Ardèche) seemed oblivious to the tricks of unscrupulous merchants when it came to weighing what they sold, using old measures long since replaced. No one stopped women or children from carrying unprotected fire, which could be carried most anywhere by the Mistral when it stormed down the Rhône. Boats on the Rhône loaded and unloaded passengers without the slightest police surveillance. In town, shouts and obscene songs echoed through the night, notably in "in quartiers specially frequented by ces polissons [little devils]." The priest directed a Sunday sermon against objectionable ditties sung near the seminary. The agent hung on until being dismissed in 1829. Only in 1836 did Bourg St. Andéol finally get a CP, and then only because the prefect forced the municipal council to allocate funds for his salary.[106]

Without judicial authority, they could not, at least in principle, make arrests or draw up procès-verbaux but merely alert CPs or the mayor or his deputies to crimes and lesser transgressions. They did not take oaths on assuming their positions.[107] Moreover, most agents still lacked any visible sign of their functions. In Rouen in 1819, the mayor urged that agents have "uniforms and a conspicuous weapon. Poorly dressed, they inspire no fear, and no one defers to their demands. Often at night they are even taken for thieves; their air of neglect and misery undermines any moral influence." Gradually in some towns they wore uniforms, in others, not. In some they attended to passports, in others, they did not. However, when the subprefect of Chinon passed through Tours in 1838, he got the impression that the agents had the right to hand out a procès-verbaux. The procureur, citing a decree in July 1814, replied that even if what the subprefect had heard was true, he would not hesitate to "overturn a judgement rendered on the p.v. of an agent, even one sworn-in."[108]

In most towns, agents had be between twenty-five and thirty-five years of age when they began their service, know how to read and write, and stand at least 1.7 meters tall. When the mayor of Niort intimated that a longtime commissaire might have to be replaced because he "had the misfortune to lose an arm," he suggested that this father of a large family would make a very good agent because he wrote well with the hand that remained.[109]

A report requested by the prefect of the Rhône and submitted at the beginning of 1836 denigrated the agents as brutal, ignorant, lazy, and venal, drawn from the lowest rung of society—"one is persuaded than an honest man could not become one without degrading himself"—treated with contempt by the commissaires.[110] Indeed one of the criticisms of Pierre Retis, fired as CP of Nancy in 1822, was the revelation that he drank in public places, "even with subaltern agents."[111] The lack advancement for agents—it was extremely rare for an agent to be promoted to the rank of commissaire—contributed to poor morale.[112] In Roubaix, the CP complained that his agents were "ignorant and incapable men, of no help at all for the judiciary."[113] Indeed, just about everybody having to do with policing complained about the work of the agents at some point or another. Many did very little work, demoralized by low salaries and a lack of respect from municipal authorities, CPs, or townspeople. Yet some stayed on for several years. In August 1830, the town of Poitiers employed six agents. Three had served between eight and twelve years, the other three less than two years.[114]

Mayors, who appointed agents, had the authority to dismiss them, usually following persistent complaints from the CPs for whom they worked. In Bastia, Santelli obtained his agent Joseph Pomonti's firing because the latter refused to go on patrols, claiming that he was too old for such activity. Furthermore, he had tried to prevent Santelli from citing a baker for a violation and routinely helped himself to goods at the market that he was supposed to be watching. He also operated a bar, despite regulations that clearly forbade agents this sort of activity for reasons that were obvious to most everyone.[115] In Le Mans, agents were fined five francs if determined to be in a state "approaching drunkenness," a single franc "for each lie while in service," and ten francs for any scandal or failure to perform their duties, with destitution a certainty for every second transgression (*carton jaune, carton rouge*).[116]

Yet whether they were assigned to a specific CP or not, agents carried out essential urban tasks. Following the orders of the mayor or deputy mayor, some agents made sure that lamps were properly lit in the evening, verified the registers of inns and lodging houses, checked passports, stood guard at the theater, watched for vagabonds, served at the police office or the mairie, and so on. In Tours in 1837, one agent was assigned to passports and livrets and another assigned to the ports (under the authority of the Ponts-et-Chaussées) along the Loire River, the scene of many crimes.[117] Le Mans employed six agents—one at the bureau de police, one serving as secretary in that same office, and one assigned to each of the four districts. Among their daily tasks was the verification that *propriétaires* and renters had swept in front of their shops and residences, that the streets were unencumbered by unauthorized *travaux,* and that their assigned districts were free of gambling. They were to monitor the busiest cafés and carry passports collected by innkeepers from their clients to the mairie, where they would be exchanged for temporary *cartes de séjour,* and, in general, to prevent any situation that could trouble the public peace. On their final round after eleven at night, they focused their attention on the theater, certain "turbulent" neighborhoods, and of course on the *maisons de tolérance,* to be sure that none were "mixed houses"—that is, offering unmarried and married women to clients—that the *filles* had been properly registered and properly (if humiliatingly) inspected for venereal disease, and that they closed their doors on time, with no clients left on the inside. In short, they were to prevent "any nocturnal orgy."[118] In Lyon, some agents worked part of the time as secret informants, although thus not in their own quartiers, haunting cheap cabarets, rooming houses, and inns where they were not known.[119] More than one CP got himself in trouble because they virtually turned policing over to their agents.[120]

Conflicts between CPs, who were hired, fired, and transferred by the state, and agents, appointed by mayor and municipal council, were endemic. In Saumur, the subprefect had to dress down the CP, a man "of extremely violent character," who had thrown an agent out of his office on one occasion and struck him on another.[121] In Rouen in 1818, a CP ordered several agents to observe the activities of a decorated army officer, who sought the hand of the daughter of a wealthy wine merchant. Apparently the family, through the CP, employed the agents to investigate the man. This angered the mayor, who, in any case, believed that such an alliance could only honor the merchant family and that it was a private matter that should in principle be of no interest to the police. That Rouen's agents accomplished little seemed to be demonstrated by the fact that the city's clocks showed different times.[122]

However, during the July Monarchy the organization of agents generally improved, particularly in large cities. By 1847 Nantes had a corps of sergents-de-ville fifty strong, divided into *brigadiers* and *sous-brigadiers*. By then they sported uniforms (for which they had to pay), indeed two outfits, one dubbed *grande tenue* (a coat of blue cloth, shirt with a collar, and blue pants), presumably for municipal ceremonial occasions, and the everyday *petite tenue*, a blue frock coat, the same turned-up collar with buttons. The municipal document "organization of the corps of sergeants-de-ville" itself reflects greater professionalization, specifying what agents were to wear when not on the job, including a vest and a round hat intended to gain more respect.

Mouchards

All three regimes used secret agents—particularly amid waves of thefts but above all for political surveillance—when the circumstances seemed appropriate, with mixed results.[123] In Besançon, a mouchard in 1816 reported that soldiers with mustaches communicated with each other by tugging at them in various directions, part of a "vast organization of agitators."[124] In Chalon-sur-Saône in 1823, in the wake of the trial of the Four Sergents of La Rochelle, a mouchard hung around the citadel on the road from Dijon to keep track of those arriving, on the lookout for a prominent liberal (although badly butchering his name). In 1840, another mouchard in Chalon provided the CP with useful information on the forthcoming election of officers in the municipal national guard.[125] The prefect's refusal to authorize a charitable association in Chalon that would bring together cabinetmakers, stone cutters, and locksmiths can be seen in the context of fears that the organizer, Roth, a republican cabinetmaker, had links to the secret society Young Europe centered in Geneva. When the CP expressed his opinion that the proposed association had no political interests, the professionally suspicious prefect engaged a secret agent, who managed to infiltrate the town's republican milieu. The mouchard reported that Roth, who had just been released from jail, admitted that he was receiving funds from socialist republicans and related a wild plan to seize power in Lyon, Mâcon, and other cities in the region. Even then, despite the success of the police spy (assuming that he related conversations that had actually taken place), the prefect insisted on the difficulty of secret police learning much of interest "in a small town where everyone knows each other all too well." However, five years later a secret agent provided the CP with useful information about preparations for the coming legislative elections.[126] Given the role of police surveillance in the two largest cities in the Saône-et-Loire, it was no wonder that when a group of young republican men gathered in a café in Mâcon in 1836, they began to shout, "Down with the commissaire de police!" when his name inevitably entered the conversation.[127]

Mouchards probably came closer to the unfavorable contemporary image of the police influenced by the notoriety of Vidocq. Pierre Blanc, a former soldier, had been employed as a secret agent in the Restoration's first year, his mission ending in October 1816. Subsequently, he was arrested for vagrancy, in the possession of his brother's passport, and had "intrigued" in Lyon and the Rhône in 1817, accused of trying to "provoke the same peasants to revolt that he had been instructed to watch, while working to create a nucleus of malcontents in order to then denounce them to the authorities who employed him." He had received a passport during one of those rare moments when no charges weighed against him, sporting a fleur-de-lys on his coat, which he claimed he had been given as a reward for his secret police work. Police soon were searching for him in Chalon, Lyon, and then in Paris. Forty-two years of age, with brown hair and brown eyes, Blanc could fade into any large city, yet he seemed "one of those men who should not be allowed to vanish from view for one instant," while in the company of a young woman who had worked in the prison where he had been incarcerated. In Chalon, he had lived out of sight near a canal, among "people of the lowest class, in general disreputable." After a reward was posted for his capture, police arrested Blanc in Lyon in April 1818.[128]

Enhancing Police Centralization: The Commissaire Central

State centralization begat centralization within the police. Gradually more commissaires central were appointed to large cities, where they stood at the top of the police hierarchy, although without question still under the direct authority of the prefect. Rouen was among the few cities that had a commissaire central early in the Restoration, in this case beginning in 1818 in the hope of putting an end to "the lack of understanding" between the office of police and the CPs.[129]

During the Restoration, commissaires centraux were named in Marseille, Lille, Rennes, Orléans, Bordeaux, and Lyon to coordinate policing. In Strasbourg, local prefectorial authorities in 1820 called for the establishment of a commissaire central.[130] A fifth CP was first attached to the prefecture in 1823. J.-M. Letz had been born in the shadow of Strasbourg's cathedral, worked as a commercial clerk keeping books, then served in the army for twelve years. He served as an account for the army during the war and then as tax collector in the village of Wilwisheim near Saverne. Letz, who was not considered very bright but whose honesty and devotion were never questioned, was paid out of the funds of the prefecture; therefore some confusion existed as whether he was really a commissaire central or only the fifth CP.

However, Letz's appointment failed to solve the apparent lack of efficient policing in Strasbourg. In 1824, the prefect claimed that policing in Strasbourg, so important by virtue of its location, cost 60,000 francs a year and yet remained woefully inadequate. He blamed the growing rivalry with the mayor. The agents, or sergents-de-ville, were "often mere spectators to disorder . . . machines mocked every day." When Letz was transferred, Ambrose Burger, a *strasbourgeois* who spoke German and French, was transferred from the prefecture de police in Paris. After having served as postal official in Italy, he had proven his loyalty to the Bourbons by going as a secret agent to Belfort, presumably at the time of the Carbonari conspiracies in 1821.

In 1825, a certain Pungnul arrived to serve at the prefecture with something like the authority of a commissaire central. Reflecting the ambiguity and confusion surrounding his functions, Pungnul wrote other commissaires centraux asking them to describe their duties. He soon complained that a deputy mayor constantly interfered with policing. The mayor wanted his own choice for a commissaire central, a certain Ehrmann, a good local family man who spoke both French and German. The prefect insisted that to have an effective commissaire central, he had to be someone from the outside whom German speakers and

"other outsiders" would obey. Pungnul himself blamed the persistence of German in the lower classes on Protestantism: "Protestants, in their heart, believe
that they are German." Most of them had supported the Revolution. In 1828, a
new prefect eliminated the post at the prefecture. This left one CP for each of
Strasbourg's four cantons and the city would not have a commissaire central
again until 1849, for reasons we will later explore.[131]

The appointment of a commissaire central placed CPs in a position of seem-
ing subordination to one of their own, rather like a foreman promoted out of the
ranks of shop-floor workers. Indeed, the minister of the interior pointed out in
1843 that under the law, all CPs were equal, and that where a commissaire central or commissaire-en-chef had been named, the result had sometimes been unfortunate. He therefore asked the prefect of the Sarthe to reconsider whether
such an appointment should be made in Le Mans.[132] In Vannes, a rivalry between the commissaire central and the other CP led to the suppression of the post
after only six months in 1831.[133]

In Lyon, CP Bardoz in December 1833 had to defend with vigor his record
against the claims of the commissaire central, Prat, who accused him of refusing
night service. Bardoz noted with pride that in two weeks he had turned over to
the *bureau de sûreté* in the town hall twelve procès-verbaux, each accompanied by
a separate report. Moreover, he had provided a requested list of the number of religious schools operating in Lyon. "Do they want more reports? I cannot simply
create events." When Prat refused to undertake night service, he had been up all
the previous night. On December 15, a Sunday, he had left his office at 3 P.M. and
done his tour through his district before heading to the theater. After the curtain
went up, he had not been able to leave for one second because of "the public
seemed ready to disturb the peace." When the curtain fell at 11 P.M., he went on
another round with his two agents, "in order to prevent quarrels and brawls that
had multiplied during the evening from continuing." Returning home, he ran
into in agent who asked him to go to the *corps de garde* to interrogate "Napoléon
Bretty, who had struck him in the face after having been stopped by him in a suspicious place during a patrol." Only after midnight had he received Prat's order
asking him to undertake night duty, instructions that had been left with his
domestic servant at five or six in the evening while he was at the theater. However, Bardoz could not walk without pain, having recently been incapacitated at
home for five days. On his patrols, "I limp and suffered considerably." Moreover,
he vigorously denied having refused to accompany an agent when instructed to
do so. His honor challenged, Bardoz asked that he be able to meet with the
mayor and Prat, "in order that in the public interest this state of things come to
an end."[134]

In Poitiers, where Legitimist activity and students broke the calm of Poitou,
policing seemed "paralyzed" because of tensions between the two CPs. Jean Davanne was a decent CP but was "too convinced of his superiority over his equals."
The prefect tried to solve the problem by promoting his detested colleague, Noêl
Lachapelle, commissaire to *commissaire spécial en chef,* to give him authority over
policing in Poitiers. Davanne asked to be transferred. Philibert Paccard replaced

him in 1838. But La Chapelle and Paccard also did not get along. Whereas Davanne had been haughty, Paccard was simply disagreeable. In Moulins, his previous post, he had been rumored to have worked as a mouchard and left behind debts and enemies. When it was learned that he would be appointed to Poitiers, a scathing denunciation (from "Blondeau, persecuted in an atrocious manner by the infernal Paccard") landed on the desk of the mayor of the latter town, attacking him as an "infamous and execrable man," who "tyrannized the best citizens, outraged public morality (it is even said that he is not married to the woman he presents as his wife)." Protected by the former mayor, the successor had made Paccard's departure a condition of his acceptance of the post. There may have been something to these charges. He had been hauled before the tribunal, finally skipping town after having promised to pay creditors at a certain time. Now Paccard also resented his subordination and, becoming the mayor's favorite, refused to recognize his rival's authority over him. He confided to the agents the names of those who were going to be replaced and "intrigued" against his new superior. Policing in Poitiers suffered. However, Paccard's small local star rose when he disarmed an armed man, breaking his own arm in the process. Lachapelle denounced the lack of cooperation he received, adding that it was "impossible to life among men who are imposters, mean, and ambitious." Yet Paccard survived in Poitiers until his transfer to Quimper in 1840.[135]

Finally, we turn to the example of Nantes, where in 1820 the prefect of the Loire-Inférieure proposed to create a bureau central, citing the port city's large population and "circumstances," an allusion to the assassination of the Duc de Berri several months earlier in Paris. He wanted the new post given to an experienced person who would be brought from the outside to assume the supervisory position. The deputy mayor in charge of policing, however, argued against such a position, citing cost, and insisting that "local policing belongs alone to the mayors" even if haute police lay behind their jurisdiction. In his view, the appointment of a commissaire-en-chef would simply add another deputy mayor to be financed out of the municipal budget.[136] Yet Nantes's first commissaire central was not named until 1831, with an eye to maintaining order with the threat of a Legitimist insurrection rising in the West, yet another example of the frequent primacy of political policing on police organization.[137] Here, too, the other commissaires resented the nomination of one of their colleagues to supervise them as commissaire-en-chef. Philippe Larralde, the nominee, at first received no raise for assuming even greater responsibilities, and the prefect argued that the municipality should pay him more. Only in 1838 did the municipal council allocate an extra 600 francs in annual salary for Larralde, who then asked for and received formal confirmation of his status as commissaire central. He fully agreed that "centralization is in every way indispensable."[138]

Thus naming of commissaires centraux or commissaires-en-chef added a new personage to the hierarchical structure of the police in provincial cities and towns. This reflected and accentuated the increased centralization of police authority under the authority of the ministry of the interior and the prefects, as well as the emphasis, in times of national political contention, on political policing.

2

CAREERS

What did a career mean for commissaires de police? Careers were dependent on the particular mix of political patronage—above all during the early years of the Restoration—or at least not becoming identified as politically unreliable, and fulfilling the increasingly bureaucratic criteria for advancement. The post of CP offered the possibility to men of relatively low social status to obtain a regular salaried position while working for the state. Having a good career usually began with receiving an appointment as CP in a small town. Then, if one demonstrated professional competency and political loyalty and all went well, promotion to a larger town, with its commensurate higher salary, might lie ahead. Being moved around in itself contributed to the construction of a collective self-identity within the police. The plum jobs in Nantes, Bordeaux, Toulouse, Lyon, or even Paris would be the reward for a small number of CPs who obtained promotion up the career ladder. For almost all CPs, however, a pension did not await at the end of their career, a term they increasingly used to describe their *métier*. As we shall see, a more consistent and tested set of expectations of competence and professional service permeated the police during the period under consideration, for all of the continued test of basic political allegiance.

We will first consider the careers of CPs: How they were hired and who they were. Then we consider arrivals, transfers, and dismissals, placing two CPs, a rare father-and-son combination, in the context of the experience of the police during the July Monarchy in Tours, the town in which they spent a good part of their careers. Amid the comings and goings of CPs, their careers exemplify not only the challenges they confronted, professional and those specifically stemming from the location and characteristics of Tours, but also the role of CPs as state functionaries.

CPs were by law to be between the ages of twenty-five and forty-five years at the time of their appointment.[1] Prefects drew up the list of candidates, based on recommendation by subprefects or mayors. But prefects and the ministry of the interior felt absolutely no obligation to name a candidate (although the official

37

appointment during the Restoration and July Monarchy was made by the king) presented by the mayor, which would have the effect of "restraining royal power and even more to render it nil in many circumstances."[2]

Clive Emsley surmises that provincial commissaires during the Revolution had been "drawn from a variety of backgrounds. There were a large number of men who had served in the army or in army administration; others had a legal background, had worked as petty functionaries, or were landowners or businessmen in the locality for which they were appointed."[3] Were the provincial (or for that matter, Parisian) CPs of the Restoration, July Monarchy, and Second Republic drawn from essentially the same milieu? The vast majority of commissaires were drawn from the lower middle classes. Many had held positions as clerks or had worked as employees of the tax or other administrations. Particularly during the Restoration and early July Monarchy, a good number had gained such experience working in Napoleon's army.[4] Antoine Jacques, appointed to Châteauroux in 1831, had participated in twelve military campaigns and had three wounds to prove it. In 1815, the Second Restoration had forced him to leave the département because of his "liberal ideas."[5] Qualities generally considered soldierly—discipline, a sense of hierarchy, and responsibility—were frequently evoked when it came time to nominate a new CP. Moreover, some retired officers enjoyed small pensions, which allowed them to suffer less the meager wages of the position.

The position of CP brought with it lower-middle-class status by virtue of its very modest salary and modicum of respect. The expansion of the métier of policeman thus can be seen as part of the expansion of social mobility within the context of the professions.[6] Moreover, at least some level of education placed a CP above many of the people he policed, and he was apt to be better lodged than most. Indeed a decision by the *cour de cassation* on March 2, 1838, clarifying the duties of CPs, made clear that he enjoyed the prestige of a magistrate, recognizing his authority as a member of *police judiciaire* and as *police administrative*.[7] Police had to be able to follow orders, but also to give them to their agents. Their previous experience and social position enabled them to understand and communicate with the lower classes, but also with the fancy people with whom they would come in contact in the towns in which they worked. CPs could hand out procès-verbaux to people of a higher social status, be invited to some official receptions, and enjoy the dignity represented by the *écharpe* of authority. There was also at least the theoretical possibility of going on secret missions for the haute police, and more than one CP liked to give the impression that he enjoyed the confidence of high officials in Paris.

Pierre Armand Leroux, fired as CP in Montmartre after allegations of liberal sympathies at the time of the 100 Days, offered his colleagues advice: "The closer a functionary finds himself close to the people, the more he has to be careful in all of his relations."[8] A commissaire should know when, where, and how to observe *le peuple,* because of his familiarity with their habits, virtues, and vices. But he should remain above, however barely. Most of their previous occupations allowed them to do so. And so the mayor of Toulon, Guieu, in 1836 complained that the port town's two CPs were "well below their functions . . . they lack tact, intelligence, and the common sense that are indispensable in dealing with a public such as in Toulon." Such faults seemed particularly grave in Toulon, where the *bas peuple* did not like the police and seemed inclined to believe stories about them spread by a local newspaper. The mayor drew the conclusion that CPs should be chosen "from a higher sphere. A commissaire de police must bring with him a certain acquired personal respect, or at least the means and the will to soon acquire it." He reaffirmed the fact that in an important town, a CP should be considered a magistrate, not as a mere agent, but as a commissaire de police.[9]

Yet it was a common complaint from CPs that they enjoyed insufficient respect and prestige. The prefect of the Haute-Saône put it this way, discussing the difficulty of finding suitable candidates in the small towns of Vesoul and Gray: "The class somewhat above them regard them as beneath them."[10] Some of their desperation becomes apparent as they write to complain about inadequate salaries or their lack of a pension.

A CP had to be able to read, and have "a sufficient notion of French legislation that concerns the public rights of citizens, the laws, and of police regulations." A CP had to know how to write at least reasonably well to draw up procès-verbaux and file reports each day, or at least each week. In 1841, the prefect of Nièvre reminded CPs that reports relevant to political policing were to be sent sealed and stamped to the office of the prefect as necessary. Summary reports were to be submitted every five days, and at the end of each month each CP was to provide a list of a infractions that had occurred in his jurisdiction. Other reports were to be sent when events seemed to necessitate them. All reports had to be legible and clear.[11]

Auguste Rouillé, who earned appointment to Laval in August 1830 to replace a man fired after the July Revolution, was "not an unlettered man." The prefect of the Mayenne could write about Rouillé, "I have been assured that he is capable of writing up a report."[12] Many CPs did not write well—their procès-verbaux reveal that more than 150 years after they turned in reports. Gaspard Berthault was replaced as CP in Angers because, among other faults he manifested "a great difficulty writing that makes him incapable of correctly putting together a report."[13] In the Rhône River town of Tarascon, L.-F. Collet, CP, endured a *charivari* mocking his lack of education, before he finally resigned in 1829. Collins, CP in Nogent-le-Roi, seemed virtually uneducated, his procès-verbaux revealing "neither style, nor proper spelling, and even his handwriting is below satisfactory." Yet he had pursued thieves with exemplary energy and performed real services during the cholera epidemic of 1849. Cafetiers and *cabaretiers* accused him of partiality, and a girl came forward to say that he had tried to attack a friend of hers in the woods, but the charge could not be corroborated. He hung on, poorly penned reports and all.[14]

Many of the successful candidates for the position of CP had held jobs that prepared them with basic writing skills, such as secretary of a mairie or working for the *fisc*. Joseph Albertini, appointed to Briançon in 1821, had served as a tax inspector in Toulon.[15] Louis Vendeville, one of the CPs of Coulommiers during the Restoration, had served as an employee in the office of the Police Générale on the rue de Grenelle in Paris.[16] J. B. Bercq, CP of Bourbonne-les-Bains, at least until the post was suppressed in 1821, had worked in a tax office before becoming, in turn, a merchant and then an agent de police.[17] Before being named to Lyon early in the Restoration, Étienne De Lasgallery, born in Montbrison in 1785, had served seven years in the army, three as a village mayor, and two as tax collector before being named CP. His Breton colleague Jean-Marie Renou had worked ten years as secretary in a mairie, for which he was paid only a pittance, before finally being named CP in Lyon.[18]

Many CPs had worked as clerks for barristers, tax offices, or prefectures. Jacques-René Thiboust's four-year stint at the octroi helped him begin to understand the people of Chartres.[19] Henri Denis Micaux, named to police both Ivry and Gentilly outside of Paris in 1826, got the job because of "the knowledge that Micaux acquired of the habits of the people who hand around the *guinguettes des barrières de Paris*," including brawling.[20] Denyvieux, CP in Nantes early in the July Monarchy, had worked eighteen years at the octroi of the town in which he would serve.[21] The link between employment at the octroi and finding a post as CP remained common.

A sample of sixty-five previous occupations of CPs (at the time of their hire) reveals both variety but also suggests the importance of prior work in "literate" occupations and military service within the context of the lower middle class.[22]

13 clerks
10 tax employees (including the octroi)
10 employees of prefecture, subprefecture, or mairie
6 former soldiers
5 former lawyers
3 former judges (military, *sénéchal*, or deputy justice of the peace)
3 in commerce or manufacturing
2 former gendarmes
1 inspector of printing shops and bookstores
1 bailiff
1 commission agent at a municipal pawn shop
1 accountant
1 mathematics teacher
1 actor
1 postal official
1 former police agent
1 employee of a hospital
1 inspector of weights and measures
1 land surveyor
1 former guard of Louis XVI
1 tailor

The occupations held by the CPs of the Haute-Garonne (for whom such information is available) at the time of their appointment confirms this impression. Of sixty-one men, sixteen had moved into the police from the army; ten had been employed as some sort of clerk, secretary, or office employee (including the army); six had administered a state office; five had been gendarmes; four were tax employees or served as secretary of a municipal council; three had been agents or inspectors in the police; three had been teachers; and the others were occupied in a whole array of occupations, including a surgeon, manufacturer, merchant, wholesale merchant, landowner, land surveyor, student, *practicien,* watchmaker, and member of a municipal council. In short, with the exception of the former soldiers (some of whom had been officers), most had been employed in occupations in which they had to read and write acceptably.[23] The previous occupations before joining Lyon's CPs in 1825 include a property owner, two former soldiers, a secretary in an army office, an employee of the civil engineering administration, and the clerk of a *tribunal civil.*[24] The previous occupations of CPs working in the Jura in 1839 included a *maître de pension,* two land surveyors, an agent de police, a notary's clerk, a guard, a soldier, and a former CP; eleven years later, their previous employment included three clerks, a student in pharmacy, a pharmacist, a gendarme, and another former CP.[25]

A few CPs emerged from a somewhat elevated social class.[26] This was particularly true in the early days of the Restoration, when Jacques Edrard, described as belonging to the "old nobility," was appointed to Cahors. He lasted only two years, his lack of intelligence compromising his best efforts, leading to his being sent to a less sensitive post.[27] Barral de Baret, named CP of Coulommiers in 1828, not only had benefited from a "superior" education but was "well born, with significant alliances, and with a number of important people in his family."[28] Louis Harnepon became a CP in Beauvais after "being cast into need" when the spinning factory that he had owned in Amiens suffered the lifting of a prohibitive tax on imported cotton.[29] Only rarely were new CPs noted as having any kind of fortune; thus Jean Julien, appointed to Cosne in 1823, was thoroughly unexceptional in having been a former soldier but had a modest fortune of 1,200 francs (more than a year's salary).[30]

Getting Hired: Patronage and Politics

During the first years of the Restoration, the appointment of CPs was most closely linked to political considerations. Article 11 of the Charter granted by Louis XVIII on his return to France was ignored from the beginning: "All investigations of opinions held or votes cast prior to the Restoration are forbidden."[31] Some demonstration of having remained loyal to the Bourbon monarchy during the revolutionary and imperial epochs was usually essential. This would again often be the case in the wake of the assassination of the Duc de Berri in 1820. Moreover, as the Restoration and July Monarchy fell in turn, questions of political loyalty inevitably surfaced in the purges of the police that followed the change in regime, although neither of the wave of dismissals in these cases was as dramatic and far-reaching as that which came with the second return of the Bourbons to the throne after the 100 Days.

Many among the first generation of newly appointed Restoration CPs could reasonably claim that they had demonstrated loyalty to the Bourbons. They did so with flamboyant language relating tales of heroic sacrifices and undying loyalty to the Bourbon cause, victims of the Revolution and/or the Empire. Some heightened the drama of their tales by using the third person.

Some men appointed to serve as CP benefited from the patronage of well-known noble émigrés, who intervened on their behalf. The Duc d'Angoulême himself made appointments of CPs as he campaigned in the Midi in 1815.[32] During the first two years of the Restoration, the support of noble deputies could almost guarantee appointment of someone with the proper political credentials to the post of CP. In the Nord, newly elected members of the Chamber of Deputies pushed such candidates as Bisiaux, whose son had been a royal volunteer in the Gard, and Bouduin, former clerk in the Cour Prévôtale, who was chosen over Jean-Baptiste L'Empereur, an unlikely name for someone who enjoyed an excellent reputation among royalists.[33]

Such patronage, most prevalent during the Restoration's first years and particularly important in the case of the Parisian police, intervened again from time to time during the period. Auguste Choinet won appointment to Dieppe in 1824 because he enjoyed the patronage of Madame la Dauphine and of the minister of public instruction, both of whom apparently wrote on his behalf.[34] Jean-François Lurin, recommended by the father of the subprefect of Dinan for his "very beautiful handwriting," had bombarded the ministry of the interior with elegantly penned letters before finally receiving a post at St. Brieuc in 1823. The son-in-law of a tax employee, Lurin had literally lived in the maison de l'octroi, an ideal apprenticeship for the police.[35]

Patronage in Paris in the early years of the Restoration could override the wishes of departmental officials. The appointment of Charles Dubrueil as CP in Beaune in 1818 astonished both prefect and subprefect. Listed as only the third candidate, he triumphed over a *propriétaire* and a retired captain in the gendarmerie. "I asked myself," complained the latter, "what bad luck attached to this post determined that after having called to serve in it the most unworthy man imaginable, today they choose the most incapable that could be found to occupy it." Dubrueil, "born into the people" with no education, constantly had to apologize for having been appointed and lasted only until 1822.[36] Fillias de Fontbouillant, a lordly sounding name for a modest CP, was appointed to Aubusson, although he had not even been among the three candidates proposed by the prefect to Paris. He triumphed because of the support of the deputies of the Creuse. But thereafter he paid only attention to his own affairs and abandoned the policing of town to the mayor and deputy mayors. In 1819, he left Aubusson for good when the post of commissaire was eliminated.[37]

The prefect of police and then the minister of the interior thus found the equivalent of a long line of entitled applicants with dossiers thickened by their own self-serving stories of courage and loyalty to the Bourbon cause, though this of course did no good following the Revolution of 1830.[38] François Simon (born in 1774), a former notary who claimed that he had to sell his practice because of the Revolution, had been arrested in 1798 because of his royalist sympathies and freed two years later. He also claimed to have led a royalist force in 1814—the kind of claim that was rampant—and to have again taken the field for the royalist cause during the 100 Days.[39] J.-B. Wallach, appointed CP in Lunéville in 1816, was a former lawyer who had lost not only his property but also his wife (the circumstances of the latter left unstated) during the ten years in which he served his king.[40]

Augustin Lefeuvre, a Breton from Fougères, had served as inspector of print shops and bookstores in Rennes before being named to distant Montpellier in 1817. Appointed in part because of demonstrable royalist convictions, he learned and enforced municipal regulations in a town considered by virtue of its location to be a difficult assignment, in addition to considerable political tensions in the wake of the 100 Days and the White Terror that followed. He was so good that the prefect had to admit that he blocked his transfer to a better post, noting that many in Montpellier also did not want him to move on. The Revolution of 1830 ended his career, as it did that of many of his colleagues.[41]

The sufferings of Lyon at the hands of the Jacobins during the Terror provided ready context for several determined claimants lining up for positions as CP. Joseph Rigod, writing in 1818, related that his store and all its goods had been burned, and he forced to flee "to escape the revolutionary fury." The monstrous Revolution forced him to take a minor administrative post that he clearly considered far beneath him, but when his position disappeared two years later, he had been left waiting in vain for a tiny pension to be paid. Since then, "he has vegetated in a state next to indigence, and in even indigence itself; his attachment to the sacred cause of the Bourbons having been the first cause of his ruin." He sought appointment as commissaire in or near Lyon.[42]

In 1822, Pierre Villefranche, "property owner and father of a family in Lyon," also recounted his suffering, relating that his fidelity to the Bourbons had brought him persecution and a death sentence before he and fifteen others managed to escape. Couthon's army had destroyed two houses he owned. He found some compensation in obtaining a post that ironically had been created by the Revolution.[43] Léon Antoine's father, a wealthy Lyonnais merchant, had been executed during the Terror. Requesting appointment as a CP in October 1814, he was named to nearby Villefranche-sur-Saône and then to the Croix-Rousse. In 1823, the prefect of the Rhône nominated him for appointment to Lyon. Antoine did well in every respect, and his career demonstrates the role of politics in the appointments of the early Restoration.[44]

The position of those men who could present themselves as having defended the royal cause during the Revolution and Empire was thus the exact opposite of the *demi-soldes,* those former Napoleonic officers pensioned off during the Restoration and then watched and hounded. While the demi-soldes languished bitterly in bars, many of those who could prove their loyalty during the bad old days—or at least present a believable case, or who enjoyed highly placed patronage—found work in the police.

Thus hundreds of letters soliciting appointments to the police poured into the

Prefecture of Police. News of vacancies traveled fast. In 1818, a certain Lanoyne-grimpré wrote the prefect to say that "the rumor is circulating that the commissaire de police of Tarare has requested and obtained another post," and asking to be named to it.[45] The letters accumulating on important desks related similar stories, with considerable colorful variation and degrees of truth, dripping with outrage and no small degree of immersion in the language of entitlement. Letters sent by men asking to be named CP were similar to letters put forward by widows of magistrates asking for pensions. These were narratives that "blend genres of autobiography, family history, and national history, and themes of honor, disgrace, and catastrophe."[46] Alan Spitzer suggests that "in no era in modern French history, save possibly the post-Vichy era, have past political commitments been recollected with such ferocious intensity as during the period following the collapse of Napoléon's empire and the rebirth of the Bourbon monarchy." (He quotes César de Proisy d'Eppe, "If the plague gave out pensions, the plague would itself find flatterers and servants."[47]) To be sure, it was extremely difficult for the ministry of the interior to verify many of the stories spun by candidates for appointment of heroic deeds and invariably honorable conduct in the worst of times on behalf of the monarchy and its nobles, as well as the claims of subsequent poverty and other claims. That there were so many letters to read itself helped swell the bureaucratic apparatus in the ministry.[48] Even though many opportunists capable of spinning a believable yarn of devotion received posts in the early frenzy of setting up a return to monarchist rule, the new authorities relied on supporting letters and information gathered by prefects to corroborate the applicants' suffering.

Even allowing for exaggeration, many of the stories told by claimants nicely evoke the drama of life during the revolutionary era. Henri Boucher, trained as a lawyer in the Sarthe, had gone before the Revolution to St. Dominique, where he served in a tax office. But, "not being able to adapt to revolutionary principles," he lost his civil rights and spent ten months in prison before managing to flee to Cuba. There, he went into the coffee trade, until the Spanish arrived and ordered all French citizens out within ten days. He traveled to the United States in 1809, and then returned penniless to France, to discover that his relatives had lost their fortune during the civil war in the West. He first found employment in the police in occupied Catalonia, but the Spanish armies returned and put him in prison. After what he wisely called "the fortunate change" that occurred in 1814, he undertook some sort of secret mission during the first Restoration, which probably amounted to no more than writing a report on the political situation in Catalonia (for which he later asked that money promised be paid). Always ready with a timely letter, he reminded Restoration officials of his family's honorable sacrifices for the royalist cause in the Vendée, and his own experience in the police. All of this finally brought the hefty reward of appointment to Paris.[49]

Jean-Baptiste Gomion was proud that he had refused to serve the "usurper" during the 100 Days. He described the plebeian origins of his family, which, from "time immemorial" had in a succession of towns—Romans, Auxonne, and Pontalier—"fulfilled those tasks awarded to *la bonne bourgeoisie*." His father had been a notary, who enjoyed the confidence of several *grands seigneurs*. His parents had instilled in him the "respectful attachment that I have always had for the distinguished class; my devotion to serve it raised my soul and inspired in me these sublime sentiments, which were so tested for the royal family." When his father was forced to flee the Jura, Gomion described himself as hiding in the house and then turning it into a hiding place for the local clergy and royalists. In 1795, he had assisted several *grands princes* in crossing the frontier into Switzerland. Denounced as a "royalist conspirator" during the Directory, he was granted amnesty by Bonaparte and took over his father's notarial practice. Gomion became deputy mayor of the village of St. Aubin. In 1814 he helped the Austrian invaders prepare the way for the Restoration, but he also claimed to have prevented the execution of a French man in Champagnole who had killed a soldier. An exemplary royalist record, even if only part of it was true, earned him appointment to Vesoul in 1822.[50]

Félix de Rochemont arrived in Nancy as CP in April 1817, rewarded for a story that touched royalist ears, thanks to the support of a prominent personage. As an adolescent, when revolutionaries had tried to force him to shout, "Long live the Republic!" he claimed that he had shouted "Long live the king!" If it was a prank, the timing was all wrong. The revolutionary tribunal of Chalon-sur-Saône condemned him to death. After the sentence was commuted because of his age, de Rochemont spent almost two years a prisoner on the Ile-de-Ré, from which he managed to escape. A battery of letters asserted that he had risked his life in 1815 when Marshall Ney sent him to report on Bonaparte's march north. When Ney went over to Napoleon, de Rochemont managed to escape arrest, bribing his way out of Mâcon. However, he did not last long in Nancy, telling people that he was also a secret agent of the ministry of the interior and assessing his own little tax on prostitutes, later claiming that such a local arrangement preexisted his arrival in Nancy, very Ancien Régime. Predictably, he then protested that he had become a victim "for having taken with firmness and loyalty the legitimate and monarchical line." De Rochemont received a harsh prison sentence of five years for misappropriation of funds. But he obtained a pardon, it appears, because of the influence of his patron, who still insisted in 1824 that de Rochement could be usefully employed as a secret agent.[51]

Born in Ernée in the Mayenne to a religious family of "mediocre" fortune, Lelasseux had magnificent counterrevolutionary credentials on which to start a career in the police. His parents had been executed during the Revolution, and he had managed to escape to fight as a Chouan. Vowing revenge, he killed two of the four judges who had condemned his parents to death, one of whom spit out that he wished that he could have killed 1,000 Vendéans before Lelasseux cut him down. With the first Restoration, he put down his arms and taught mathematics, then took up arms in Lower Anjou during the 100 Days. Ordered to hide the munitions of the Royal Army, he came on a château he believed was held by troops loyal to the Bourbons, optimistically called out, "*Vive le Roi!*" and then realized—too late—that Bonapartist troops were inside. He was beaten, stabbed, imprisoned in Nantes, and then freed on Bonaparte's fall. His reward for all of this was nomination as CP in Nantes in January 1816. There Lelasseux not surprisingly became known as a hardened Ultra. His provocative behavior brought transfer to Caen in 1818, when the government yielded to anti-Ultra sentiment; he was then reassigned to Nantes years later, returning as CP again in Caen in 1827.

Lelasseux had become a small legend in part of the West. His rage against the Revolution again got him in trouble when someone selling images of Bonaparte received an unusually harsh sentence, thanks to Lelasseux's single-minded determination. A subsequent transfer to Brest was presented as a promotion, although Lelasseux, who had to sell his furniture to pay for his move to Brittany, did not see it that way. In 1829, he requested transfer to Paris, Rouen, or Bordeaux; his wife was "languishing" in Brest, complaining endlessly about the rain. More than this, Lelasseux did not get on with one of the deputy mayors of Brest, whom he claimed "only speaks of the sovereignty of the people, of popular laws, of the destitution of royalists, and insults as brigands those who defended the royal cause in the Vendée." He also did not like having to work on Sundays and holidays. Lelasseux survived the entire Restoration when other Ultras of temper and vengeance did not because he was a reasonably good CP and because he served only in the West. His four transfers were not at all unusual, but rather the norm. He lost his position after the Revolution of 1830, which was the work of men such as the liberal deputy mayor of Brest. Lelasseux thus took his convictions and stories of royalist heroism into retirement.[52]

Jean Rivière, appointed to Poitiers early in the Restoration, seemed a case of downward mobility for which he blamed the revolution. He had been a lawyer during the last years of the Ancien Régime, and then *juge sénéchal* in the Charentes. In 1802, he was an *avoué* in Poitiers, before being appointed CP there in December 1815. Sixty-two years old in 1820, he complained that he could barely survive on an annual salary of 1,000 francs. Moreover, complaints had started to surface about his inability to command respect. But weakened health and the size and hills of Poitiers worked against him. And so did his poverty: He seemed ill at ease among those he was supposed to police. [53]

Poitiers would have been better off if Rivière had been kept on in 1819. Jean-Marie de Gallemont, a former émigré who had fought against the Revolution and had the scars to prove it, succeeded him. After two years of service, he still had not mastered his responsibilities and demonstrated only indifference and negligence. He had made "dishonest" comments to the daughter of a count as he tried to coax her into visiting his room, and the count had complained. Moreover, he, like Rivière, was poor, hounded by creditors, and therefore ill at ease in aristocratic Poitiers. The procureur and mayor both wanted him out. He was asked to resign to avoid the fatal word *révocation* (though he then claimed that this news hit him so hard that a doctor said that he could have died from the "bolt of lightning"). De Gallemont then asked the mayor for money so that he could go to Paris to look for a job, reminding him of his services to the dynasty, "riddled with wounds" for the good cause.[54]

Yet the Restoration had to turn to some CPs who had served during the Empire, which had lasted so long that very few men with experience in the police had not served during the Napoleonic period. More than a few CPs during the first years of the Restoration who had survived imperial origins had worked in that capacity in conquered regions transformed into French départements. Jean Lançon had served in the police in occupied Austrian Netherlands and in the Netherlands and then in Aix early in 1814. He continued to serve during the 100 Days. After retiring briefly because of infirmities in 1818, he was reappointed in La Rochelle the following January, before being dismissed in 1821. He headed rapidly to Paris, leaving many debts behind.[55] Schaueffle, CP for Colmar until his death in 1820, had served in the same capacity in Gand in 1812.[56] Moreover, most CPs who had served in the army had obviously fought for "the usurper," whatever they thought of Bonaparte.

After the Revolution of 1830, similar stories about unyielding devotion—this time to the liberal cause—arrived in the ministry of the interior and in prefectures. When Laurent Tarriault asked to be appointed CP in Nevers following the *Trois Glorieuses,* he related that, on Napoleon's return during the 100 Days in 1815, he had hoisted a tricolor in Chalon-sur-Saône, a brave act for which he claimed to have been sentenced to death. However, the prefecture checked out his story and found that someone else had run up the tricolor flag and no one in Chalon had ever heard of Laurent Tarriault. He had also lied about his military record. He never attained the rank of lieutenant or served in Ancenis, as he had claimed.[57]

During the July Monarchy, powerful patronage could still count for something, as in any bureaucracy, even if less than during the early years of the Restoration. Henry, appointed CP in Toulon in 1832, had had the good fortune to have impressed de Joinville, Louis-Philippe's son, toward the end of his career in the navy.[58] In the last years of the July Monarchy, a certain Guizot living in Nîmes wrote the ministry of the interior on several occasions seeking the post of CP. He was "somewhat the relative of a very great personage." This particular Guizot had been a soldier and then a notary of means, but had somehow lost this position, and his family refused to come to his aid, in part because he never could hold on to places obtained for him. Honest but also lazy in the view of his superiors, he sometimes depended on the charity of some of the people he once policed.[59]

The Métier

What abilities led to a successful career as a CP? Victor Hugo describes the work of Javert, the policeman in *Les Misérables,* perhaps with some exaggeration:

> His whole life was contained in two words, wakefulness and watchfulness.
> . . . His life was one of rigorous austerity, isolation, self-denial and chastity without distractions; a life of unswerving duty, with the police service playing the role that Sparta played for the Spartans—ceaseless alertness, fanatical honesty, the spy carved in marble, a mingling of Brutus and Vidocq.[60]

In Lyon, the CP for the district of the Hôtel Dieu in 1843 claimed to have worked 18 hours a day, making 320 arrests, drawing up 550 procès-verbaux, handing out 200 certificates or attestations for this or that, reading 300 letters (and responding to many of them), and writing 450 himself, all in a period of six months.[61] Louis Canler's description of the difficulties of finding the ideal sergent-de-ville of Paris applies to CPs:

> [The sergent] must possess an acute understanding, sensible and speedy judgement, and above all must never become angry. Now where is the man who, finding himself in constant, direct contact with the working population and with street sellers, called upon by the nature of his job to reprimand a number of small offences, a number of disturbances of public tranquility or safety, before reporting a number of contraventions of the law or of bye-laws, which action of course alienates the offenders who often show their discontent with abusive language, where is the man, I say, who will not let himself be carried away by anger?[62]

In February 1850, David, one of Lyon's CPs, penned his reflections on his métier, hoping to point the way toward a "new organization of the police in France." In his view, "Simplicity, politeness, dignity without haughtiness and pomposity, the severity of justice is the best and surest way to provide strength and bring respect for the state [*pouvoir*] and the functionaries who represent it." Darcy, the former prefect of the Rhône to whom David dedicated his thoughts, had told Lyon's CPs, "The police should have a hand of iron, but this hand should have a glove!" But in his years of police work, David had instead too often seen that these two approaches had been put into practice without relation to the other, one, "intemperate and brutal, stands for inflexibility in action. . . . The other, lazy and almost ridiculous, characterized by the lack of tact and of appropriate action." In David's view, many policemen arrived at their post without the least idea of their duties. Newcomers began to copy without reflection the methods of the old hands, resulting in a "heavy-handed policing, done without intelligence," for which ordinary people, who counted on an efficient and moral police, blamed government authorities. The ministry and prefects should ensure that only suitable candidates were selected to serve in the police, thus enhancing the credibility of the institution.

David cited Napoleon's contention that if military victories were the glory of his Empire, "effectively, the police of the Empire was what it should have been: the principle of government." In David's view, the police had to dominate from "the heights of its healthy influence" all events "that surge inopportunely in a society, and that political tempests so often put at the discretion of subversive and catastrophic ideas." In such situations—he was writing at the height of the *chasse aux rouges* in 1850—political repression took precedence over understanding. Yet he emphasized that the police should always show itself to be "just, wise, and prudent. . . . That failing, it loses general respect, and is reputed to be unfair, thoughtless and angry." To accomplish these ends, "the bare hand of iron for the criminals, anarchists, the instigators and trouble-makers of all kinds," but "the gloved hand as long as one is dealing only with the accused and not the guilty."

Why did some CPs, in his view, fail to live up to their chosen profession? Those who tried to overcome their complete "uselessness in service, whether because of a dose of pride, mixed with arrogance and pedantry" were quickly seen by sensible people as "expert charlatans, or dandies on their departmental inspection tour . . . [with] dazed looks of gaping provincials." Others were "louts and vulgar people, appearing to have only studied in the dictionary of the market! They treat the public very badly, especially people from the working class." And then there were those with "affected manners, spending most of the time at the café," trying to satisfy everyone. The CP, "a public man," should be a simple citizen, "conscientious, hard-working, loyal, and of unfailingly good conduct, resolutely enforcing the law."

Each commissaire should realize that he was at the same time a magistrate, an administrator, a conciliator, and above all a *juste appréciateur de l'esprit public*. David's description exudes proud professionalism. The métier required tact, common sense, "an exact knowledge of the human heart," and a sense of "practical morality," all "urgent qualities." As the police stood as "direct intermediaries between the people and superior authority," brusque behavior, rudeness, and insolence could only "engender hate, contempt for repressive institutions and the desire for vengeance." All of this was complicated by the ignorance of the people, who had a "profound ignorance" of the government's administration. "Disastrous days" could lie ahead, with "awful reprisals" from the people.[63]

The word *zeal* (or the absence of) emerges repeatedly in reports assessing police performance. CPs had to be prudent and discreet, sometimes acting as judges, as well as police, but also as father confessors, while remaining "firm" enough to "resist the demands of local interests."[64] They had to know very well the town or neighborhood to which they had been assigned, retaining an amazing amount of information. Yet the prefect of the Rhône in 1826 estimated that a CP could at best know one-sixth of the people in the arrondissement to which he was assigned, because, among other obvious reasons, people moved in and out of every town and every quartier. Moreover, most policeman in Lyon stayed less than five years in that city and just three in any individual district.[65] CPs had to use good judgment in handing situations, avoiding confrontations and violence as best they could.[66] They had to anticipate events, which was more important than simply being engaged in repression. Tact, not condescension, was required to earn and retain the respect of the lower classes.

Désaignement, CP in Marseille, treated everyone in his arrondissement with a high-handedness that irritated workers, who in general respected the police, at least in 1817. He carried on as if he were on some sort of secret mission authorized in Paris. He arrogantly handed out *mandats d'amener* and announced new regulations on his own. Deciding for no apparent reason that a barber shop was suspect, he turned up at six in the morning and demanded the names of all those waiting their turn for a shave. This hurt the barber's business. Moreover, Désaignement was an outsider and did not know Provençal, which certainly antagonized much of the population of his district, compromising the sense of impartiality that was so essential to the position.[67] Désaignement's colleague Arnaud also failed to earn the respect of ordinary Marseillais. His had been an actor, "well known to the public." Thus the lower classes lacked respect for him—actors, it will be remembered, were only made citizens by the Revolution: "Instead of calling him by his name, he is designated by the ridiculous and buffoon-like roles that he had to play." What counted in Marseille, and in other teeming cities as well, was "the particular merit . . . to be able to impose himself on the multitude in a moment of danger."[68]

A CP respected by townspeople could bring arguing, insulting, even brawling opponents to conciliation. In April 1848, less than two months after the February Revolution, the municipal council of Angers, making the claim that a second commissaire was indispensable because of the town's growth, put forward its idea of good policing: "The most desirable police is a police of peace and conciliation: it should anticipate and prevent trouble and crimes rather than preparing the means of punishing them. The police should intervene not with the goal of drawing up a report, but rather to bring people together and to conciliate."[69] Considerable tact and discretion were necessary. On successive days in June 1831, CP Bertrand Cazeaux in the western district of Tours "arranged" a dispute between a passer-by whose clothing was damaged by "strong water," as it were, tossed carelessly from the third floor of their house, and the bloodied victim of a punch thrown in anger. When Louis Dunais, a cabinetmaker, alerted the police that *la fille Deniaux* (with whom he apparently lived) had beaten her child, no evidence could be found. The policeman was able to arrange a reconciliation. To be sure, sometimes such attempts failed. When in Tours, Alphonse Bernard from Paris claimed that a certain Cauvin, rue Colbert, a neighbor of his own uncle, was trying to steal the latter's "fortune"—such as it was—and threatened family members like himself who came to visit him, the commissaire convoked the warring parties. Animated discussion followed, but the policeman was unable to conciliate the quarreling parties and sent along the case to the courts.[70] And of course commissaires intervened in incidents of domestic violence (as did neighbors). An astonished military officer, sent in 1844 to the Aveyron to prepare a *reconnaissance militaire,* reported that in Nasbinais he had personally seen a wife knock out her husband with an iron bar. It was a little late for police conciliation.[71]

Pensions

The problem of pensions—specifically the unwillingness of municipal councils to award them except in absolutely exceptional circumstances—sheds light on three essential aspects of the development of policing in France during the first half of the nineteenth century: the conditions under which the police labored; their growing sense of being professionals; and, finally, tensions between the centralized state and municipalities that arose due to the contradiction between a national career hierarchy and local financing of police salaries.[72]

During the Ancien Régime, the Revolution, and the Napoleonic periods, *fonctionnaires* fortunate enough to have the right to a pension looked to the state. By virtue of the Law of 28 Germinal, year 6 (April 17, 1798), gendarmes could receive a pension at age sixty. In 1806 and 1807, the imperial government began to study the question of retirement. The decree of September 13, 1806, required thirty years of service and sixty years of age before a magistrate could request a pension, cases considered one at a time. This was a start, as one of the results of the Revolution and Napoleonic period was that "more and more people began speaking a language of social rights." During the Empire, individual pension plans were created for employees of the Ponts-et-Chaussées, Mines, Relations Extérieures, Préfecture de Police, and the Ministère du Commerce. Royal ordinances in 1814 and 1815 made it possible for judges and other functionaries of the ministry of justice the right to request retirement pensions.[73]

The situation for CPs was very different. The ministry of the interior moved the CPs around without giving any consideration to whether such a transfer would cost them the possibility of receiving a pension, despite the fact that ministry employees themselves. Magistrates, in sharp contrast, carried their years in service with them from post to post.

In a few cases during the Restoration, the minister of the interior and the prefect pressured the municipal council to fund a pension for the departing commissaire with proper royalist credentials. When Claude Curie, whose family had lost its fortune during the Revolution, was gently fired in Besançon in 1820, the minister of the interior asked the municipal council to accord him an annual pension of 550 francs. When this was too much for the municipal budget, the council awarded Curie that sum as an unforeseen expense and then a pension of 250 francs a year.[74] A few CPs who retired actually did indeed receive pensions. Louis Linet (who blamed the Jacobins for his loss of a position in the magistrature in 1792, claiming that "providence and friendship tore me away from the hands of the executioners who wanted my blood") received in 1821 at aged seventy-two an annual sum of 387 francs from the municipal council of Reims, where he had served since 1807. But Linet was in a tiny minority of CPs who eventually received a pension.[75]

In 1825, the Chamber of Deputies, even as it debated the right to a retirement pension among magistrates, affirmed that municipal councils were free to refuse a pension to a CP, because no law required that they do so.[76] Lyon's CPs bitterly complained about these restrictions, noting that they could be transferred after twenty-four years in one place.[77] Moreover, everyone knew perfectly well that the odds against that were monumental: Four or five years was a normal stay in a post, and rare were those who lasted more than fifteen years without being transferred (or fired). They asked that the city put some sums into a fund for their retirement, to which would be added funds withheld from their salary. The mayor of Lyon proposed—and would again four years later—that the municipality set aside 2.5 percent of a CP's salary and put it in the bank, where the funds would remain until his retirement. However, the municipality would contribute nothing unless the CP managed to last twenty-five years. Several other towns, including Laon, offered the same arrangement. In Lyon the *caisse de retraite* may not have functioned until 1829, and, from the wording of the offer, it seems unlikely that any CP had yet been able to afford to participate.[78]

Nicolas Ménard had been appointed to Lyon in year 4, but had been dismissed in the wake of the coup of 18 fructidor, "an era when a revolution took place among officials, and those called to functions held different opinions than his"—an occupational hazard in France. He had the good fortune to be reappointed in 1815 and then transferred to the peace and quiet of Montbrison in 1820, until he returned to one of Lyon's suburbs in 1823. The mayor found him a "kind, affable, and honest man." But Ménard could not afford to relinquish 2.5 percent of his pay, which he needed to support himself and his seventy-nine-year-old wife, who was senile.[79]

In fact, Lyon was one of the few towns whose municipality even considered the matter of pensions. In 1829, the municipal council formally proposed that the small part of the salary of participating CPs be turned over to the state, which would administer this pension, one that did not require twenty-five years of service in the same town, and would add 5 percent interest. Nothing came of this.[80]

In Lyon, CP Vaché lost his post in 1831 at age fifty-four. He had little money or hope, but he passionately and accurately described the plight of the CP, hoping to obtain a pension: "Thus, because of the lack of any legislation in this regard, a commissaire de police who has passed a great part of his life in serving the state in a post that is always difficult and often perilous is reduced to fight for, penny by penny, a small pension that a municipal council may award him with bad grace, in the best outcome, or he should be resigned to die of hunger when age and infirmities earned in the career that he has had force him to leave it behind."[81]

The persistence of commissaires asking for higher salaries and pensions reflected the way in which CPs increasingly saw themselves as a corps, identifying the state as the ultimate authority. In 1828, the commissaires of Orléans, well aware of what the state had done for magistrates and other functionaries, collectively complained. "Since the creation of the commissaires de police," they wrote, "none of the successive governments have considered their fate." The commissaires seemed properly remunerated and respected only in Paris. "Deprived of respect," the police of Orléans asked that the government consider the burdens of their position. Few other jobs of such relatively low status required as much aptitude and experience. As an officer of the judiciary, the CP could condemn or absolve the accused. His moral influence frequently led to mediated disputes. Yet only in exceptional circumstances could they receive a pension, despite representing the state as the front line of defense against "the most immoral part of society." Their specific request was modest indeed: They asked that 3 percent of their salary be withheld for their retirement.[82]

The July Monarchy, too, failed to provide a pension plan. Not long after the July Revolution, the minister of the interior rejected the request of Pierre Couture for a pension, ruling that it was the decision of the municipal council to award one. The municipal council of Le Havre had rejected Couture's request in 1817, because he had not served twenty years, having begun in year 8—a tenure of service that in itself was extremely long.[83] Yet a few municipalities seem to have followed Lyon in withholding, at the instigation of the CP, a small sum from his salary as a type of caisse.[84] At least the law of July 18, 1837, formally established the possibility of pensions for CPs for those policemen who had twenty-five years of service in the same town, however improbable.[85]

In 1845 the CPs of Nîmes sent out a letter to their counterparts in several major cities asking for their support in their attempt to be declared fonctionnaires worthy of a pension. They were increasingly curious about the status of and advantages fonctionnaires enjoyed and resented them for it. They also wanted the right to address the state as functionaries, and to have a pension that would reflect the respect the state had for them.[86] Here, too, we observe the emergence of a professional sense of self-identity as something of a corps among the police, with the right to address the state that employed them, in harmony with similar self-identification among other emerging professions. Only a commissaire in Paris had the esteem of the public. It was not fair. The Chamber of Deputies had already established that the CPs were principally fonctionnaires of the state. But they did not have the right to a pension.[87]

In Lyon, CP Paulin had resigned on July 8, 1829. He did so with unconcealed bitterness. He had begun his career in the police in Beaucaire, a major market town on the Rhône, before moving on to nearby Nîmes in 1801. He had subsequently refused a transfer to Grenoble, as he mourned the death of a son. Like many of his colleagues, he hoped one day to be elevated to Paris with its lofty salary, but his *patron* and distant relative, the Comte de Lamartillière, had died, so there was no one to put forward his name. Lyon proved to be an excellent consolation prize. In the late 1820s, despite having accumulated thirty-eight years of service, he would not be eligible for a pension until 1843, because his tenure in Lyon had begun only in 1818. He would be seventy-one years of age—with luck. The municipal council of Beaucaire refused to accord him any reward for his earlier services. In a letter to the minister of the interior filled with pride and despair, Paulin put forward a strong case for the CPs. He and his colleagues were responsible for defending society "against the attacks of criminals." The CPs were nothing less than "the advanced sentinels of government." Paulin lamented, "Magistrate of every hour, of every minute, the commissaire is the born guardian of the public security of his quarter," the first person to whom those threatened by misfortune turned. The commissaires were nothing less than the front line against "the most immoral part of society." Paulin had a profession but not a pension, despite compelling letters of support. So Paulin left the police. He did so with great regret: "I am not rich, but I am an honest man. I am the father of a family. I embraced the career of a policeman without hesitation and followed it with honor. I spent the best times of my life in it. I had a career."[88]

Career Advancement

Careers depended on the regular reports written by mayors and by prefects and subprefects assessing their performance. Such reports were at least to be submitted annually, sent by the mayor to the ministry of the interior via the prefect (though in practice such thoroughness of reporting varied from place to place).[89] These could be extremely critical: In Lyon, only about a third of reports assessing the performance of CPs contained only favorable remarks.[90] The evaluation of the police of Nantes for 1836 offered comments on eight of the ten CPs then in service in the Loire port. Calbris, a former wholesale merchant, had exhibited none of the necessary qualities to serve and lacked "zeal"; Larralde was educated and capable, attached to the government with "zeal," clearly already marked for modest police stardom; Bretaut was capable, but his daily work left something to be desired; Denyvieux was impatient; Miller had ordinary ability but compensated for this by closely studying the laws; Horrie, a former royal guard and a CP since 1822, had an unfortunate marriage, but this was no reason to lose confidence in him; Martin enjoyed a good reputation, but was somewhat abrupt in his dealings with his superiors; and Triomphe, a former soldier who had served in Spain, maintained sufficient "activity," despite his sixty-eight years, but sometimes not very polite. Thus only two of the CPs were praised without some qualifying statement.[91] By 1843, Denyvieux's impatience had become a "nervous disorder," severe enough that someone had to be added to assist him in writing reports because his writing had become illegible; he would soon be forced into retirement. Byvoët, who had been added in the interval, had become obese and demonstrated little zeal, but if forced to retire would be in a terrible financial situation, so that the mayor asked for indulgence.[92] By August 1848, of the ten CPs of Nantes, only five had been in service before the February Revolution and one of them had retired in 1845 only to be reappointed with the advent of the Republic.[93] The regularity of reporting to the ministry of the interior itself reflects the bureaucratization and professionalization of the police.

Some CPs enjoyed long, successful careers. Before his death in 1826, Lucien Coutans had accumulated forty-three years and eleven months service in the employ of the state, thirteen years in the police before 1790, more than four years employed in a military hospital, a short stint as a clerk in the central office of the Paris police, and then more than twenty-five years as CP in Paris, surviving the accusation in 1825 that his conduct provided "a very bad example in his neighborhood" because he lived with an unmarried woman.[94]

Some policemen had long terms of service in the same town. In Paris, the average CP during the Restoration served about ten years.[95] In the small, industrial Rethel (Ardennes), Jean-Baptiste Camus-Lefranc patrolled the streets from 1814 until his dismissal in early 1831—thus he survived the 100 Days. Hippolyte Laviron was appointed in 1810 in Besançon. Despite receiving what were sometimes less than rave reviews, he survived until he lost his post in the purge that followed the Revolution of 1830. Philibert Rolly, a decorated soldier, worked almost thirty years in the calm of Chaumont (Haute-Marne), and in Sedan Jean-Baptiste Kaulin, a brewer ruined by the Revolution, lasted from December 1815 until 1838. Nicolas Petit-Jean lasted in Langes from year 8 until October 1830. Couderc served in Nevers for almost twenty years before retiring in 1841. Early in his career in the police, he was valuable enough (he had saved a boy from drowning, among other accomplishments) that the municipal council raised his salary, a most unusual compliment.[96] In Versailles, Charles Herminé lasted from February 1815 until May 1831, when he was succeeded at age seventy-four by his son. Then Jean-François Blanchard served in the shadow of the château until he retired because of illness in December 1847.[97] In Villemur (Haute-Garonne), Junien lasted from the creation of the post in 1810 until the Revolution of 1830. In Vaucluse, Cavaillon and L'Isle each had a CP who served throughout the entire Restoration. Le Havre's two CPs both survived the entire July Monarchy and the Second Republic. Ferdinand Engramelle, who had worked eleven years at the prefecture in Arras, his place of birth, was named CP shortly after the Revolution of 1830. He served with Pierre Baillard, a former employee at the bureau de police in Calais, who had served as commissaire in Rouen and Yvetot during the last years of the Restoration. Both men were still in place in September 1853, by which time they had been joined by two new CPs added during the Second Republic.[98]

Each of the four cantons of Strasbourg, a key post, enjoyed remarkable stability in terms of policing during the July Monarchy: In the west canton, Collignon served from 1838 to 1850; in the south canton, Pfister lasted from 1830 to 1849; in the east Mehl served from 1841 to 1849; and Bonnisant policed the northern canton for ten years beginning in 1840. The relatively small pool of potential candidates who spoke the Alsatian dialect contributed to this surprising stability in a town considered one of the most critical for political policing. The Second Republic brought dismissals, retirements, and the appointment of a commissaire central to oversee policing in Strasbourg.[99]

Yet long terms of service in one town remained fairly unusual. Four CPs served in Mâcon during the Restoration, and five in Chalon-sur-Saône, two towns with just one post; in both cases one was fired for negligence, the others resigned or were transferred. In Quimper, Béziers, and Narbonne, five CPs served in each town during the same period. Thus the average terms of service in these four towns was between three and four years, compared to Troyes, where the survival of Jeanson from 1815 to 1831 considerably raised the average length of stay for the town's CPs, as was the case in Châlons (Marne), where François Lérard served from 1815 until a week before the Revolution of 1830. And in Nevers, five men occupied the post of CP during the July Monarchy, thus serving an average of 3.6 years (despite two long terms of service during that time, separated by three extremely short, unsuccessful tenures).[100] St. Gaudens (Haute-Garonne) had four CPs during the fifteen years of the Restoration, thus again a term of service was a little less than four years.[101] St. Brieuc, chef-lieu of the Côtes-du-Nord, had eight CPs between November 1815 and 1831, of whom five were dismissed from their posts and three resigned.[102]

Indeed, despite many exceptions, five years was a lengthy tenure in one place. However, although transfers were almost inevitable and sometimes vexing (although in some cases, prefects advanced money to facilitate a move[103]), it was not unusual for some CPs to serve much if not most of their career within a specific region. Of Rouen's CPs early in the July Monarchy (eight of nine of whom had survived the purge following the Revolution of 1830), most of those who had begun their careers elsewhere had served as CP in another Norman town: Dieppe, Yvetôt, St. Valéry-en-Caux, and Neuchâtel. Of the nine CPs in place in Rouen in June 1848, terms of service had begun in 1826, 1829, two in 1836, 1840, 1843, two in 1846, and the most recent appointment immediately after the revolution of February 1848. During the Second Republic, three new CPs were appointed. The longest-serving men in March 1851 had twenty-five, twenty-one, fifteen, eleven, and eight years experience as CP.[104]

Commissaires who did well earned promotion, and prefects and subprefects assessing their work kept this in mind. Successful careers carried older men toward the higher salaries and greater prestige of ever larger towns. The move of Horrie from Bourbon-Vendée (La Roche-sur-Yon) to Brest in 1827 typifies such a successful jump, carrying with it a somewhat higher salary. Jean-Antoine Estivalèze, CP in St. Étienne, enjoyed an extraordinary reputation during the July Monarchy. Born in Carman (Tarn), he had been a law student before entering the police. He was "zealous, active," and well respected, responsible for surveillance of former convicts. Estivalèze merited advancement, in the subprefect's informed opinion, although he did not seek it, but he was talented enough to be somewhere appointed commissaire central. In 1838, the prefect of the Eure-et-Loire put forward a request that the CP, whom he knew from previous service and had helped him obtain the post in St. Étienne, be transferred to Chartres. However, this would have reduced his annual salary from 2,050 to 1,850 francs. Moreover, his counterpart in the Loire noted that policing in St. Étienne, a considerably more challenging town, would suffer because of the transfer. The prefect of the Eure-et-Loire withdrew his request, and Estivalèze stayed on. He was so good that the next year the prefect of the Loire accused the authorities in Lyon of trying to arrange to steal him by obtaining his transfer.[105]

Logically enough, CPs in the more important posts were often somewhat older, more experienced men. In 1828, the CPs of Lyon included men who were sixty-four, sixty-one, fifty-seven, fifty-six, fifty-five, fifty-four, and forty-nine years of age, which was impressive given relatively short life expectancy; a CP appointed in 1829 was a former soldier of fifty-three years of age.[106] Of Cargue, CP in Muret near Toulouse, the subprefect noted in 1850 that "the day will soon come when his services will call him to a more considerable stage."[107] However, it is highly likely that here and there mayors, eager to rid their town of someone with whom they found it difficult to work, put forward the case that a CP deserved promotion.

As in the case of Estivalèze, assessments of the performance of CPs often frequently included mention of whether they could be considered for promotion to more important posts. Thus in Tours, the report on CP Georges Painparé praised the policeman for his zeal and devotion to his duties and to the government but added that he was "not susceptible for advancement." And of course some CPs who received poor notes but who had not done anything to merit dismissal were transferred to a lesser post (and smaller salary), as in the case of Vanbambecke, who, after being promoted from Cluny (Saône-et-Loire) to Nevers, was demoted to the very small town of Montagne (Orne) in 1842.[108]

The appointments, transfers, dismissals, and general organization of the CPs in Toulouse were typical of the experience of major cities in France. A major administrative and commercial center for the southwest, Toulouse was France's sixth largest city, its population increasing from about 60,000 in 1830 to 111,000 in 1872. The proud *parlementaires* were gone, but judges and lawyers held sway on the elegant Place du Capitole.[109]

With Napoleon's amazing return to France during the 100 Days, three of Toulouse's five CPs were replaced. The emperor's Waterloo brought the replacement of all five CPs. During the next two years, the turnover was again complete in the purge of Ultras, in the wake of the White Terror in 1815, of which Toulouse was a center.[110] At least two of them seemed more opportunists than hard-core Ultras. During the Revolution, François Pécharman had adapted himself "in succession to each opinion that he believed held sway and could profit him"; a report condemned his colleague Glassier as "a sot who assumes each color that he thinks will be advantageous . . . as for his opinions, we do not give him the honor of believing that he has any." Beginning in 1817, changes in the composition of Toulouse's CPs, who had been denounced by the mayor in 1819 as "inadequate to fill the important and delicate functions that have been confided to them," during the next four years included four dismissals as well as two resignations and two transfers.[111] In 1822, the police of Toulouse, as in many other cities and towns, was purged under the influence of the assassination of the Duc de Berri. Four of five heads fell. Pécharman got his position back, having been noted for "zeal" and "good" political opinions. There was more: His brother was secretary of one of the offices of the future Charles X. The purge of 1822 brought stability to the police of Toulouse. Counting the four new appointments, the five CPs were still at their posts six years later.[112]

Exemplary Careers on the Loire

In 1835, Jean-Bertrand St. Lary arrived at his post as CP in Blois. He had been a decorated gendarme and had applied for a position in the police even though leaving the gendarmerie meant that he would forfeit any chance of a pension. His first post had been in nearby Romorantin, where he had done well. Fifty-six years of age, he was selected over an insurance employee and a former clerk. With the support of the mayor, he had first cleared the marketplace of old furniture and piles of wood that took up a third of the space. He then ordered the removal of women selling secondhand goods from the Place Louis XII and the gambling tables that stretched from the bridge to the Promenade du grand mail, "the rendez-vous of all the town rogues, a veritable school of mischief." On his arrival (he of course felt inspired to claim), "when public coaches arrived, travelers were besieged by an insolent and disgusting throng," beggars blocking their path and harassing them until they coughed up a sou or two. Indeed, beggars with real or fake infirmities had been showing up in greater numbers. Every Monday, a group went from house to house, spending what coins they received on drink. The bishop agreed to stop giving beggars who came to his residence anything, and St. Lary himself went to houses that had proven reliable targets for beggars and asked residents to follow his lead. Several judicial convictions seemed to help. A certain Lespagne who was the leader of a band served three months in jail after being convicted of begging. St. Lary then went after his friends, harassing them "for the littlest thing, and several simply left." After Lespagne joined the army, St. Lary began to file charges against *compagnons* for the slightest misdemeanor, and several convictions discouraged them from meeting. At the cemetery, he insisted that deeper graves be provided, to eliminate the unsightly presence of bone fragments. Finally, the cabarets of Blois had always had corks protruding from their walls to beckon the thirsty. To St. Lary, cosmopolitan policeman that he was, "their disagreeable appearance . . . gives a countryside aspect to the streets, which is ridiculous in a departmental capital." A small but intense campaign for fancier signs was successful. The *police correctionnelle* handed down 852 condemnations. In 1840, St. Lary asked for a full-time secretary, although he had to settle for having one of the three agents to work in the office. In 1844, Blois was the scene of a number of attacks on people, including an atrocious murder in a guinguette on the edge of the city that sent shivers throughout a good part of France, and the municipal council raised his salary to 2,400 francs. But St. Lary, now sixty-five, was nearing the end of his career, "his forces no longer equal to his good intentions" (although the announcement of his death in 1842 had turned out to be premature). The prefect asked for the appointment of a younger and more vigorous CP. St. Lary was out of a job in January 1845 and died two years later. Yet he and his superiors might well consider that his career had been exemplary.[113]

Bertrand Cazeaux, who was posted in Tours during the July Monarchy, and his son, Philippe-Louis, were a father-son combination that represented a very Ancien Régime situation, however atypical in the nineteenth century. Cazeaux *père* provides a good example of the emerging self-image of the CPs as state functionaries. Restoration authorities had dismissed one CP after another in Tours.[114] In the month following the July Revolution, Bertrand Cazeaux, a former lieutenant in the infantry, was named one of the two CPs. His predecessor had fled the city on July 31 after news of the revolution. Cazeaux served until being forced into retirement in 1837. He was a professional and proud of it. His career provides an example of the emergence of the self-image of CPs as state functionaries.

Two CPs shared responsibility for policing Tours. The first CP appointed to serve with Cazeaux died almost immediately, and his replacement transferred to Dijon in April 1831 in what amounted to a trade for James Chameroy, but the latter was dismissed less than a year later. The latter prepared a "Situation de la police de Tours au 28 juin, 1831," sketching the problems of policing in the city in which he and Cazeaux would serve. He complained bitterly that the city was inundated with prostitutes, most of whom were minors without papers. Cabarets, cafés, and brothels stayed open until their owners felt like closing them. Many young men, including even some "well brought up," were becoming addicted to gambling, a few losing considerable sums at the tables. In some more plebeian places, one could find "fathers of families, workers who spend in one hour what they have earned during the day and who leave their household to spend part of the night in clandestine places, which they leave overheated by drink." When they poured into the street, they sang loudly and caused disturbances. In the absence of patrols by police, gendarmes, or national guardsmen, the town was victimized by frequent thefts, brawls, dealers in secondhand goods selling stolen property, the sale of unhealthy meat by itinerant traders, and encumbered streets. He blamed the July Revolution, "because people confused the word liberty, taking it to mean nothing less than license, no longer subject to laws and police regulations." Given his attack on the revolution that had brought the prefect to power, Chameroy should not have been surprised to receive word of his dismissal in February 1832.[115] Cazeaux's next partner was Georges Painparé, who was transferred to Tours, his hometown, in 1833. Painparé had overcome a "mediocre" education with great "zeal," earning public esteem.[116]

In the meantime, Tours was growing, with well over 20,000 people. The town itself lay in the form of a nearly perfect rectangle, stretching 2,000 meters along the Loire, some of its towers remaining from the fortifications that had been built at the order of Henry IV. Its emerging suburbs included St. Symphorien (301 houses in 1828) across the Loire; St. Cyr, with but 20 houses in 1828; St. Pierre des Corps, still a village; and St. Étienne and La Riche. Each offered an imposing number of inns and cabarets (fifteen in La Riche and seventeen each in St. Pierre-des-Corps and St. Symphorien).[117]

Police reports for Tours do not suggest that Cazeaux and Painparé had to confront a wave of criminality. February 1830 brought four thefts, a duel between two soldiers, an attempted murder during an attempted robbery, one suicide, and one infanticide, as well as a boat sunk by ice and an accidental fire. In April, a boat sank in the dangerous Loire River, and there were two accidental deaths, a suicide, a drowning, two fights between soldiers, one of which resulted in a death, one theft during high Mass, and the suspicious death of an elderly man, perhaps because of poor treatment by his daughter-in-law.[118] Yet there was much to do: In 1831, the CP for the western district of Tours handed out 568 passports and stamped another 2,154 passports, all during a period of seven months. He also handed out 663 cartes de sûreté. During the year, he also handled 99 cases of nocturnal noise; investigated 30 cases of fraud, 10 incidents involving prostitutes, 86 thefts, and 11 sudden deaths; followed up 23 complaints about bakers; confronted at least 34 cases of streets being blocked or encumbered; received 341 various complaints about this or that; handed out 48 certificates of indigence and 83 certificats de bonne vie; provided information on 178 different occasions, as well as drew up various other procès-verbaux.[119]

No such statistics are perfect, of course. Two arrests were registered in July for begging or vagabondage, seven in November, and five in December, but none for the other months. The latter seems highly unlikely, as do ten cases of assault and battery that same month, six in October, with none noted in the other months. Two young women declared their pregnancies in November, and two more the following month, but none in other months. There were two acts of resistance against police authority, one "crowd," one strike, one abduction, one abandoned child, a smattering of suicide attempts (two of which succeeded), and surveillance of several foreigners, including a (presumed) English man who, with a French accomplice, hoodwinked a naive peddler out of 300 francs, an unknown convincing him to exchange them at least temporarily—and as it turned out, permanently—for forty sous.[120]

Cazeaux based a request for an additional agent on the fact that many thefts occurred, as well as brawls in the *quartiers bas,* about which the national guard (still in service in the wake of the Revolution of 1830) did not want to be bothered. His solution was to propose that if *logeurs* were ordered to pay five sous for cartes de sûreté, as in some other towns, another agent could be added to the western section. Workers may have grumbled about the lack of jobs, but at least in 1831 roadwork kept some of them employed and, as long as municipal workshops could be continued, all seemed relatively well. However, Tours, like other towns, was inundated with poor outsiders and handed out tiny sums "to the imprudent who sometimes have the habit of wandering through the world." Some of these Cazeaux considered capable of participating in any kind of disorder "or of deceiving those who help them for reasons of humanity."[121]

In 1835, Cazeaux eagerly offered to his superiors his views on policing in Tours. He emphasized that the periphery seemed to attract marginal types, so that the communes on the outskirts required more systematic policing. Three years earlier, he had asked that the surveillance of former convicts and foreigners be separated, warning that the movements of "the English, Spanish, Italians, and others who are always trying to keep us from knowing where they live" be watched. The neighborhood of Poissonnerie, with its surrounding streets "in a permanent state of agitation and very often even disorder," required particular attention, with its fishmongers, vegetable sellers, and poor workers, along with about forty drinking places, particularly in that the garrison was far away.[122] In his view, Tours required more police attention than other places by virtue of its size, location, and complexity. All this took a toll on the two commissaires, inevitably contributing to tensions between them. Insisting that insufficient administrative organization was destroying "legal and moral authority," he presented an unsolicited plan of sixteen pages predicated, not surprisingly, on more money for Cazeaux and his colleague, a raise from 1,200 francs to 1,500 francs. He also stressed the necessity of a third commissaire and two more agents. By Cazeaux's reasoning, the agents' salaries could be reduced from 800 francs to 600 francs per year, which would cover the raise in the CPs' salaries, and further savings could be had by eliminating the position of the man who inspected the town's lighting. This would leave Tours with three CPs and twelve agents, each paid 600 francs, at a total cost to the municipal budget of 11,700 francs. Cazeaux added that if the mayor followed these ideas for reorganization, he would be remembered even more fondly by the inhabitants of Tours.[123]

Two years later, Cazeaux seemed positively overwhelmed by the tasks of policing: "The commissaires of police and their agents do not have a minute to themselves, no rest night or day, caught between an ungrateful public and an administration that finds fault with them. They are in an awful situation." Too many people came through Tours. There were too many workshops, too many compagnons—Tours was a capital of the *compagnonnage* and thus an important stop on the Tour de France. Compagnons, prostitutes, beggars, and various "traveling entertainers [*saltimbanques*] and other rogues and adventurers," all requiring constant attention. And so did catching thieves and ordinary rowdies, verifying lists of electors, gathering information on convicts, providing political information required by the prefect and that requested by the mayor concerning the operation of the hospice, *bureau de bienfaisance*, and markets, as well as the policing of butchers and bakers, outsiders arriving in Tours, illegal gambling, abandoned children, seditious songs, dances, spectacles, policing the mentally retarded, and much more. One hundred fifty people turned up at the police office every day. They included an endless stream of those seeking passports, hoping to gain admission to the hospital or *secours de route,* desperately wanting to find relatives or friends, complaining of thefts, vagabonds hauled in by gendarmes eager to get rid of them, and angry Tourains howling against procès-verbaux received. All this amid "the shouts and pounding coming from the jail ["le violon"], announcing that the night was stormy." It was like this 365 days a year. With just two CPs and four agents, much fell by the wayside.

Cazeaux, something of a petty bourgeois urbanist, recommended the division of the city into three arrondissements and nine sections. The agents (reversing himself) should be better paid because of the "difficult" nature of their work; uniforms would lend them some degree of respectability. Cazeaux, a well-read policeman, then quoted Cicero, responding to someone who asked him how to become rich: "Have many animals and feed them well, have many of them and feed them less well, have many animals even when you are forced not to feed them well." Tours cried out for a third CP and more agents. In his view, the uniform reorganization of the police was essential in all of France.[124]

Citing the organization of the police in Orléans, Lille, and Rennes, Cazeaux's plan also called for one of the commissaires to serve as the "principal authority," the equivalent of a commissaire central (which had existed in some other, larger towns), to whom the other CP and the agents would report. Tours required a central office of at least three rooms ("appropriate and decent") at the mairie. Along with a secretary, at least one agent would be available there at all times from 9 A.M. to 6 P.M. The principal CP would also be specifically assigned duties of haute police, including checking *livrets,* passports for indigents, assistance sums for impoverished travelers, carrying out judicial warrants, and much more. In his plan, the CP would oversee the payment to agents, deducting sums for negligence or adding to them (giving small bonuses for supervising the slaughterhouse, for example).[125] The second CP would take on "in some way the functions of a police inspector," running the office with the help of a secretary when his colleague was absent. The division of the town into arrondissements would eliminate some of the confusion, miscommunication, and duplication of tasks.

Cazeaux's proposals also suggest an emerging sense of corps among some CPs. He complained that the police were "the only corps not submitted to fixed and unchangeable rules." If this were the case, respect for the police and its authority would increase. Moreover, reorganization could make the police attractive to "many distinguished and educated young men," who fell short of a career in law, medicine, or education. They would enter the police "without a grudge," and they would do well. He then went on to an extremely important point, undoubtedly drawing on what he knew about the situation of other functionaries who were fortunate enough to be paid by the state: "In order for this to happen, the question of retirement and salary deduction to create a fund [to permit a pension] has to be considered." Agents and other police employees would be eligible to participate, thus providing encouragement to all.

But the problem of jurisdictions and rivalries remained, even though CP Cazeaux and his current colleague got along well enough. In Tours, "each commissaire views the area confided to his surveillance his property and thus absolutely off-limits to his colleague." In his view, the mayor of Tours should be the center of policing. But because the police lacked "a common center," communications between the mairie and the CPs were slow and difficult. Each CP maintained an office at home, but stamped passports and livrets at the mairie, and one of them was also assigned to the *tribunal de simple police*. The mayor, too, believed that it was essential to create a central police office; Tours had "elements of a police, but not a police." The CPs often gave the four agents contradictory orders and had virtually converted them into office clerks who ran errands from eleven until at least three in the afternoon.[126]

After seven years in Tours, Cazeaux had asked without result to be posted in a larger (and thus better-paying) post. In the meantime, Cazeaux's son, Philippe-Louis, a former agent in Tours, received the commissariat in Amboise. Born in 1806 in St. Gaudens, the younger Cazeaux had studied Latin, Greek, and the law, and now was married and had a sixteen-year-old daughter. Several times he wrote the prefect to request that he be transferred to a more important town, assuring him that he had studied "all the aspects of my functions" as CP. The son had done well enough in Amboise, particularly in political surveillance. And a flattering letter from the state prosecutor overcame a letter of denunciation that attacked the younger Cazeaux as a "libertine" who had spent more than two months of his salary "amusing himself in Paris in the company of a young girl sixteen years of age."[127]

In 1837, the prefect encouraged Cazeaux père to retire with the understanding that his son would be transferred from nearby Amboise to replace him. Such successions were extremely rare.[128] And so Cazeaux, who had complained that he had not been able to return to his pays—St. Gaudens on the edge of the Pyrénées in the Haute-Garonne—for seven years, resigned from the police. The prefect believed that the natural subordination of the younger Cazeaux to Painparé would put an end to damaging rivalries between the CPs. His appointment could end the certain "weakness" that had characterized policing in Tours, something for which Cazeaux père had perhaps unfairly been blamed. The latter implored the prefect for some reward for his work.[129] Cazeaux père disappeared into retirement with apparently nothing but his wits on which to fall back, leaving Cazeaux fils behind in Tours. Writing from a modest hotel in Paris, he asked to be informed if a suitable post became available in the police, a prison, or somewhere else: "I am still robust, very devoted to the dynasty, and I have no future."

Philippe-Louis was appointed in November 1837, but he never fulfilled the hopes of the prefect who had appointed him to Tours and drew blame that policing seemed "badly done."[130] Unlike his father, the younger Cazeaux had a difficult personality. He and Painparé had several violent disagreements, capped by an angry confrontation in front of the agents. Cazeaux spit on his colleague, challenged him to a duel, and then called him a coward because he refused to fight to the death because he had six children. After having requested assignment to Marseille, in December 1840 the hot-headed Cazeaux was shuttled off to St. Esprit, a faubourg of Bayonne. This reduced his salary and seemed to the policeman to be a step backward. The prefect's reassuring insistence that the cost of living was lower in the Landes and that his new post was important because of the proximity of the Spanish border could not overcome a sense of disgrace. Cazeaux fils took his time arriving in Bayonne, sending along a series of lame excuses, and finally was threatened with losing his job if he was not at his post by January 15. He sent a pathetic letter to the prefect, his protector, who had obtained his transfer from Amboise years before, begging him not let him fall into "discouragement and misery." His sights were still set on the port of Marseille.[131]

The successor to Cazeaux fils in Tours died within six months of his appointment, and he was replaced by Alexandre Legrand, sent from Dunkerque. In 1843, the minister of the interior appointed Jean-Charles Lascomerer as commissaire spécial in Tours, with the specific task of overseeing the policing of the construction of the Orléans–Tours railroad.[132] In the meantime, complaints about Legrand began to pile up. He insulted an agent for no apparent reason, drank with various suspicious characters, and called the long-suffering Painparé a "brigand" and a "rascal." Legrand was transferred to Gap, a world away.[133]

In the meantime, beyond the octroi, the commune of St. Étienne continued to grow rapidly, its population reaching more than 1,500 by 1843. With its attractive gauntlet of cafés and cabarets offering travelers and residents of Tours cheaper drink and less expensive lodgings, it received "most of the workers and beggars of town." Workers and soldiers carried their festivals and celebrations to the edge of town. In addition, the railway tracks were inching their way to Tours, bringing "a great number of outsiders." Tours, with its population now approaching 30,000 inhabitants, should by law have had a third policeman, but the municipal council refused to pay a third salary, and the prefect helped them out by arguing that Tours's "floating population" should be subtracted from the official number of residents. In 1843, St. Étienne received its own CP. When the suburb was incorporated into Tours, Louis Bacquez, seventy years of age at the time of his appointment, became the city's third CP in 1845. Tellingly, the mayor complained that Bacquez had been imposed on Tours by the administration and that he "corresponds more with the prefecture than with the mayor."[134]

In 1847, the municipal council finally asked that a commissaire central be appointed to oversee policing in Tours, while objecting to having to pay his salary. The February Revolution put such debates on hold. Painparé and his colleagues survived, but Bacquez was suspended by the president of the provisional commissaire on March 9 and dismissed by the minister of the interior on March 14.[135]

Tours finally received a commissaire central in July 1850. Jean-Antoine Estivalèze, the star of policing in St. Étienne, became commissaire central in Tours, responsible for all that concerned public order.[136] Tours remained divided into two districts, separated by the rue Nationale and the bridge crossing the Loire. Twelve uniformed agents (four assigned to each commissaire and four to the commissaire central) and a secretary would take turns patrolling at night and manning posts at the hôtel de ville.[137] Reflecting the obsession of the regime of Louis Napoleon Bonaparte with haute police, policing in Tours had become more centralized and more organized. Cazeaux père would have approved.

3

GETTING FIRED

Commissaires de police like Bertrand Cazeaux increasingly referred to their careers, a term that itself reveals increased professionalization within the context of the centralized state that was nineteenth-century France. Yet that state could and did frequently intervene to end careers in the police, firing CPs who in the view of prefects were incompetent or dishonest. Some CPs lost their jobs during the politically motivated purges that followed changes in regimes. They also accompanied political shifts within regimes, notably the move against the Ultras early in the Restoration and the purge that followed the assassination of the Duc de Berri in 1820.[1]

Being fired (*révocation*) was the nightmare of the CP. The dismissal of CPs during the course of the Restoration above all reveals the growing professionalism of the police within the context of increased state centralization. Prefects, not French municipalities, ultimately called the shots, establishing a code of responsibilities and allegiances that reflected the emerging police bureaucracy. The Restoration, crucial in this evolution, is the focus of this chapter.

Although without question political loyalty to each successive regime— Restoration, in particular, July Monarchy, and the Second Republic—remained essential for any CP, the significance of the Restoration lies from this respect in the fact that early in the Restoration, the regime dismissed many CPs who had not demonstrated competence. Their frantic claims that they had selflessly and heroically served the royal cause during the bad old days of Revolution and Empire could, in most cases, no longer help them. Politics still could count for much, but competence became increasingly important in the official assessment of CPs, making or breaking careers. The Revolution of 1830 again brought political antecedents into play, and during the Second Republic an active role in the political repression of the Left again became paramount in the assessment of CPs, but overall professional competence and behavior increasingly held sway.[2]

From Purges to Dismissals during the Restoration

During the First Restoration, the Bourbon administration began to purge the police of those suspected of Bonapartist sympathies, dismissing seventeen CPs in Paris. In Toulouse, three of five CPs were replaced. Following the 100 Days, the Second Restoration had considerably more time to turn its attention to the dismissal of commissaires who had served the Empire (just as the interim regime of Bonaparte had dismissed many policemen appointed during the First Restoration). Not long after the Duc d'Otrante sent each prefect a letter asking for an assessment of the loyalty of the CPs to the Empire, another missive, dated July 27, 1815, stressed the urgency to "regularize" the police, asking the newly named Restoration officials to list three candidates for each vacant position. The fate of CP Manas in Auch was typical. Described as "active and zealous in the service of Bonaparte, but absolutely useless in that of the king," he was suspended from his duties and then dismissed in December 1815.[3] In Paris, seven of the seventeen commissaires dismissed during the First Restoration had been restored to authority during the 100 Days. A new purge inevitably followed. In the Hérault, three of nine CPs were replaced following the 100 Days. For all five CPs in Toulouse, their Waterloo was getting the bad news that they had been fired.[4]

Poitiers, a town dominated by nobles and clergy, lost both of its CPs in the Ultra-inspired purge at the beginning of the Restoration. CP Ginot had loyally served during the Empire, but the Second Restoration immediately brought the wrath of Ultras down on him. The Ultras, some of whom were émigrés who had fled France during the Revolution, were the most intransigent of the supporters of the Bourbon monarchy. They refused to accept Louis XVIII's compromises with the Revolution, most notably the Charter he granted on his return, and were determined to exact vengeance on those who had supported the Revolution. In 1822, they won a resounding electoral victory, the assassination of the Duc de Berri again giving them an advantage they consolidated during the rule of the reactionary Charles X. Ginot's claims that he had lost everything during the Revolution were ignored. Seeing dismissal heading his way, he resigned to avoid the disgrace of being fired, the fate of his colleague who had served in Poitiers since 1802. The other CP in the département, in Châtellerault, also was dismissed.[5] Despite the fact that the procureur admitted that he had been a very good policeman, Louis Toustain lost his position in St. Amand (Cher) in 1816 under Ultra pressure, because he had been an imperial appointment four years earlier. The deputies of the Vienne had supported him, and in 1819 there was some recognition that he had been deprived of his position at a time when the government "was far from ours . . . it remains a wrong left over from the system of 1815 which remains to be repaired."[6] Pierre Armand Leroux, who had managed to survive since 1800, was replaced in Montmartre in January 1816. Several years later, he tried in vain to get his job back, claiming that he had been the victim of Ultra calumnies.[7] Ultra influence led to dismissals in small towns, as well, for example in Revel (Haute-Garonne) in 1816, where André Cailhasson had served the Empire as a CP, even though no complaints had ever surfaced about his work.[8]

Some CPs who served during the Empire were saved from dismissal in the first days of the Restoration because they were able to provide evidence that they had previously served the Bourbons, claims that sometimes required deft packaging. In Narbonne, Dominique Cadas had served as commissaire since 1799. Despite having stayed on the job during the 100 Days, he retained his position into the Second Restoration because he had achieved certain local notoriety as the savior in 1792 of royalist suspects who had been imprisoned. When soldiers who had arrived from the Hérault threatened the royalists with "horrible shouts" and seemed on the verge of massacring them, Cadas stood them down. He thus survived the purge of 1815, and when his position was threatened in 1822, a letter from the former archbishop of Carcassonne and from seven of the men whom Cadas saved spared him.[9]

CPs identified with the Ultras themselves fell to the next wave of purges during the Restoration. This was particularly the case in the Midi, where the purge must be seen in the context of the bloody White Terror Ultras launched against those who had supported and in some cases benefited from the Revolution and the Empire. Many of the victims of the White Terror were Protestants, particularly in Nîmes, Toulouse, and Montauban.[10] Many Ultras, as we have seen, refused any accommodation with even a Legitimist monarchy because it accepted the charter, and because the king refused to return *biens nationaux* to the families that had originally owned them, fearing civil war. The government thus sought to weed out Ultras in the ranks of the police, particularly those whose provocative presence threatened to compromise acceptance of the restored monarchy and thus public order.

Lamiscarre, a former artillery officer, was replaced as CP in Marseille in March 1816; he had run around claiming to reveal plots but only provided a series of insignificant facts that added up to nothing.[11] De la Fosse, appointed in June 1816, was a fanatical royalist who suspected everyone of Bonapartism. He was dismissed the next year, as an "enemy of peaceful people"; he had incurred the wrath of the mayor for not being familiar with the duties of a CP and not bothering to learn them.[12] Antoine-Adrien Gaulthier, appointed in January 1816, lasted less than two years in the police. The Duc d'Aumont then helped Gaulthier find a position that the latter considered beneath him, working in the shoemakers' placement office. Although Gaulthier ended up better off than almost all of his dismissed colleagues, he viewed his new position as an inadequate consolation prize, leaving him at the mercy of men who "have not ceased to test me with vexations that have included threats." And this after twenty-nine years of serving the Bourbon cause.[13]

When Raymond Pétiton was dismissed as one of Brest's CPs in late 1816, he bombarded the ministry with one indignant letter after another. "Vile calumnies" of course had brought about his disgrace. He took full credit for having saved the monarchy 20,000 francs by uncovering thefts from the naval warehouses of the port city. Moreover, he claimed that when he had first been appointed, policing in Brest had been illusory, "laws and regulations without force and the rights and guarantees owed the people unrecognized or scorned." He had restored order in the market, enforced a ban on the selling of grain and bread in other places, ended speculation so that the markets were sufficiently provisioned, and enforced the application of the metric system. He could only blame "muted and obscure maneuvers in those days, the work of ambition and malevolence." Letters of support for him arrived in the office of the director of police. However, a note attached to Pétiton's file indicated that he "carries out his functions badly," refusing to report to his superiors. Moreover, he had lived "in concubinage," an unforgiven sin during the Restoration. A subsequent prefect noted that he had indeed lost his post because he was an Ultra. Despite his vigorous campaign on his behalf, he failed to gain reappointment.[14] In Dieppe, another blatant Ultra appointee, commissaire Robion had a modest racket going in 1817. He collected an arbitrary tax on travelers entering or leaving the port, discovering that few voyagers would risk putting themselves in the dreaded *situation irrégulière*.[15]

The CPs of Paris were subject to particularly close scrutiny. Demonstrated loyalty to the Bourbons was no longer enough. In 1817, a certain Vincent submitted a secret report on the "Bruits Publics, Témoignages sur l'inconduite et les prévarications de neuf commissaires de police de Paris." It denounced Ultras, such as Gautier, CP for the "faubourg Montmartre," who owed his appointment to the "princes" and was so *fanatique* that he refused to give workers a passport unless they brought with them "a certificate of confession" signed by a priest. Bastion de Beaupré, who survived this purge but was later fired for selling certificats de bonne vie in 1828, was "hard, mean, and very vindictive," and had even refused to make the customary New Year's courtesy visit to the prefect of police on January 1. He was alleged (and probably correctly) to report directly to an underling of the Comte d'Artois, an Ultra CP said to be in the pay of the Comte de Bruges, and went so far as to circulate lists of the "enemies of the king" before elections.[16] François Simon was another Ultra who, "by his inflamed views has made many enemies for the king . . . drinking in cafés and tobacco stores with whomever shows up." In fact, Simon had been forced to sell his *étude de notaire* because he had been a cheat, and was considered a *pédophile* in the neighborhood he policed. Now, he eagerly awaited the advent of the Comte d'Artois to the throne, believing that he would put things right again. After moving from a boulevard café to the Café de la gaïté on the plebeian side of one of the southern gates of Paris, he became "one of the most unflagging habitués of a *table d'hôte* and of a *cabinet littéraire* . . . after for some time having called attention to this gathering as dangerous." There he required the patron to admit for free those carrying a card with his seal or stamp on it, disingenuously claiming that this was an excellent means of surveillance. Simon was one of four CPs then fired in the capital.[17]

It was a sign of the times that a highly placed personage who could have virtually assured someone of appointment in 1815 and 1816 could no longer save an incompetent CP. This point is illustrated by the sad case of Justin Bellier, CP of Abbeville. At the time he was named CP in May 1816, Bellier's credentials seemed impeccable. An émigré captured by republican troops in 1792, he had escaped execution by virtue of an exchange of prisoners. By the time he returned to France, Bellier had lost whatever fortune he had once had. However, the support of Cornet d'Incourt, deputy from the Somme, made possible his appointment. But Bellier did not even survive a year as CP, dismissed on February 3, 1817. He claimed his replacement was due to his identification as an Ultra. But in fact, a search he undertook without authorization in a high-handed manner was his undoing. Bellier protested bitterly, heightening the drama by describing his situation in the third person: "Without his post, he finds himself and his family reduced to a state approaching misery." Letter after letter to the prefect of police went unanswered. His last hope was that his patron might intervene on his behalf. Bellier journeyed to Paris in April 1821 in the hope of convincing the deputy to do so. The trip must not have gone well, as gendarmes found him hanging from a tree in the village of Esquennoy near Breteuil in the Oise northeast of Beauvais. It was a short distance from the limits of the Somme, to which he had to return, once more, in disgrace. In the pocket of his coat was the letter he had carefully penned to his former patron.[18]

The year 1818 brought another wave of dismissals of CPs whose work seemed to be compromised by Ultra allegiances. In Agde, Pierre Arnaud, who had first been appointed in 1813 but had been dismissed on Napoleon's return in 1815, also lost his position. His subsequent indignant letter related fifteen months of suffering as revolutionaries had moved him from one prison to another, once taking him to the foot of a scaffold, where he somehow escaped execution at the time of the fall of Robespierre. But he had to explain how he could have been appointed CP by a letter bearing the imperial eagle in 1813: After all of these dramatic events, he had "spent a considerable amount of time in strict isolation, communicating with very few people, whose simple and gentle way of life complimented my own." Then, to "his great surprise," he learned that he had been named CP. He would have refused the post, of course, had it not been for a number of people who convinced him that he would be an excellent CP. That he had been dismissed during the 100 Days meant that his earlier imperial service counted less against him, particularly because Bonapartist authorities had issued a warrant for his arrest. Recalled to his post with the Second Restoration, he claimed that three "troublemakers" persecuted him, including a certain Jacques Autié *dit l'organe du peuple*. Just as he was trying to prepare for their arrest, he received news that he had been replaced. Why? Agde, like many other towns in the Midi, remained bitterly divided, in part because of Ultra influence. Convinced Ultra or not, Arnaud's presence made calm in Agde unlikely.[19]

Likewise, Jean-Louis Augier, appointed for Laon in December 1815, had seemed a natural for appointment. His father had been the secretary for the Comte d'Angevilliers, who had looked after the property of Louis XVI and was Jean-Louis Augier's godfather. His mother had served the Duchesse d'Angoulême. When Louis and Marie-Antoinette were carted off to prison in 1792,

Augier's father had been sent to the Tuileries to fetch their personal belongings. One could not get much closer to royalty than that. He had carried out several "secret and difficult" missions in 1815 and 1816. However, Augier, too, lost his post in Laon in 1818 after having been accused of arbitrary detention by an influential local man who had insulted him. Augier's indignant letters blamed his bad fortune on a politically motivated denunciation and the lack of support from the prefect: "Since 1818, I have been miserable." It was little consolation that he was acquitted of the legal charges and received 200 francs to tide him over.[20]

Thus departed from the police many of the professional spinners of conspiracies, whose *mentalité* was shaped by the specific historical circumstances of the last years of the Empire and the first years of the Restoration. Their successors increasingly manifested more professional characteristics. Although allegiance and service to each regime remained paramount, the state increasingly judged the competence of the CP in determining their future in their chosen métier.

A strong royalist record could not save the rascal François Roustaing from losing his job in Bordeaux in 1822. He had been among those called to duty because he seemed "a good man who did good things on behalf of religion and the monarchy." But Roustaing neglected his police duties. The prefect of the Gironde contended "that no where else is policing as badly done as in Bordeaux; I would have been justified in getting rid of six commissaires when I arrived here, instead of only three." One could not count on Roustaing. He had been bribed by a Bordelais wanting to avoid a procès-verbal and he extorted a small sum from a woolens merchant. While his acerbic character antagonized people coming to see him, he proved more accommodating to the inmates of the prison, allowing one of them, a man of some wealth, to entertain a prostitute (or the other way around). He had also insulted a nun. It could no longer be overlooked that in 1813 a father had accused him of having kidnapped his daughter, age thirteen. Not even a string of letters from influential people could save him.[21]

Pierre-François Retis's unquestionable loyalty to the Bourbon throne could not prevent his dismissal from Nancy after little more than two months' service in 1822. He had served in the army of the Vendée and had remained loyal to the throne during the 100 Days. He claimed to have been a surgeon, not then a position of great status. In Nancy, Retis angered townspeople by drunkenly denouncing them as "conspirators and rebels," boasting "that his dog was more royalist than they, and that several Vendéans like he and his dog would soon show them what's what." He had to be rescued from a brawl that began in a café when he insulted a man wearing the legion of honor by saying that only "brigands" wore such a decoration. Retis tried to counter mounting disapproval, including that of the prefect and mayor, by claiming that he had enjoyed the patronage of the Duc de Berri and that highly placed police authorities in Paris had entrusted him with crucial political missions in Lorraine. When word arrived that he had cheated a widow out of 2,000 francs and had left behind debts in Blois and Le Mans, he was finished in the police.[22]

Jean-Marie de Gallemont claimed near perfect royalist credentials when he was named in 1822 to Poitiers, faithful to altar and throne. Having emigrated during the Revolution, he had been wounded fighting against the armies of the Republic and had been named chevalier de St. Louis. But he was very poor and thus ill at ease in Poitiers; moreover, he still owed more than 300 francs to a Parisian tailor who sent him nicely dressed to Poitiers. De Gallemont was negligent and made inappropriate comments to the daughter of a count, trying to talk her into his room. Moreover, creditors still hounded him; he threatened a witness to get corroborating testimony; and he behaved so badly toward a woman who disrupted mass that the offended priest turned to defend her. By 1824 the procureur général and the mayor had concluded that he was inadequate as "un homme public," a telling phrase. When he was told that he must resign—a far more honorable ending to a career than being fired and one that for the most part was reserved for those who could produce such political pedigree—he asked for a delay of fifteen days "in order to have the time to alert my friends and protectors to my unfortunate position." Furthermore, he dared ask the prefect for money to go to Paris and search for a job, rambling on about his services to the legitimate monarchy, for which he had been "criblé de blessures." But to no avail.[23] Tellingly, not even the pedigree of having been named on the recommendation of the Duc d'Angoulême in 1815 could save Moncontie, fired in 1822 for negligence.[24]

As in the case of letters sent by those asking in the first years of the Restoration to be named to the post of CP, those sent to protest dismissal put forward dramatic accounts merging the stories of their lives with France's intense recent history, describing themselves as honorable men of sterling reputation and unshakable principles.[25] They unfailingly evoked their distinguished services to the monarchy before the Restoration. From Dax, in 1817 Lescala sent a twenty-five-page letter with fifteen separate accompanying texts defending his record of service. Lescala described himself as a victim of his loyalty to the August Dynasty of the Bourbons and reminded the prefect of police that he had suffered in prison during the Terror.[26] J.-B. Dutertre-Desaignement, who had been fired in Marseille in 1818, bombarded the ministry of the interior with missives asking for reappointment. Naturally, his self-serving printed "Notice sur M. Desaignement" skipped delicately over the causes of his dismissal, which stemmed from his indecision and tendency to talk too much at the expense of his service. His file still bulges with more than forty letters.[27] Following his dismissal as CP in Toulon that same year, Jules Feraud protested that two years earlier he had caught a *conspirateur,* who subsequently was executed. He sent several couplets that he had written to celebrate the birth of the Duc de Bordeaux (it would be too cruel to quote from them, even though their author has been dead for well more than a century and a half). Years later, he proudly wrote that he had written several stunning stanzas to grace an arch of triumph erected for the arrival of the Duchesse d'Angoulême in 1823.[28] The very language of such defensive accounts of service in the police in itself reflects some growing sense of professionalism in expectations and standards, something they shared with judges, as David Troyansky's research demonstrates.[29]

Larivière, removed from Chartres in October 1818, was still protesting disgrace four years later, claiming—correctly—that he had been dismissed because he had been an ultra-royalist. But Larivière had been fired because of negligence, and in any case, his reappointment would bring back "pénibles souvenirs," not all of which had anything at all to do with politics. Larivière had failed to enforce municipal ordinances on the draining of *fossés d'aisance* during the dry months of the summer. Three brothers who lived across the street from him in the most densely populated quartier in Chartres had been killed when their ditch collapsed, asphyxiated when their father sent them in, one after the other, to try to rescue the first who had fallen.[30] Claude Broissonnard, dismissed from Brest in 1825, described the disgrace of "being fired, today a condemnation to moral and civil death . . . with neither a job nor means of existence, with no other hope than your extreme kindness." He promised to send along "numerous attestations to my good conduct."[31] And this he did, but to no avail.

Charles Louis Prévôt began his career in La Rochelle, where had earned the support of the mayor, with whom he had fought in the Vendée against the soldiers of the Revolution. Having been decorated by Louis XVIII and the Duc de Berri and named to the Compagnie des gardes de la porte du Roi, he carried provocative views with him to Montpellier in 1817. There, the mayor, who believed he should have the right to name CPs, had been hostile to his nomination, describing him as "too much of a hot-head, who could compromise public peace if the higher authorities do not compel his moderation." The mayor's assessment proved correct. Prévôt announced to everyone who would listen that his father-in-law had been a mayor under the "martyred king" and that the Revolution had taken his shipping fortune but not his honor. He treated his promotion from La Rochelle, then a town of 13,000 people, to Montpellier, a town of 35,000, as a demotion. Prévôt described himself as surrounded by enemies, "vampires" out to destroy him, while singing his own praises as an efficient policeman who pursued "guilty parties from all classes . . . with complete impartiality." He had provided security for the missions in 1821, while saving a man and his wife from a crowd that believed they had insulted the missionaries. He had extracted one confession of a crime by using persuasion based on the principles of religion, or at least he had shrewdly made such a claim in language that he believed authorities of the restored monarchy wanted to hear. He had also provided essential services during the epidemic of yellow fever in 1821, inspecting sewers and cemeteries to make sure that bodies were properly buried. But now, as an official in the ministry in Paris put it, "there is nothing that can be done." He was through.[32]

In the Norman town of Falaise, Jacques-Jean Esnault had been appointed in 1816. Born in 1767, Esnault claimed that he was preparing for the seminary when the perfidious Revolution came along. To save himself from "the revolutionary axe," he had joined the army. Good fortune brought him home to Falaise in 1797, where he found work in the Bureau des hypothèques. But his royalist opinions got him imprisoned, until he was freed after the 18th Brumaire. He married on the first day of the new century. Now what was he to do for a living? Desperate, "not having a trade, I became a humanist!" ("N'ayant point d'état, je me fis humaniste!") Indeed he embarked on a career teaching Latin. This lasted until he was forced to pay a fine of 3,000 francs (so he claimed) for having taught without authorization. In 1823 his career in the police came to an end because of what he called "several insignificant events" that he blamed on "the goodness of my soul." With six children to feed, he supplemented his meager salary by taking bribes from those wishing to avoid being slapped with a procès-verbal; he forced the entrepreneur of municipal lighting to provide him with free services; and he demanded free drinks from a cafetier, who then blew the whistle on him. Perhaps even worse, in three years, he had drawn up but three procès-verbaux and made only one arrest. He was through, despite a petition on his behalf, and his own massive, predictably self-indulgent *mémoire justificatif*.[33]

Henri-Louis Arnault, an émigré in 1791 who had been rewarded a chevalier de St. Louis, was a disaster as CP in Limoges, "almost incapable of writing a letter or a procès-verbal of more than ten lines." In 1818, the mayor considered him "firm, someone of integrity, honest, and loyal," but the former soldier with a small pension had conserved his old military habits, smoking, drinking, swearing, and chasing women. He preferred "justice dispensed by blows from a truncheon than the slow and wise procedures that the law represents," showing more bravado than prudence, while ignoring the minor but essential details in policing Limoges. In 1822, the ministry of the interior dismissed Arnault for having contributed by his conduct to the "demoralization" of Limoges. His "roguish" (*crapuleuse*) conduct included gambling, corrupting young men by introducing them to young women of uncertain morals, and tolerating if not subsidizing a brothel, where "young girls, sometimes not even nubile—daughters of artisans or of bourgeois—go furtively while their parents think them at work or in church." He lured several "unsuspecting" girls to his apartment, threatening to denounce them to their parents if they resisted his advances. Even his continued good standing among Limoges's Legitimists could not save him.[34]

Who could have had better antecedents than Boudin, commissaire in Metz? He had been wounded defending the royal family at the Tuileries on August 10, 1792. But this "honest and even pleasant man" was in his police work "an old lady who has no other ambition than to please everybody and to get in the way of no one." He, too, was dismissed in 1822. Even the enthusiastic recommendation of a deputy could not get him appointed to a smaller town, where he could do less damage.[35]

With a good royalist name, the patronage of a noble deputy, and excellent political antecedents (his family had been trapped in Toulon during the British bombardment and he had been subsequently imprisoned by the revolutionaries), Jean-François Maistre seemed to have everything going for him. The CP for Brest had learned Breton while taking refuge in Quimperlé and could also speak with Provençal sailors in their own language. But none of this could save him from dismissal after he was accused of compromising the virtue of a fourteen-year-old girl by writing her passionate letters addressed to his "future wife," missives that his current wife could not have appreciated. His protector managed to get him 200 francs for past services but could not save his career in 1824.[36]

The case of Étienne Arnaud, a former grain merchant turned CP in his native Lyon, demonstrates how tensions—indeed the rivalry—between a prefect and a mayor could sometimes protect a beleaguered policeman from dismissal. Benefiting from the support of the mayor, who was in a cold war against the prefect over the question of police authority, Arnaud held on despite accusations that he was being paid off by a *hôtelier* to ignore the presence of certain guests about whom the authorities had every reason to worry. Prostitutes solicited with impunity in the district to which he had been assigned, and wagons parked haphazardly, blocking circulation. Arnaud had connections: His daughter was the wife of a prominent grain merchant in Mâcon. His major vice, gambling, was probably also his greatest asset, as he was a big winner, rumored to have won and tucked away a fortune. Arnaud died in 1827 before he could be dismissed.[37]

The story of Jean-Baptiste David-Claret in Montauban illustrates the tension between royalist pedigree and competence during the Restoration. The task of policing the red-brick town of 26,000 people in which fanatical royals hated Montauban's Protestants was divided between two commissaires. Jean-Marie Ansas lasted from December 1815 until September 1823, when he lost his job because of complaints of frequent absences and uneven application of the laws. But if some people in Montauban viewed the dismissal of Ansas as inevitable, many, including the mayor himself, considered the survival of his colleague Jean-Baptiste David-Claret to be nothing short of miraculous.

Because of his unwavering loyalty to the Bourbon cause and his reputation as something of a man of letters, David had acquired patronage in the highest places, including—perhaps—the Comte d'Artois, the future Charles X. To listen to David tell it—which few in Montauban could avoid—"the fatal and infernal Revolution" had cost him some 80,000 livres and his house. He had been "a distinguished master of writing" before 1789, an "associate" of the Bureau académique d'écriture, teaching orthography in Paris. The Revolution found him in Montauban, where he formed a force of 150 "elite citoyens," who attacked "vigorously those cannibals, who were carrying out their orgies" in a château near Montauban. After being imprisoned in 1791, he had made his way to Spain, where he continued to voice his strong hatred of the Jacobins, denouncing them in French, English, Spanish, and Latin.

David thus saw his nomination as commissaire in Montauban in December 1815, through the support of the department's deputies, as a modest reward for suffering the purgatory of Spain. Named in September 1823, Pinot de Moira arrived in Montauban with all good intentions, hoping to find an able, energetic colleague. Instead he found David. "In the first days after my arrival," Pinot de Moira reported, "M. David didn't do anything, appearing in our office only very rarely, claiming to be sick. I went along with his absence and inactivity easily in good faith." But Pinot de Moira soon learned that David was a spry man of seventy years. Pinot de Moira worked far into the night to accomplish the work of two men. He soon became convinced of the inability and absolute *nullité* of David.

Yet the prefect still wanted David to stay on. Thus, the municipality found itself helpless before the authority of the state. Prefect Charles-Antoine Limairac, former deputy from the Haute-Garonne, ignored David's obvious incompetence, as well as certain habits that bordered on theft. David walked off with some items saved (by someone else) from a house fire. And while ignoring almost all of his duties, he did "visit" the bakers, not to check on their supplies, weights, and prices but to pick up large, expensive cakes for his family that he insisted be given him. It was the same at the grocers of Montauban, where he filled his pockets with goods. When he did show up at the police office, it was only to spy on his colleague and take what paper and pens he could find there.

When Montauban's mayor again complained, David assured him that the prefect would protect him. So the mayor was left musing about possible replacements, any of whom would have been better than David. These included "a type of saltimbanque" without talent, a man whose business had recently failed, a usurer, a debtor lucky enough to enjoy the protection of his creditor, and someone who lived the good life and crooned drinking songs. Even if David left, the relatively low salary attached to the post would discourage most competent candidates. David was protected by not only the man the mayor referred to as "this monkey of a prefect," but such Restoration luminaries as Baron Portal, the minister of the navy and colonies. Moreover, the prefect thought it would be barbaric to toss out an elderly gentleman "blanchi dans la fidelité," particularly in a town in which even the Catholic lower classes supported the monarchy with fervent passion.

At last the prefect found a solution that allowed David to leave with his dignity more or less intact. He named five new members to the municipal council willing to offer the colorful, aged policeman an annual pension of 200 francs. David resigned in January 1826. This eccentric old man with the flamboyant handwriting had been one of the notable survivors of the system of pure political patronage.[38]

To be sure, politically motivated dismissals still occurred.[39] Obviously, any commissaire who expressed liberal political sympathies, or who failed to carry out the tasks of the haute police by watching for conspiracies and signs of opposition, or who stood accused of being too soft on liberals, would soon be through. In 1822, Jacques Coutancin lost his post in Bourbon-Vendée, that pathetically artificial capital of the Vendée, constructed on Napoleon's order in the middle of the bocage on the ruins of a small bourg with the goal of bringing "civilization" to the fanatical hotbed of clerical counterrevolution. If there was any part of France in which a functionary should have stayed away from any festivity—even if in honor of a baptism—that had been unthinkingly scheduled for January 21, the anniversary of the execution of Louis XVI, it was the Vendée. The guests ate, drank, and danced far through the night. The CP walked out into the early morning hours and to unemployment.[40] Pierre Biers, dismissed in Béziers in 1828, blamed in ten virtually identical letters his fall on the "philosophic illness" that had brought the Revolution.[41]

However, as French cities and towns increased in size and complexity, the rich dossiers of the police reveal the gradual professionalization of the municipal police. But "professionalism" did not necessarily mean "neutrality," as political considerations inevitably lurked behind some decisions of hiring and firing.

However, ability and performance began to count for considerably more during the Restoration, and purely political antecedents came to matter less. Competence became—barring the folly of political opposition—arguably the most important measure for assessing the police. It could be assessed, if not quite measured, by reviews of how well a CP fulfilled the tasks assigned to him. Indeed, the language of official reviews increasingly reflected this preoccupation.

Impeccable political antecedents could, here and there, bring a second chance. Emilien Martelly, who had served as a captain in the royal volunteers of the Duc d'Angoulême, served as CP in Montpellier, remaining obsessed with conspiracy. Yet clouds of doubt surrounded him, because he hung around cafés and protected illegal gambling. He may have temporarily saved himself from dismissal by sending to the minister of the interior a copy of what at least appeared to be a secret alphabet used by conspirators against the Bourbon monarchy, taken from a *demi-solde* passing through town not long after the discovery of the conspiracies of Belfort and of the Loire. He earned transfer in 1823 to Marseille, to a district with relatively few cafés to tempt him.[42] Barral de Baret, appointed to Corbeil in February 1830, in what turned out to be the Restoration's last months, simply never showed up. Serving in Coulommiers for two years, where, despite being from the Hérault, he had family connections, he had fallen into serious public disrepute because of what was considered an egregious lapse in morals, what Barrel de Baret dismissed as "des bruits infâmes." A transfer seemed the only way of resolving the situation. Humiliated, Barral de Baret pouted, staying in Coulommiers. Yet because he had served with the Duc d'Angoulême in the Midi in 1815 and been decorated for his loyalty, he received only a stern warning from the minister of the interior: "It's up to you now to justify our hopes, in exerting all your efforts to destroy, through conduct thereafter exemplary, the unfortunate impression that your faults have left and for which you are still reproached." He took up his post, lasting until the purge that followed the July Revolution of 1830.[43]

The Increasing Primacy of Competence

Negligence and incompetence remained high on the list of reasons CPs were dismissed as the policing became more centralized and more professional. An inability to read and particularly write adequately could increasingly doom a CP. To take one example of many, Guilhaume Cazat, a former wood merchant, had become CP in his small hometown of Fos in the Haute-Garonne. But despite his energy, his work drew criticism because he barely knew how to write and was of mediocre intelligence. The fact that he spoke some Spanish was not enough.[44]

No one could have been more humiliated by being dismissed than Julien Alletz, commissaire in Paris from year 8 until his dark day of June 7, 1820. Alletz, a topographer who had first been named commissaire during the Directory, had published, at his own expense, the four-volume *Dictionnaire de police moderne pour toute la France,* which appeared in an increasing number of police offices. Since his appointment in the wake of the Ninth of Thermdor, Alletz had spent thirty-five years in the police and other administrative posts, twenty of them in the quarter of the Place Vendôme in Paris, where he had "survived all the revolutionary storms, not without great peril because of his anti-revolutionary views." However, in 1820, Alletz was immediately suspended and then dismissed for having released from custody three men, including a decorated general who was to be arrested, even after they had refused to reveal their names. Several months after the assassination of the Duc de Berri, this major gaffe could not be forgiven. Despite "much testimony on his behalf," Alletz was out of work. Owing his publisher 15,000 francs, Alletz was left with nothing but "his honor."[45]

Antoine Desribes, CP in St. Flour (Cantal) was dismissed in April 1823, "being immoral, negligent, *mal pensant* and dangerous." He had found work in the supply corps for the army of Spain, after which he went to Bordeaux, where he presented himself as a faithful servant of the king. Desribes told police there that he could deliver to them "a forger, and perhaps a conspirator," which he tried to do in the company of a disguised gendarme, a minor scene that failed. A relative wrote on his behalf, stressing his miserable solution and his "royalist heart." But notes in his file stressed instead his debts and lack of *considération* in St. Flour, where the mayor noted that he was "somewhat lax" in the fulfillment of his duties, alternating between underreacting and overreacting. The municipal council had tried to get rid of him by refusing to allocate money for his salary, particularly after he had been involved in a violent dispute over stolen flower pots. Desribes, however, was proud of the job he had done: "I fulfilled my functions to the extent that my lack of knowledge permitted"—which pretty much summed it up. He asked the minister of the interior for "some instruction about the post in which I am still quite a novice." He also sent along a list of his professional accomplishments during the four months he had been a CP, while complaining about the incapacity of his two agents, whom he described as "the valets of the town hall," and who spent most of their time working at the octroi. But he was through in the police.[46]

With the firming up of the administrative hierarchy, disobedience was often cited as a reason for dismissal. François Sablon lost his post in Bourg-en-Bresse after failing to heed the instructions of the prefect of the Ain, Christophe Jussieu, who ordered him to stand ready in the theater in case of seditious behavior on the part of spectators. The CP was not there when an expected seditious couplet was repeatedly sung.[47]

A few CPs were dismissed because they ignored their posts but not businesses they had going on the side. Michel Cheri lost his job in Paris in April 1830 after four years in service because he spent most of his time in Courbevoie, outside Paris, where he had a wine business and loaned money at usurious rates (12 percent and even 15 percent), his clients in the latter business including some of his colleagues in the police.[48] Likewise, one of the CPs of Lille fired in 1815 had an interest in the small company that had a contract to look after the city's lighting. He managed to arrange his schedule so that he could extinguish the lights before the time agreed on in the contract, so as to save his company money.[49]

Advancing age, inevitably reducing the "zeal" of CPs, could lead to dismissal. In Villemur (Haute-Garonne), a town of 10,000 people, Bernard-Antoine Junière served as CP from 1810 until after the Revolution of 1830, when he was eighty years of age. Each year the town's hamlets seemed farther away.[50] In Paris, Edmond O'Reilly, a chevalier de St. Louis who had served ten years with the army of Condé, seemed to be losing his mind. He forgot orders that he had received two hours earlier and wasted four days looking for a monkey he believed had been strolling about the rue St. Florentin. He took men playing *boules* on the Champs-Elysées for conspirators, and, armed with his sword, tried to go to St. Cloud to warn the king about another conspiracy he had uncovered. He hauled people into his office and harangued them, *bâton* in hand, and on several occasions forced his victims to beg for his pardon in public. O'Reilly was allowed to resign.[51]

Louis-Charles Richart, appointed to Lyon in January 1818, was dismissed in the quartier of the Metropole in December 1824. It turned out that the commissaire was not really Richart at all but an indebted "mauvais sujet" known as Peluche. After going broke in the grain trade in Noyon in the Somme, he had taken the identity of Richart, a local surgeon who still lived in Jean Calvin's hometown. Peluche had even managed to have a false birth certificate registered with a notary in Paris. In 1826, after working for a mining company in St.-Étienne and then talking his way into the job of secretary at the town hall, he returned to Lyon. There he could be found hanging around the cafés of the Presqu'ile, denouncing Lyon's mayor as "too stupid and too much of a Jesuit in that he supports only the rabble." A liar and a cheat, Richart was aptly described as "dangerous," one of the few CPs to fit the Vidocq stereotype of the métier.[52]

The past of Charles Chailan de Mories, appointed CP in Orléans in September 1816, also caught up with him. He had asked for the job, because of his perfect knowledge of the inhabitants of the region and his experience watching troublemakers in the region of Gex and the Swiss frontier. Even his status as chevalier de St. Louis could not prevent rumors that the CP had been implicated in a counterfeiting scheme by the tribunal of Vaud in Switzerland. He had been acquitted, but only because of the lack of sufficient evidence. Chailan de Mories then accused the Bonapartists of harassing him. But there was more. His wife in Orléans was but one of two; the first Madame Chailan de Mories was still very much alive. When the mayor called him in about this unfortunate rumor, he insisted that the woman with whom he lived was his legitimate wife but could not produce any proof. Mories was, in the opinion of the prefect, one of those men "that one calls dishonest, and as for his abilities, they are absolutely *nuls.*" The proof also lay in several selected reports, such as one that rambled on, "Nothing new, except a man hung himself," and one that simply noted, "Let's say that in passing along a street . . . I saw a great stream of blood that was running into the stream running from the sewer of Madame N." A little vague. Furthermore, his experience on the Swiss border had stamped Mories with a permanent sense of intrigue; few days passed without his announcing the discovery of one conspiracy or another. This when he was not poaching and exchanging his catch with certain unscrupulous butchers for meat. He had also pulled off a minor coup, marrying off his nineteen-year-old son to a Parisian baroness sixty years of age. When the baroness turned up in Orléans, having for whatever reason been sent to Mories in the hope he could find her a suitable companion, the CP had chased off her escort by accusing him of theft, driving him away from Orléans. Mories never got his job back.[53]

Most dismissals met with little local opposition. Some even brought smug condescension from those smirking at the former CP, now skulking about without his *écharpe,* that emblem of authority not long before so proudly—even arrogantly—carried. But when Maurice Tristant was let go in Verdun after complaints of him lacking energy and failing to arrest some soldiers for seditious shouts, protests were heard because people of all classes seemed to like him. His appointment to Chartres in 1819, a post he held until his death in 1824, made him one of the very few CPs to be reappointed after being fired.[54]

Occasionally, the dismissal of a commissaire brought not only letters on his behalf that he solicited but also petitions of support from townspeople. Sagot, popular in St. Germain-en-Laye since being named to the post in the 1800, had battled revolutionary insurgents at the Tuileries in 1792 and claimed to have loaned nobles money so they could flee France. In 1815, he had been dismissed by Napoleon and then braved popular opposition by removing a common incendiary placard from near a church—"house for sale, priest to be hung." He was fired in 1817 for having failed to prevent seditious whistling in the theater. But, "incapable and negligent," he had to go. A petition protested, announcing that "the inhabitants of St. Germain all want M. Sagot to be their commissaire de police." The petitioners undoubtedly felt some sense of vindication when the successor lost his new position the following year after taking bribes.[55]

Disrepute

Once it became painfully clear that a commissaire had lost the respect of townspeople—the nightmare of disrepute—he was through. Despite his royalist credentials, Jean-François Lurin, whom we met earlier, lost the respect of all St. Brieuc, and soon his job, after being seen brawling in public with one of his agents. His "beautiful handwriting" could not save him.[56] Jean-Joseph Copin's tenure in Romans ended in 1821. Faced with political agitation, he neglected to write down the names of witnesses, making prosecution impossible. Perhaps even worse, his son had been among those singing the *Marseillaise.* When Copin père had ordered the group of young men to disperse, "his son had been the first to resist him . . . the father did not have enough authority to make him obey." Townspeople lost all respect for the father, who henceforth could hardly command much authority.[57]

Some CPs were also fired for what were considered moral failings. During the purge in Marseille in 1823, Joseph Bourguignon was among several let go because they were suspected of dishonesty. "His probity has not always been above suspicion on the part of the public" was the way the prefect had put it. At the border crossing with Savoy of Pont-de-Beauvoisin in the Isère, Jacques-Antoine Théol also was on to a profitable undertaking, preying on workers crossing into France from Piedmont. His job was admittedly not easy: verifying some eighty to ninety passports each day in addition to the usual tasks of policing the town and watching out for those entering France illegally. The considerable booty taken from those passing the frontier lightened his load. He was fired in April 1826, just as his lucrative *haute saison* was beginning.[58] Likewise, in Le Havre, Deloynes and Manuel lost their jobs when it was discovered that they were raking off enormous sums (as much as 20,000 francs) from the port city's innumerable prostitutes, splitting the take with the prison doctor who inspected the women.[59]

Jacques Faroux's career as the CP for the Arcis quarter in Paris could not have ended in 1825 in greater humiliation and tragedy, because he lost the possibility of a pension after twenty-six years of service because a CP dismissed from his post lost all claims, however remote, to a pension, saving municipalities money but leaving the policeman with nothing. Faroux suffered the fatal révocation, "a stain for a public man." It happened that the CP for the quartier du Luxembourg was making his nightly rounds, "as he does frequently, in the almost uninhabited streets" that bordered the nursery of the garden of the Chamber of Peers. His goal was "to chase away the debauched, prostitutes, and even more men given over to infamous practices [*livrés à des gouts infâmes*] who, despite surveillance, gather habitually there." He came on a man and "young woman very close to one another." The man turned out to be his colleague, Faroux. Admittedly in an awkward situation, with the "pont de son pantalon abattu," Faroux bravely tried to explain his way out. He had been on duty in his quarter but had left to go beyond the Montparnasse city gate to eat at the Moulin Janseniste, returning through the gate at about eight in the evening. He had taken the most direct route back to his quarter, which took him through the gardens of Luxembourg. He stopped "to take care of a need, which naturally explains my position against a wall." It was then that a prostitute suddenly approached him, making "indecent propositions" that of course he "did not accept." But before he could even arrest the offending woman, his colleague arrived. This led, of course, to some "humiliating suppositions" that wounded this *brave royaliste* who had been ruined by the Revolution, and who had served in the administration of military transport for years before becoming a CP, and who had served so loyally during the elections of 1822 and 1824. No one seemed to believe him and, at age fifty-nine, he was out of a job.[60]

As the number of *débits de boissons* and the amount of alcohol consumed in

France's urban world rapidly rose, the demon rum took its toll on some CPs. Simon Marcon lost his job in Tarbes in 1819 because of "his habitual intemperance—he is often *dans le vin*—as well as his brutality, his scandalous behavior."[61] Marc Rapallo sometimes went about his job in Toulon completely drunk— another sense of the "spirit of Rapallo"—dipping in and out of the tough, cheap bars of the port. He patronized brothels as a client, not as a policeman, and even set up his office in a house in which prostitutes lived. The Restoration was not as *pudique* a regime as it has often been characterized, but this was going too far. Rapallo's brief career ended several months before the Revolution of 1830.[62]

The fates of several commissaires offer at least a brief glimpse into the world of homosexuals in Restoration France. J.-B. Bercq's alleged "shameful vices" may have contributed to the suppression of the post of CP in the small spa town of Bourbonne-les-Bains (Haute-Marne) in 1818.[63] Adolphe Carbonneaux de Laujol lost his position in Niort in 1824 because "people attribute to him with an heinous vice, [and] a pronounced repugnance for women and a marked penchant for licentious discourse." A boy whose father worked at the prefecture accused him of "having tried to commit acts on him that indicate a heinous vice and brutal passion." The boy related in the presence of a gendarme that Carbonneaux had been guilty of suggestive language, indeed of certain "fondling." This was not the first time Carbonneaux de Laujol had faced such accusations; moreover, others evoked "his horror for women and for marriage. He has been heard speak in an extraordinary way about his friendship for a man of his age, today married, a merchant living in Saumur." Complicating the search for the truth were tensions between the prefect of the Deux-Sèvres and the mayor of Niort, who at first had supported the CP. At a minimum, Carbonneaux stood accused of spending too much time in Paris, the implication being that his time in the capital was related to "his most perverse inclinations." Carbonneaux penned an impassioned defense, blaming the accusations on vengeance, stemming from the fact that the mayor, his patron, had worked against the royalist candidate in the elections. But Carbonneaux was finished in the police and presumably returned to the anonymity of Paris for good.[64]

Heavy debts could engender disrepute. Rulings by the Tribunal de Commerce of Le Havre against Alexis Manuel, who had been named to that port city in 1818, left him in a state of "complete discredit, which make his services almost non-existent in Le Havre." His successor himself never recovered from debts contracted during the Revolution.[65] Nicolas-Pierre Haillot de Sellincourt lost whatever respect he had enjoyed in Auxonne because his debts put him in the embarrassing position of owing money to some of the same people he was supposed to be watching. In 1820 he was reassigned to a smaller town, far from his creditors.[66]

Likewise, family disputes could weigh heavily on reputation. René Fouquère in Paris was considered in the higher reaches of the administration one of the finest CPs in France. But when his wife began having affairs, Fouquère's reputation suffered (although one report suggested that he abandoned her). Yet he survived until the purge of August 1830.[67]

Denunciations

Many CPs faced denunciations or sheer calumny at sometime during their careers. Depending on circumstances, they could be the kiss of death, particularly if there seemed to higher authorities to be something to the allegations presented. Jean-Marie Durand, CP of Hyères, served from November 1815, when his "devotion to Legitimacy" was rewarded, to 1823, when he was denounced as "a hideous vampire and the most immoral man one could ever find." Not only did his detractors claim that he did not do his job, but he was guilty of abuses of authority and other acts so awful that "the pen refuses to relate them," including "immoral caresses" that he lavished even while wearing the sash emblematic of his police authority. Durand's detractors, some of whom were also his creditors, finally did him in.[68]

Yet many survived such letters, even those penned by experienced hands. Senior officials ignored most denunciations. François Camet was accused of demanding fifteen francs to conceal the fact that a man found dead had killed himself, when he had not. Then he was accused of intimate relations with a women who was in principle a *limonadière* but was reputed to run a brothel. To hear him tell it, the policeman had visited the house only in the line of duty. A former officer of the Royal Army of the Midi during the 100 Days, Camet outlasted these denunciations, as well as four others.[69] In Châteauroux, commissaire Jacquet survived an anonymous extravagant attack that arrived at the prefecture in 1832. The fact that the letter was sent to the prefecture and not the mairie was itself telling. The denunciation began, "You have been misled [*on a trompé votre religion*] by those telling you that Jacquet is worthy of being commissaire de police in this town. This man only knows the occupation of a soldier from the ranks, more brutal than an animal and similar to a tiger, he shreds without pity all the unfortunate souls who fall beneath his claws, that is to say, have the misfortune to displease him. He frequents prostitutes…and spends part of the night in cabarets and cafés."[70] Lachapelle, CP in Poitiers, learned that he had been denounced—indeed, that he was going to be fired because his authority in Poitiers had been "paralyzed" for whatever reason. The denunciation had been sent anonymously by "some highly placed person," sent to "one of the leading officials of our town." Thus forewarned, Lachapelle prepared a defense, blaming implausibly "implacable enemies" in Troyes who still persecuted him from afar: "My blood runs cold—I am and always will be without reproach. Yes, I go to cafés. That's where a commissaire de police should be to keep track of habitués."[71]

Obviously many CPs, facing sharp criticisms from mayors and prefects, assumed that someone was saying something nasty about them, and must have spent no small amount of time trying to guess what had arrived on the prefect's desk and who had penned it!

The Tricolor Returns in 1830, the Republic in 1848

The Revolutions of 1830 and 1848 also brought predictable purges of the police. In both cases, the sudden transfer of power temporarily reversed the trend toward the adoption of professional criteria in the dismissal of CPs, as each regime embraced the purge as a weapon of political assertion. Yet during the July Monarchy and the Second Republic, the professional criteria for hiring new policemen was considerably higher than had been the case at the beginning of the Restoration.

As the fighting on July 28, 1830, swirled around him in Paris, CP Gombeau found himself at the Place Maubert, where he was told that "a price has been put on your head in the neighborhood for your head," and that there were people prepared to slit his throat. He hid for two days, returning to the prefecture of police on the July 30, where he wisely took the precaution of picking up a tricolor flag to take back to his office. There he found that his secretary, who had coveted his job, had taken over, with the support of the national guard, and had even moved into his residence. Naturally, Gombeau's letter of protest rang with his liberal principles; however, it offered a sharp contrast with his letter the previous year when he had proposed a plan for countering the "sinister projects" of the liberal opposition. Needless to say, he did not get his job back.[72]

In Toulouse, the purge was inevitable because of the memory of the White Terror that had accompanied the (second) return of the Bourbons in 1815. When news of the July Revolution in Paris arrived, only two CPs were available, Turies and Dunogués. The new mayor recommended the appointment of two CPs who had been fired earlier in the Restoration, Arthaud and Plain, both of whom had served during the 100 Days. The provisional prefect suspended De la Tour on September 21. He had hesitated when ordered to pick up a bust of Charles X that stood in the municipal tax office. It would no longer be needed. De la Tour had asked for a written order, and, on receiving that, had taken the bust and placed it at the door of the prison. It had not been the time to hesitate. Another CP accepted reappointment. As for Turies and Dunogués, both were fired. Turies had been absent on the night of August 3, when a provisional administration set up shop at the Place du Capitole, and appeared only the following day. Naturally he protested bitterly—he had been sick in bed.[73]

Two CPs survived the change; both had held their posts in Toulouse only for a matter of months. Two seasoned veterans of Napoleonic military campaigns appointed in August and December provided a nucleus of stability in Toulouse in the early years of the July Monarchy.[74]

In Paris, thirty-three of the fifty-seven CPs were "allowed to retire."[75] The purge was thorough in Marseille, where a local newspaper, the *Sémaphore,* on August 22 demanded the dismissal of all CPs to prevent "machinations" against the "new order of things." The mayor had already three days earlier asked that all the CPs be suspended until their cases could be reviewed. Of Marseille's eleven CPs, only four were kept on. Officials in Marseille and Paris thus sifted through the dossiers of candidates for the seven open posts. Sénès, a member of "a respected family in this town" and who was employed in the mairie and known for his intelligence and exactitude, was named without hesitation. Moinier, from St. Rémy-de-Provence, and Marbeau, from Brive, who had fled France in 1815 for fear of the Ultras, were easy choices given the circumstances, as was Coutelle, a former gendarme let go for political reasons in 1827, recommended by one of the new deputies from the Gard, and Jacques Imbert, a former national guard officer in Marseille, who had had the good fortune to have participated in the "Three Glorious Days" in the capital. Duranty, who had worked ten years *sans histoires* in the bureau of the commissaire général in Marseille, had enjoyed a kind of apprenticeship in the métier. Naturally, all sang wild enthusiasm for "the new order of things," and, as we have seen, a few of them had indeed good reasons for doing so.[76]

Some very good CPs lost their jobs in the purge. In Blois, the municipal council in August protested the firing of Robin after twenty-three years of "zealous" service.[77] In October 1830, the minister of the interior admitted that "some intelligent and active commissaires de police, who have good political opinions, were nonetheless replaced after the events of July, only because they were obliged to carry out unpopular measures and thereby lost the influence necessary to subsequently exercise their functions in the locality where they were serving" when the Bourbons fell. Some could now usefully serve in other places, along with others who been fired between 1822 and the July Revolution, most accused of having "opinions similar to those that in the end triumphed."[78]

Many CPs who had been fired during the Restoration came forward to ask for reappointment, routinely claiming that their "liberalism" or their "patriotism" had done them in at the hands of the Bourbons. Yet many of these were not rehired, because their dossiers recorded the reasons for their dismissal. Claude Gaudemar, former CP in Marseille, wrote in the hope of convincing the minister of the interior in 1832, fifteen years after having been fired (for the second time), that his disgrace had been unjust because he had been falsely accused of incompetence. Although he had somehow managed to get a pension in 1829, he wanted assignment in any department. But his slim chances became none when it turned out he had been fired for taking bribes.[79]

Joseph Palis also stepped forward in 1830, at least by letter. After beginning his career in the police in Turin during the Napoleonic era and then being transferred from Grenoble, he had served as CP in Toulouse from 1819 until 1822. Shortly after his arrival in Toulouse, he had penned a lengthy document called "Quelques observations sur l'organisation de la police," drawing on his experiences in Turin during the Empire and then Grenoble.[80] However, he had been dismissed in 1822, accused of failing to take decisive action when a theatrical presentation turned into a political demonstration. After six years, he had finally been appointed early in 1830 to Bagnères. He wanted the big time of Toulouse. A sixty-one-year-old widower with three children, he now noted that "exact" information could be found on his previous service, correctly noting that a prefect had sung his praises in 1822. Moreover, his former prefect in the Isère affirmed that Palis was "one of the most capable men I know. His sense of moderation and tact were of great utility to me." Indeed he would be happy to have him back if there were an opening.[81]

Palis summarized his twenty-one years on the job, reliving his finest moments, including the arrest in Grenoble of thieves who had stolen 25,000 francs and the recovery of the money. His account of the incidents that had cost him his job now predictably sang the new language of liberty: The young liberals who had disrupted a theatrical performance were transformed into "youth passionate for liberty and our constitutional institutions," having rejected "a despotic and bloody authority." A "secret committee," led by none other than de Villèle, had pushed the prefect, whom Palis now described as suffering from mental illness, to seek scapegoats within the police. He had been refused a pension, which would have been his "last resource, like a plank of wood in a shipwreck." He had finally taken back into the police in April 1830, three months before the Revolution, posted in what he considered the purgatory of Bagnères. Now of course he was ready "swear fidelity to the King of the French and to the Constitutional Charter with as much pleasure as I saluted with enthusiasm the first dawn of liberty in 1789."[82] We do not know where Palis ended up, but it was not in the police.

Pierre Lequet could look back over three different regimes. A former CP in Rouen during the Empire dismissed with the Restoration, Lequet had gained reappointment to Toulouse in 1817 and then Lyon a year later. He had resigned three years later, but must have done so in the good graces of the government, as he was replaced by his son. In May 1831, he wrote the ministry of the interior, asking for reappointment, because "the present system of government corresponds to my principles . . . in [17]93, the priests and émigrés were the enemies of France. They have been replaced today by Carlists and republicans."[83] His understanding of the politics of the new regime was impeccable, but he was not reappointed.

Gabriel Baille served as CP of Épinal, Rouen, and St. Denis before reaching his dream, appointment to Paris with its commensurate salary in January 1829. Baille had been the chef de bureau and an inspector for the weights and measures office in the Nièvre in 1815. In 1825, a series of indiscretions (including demanding and receiving gifts from merchants coming to Rouen's largest fair and borrowing money from prostitutes) led to his being fired from his post in Rouen (he preferred to speak of his "retirement"). He protested vigorously, but a brief investigation determined that Baille had been even worse than suspected. The former policeman wrote to Franchet d'Esperey, the director of the police générale, about his fifteen-year-old daughter, who was in the convent of the Ursulines in Rouen, "well known for the practice of all of the virtues. Her childhood was so happy, but with the fatal word [*révocation*] that you just pronounced, you have destroyed all my hopes and brought me the greatest of my misfortunes." His robust son, seventeen years of age, would be all right, "at least he still has the profession of soldier. But his sister!" Baille could hardly go on. "Divine Justice cries out to you! Stop! This man is not whom you think!" Baille had mailed a bulky, boring mémoire justificatif, citing a few modest triumphs, having closed down a gambling operation, preventing seditious songs from being sung when the Duc d'Angoulême had visited, when the policeman was posted in Épinal. Grateful, the duke, Baille claimed improbably enough, had promised his promotion. Yet reports had followed him from the Vosges that had noted that he was "riddled with debts"; Baille confessed that he preferred that it had been noted less scathingly that "he owes 4,000 francs," because of bad luck and family misfortune. Here, hefty patronage paid off, and Baille was appointed to St. Denis at the end of 1828. In his file, his 1825 révocation was changed to "retired." But nothing could help him ten months later, in November 1829, when he was fired again, the "fatal word" révocation seared in his dossier and the historical record.

However, the Revolution of 1830 seemed to offer Baille another opportunity, one he could not have expected. The former policeman enthusiastically portrayed himself as "still a victim of absolute power," having supported Napoleon during the 100 Days. A veritable weathervane, he now looked to the ministry of justice to bring justice to "this father of a family, without fortune . . . Baille could cry out, 'Oh, if the king only knew!'" Shifting into the third person, he claimed that "dignitaries are interested in the fate of Sr. Baille," including none other than the bell ringer of liberalism, Benjamin Constant, as well as three deputies. However, Baille received a discouraging official letter telling him that a surplus of candidates prevented his reappointment, while holding out the promise "that later justice would be rendered."[84]

Pierre Leclerc, who had been hired in 1809 under the Empire and fired in 1817, within several weeks after the Revolution of 1830 figuratively prostrated himself before "the auguste, philanthropic, benevolent, most just, greatest, and most accomplished of all monarchies" to gain reappointment. He blamed his firing in 1818 on the former mayor of Meaux, "at whose home Charles X had slept on his return to France." Leclerc wrote that if he were not reinstated that he would be "reduced to shame and would perish of hunger and misery" (the same stock phrase he had used when he had been fired in 1818). The latter was very unlikely, but the former undeniable. Yet his file contained a damaging official letter that the previous year had described him as "a weak man, without talent, given over to excess with strong liquors, and neglecting the duties of his post."[85]

As ever, good luck could still come to the rescue. Pierre Laval had the good fortune to be one of the commissaires to have been appointed early in the Restoration after having served the regime of the "usurper." Reappointed in Tulle on February 8, 1816, Laval was fired seven years later. During the July Monarchy, he naturally enough blamed his disgrace on the "deplorable Ministry" that had sought to eliminate "all the true friends of the Charter," a familiar refrain after 1830, when one could more easily talk of "all those liberticidal projects" with the Bourbons long gone. (A namesake and possibly a distant descendant merited far greater disgrace more than a century later.) But the truth was that Laval "proved himself unworthy of confidence by his negligence on the job, and by his immorality and liaisons with dangerous men," after having squandered a fortune acquired through "usurious loans and totally unacceptable investments." Furthermore, he had simply invented the story of having been an émigré. He, too, was not rehired.[86]

In Paris, the tenure of Henri Gisquet as prefect of police from October 1831 to 1836 again firmly placed the surveillance and repression of political opponents at the forefront of police preoccupations, the full use of la police générale, against the backdrop of petitions, protests, riots, and even insurrection.[87] The police again faced evaluations that were as thorough as those in the early years of the Restoration. When a new prefect of Vienne arrived in Poitiers in late 1831, he looked over the dossiers of and sought reliable opinion about the town's two CPs, firing one outright and obtaining a transfer for the other. Gueudin, a former cavalry officer from 1794 to 1800 who had served as CP in Besançon, had already been replaced because he had been unable to maintain the respect of its inhabitants, notably "the most turbulent part of the population." But his evocation of his "honorable wounds" in the army and prevention of a massacre of Catholics by Protestants at Le Vigan during the 100 Days helped him win appointment to Châtellerault.[88]

Poitiers's other CP, Pierré, named after the July Revolution, had also served in Besançon during the last years of the Restoration. But now he did not send a single political report to the ministry of the interior, the prefect, or the mayor, noting that such reports would take away from other duties. But politics took precedence in the regime's first months, indeed years. An undated denunciation accused Pierré of having "morals as lax as those of the court of Louis XVI" and claiming that in Besançon he was considered "a protégé, an agent of secret government. That he is not a thief is about all he has going for him."[89]

A final example here stands for many. Louis Murat, dismissed in Narbonne in November 1830, attributed his demise to the fact that he was hated by "several people who are hard to please, as there are so many after every change of government." To hear Murat tell it, the subprefect and mayor had assured him that he would be spared, but he should perhaps look for another position. And so the bad news did not really come out of the blue.[90]

Patronage still played a role during the July Monarchy (and after). Michel Bouillay-Bonneville, CP in Mâcon, had protectors in high places. However in 1840 the mayor considered him not up to the challenges of policing the town. That January, several butchers refused to sell meat, saying they had nothing to sell (although several lambs could be seen inside their shops, almost taunting potential clients) and the next day announced that they would sell only chicken. They were protesting an increase in the octroi tax. The next day, two of the butchers convinced their colleagues to end their rebellion. But a large, hostile crowd gathered, egged on by a mentally retarded woman who shouted out that the meat for sale was not fit for the "dogs of St. Laurent," a reference to Mâcon's bitter rival across the Saône River. The 100 troops that had to be called in seemed to lay bare Bouillay-Bonneville's lack of ability. To the mayor, he seemed better suited to a large city than a town, because he followed orders better than he gave them. He lacked firmness and the ability to intimidate when necessary; thus, when push came to shove, troops had to be called: "Here, as everywhere, the police lack all respect." Moreover, he had an affair with the wife of a grocer, who sent her new man compromising love letters. When the affair ended, she asked to have them back. Boulay-Bonneville returned only some letters, saving the most lurid and then, if one denunciation had it right, tried to blackmail her, after telling his own disappointed wife all about the affair. However his wife might have felt about this, she accepted 600 francs from her husband's former lover. By 1842, most people in Mâcon knew about the whole mess. This affair and his inability to end a riot in 1841 that led to troops shooting three people, ended Bouillay-Bonneville's career in the police. Yet almost miraculously, he landed on his feet in Paris in the bureau of personnel of the prefecture of police. He then claimed that his own wife— whom he had apparently left without resources—had been alone in trying to blackmail the woman, who was trying desperately to save whatever of her reputation remained. Not much remained of that of Bouillay-Bonneville.[91]

Another politically motivated purge inevitably followed the Revolution of 1848, often carried out by *commissaires de la République*, who served as provisional prefects in the first month or more of the Second Republic. On April 11, the minister of the interior asserted that commissaires de la République had the authority to replace CPs on the spot, if such a move seemed urgent. An increasingly conservative republic took root, particularly following the bloody June Days, at the end of the republic's fourth month. On December 10, 1848, Louis Napoleon Bonaparte was elected president. However, the party of the left, the Montagnards or *démoc*-socs, increased their support, particularly in southern France. In the legislative elections of May 1849, they earned more than a third of the votes, and did well in by-elections a year later. CPs were fired if their loyalty to the regime could be questioned in any way. But overall, they became part of the repressive apparatus that helped prepare the way for the ultimate destruction of the Republic with the coup d'état of December 2, 1851.[92]

The Revolution of 1848 and the Second Republic, then, replicated in some ways the first months and even years of the July Monarchy. Politics played an important role in the hiring and firing of CPs. Yet in the wake of the Revolution of 1830, even the hiring of commissaires reflected professional criteria that had often not been present early in the Restoration. When the subprefect of Tournon in 1831 assessed the qualifications of Bachelot in Annonay, he noted that "his political principles are little know, but I believe him disposed to fulfill his duties to the state."[93] This sort of comment was virtually unthinkable little more than a decade earlier, during the first years of the Restoration.[94] This was also the case following the Revolution of 1848, which brought a small purge of the police. To take just one example, in the Nièvre in August 1848, four of the nine CPs serving in nine towns had been appointed since the Revolution.[95] However, the Restoration played the crucial role in the professionalization of the CPs, even if political considerations could and did subsequently intervene in important ways following each of France's next two revolutions. Only the Restoration had hired incompetent CPs solely on political grounds, a practice that it largely ended, even if political instability following each of the subsequent two revolutions made politics the primary determinant of assessment.

4

POLICING POLITICS

"Never let a riot swell, because it will resemble a gale, growing
from hour to hour."

Advice given to General Cavaignac, July 5, 1848

Hébrard dit Laquet was to be guillotined in Albi in front of its splen-
did fortified cathedral in September 1831. A huge throng assembled
in the square,[1] as was customary on such festive occasions, straining to catch a
glimpse of the convicted murderer as he was led up to the scaffold to confront the
executioner. Albi's commissaire de police took every precaution to ensure that order
would be maintained; gendarmes, too, stood ready. The executioner's two assistants
tied Hébrard to the board, forcing his head through the "the little window"—as
they called it during the Revolution—to await the fall of the razor-sharp blade. The
hushed crowd anticipated the instantaneous severing of the victim's head from his
body. The rope cut, the blade began its speedy descent, but it stopped centimeters
from Hébrard's neck. The multitude roared its shock. Twice more the executioner
hoisted the blade, and twice more its fall was stopped just above the murderer's exposed neck. Bedlam. Shouts described as "horrible" and then rocks rained down on
the executioners. To many, it seemed that the man should be freed, the guillotine's
failure a sign from above of the convicted man's innocence. One *homme du peuple*
climbed onto the scaffold, before a magistrate's stern warning brought him down
again. During this time, the astonished Hébrard had somehow managed to pull his
head out of the guillotine's window and staggered to his feet, still strapped to the
long plank of wood. The crowd howled even louder. The executioners having been
humiliated in their métier, one of the assistants grabbed an ax and, seizing the condemned man by the hair, dispatched him with several blows, a bloody spectacle that
roused the throng to fury. The assistant ran for his own life, hiding behind the
horses of gendarmes until he could be escorted out of town to safety.

What had happened? After the police and gendarmes had finally succeeded in calming and dispersing the crowd, they joined higher officials examining the "infernal machine" to see what had gone wrong. They discovered that some-one—not just anyone, but someone quite knowledgeable about such things—had tampered with the guillotine so that the blade would stop exactly short of its mark. Suspicion immediately fell on a carpenter's assistant whose master, charged with constructing the scaffold and preparing the guillotine, had recently dismissed him. The assistant had lost his job but not his skills. He had exacted revenge on his former master by ensuring his public humiliation. The incident was not quickly forgotten.[2]

We enter the world of the first half of the nineteenth century, the stuff of social, political, and cultural history. There was a "crowd," with its potentially incendiary aspect, reflecting revealing continuities with the Ancien Régime. Capital execution remained "a spectacle, a theater piece, a divertissement that urban residents sought."[3] Some in attendance—how many we cannot say—believed that the guillotine's failure was a sign from above of innocence. Then there were the "forces of order," including Albi's CP, the urban face of policing, backed up in such circumstances by gendarmes and troops.[4] When the gendarmes and troops departed several days later, Albi's CP would still be there, his duties as the town's policeman more or less returned to those of everyday life. This remained true even in a time of heightened political contention, as the fledgling July Monarchy sought to keep in check the opposition of Legitimists, and of liberals whose disappointment with the relatively minimal change brought by the July Revolution pushed them increasingly toward republicanism.

The delayed, traumatic execution of Hébrard dit Laquet brought the kind of incident of collective violence that historians have long associated both with the Ancien Régime and with the "rebellious century"—the nineteenth century, particularly its first fifty years. Yet most CPs never confronted a riot or large demonstration, despite cascades of orders during national political crises that overwhelmed the routines of the policing of daily life and for a time turned their attention toward political policing.

In France's growing cities during the first half of the century,[5] political policing stood as a central preoccupation of CPs, caught between the determination of the regimes they served and increasingly organized opponents, particularly liberals, then republicans and socialists. We will first consider the prevention or repression of social protest, in particular the policing of public spaces that could be considered possible staging grounds for political opposition. Then we will look at the haute police, essentially during the Restoration the targeting of well-educated liberals who were suspected of conspiring to overthrow the Bourbons. During the July Monarchy, in turn, the police were ordered to pay particular attention to Legitimists and republicans, even as social protest and political dissidence began to converge, which is indeed one of the most important aspects of that crucial period. Indeed, arguably the politicization of social protest in the wake of the Revolution of 1830 affected the political role of CPs in provincial towns, as ordinary workers fell increasingly under police surveillance because of suspected political activities and the development of the strike as a form of more organized protest and political contention. As French cities and towns grew, such a transformation made the CP an even more important figure as the guardian of public order, as was defined by the Orleanist regime. This was also the case during the increasingly conservative Second Republic headed by its prince president, Louis Napoleon Bonaparte, even as he set up destroying the regime he had sworn to defend.

Describing the police of late-eighteenth-century Paris, Richard Cobb could as easily be discussing their successors during the first half of the following century.

> A good policeman . . . could always expect to be a couple of steps ahead of a riot, a sedition, a turbulence, and so to be forearmed. He could pride himself on being able to distinguish between habitual, almost permissible, disorder, and a commotion that overstepped the boundaries tacitly agreed upon between the repressive authorities and those who were most likely to be repressed. . . . The police [had] to be two steps ahead of potential violence, wherever it might spring up in its swift obscenity, and to recognize a prevalence to violent solutions among certain trades and people from certain regions. They therefore also need to be well acquainted with the calendar of violence and riot, almost as fixed as that of the saints. . . . They were, in fact, going on a mixture of common sense, experience, and feasibility.[6]

Justes appréciateurs de l'esprit public, the CPs were informed observers of public opinion who carried out the will of the ministry of the interior and its prefects.

Having reason to fear popular solidarity, CPs sought to avoid protracted incidents that could attract crowds and degenerate into "tumults."[7] Most policemen went through their careers without confronting a potentially dangerous crowd. Yet such a possibility was in the back of every CP's mind. A good many, including some newly appointed, confronted political demonstrations in the wake of the Revolution of 1830, as the Orleanist regime confronted its new political enemies.[8] Even in sleepy Yssingeaux (Haute-Loire), the subprefect in 1832 became convinced that "germs of disorder have been fomenting for several days in this town." The symptoms were the fury of tailors against competition from itinerant merchants, this following some agitation by carpenters and masons several days earlier. Moreover, butchers seemed on the verge of refusing to move their slaughtering into the slaughterhouse. The discourse of political paranoia highlighted the fear that "agents of a party" might profit from these competing interests to direct unhappiness against the government. By the time the subprefect had finished his account, Yssingeaux loomed as a veritable faubourg St. Antoine or Lyon's silk-weaving faubourg, the Croix-Rousse. When nothing happened to break the calm, he might even receive some credit for that fact.[9]

Lyon was something else. Relations between the police and ordinary people were particularly bitter, and large crowds formed with unusual speed. Lyonnais rich and poor always have appreciated a good spectacle (the puppets of *le guignol* not the least of them). Any noisy, public incident quickly generated interest. Thus, the prefect's instructions to the CPs in Lyon in 1822 stressed the urgency of preventing "all popular movements by being present in any crowd that could form for any reason: more often than not, your very presence will be enough to prevent any disorder."[10] Yet a policeman's presence offered no guarantees. When CP Vaché in 1822 tried to separate two drivers who were "mistreating" each other, they resisted and tried without success to turn a rapidly forming crowd against him.[11] The Place des Célestins, in particular, had to be watched, as "the rendez-vous of a multitude of dishonorable people who every evening besieged the doors of the theater and the idlers who hang out in cafés, leading to quarrels and brawls." The CPs, even with the help of their agents, seemed unable in 1828 to "make themselves respected." Sometimes the police had to give way, which led the mayor to request a permanent military post for the Place des Célestins.[12] When the police approached the Pont La Guillotière that led from Lyon across the Rhône, trouble could come quickly. When the next year police near the bridge arrested someone who had broken some windows during the Lyon fair, a crowd tried to free him the next day, attacking soldiers with sticks. The crowds quickly swelled in size, such that the arrival of a detachment of twelve soldiers from Brotteaux across the Rhône was not enough to restore order. Protesters scattered only with the arrival of more soldiers, including cavalrymen. Even then, crowds hurled rocks at troops escorting the carriage hauling off several prisoners to jail. Protesters reassembled on the Place des Jacobins and shouted against the soldiers.[13]

In Lyon, insurrections of the *canuts* in 1831 and 1834 enhanced coordination between the police and the army, even amid sharp disagreements between the municipality and the ministry of the interior and the prefect of the Rhône. During the mid-1830s, following bloody revolts by silk workers in 1831 and again in 1834, three military posts were eliminated and then reinstated a year later, with the warning that having too many small, separate posts made them vulnerable to being taken one by one by insurgents. The commander of the Military Division suggested having fewer but larger posts that could more easily be defended in the event of another uprising. The mayor agreed to pay for the reestablishment of the post at the intersection known as "La mort qui trompe." In 1838, military authorities established a post at Perrache, then an isolated and occasionally dangerous quartier of the Presqu'île.[14]

In Paris, during what amounted to a general strike in 1832, the police were advised to avoid any action that would make things worse: "Without doubt the cessation of work . . . and a coalition of workers are evils; but the behavior of the administration and even of justice, must have as its principal aim the prevention of worse developments."[15] The perception of overreaction could encourage opposition. If police went too far, they defied the popular sense of a quartier or a town of what was proper. In Draguignan in 1839, the CP arrested four young workers for having insulted him, and the popular feeling that he had overreacted following their conviction in court led to several crowds demonstrating against him. One hostile crowd reached more than 200 people in number, "brought together at the sound of drums" before the prefecture. The CP was roughed up, "his sash [of authority] was disrespected, his clothes torn, and he had several scratches on his face." Obviously more lay behind the incident than the insults—the CP was already engaged in a small war with a faction in town.[16]

CPs were of course to take down the names of people participating in any demonstration. But in Metz in 1833, when resistance against the police turned an outburst against Legitimists into a full-fledged anticlerical demonstration, how many faces and names could be remembered and written down as a crowd of something like 2,000 people surged along the quais?[17] Police took note of the young men serenading political visitors with song (as in Arbois in Jura, which had a remarkable republican nucleus[18]) or those attending "royalist" dinners in the early years of the July Monarchy, particularly during attempts to revive *chouannerie* in the west. During that period, police identified people attending Mass on January 21, the anniversary of the execution of Louis XVI in 1793, in towns with committed Legitimists. During the campaign on behalf of political reform in 1839–40 and 1846–47, CPs turned up as nonpaying guests at banquets to identify republicans who showed up to toast an expanded electoral franchise, writing down what exactly had been toasted.[19] The opponents of each regime may have changed, but the responsibilities of the CPs did not.

Les points chauds: Market and Octroi

The market, the center or stomach of any town, and the octroi, not only standing as the entry to town but the point at which taxes were collected on goods, offered potential for collective action. Steven Kaplan's insistence that "police and provisioning formed an inseparable couple in old-regime society" fully applies to the first half of the nineteenth century.[20] In eighteenth-century Paris, the posts of the *guet,* or city guards organized along military lines, had "generally (been) situated close to markets and the posts which supplied them, reflecting concern about food riots."[21] Mayors continued to provide prefects with daily reports on the price and availability of grain and other foodstuffs at the market, and markets drew increased police surveillance when the price of grain was high.[22] CPs were to monitor the quantity of grain brought to market, the price of grain and bread, and "all events and rumors related to the movement and high cost of grain."[23]

Grain riots lingered in the collective memory of virtually every market town in France. Poor harvests and high prices brought waves of grain riots in 1816–17, 1826–27, during the first years after the Revolution of 1830, 1840–41, and 1846–47. Julien Alletz's *Dictionnaire de police moderne* (1823) listed dearth (of grain) under "ALARME," as a major threat to public order. In times of grain shortage, the municipality was forbidden to arbitrarily set a lower price of grain or in any way interfere with the functioning of the free market. It was permitted to send representatives to other markets to buy grain at the market price (which occurred during the Revolution), which might lower the price of grain at home.

Here, again, we see striking continuities between the Ancien Régime and the first half of the nineteenth century.

The shortage of grain and high prices were not in themselves enough to lead ordinary people to take matters into their own hands. For those without enough money to purchase grain at inflated prices, the feeling often prevailed that somewhere else grain was available in great supply, and that hoarders and inept officials were causing local hardship, violating the "just" price. Most grain riots were directed at outsiders taking away grain purchased at prices few locally could pay, although hoarders, local officials, and bakers could be targets.[24]

If a grain riot occurred, a CP could be faulted for failing to master the situation before protest turned into riot. To be sure, prefects and subprefects were often quick to blame the police, deflecting possible attention to what the ministries in Paris might consider their own failings. Grain riots quickly took on political connotations during one of the highly charged periods when a regime felt its back was to the wall. For example, during the famously hungry spring of 1847, insufficient provisions and high bread prices in Le Mans took on a political context in a town in which nostalgia for the departed Bourbons remained strong. Young workers "circulated" in town, some shouting "Long live Henry V!", the Legitimist pretender to the throne, the Comte de Chambord (born the "miracle baby" to the Duchesse de Berri months following the assassination of the Duc de Berri in 1820). "Bands" of beggars went from house to house asking for bread. Police and gendarmes were instructed to arrest "habitual beggars who are ablebodied," who went about at night, particularly those who used tactics of intimidation in the quest for money or bread. As a general strategy, mass arrests were avoided for fear of swelling active political opposition.[25]

CPs were apt to know some of the participants in grain riots, sometimes manifesting sympathy for the victims of high prices, even as they, along with gendarmes and sometimes soldiers enforced order, ensuring the departure of grain. In 1831 in the Breton département of Morbihan, "twelve unfortunates, most of them fathers with several children, some still in the crib," had been condemned to six months in prison by the tribunal in Vannes for having stopped the free circulation of grain in a nearby town. "In the eyes of the law, sir," they wrote the prefect, "without doubt we are guilty, but this guilt comes from the rise in the price of items of first necessity, the frequent departure of grain, the uncertain harvest, and the fear of an unhappy future, these are the motives that led us astray."[26]

Several other examples will stand for many, as CPs tried to cope with popular indignation at the market over high grain prices and confronted collective action. Early in June 1816, at the instigation of cutlery workers from Thiers, people from nearby villages of St. Rémy and Celles prevented wagons filled with grain from leaving. After an estimated crowd of 1,000 people had blocked the departure of wagons of grain on June 2, the next day the wagons departed, escorted by gendarmes. In St. Rémy, the tocsin sounded its cry of alarm, and villagers, their number swollen by those arriving from other villages, forced the wagons to turn around on the road to Lyon and return to Thiers. All along the route the wagons passed hundreds of people of all ages, some armed with sticks or pitchforks, a few with swords and even guns, all demanding that export of grain from the region be forbidden. The subprefect, evoking the "abysse that is opening before us," finally managed to disperse the crowd. At the gates of Thiers, Swiss guards, part of the allied occupying forces, stood ready for action. After the subprefect and mayor announced the equivalent of martial law, some of the guards fired on demonstrators, wounding several; those fleeing headed for the hills and mountains. The arrival of troops seemed to calm the workers of Thiers but not the poor of the environs. More than twenty arrests followed, including that of one worker who kept repeating "we need only grain," which was true enough. A single CP could do nothing; the arrival of troops dramatically raised the cost of popular protest.[27]

Grain riots virtually disappeared in the mid-1850s, providing another reason for us to consider the middle of the century as the major turning point in the construction of modern France. Food supply increased and distribution improved, combining to eliminate sharp rises in prices that had led the poor to protest against and often prevent merchants from buying up grain at local markets at high prices most local consumers could not afford. Moreover, *le grand départ* began from poorer rural regions; two thirds of the départements of France had a larger population in 1851 than in 1939.[28]

In addition to watching out for thieves (pickpockets and others), the police at markets assessed common complaints that merchants were not using proper weights and measures. Moreover, what could be sold had to be kept in mind: For example, in Nantes, among other places, oysters could only be sold from October 1 to May 1, and mushrooms, some of which could kill, had to be inspected.[29] They also adjudicated complaints from merchants against outsiders. In Amiens in 1837, a merchant from Paris announced a "public sale at low prices." His competitors prevented anyone from hearing the prices as he shouted them out, and the next day a crowd set fire to the tables on which goods were put out for sale.[30]

The monitoring of butchers, making sure that they were following municipal regulations about the slaughter, sale, and taxation of meat (which was not to be exposed outside of any shop or the market), was part of daily routine. Butchers, a tough bunch, could be defiant, difficult to police, and none more so than the corporation in Limoges.[31] In Caen in November 1815, the CP managed to restore order when a butcher refused to open his shop for inspection by tax officials, as locksmiths prepared to open the door and a crowd shouted against the taxmen.[32] In isolated Barcelonette (Basses-Alpes), the butchers' refusal to submit to any kind of payment—one of them had added that he would "cut off the head of any official who dared enter his shop"—caused the municipal council in late 1830 to suspend temporarily the collection of taxes at the octroi, which had only been established two years earlier.[33]

Unlike markets, which were weekly or biweekly, most fairs were annual. They attracted huge throngs, an estimated 30,000 in Alençon in 1834.[34] If a major fair held annually in Bordeaux seemed unusually calm in 1823 with just a few thefts, the mayor took credit for having ordered the police to "drive from

Bordeaux all those so-called traveling merchants and their many assistants who previously have come to town and gone into houses not to sell merchandize but to check out what was there" so that they could return to exercise their real métier of thieving. CPs patrolled night and day during fairs, aided by their agents and in large cities even infantrymen to assure that cafés, *cercles,* and other establishments closed down at the appropriate times, while watching the "gambling houses . . . in order to discover the machinations and habits of the suspicious people who frequent these dens."[35] Part of the policing of fairs included keeping an eye on those—outsiders all—who turned up putting on "various spectacles, such as mechanical theaters, exhibits of fantastic figures and other things, that they mix with explanations, parades, amusing scenes, and song." Such spectacles required local authorization, and the exact program had to be provided for perusal and acceptance in advance, to prevent (at least in principle) anything deemed inoffensive to the government, religion, or good morals or that which would "mislead public opinion."[36] For example, the fair of Mammès in 1849 Langres brought to town "a number of street-entertainers and traveling actors," who set up shop in a narrow space alongside the military hospital and went about their business making as much noise as possible to attract the curious. Yet despite the presence of more than a thousand workers employed constructing fortifications, police made only one arrest in three days at the fair, taking away a saltimbanque who had insulted a tax official.[37]

To enter town with more than 5,000 inhabitants, anyone had to pass through the gates of the octroi (toll gate). As we have seen, the octroi provided most of their modest budgets, which went to pay the salaries of the commissaire(s) de police. The octroi took on great symbolism for those sitting astride wagons outside cities and towns with gates, waiting for them to open in the morning.[38] Standing as a fiscal and physical barrier against the free passage of goods, farmers, merchants, and consumers resented the octroi.

In some places, the octroi barrier marked the limit of the commune and thus of municipal policing.[39] However, in certain cases, the octroi itself did not limit the jurisdiction of a CP, for example, in Châtellerault, where during the July Monarchy the authority of the police was extended several kilometers beyond the faubourg of Châteauneuf, site of the arms manufacture, across the Vienne River to encompass the adjoining commune of Naintré, where the CP served under the authority of the mayor.[40]

The octroi also stood as a "visual signifier" between city and country. Some towns, like Niort, had lost their walls long before, even if the octroi remained (thus sneaking untaxed goods into town was easier). Only four of the seven gates of Chartres remained in 1831, the others demolished to embellish the town. Gardens had replaced the walls around Guéret. In the Nord, Vauban's fortifications still embraced Lille, Cambrai, and Douai. But the octroi also represented *une fausse coupure* between city and countryside. The rural world still impinged forcefully within the limits of most cities and towns. The *agro-villes* of the Mediterranean region and Alsace are only the most obvious examples: Perpignan, Béziers, Narbonne, Ribeauvillé, and many others. In fortified towns (villes fortes), the contrast between town and country was more marked, because of a ban (in principle) against building within a certain distance of the ramparts, for purposes of defense. City dwellers passed through the octroi on Sundays and Mondays to amuse themselves not only in the cabarets just beyond the walls but in the countryside farther out.

The octroi thus remained a principal police preoccupation. The octroi could be tough work. When Paulin, CP in Lyon, sent to the ministry of the interior in 1829 a moving account of the duties of the police, poorly paid and in almost no cases with the possibility of having a pension, he proudly noted the role he and his colleagues played in helping catch smugglers and others seeking to avoid the octroi.[41]

Because of its obvious association with the *fisc* (the state taxing apparatus), the octroi stood as a privileged place for "disorder." In July 1789 and in the wake of the Revolutions of 1830 and 1848, the customs offices at the barrières of Paris became targets of popular anger, the offices of many sacked and registers burned. After the July Revolution, shouts of "Down with the rats!"—the tax officials who came to check the wine cellars of merchants, for example— echoed in a good many towns. Ordinary people hoped that the revolution and the "liberal" regime that it brought to power would end the indirect taxes collected at the octroi, especially on wine. Here, again, the octroi stood as a symbol of urban identity while symbolizing tensions between city and country.

In Aurillac crowds protested taxes after the Revolution of 1830, shouting against tax officials in several quartiers. The mayor had "no other means of repression besides moral force." On August 15, a crowd of 150 to 200 workers and "several publicans in general excited by having drunk too much" raged through the streets, demanding that the mayor burn the tax registers, while rumors spread that tax officials would be forced to drink from a certain fountain. As for the CP who had been ordered to help keep order, he simply did not appear.[42] In Moissac (Tarn-et-Garonne), a crowd burned the octroi itself as well as the tax registers, as they did in Bordeaux and Issoire (Puy-de-Dôme), whereas in Bas-Languedoc trouble raged in and around Béziers. In Burgundy, vintners took over the hall where the tax on bread was assessed in Auxerre and sold it at a lower price.[43] And in Cahors, a town of fewer than 12,000 people, a full-scale riot took place on October 23, 1831, including the invasion of the hôtel de ville by "an insurrectional mass of people," in the words of the mayor, a throng that included some national guardsmen in uniform.[44] Two years later, troops shot down nine people during an "attack" on Clermont's octroi. The next day, when *vignerons* returned to protest, the soldiers killed twenty people and wounded twenty-five others, with three killed and fifteen wounded among "the forces of order." This case is interesting because as people from town joined those from the faubourgs beyond the wall, the octroi was identified not with town but with the state, suggesting another way in which the octroi stood as an arbitrary dividing point between town and country, the economic and political interests of both of which could be interdependent.

Elite Associations

Voluntary associations stood in an ambiguous position between public and private space. During the first half of the nineteenth century, their rapid proliferation characterized French urban life. Every town of any size had at least several associations essentially bringing together upper-class males for leisure activities, for which they paid an annual fee, sometimes very steep.[45] Each association had to send the prefecture a copy of its proposed statutes, and prefects and officials in the ministry of the interior went through them carefully, attentive to the politics of members. Such private associations were in some ways extensions of the intimacy of a bourgeois apartment. Their doors remained closed to CPs, whether members met in private houses or apartments, or, in the case of those under ecclesiastical patronage, in church buildings or in the back rooms of cafés (which were technically public places). Thus, the commissaires may have been excellent sources as to the regularity of meetings, but, unlike cafés and cabarets or the political reform banquets of 1840–41 and 1847–48, they could not in principle listen to what was said.

For example, Alençon in 1833 boasted a literary association and a reading club, both standing as signs of growing cosmopolitanism, and a Masonic lodge, which had been there since "time immemorial," which probably meant since the mid-eighteenth century. The "constitutionnels," that is, those who backed the Orleanist regime, joined the Société littéraire (although their number included several "progressives," including a few republicans), which had started up after the July Revolution. Legitimists had their own association, whereas "ardent republicans" belonged to the Masonic lodge. During the Restoration, some royalists had been Masons, but they had stormed out of a gathering when political debates heated up. After the Revolution of 1830, some "constitutionals" joined as well, but they, too, had left for similar reasons. This departure left about twenty-five or thirty members, one of whom had the audacity to smash a bust of Louis-Philippe. Intriguingly enough, the perpetrator had acted "in a euphoric moment, caused, it is said, by having smoked *les fumées bachiques*." Where were the police? Again, they were sometimes outside, observing who came, who left, and how long the gatherings went on. It would never have occurred to them to go in, unless shots or bloody screams suddenly emanated from the gathering.[46] In the Hérault, prefects carefully distinguished between clubs bringing together the "republican aristocracy," those that grouped liberals who were "not very fervent," those of the "hotheads," and, finally, "all the young Legitimist aristocrats" of Montpellier, and the association of "Les coeurs réunis" of the same town, "rather a gastronomic gathering than anything else. They eat constantly."[47]

In Amboise, the members of the Masonic lodge met monthly, attracting the surveillance of the commissaire, who in 1822 had to admit that he had no interesting information to relate, except that the meetings were not particularly well attended and that those in attendance played billiards. He knew that their gathering was breaking up at 11 P.M. when the clack of billiard balls stopped and the members left.[48]

Cafés and Cabarets

Cafés and cabarets (the latter including various *débits de boissons* known as bouchons, guinguettes, *estaminets,* and so on, often depending on the region) served as rallying points for political dissidents throughout the entire period, as well as providing places for workers to meet. Moreover, more cafés subscribed to newspapers. They also provided a natural feeding ground for rumors, carried by travelers of all sorts.[49] The political surveillance of drinking spots was an important part of police activity during periods of heightened political contention.

For example, in Agen, liberals gathered every day in the Café Foy during the last years of the regime to "devour the revolutionary newspapers."[50] Down the Garonne River, in Bordeaux, Legitimists favored the Café Helvétius and the adjacent Salon de lecture during the early July Monarchy, while republicans drank at the Café de la Jeune France, the very name of which had political resonance in the era of "Young Italy" and "Young Germany."[51] In Roubaix in 1841 the CP carefully drew up a list of cafés and private clubs and the newspapers to which they subscribed.[52]

The role of cafés, cabarets, and Provençal *chambrées* in the Montagnard movement—that is, the radical Left, the democratic socialists or démoc-socs—during the Second Republic is by now well known. Prefects ordered the police to shut down many cabarets, some for having red signs or provocative names (Le Prolétaire, for example), which could be construed as violating the law by "exciting the hatred of one class of citizens against another."[53] The minister of the interior announced two weeks before the coup d'état of 1851 that "cabarets become clubs in the evening, and it is principally there that are formed the dangerous secret associations that threaten the public peace."[54]

The Surveillance of Workers

If in principle everyone (at least all males) were equal before the law, workers were less equal than others. We have seen that police directed particular attention to the compagnons, whose rivalries and brawls were both legendary and predictable. In general, the laws, regulations, and administrative instructions under which the police operated were particularly weighted against workers. Each worker had to maintain a livret, which listed his past employers and their comments, if any, which made it easy to blacklist anyone. Strikes were illegal, and remained so until 1864, as were *syndicats* (legalized only in 1884) and, for that matter, public meetings unless previously authorized. Thus one list of duties given to the CPs specified "measures necessary to prevent or break up groups, coalitions of workers with the goal of increasing their wages, or tumultuous gatherings that threaten public peace."[55]

The policing of workers probably comes closest to the hypothetical attempt to impose perfect order in some sort of Foucauldian way. In Lyon, CP Paulin noted that the workers of his arrondissement of Palais des arts "do not like the police because we are in constant contact with them."[56] The legal obligation of workers to have and travel with a livret certainly aided the police. The prefect of the Seine-et-Marne, five weeks after the July Days, reminded the police that in the present circumstances, "surveillance becomes even more urgent, in that malevolence can seek to instigate agitation, notably among the less enlightened classes of society. I principally call your attention to workers gathered in one place."[57]

Here we see the convergence of two threads of surveillance: that of upper-class political dissidents, such as those so closely watched during the Restoration, and markedly increased attention to workers, whose burgeoning protest and political interest stands as one of the defining themes of the history of the July Monarchy. For example, in Lille for several days in April and May 1832, the police noted a large number of workers assembled on la Grande place in several groups, among whom could be seen "people who do not appear to belong to the lower class." The police, always on the lookout for political enemies of each regime who might try to "corrupt" workers by giving them "bad" ideas, were particularly careful to observe the behavior of those who seemed to be from a different social class.[58] We may be skeptical about this trickle-down theory of politicization, to be sure, but this remained a common view during the first half of the century.[59]

Well-dressed bourgeois were no longer assumed to be encouraging or standing behind the mobilization of workers in this period of precocious nascent class consciousness.[60] Strikes by artisans were an increasingly common occurrence. Police were to enforce the "freedom" of work established by the Le Chapelier Law of 1791. The police were also expected to enforce laws against public gatherings, notably those of workers planning strikes, often beyond town to avoid the prying eyes of the CP. For example, in Le Havre in 1831 the police had to intervene to stop workers from preventing the use of wood paneling and floorboards that had been produced by machine, despite their scrawled warnings several weeks earlier, "under the pretext that this new kind of woodworking could annihilate their trade and deprive them of work." The workers forced their way into the house, smashing the new paneling; only the arrival of national guardsmen prevented the workers from crossing a bridge to destroy the offending machine and led to the conviction of twenty men.[61] In Poitiers, "thanks to the good work of the commissaire de police," four leaders of the apprentice tailors were prosecuted in 1835 after having "coalesced to obtain an increase in salary."[62]

The police were responsible for watching both traditional forms of workers' organizations, above all, the *compagnonnage,* and evolving new ones. Following the Revolution of 1830, artisans took "liberty" to mean the right to organize and put forward their demands, an important step in the emergence of working-class politics in France. Many workers' associations were established in the wake of the "liberty" supposedly brought by the July Revolution. Because the Le Chapelier Law had made such associations illegal, they faced increasing police scrutiny. Indeed, the development of the strike as a weapon of workers increased police surveillance. Mutual aid societies, the French equivalent of British "friendly societies," could be easily transformed into "resistance associations" (*sociétés de résistance*) capable of sustaining strikes. CPs provided information and enforced laws regulating them. When in Nantes, where police had focused their attention on compagnonnages that had existed for centuries, surveillance during the 1830s increasingly fell on newer kinds of workers' organizations. In 1833, the prefect refused to approve a mutual aid society of printing workers because its existence could undercut the interests of the master printers. When the prefect balked at approving even an association of master shoemakers, their lawyer complained about the authorities' fear of association itself, and promised that his clients, relatively well-heeled masters all, were incapable of causing any disorder in Nantes. However, mutual aid societies of wheelwrights, cabinetmakers, saddlers, weavers, and other trades also sprang up, some of them meeting in back or upstairs rooms of cafés. The association of printers wrote of the "general interest" of all workers and contacted workers in Limoges. Such new associations, some approved, some tolerated, and others meeting in secrecy, added to the work of the CP.[63] In Chalon, CP Jacquemont in 1834 provided commentary on all of the statutes submitted by workers who wanted to begin a Société philanthropique; "general meetings," he believed, had no use in a mutual aid society, and he suspected it to be "a veritable club," perhaps linked to the Society of the Rights of Man.[64] During the Second Republic, the repression of workers' associations was part of the overall campaign against the Left, preparing the way for the coup d'état of Louis Napoleon Bonaparte. In this surveillance, too, CPs played an important role.[65]

However, CPs sometimes played a conciliatory role as they policed workers. In Béziers in 1833, the presence of a CP was enough to convince agricultural workers gathered outside of town to go back to work, when he promised not to prosecute them for a *délit de coalition*.[66] Even in the small Auvergnat town of Ambert, a center of paper production with only about 4,000 inhabitants, when workers met with the intention of demanding a raise "and imposing fines against the masters and against certain compagnons as well," the CP accompanied the mayor to the gathering. Their combined presence convinced them to return to work. Here, too, the CP could be a calming, conciliatory influence, at least if he had served some time in town and had earned the workers' respect.[67]

As the world of work expanded into the periphery of faubourgs and *banlieues,* the police had more to do on the edge of the city.[68] Cabarets offered cheaper drink by virtue of being beyond the octroi, the edge of town providing meeting places for workers. In Dijon in 1848, at the time of the June Days, a CP came on workers gathered—and presumably "plotting"—near the Porte St. Pierre, as rumors of an insurrection even there circulated.[69] At virtually the same time, Bourg-en-Bresse's CP heard a rumor that "a meeting of insurgents was to take place at the Pont des chèvres northeast of the faubourg of Mâcon . . . with the intention of burning a building known as *le bon Pasteur* where munitions are stocked," while other accounts had insurgents planning to construct barricades.[70]

Pressures built up first for the extension of police authority into peripheral communes and then, as we saw in chapter 2, for the creation of commissariats there, and finally for incorporation.[71] A decree in 1847 extended the authority of the police of Nantes into the surrounding communes and in 1850 even further out. This extension of police authority led other prefects to inquire about similarly extending the territory in which the CPs could operate on the outskirts of their own cities. The commissaire central then proposed that his authority be extended to the entire département, a request rejected by the minister of the interior (but one that anticipated reforms in the first years of the Second Empire).[72]

Police attention was above all directed at the working-class faubourgs of Lyon's periphery, particularly after the insurrections of the canuts in 1831 and 1834 (see chapter 7). The military survey of the environs of Lyon that latter year in October reflected the impact of the recent insurrections, insisting on the "filth" of the *canuts*. Another military survey taken of the Croix-Rousse in 1841 might have been taken in North Africa or some other place considered to be a colony by occupying forces: "Their behavior (*moeurs*) is crude and one can easily see why: situated near a large city that is so thoroughly corrupted, with residents whose precarious situation puts them in the lowest class of society and who receive as a result very little education, the Croix-Rousse is, one can say, a place which can only be considered as the dumping place of a large and miserable population. Civilization is very little advanced there."[73] At least this was the misleading view from the center.

Politics and Contested Public Space

Theaters were, to be sure, public spaces, thus part of the beats of the CPs. During the Restoration, in particular, theaters became hot points of political protest, a miniature political arena, "the primary schools of enlightened men."[74] Opponents of each regime used allusion in the lines presented by actors to make political points, shouting "again! [*bis*]" whistling, or yelling, "Down with [whomever]!" In principle, a CP or at least an agent had to be on hand at each performance. Relative darkness in the theater made difficult the identification of those doing the shouting or singing. CPs were sometimes left the choice of clearing the house or tolerating expressions of political opposition.

For example, in Bordeaux in 1820, the play *Le faux Stanislas* provided an occasion for liberals and conservatives to taunt one another. When an actor came to the line "one must respect the constitution!" thunderous bravos echoed through the theater, along with shouts of "again! again!" From the loges came contrary shouts of "non!" and, in turn, from the *parterre,* "Long live the constitution! Long live the Charter!" This drew the predictable retort, "Long live the king!" The prefect then banned any more performances of *Le faux Stanislas.*[75] In Bayonne a year later, part of the audience demanded the repetition of a line in a vaudeville presentation; the occasion for the tension was the role of French armies in putting down a liberal movement in Spain on behalf of the Congress of

Vienna. Here a police agent bore the brunt of audience anger, showered with "insults too awful to be repeated."[76]

As Sheryl Kroen has demonstrated, Molière's *Tartuffe* presented authorities with the greatest challenge and the enemies of the Restoration with unparalleled theatrical inspiration. In Rouen, the presentation of Molière's masterpiece coincided in the spring of 1825 with mounting hostility to the archbishop amid the beginnings of an economic crisis and mounting unemployment. After the prefect banned *Tartuffe,* and the *Nouveau Seigneur* was announced, small riots broke out in the theater on two nights. A CP cleared the theater and made arrests after those in attendance shouted for *Tartuffe.* During one performance, a man stood up and announced his intention to read aloud *Tartuffe,* a copy of which he had brought with him. He was arrested, along with six others, most of whom were workers, in the pushing and shoving that followed. But that was not the end of it. Following the archbishop's pastoral letter, several satires turned up mocking a vicar, including what was by then the almost inevitable "Our father, unworthy of this title, who lives in the archbishop's palace, that your name be removed, that your reign be destroyed, that your will be abolished, as elsewhere." Rumors then spread that workers from the industrial towns of the valley of the Seine would come to Rouen to protest at the prefecture. Significantly, the cheaper seats of the theater had been more filled than usual, and workers certainly represented a majority of the crowds gathered outside the theater, mocking the clergy in song. A rumor spread that well-heeled liberals were stocking a fund that would free from jail those arrested for protesting *Tartuffe* (an interesting rumor in a country that has never had a system of bail), or, alternately, that 2,000 francs had been gathered to force the playing of the play. The new season, after the Lenten break, brought more trouble, with Molière's classic banned again. The minister of the interior then decided that it would be safer to let *Tartuffe* play. The prefect ordered the gendarmerie readied and informed the CPs that the maintenance of order would be their responsibility. *Tartuffe* played, in calm.[77]

Police confronted other incidents in theaters that had nothing to do with politics. Thefts were frequent. Moreover, "tumultuous scenes" occurred here and there when the rivalry between soldiers and civilians burst into the open. Competition for the attention of ladies led to duels—two of which were fought in Rouen on one day in November 1826.[78] Confrontations occurred between occupants of loges and the parterre, including arguments started over the view of those farther back being blocked by coats or by the hats of officers, who refused to take them off as a matter of pride.[79] Shrill disagreements echoed over the choice of the plays, the quality of presentations, and the performances of new and, for some, favorite actors and especially actresses, reprobation sometimes followed by fights, as in Perpignan in 1824.[80] In Boulogne-sur-Mer the next year, an employee at the customs office took on a musician who had asked that he and his friends, "sacrés bavards," make less noise. He then insulted the CP who intervened as being "unworthy of wearing the sash [of authority]."[81] Occasionally dissatisfied audiences tossed cherries, oranges, or, in the southeast, olives (which would have been carried into the theater in anticipation), and even chairs landed on the stage. In Reims, chaos understandably enough followed a rumor circulating that an actor, who served as director of a troupe in the city, had raped an eight-year-old girl. After trying to defend himself on the stage against these charges, he fled the theater in his costume, and then the city itself.[82]

But it was the juxtaposition between "disturbances" within theaters and subsequent confrontations on the sidewalks, streets, and *places* outside that brought disturbances even more forcefully into public space, for no one needed a ticket to be outside. In Lyon in June 1830, just before the July Revolution, the debut of new actors led to dissatisfaction and so much noise that the CP could not be heard reading the relevant regulations, and a "tumult" followed outside the theater on the Place des Terreaux, the first of several contentious nights of trouble that led to violent confrontations, various "outrages," including a CP being struck. When a large crowd practically blocked the Grand Théâtre on June 12, a gendarme observed that "this gathering, like that on the 10th, should be considered seditious, given the fact that it was no longer inside the theater that the disorder took place, but outside, and this time carried out by the working class."[83]

Political differences could transform other urban public spaces into points of contention. The arrival of religious missions during the Restoration provide another example, in this case the reappropriation of public space in the name of the Church. Lasting from several days to two weeks, the missions combined an attempt to inspire a regeneration of religious fervor in France, encouraging a mood of collective penance for the sins of France assumed to have led to the Revolution. The controversial Abbé de Rauzon, the superior general of missions in France, orchestrated the missions. These had to be authorized by bishops, although the impetus to bring the mission to a city or town often came from the local clergy and the faithful.

Missions drew throngs of amazing size. As many as 15,000 people from all over the region poured into the tiny bourg of Billom (Puy-de-Dôme) for a mission. In Clermont in 1818, the missionaries drew 20,000 people, including faithful villagers arriving from the hinterland who heard the preachers call for "the restitution of usurious sums, of which a great number appear to have occurred." Fleurs-de-lys lined some of the routes, along which processed girls dressed in white, and priests stood for the alliance of altar and throne in France. In Nemours, perhaps three-fourths of the population heard two Lazarist missionaries preach; the subsequent procession included "all the officials, the *notables,* and thirty young girls dressed in white carrying candles and singing canticles."[84] The missions, some of which took on the character of triumphant marches, made clear the link with national and local politics. Indeed the bishops noted with pleasure—and again in 1824—that the success of the missions would have a salutary effect on the upcoming elections.[85]

Missions concluded with the planting of mission crosses, some weighing tons, at the entrance to town or in public squares. These crosses were expensive (one erected in Nemours in 1820 cost 1,500 francs), paid for by funds voted by municipal councils, money collected from the faithful, and by donations from families of means. Thousands of mission crosses—or parts of them—still stand in France, most erected during the Restoration or during the Republic of the "moral order" in the 1870s (or in the late seventeenth or early eighteenth century). In Clermont, the prefect had wanted the cross planted on the land between Clermont and Ferrand, the two rivals then still standing apart. But Rauzan insisted that the cross be placed inside the cathedral, carried by 600 men. The crowd remained calm and respectful, as commissaires de polices and gendarmes stood by. Townspeople and villagers alike scrambled to take home a piece of the remains of the giant *brancard* that had made transport of the giant cross possible.[86]

The missions raised issues of public order. Some priests added their political views to their fiery sermons, for example by denouncing purchasers of *biens nationaux*.[87] Some Restoration authorities tried to keep the missionaries in line. In the Seine-et-Marne, outdoor sermons appear also to have been, in principal, forbidden, at least until the assassination of the Duc de Berri. Even thereafter, concern for public "tranquility" or order predominated, as a royal ordinance of April 20, 1820, allowed prefects to ban these "exterior" ceremonies in the interest of public order.[88]

The placement of mission crosses brought some controversy. In 1819, the subprefect of Fontainebleau forbade the planting of mission crosses on public land. In Coulommiers, the municipal council asked that the cross be erected halfway up a considerable hill along the road leading to La Ferté-sous-Jouarre and not along the road itself, as had been originally planned. It was the same in Fonteainebleau, where the location at which the cross was to be erected on the second Sunday of the mission was changed from along the side of a major road to the court of the church presbytery.[89]

The missions drew the condemnation of Restoration liberals because prefects, subprefects, and other officials invariably attended them.[90] In 1821 in Reims, two men were arrested for having insulted a missionary in the church of St. Jacques during his sermon, as well as a servant living in the plebeian faubourg de Cérès "for having said insulting and seditious things at the foot of the cross."[91] Someone covered a mission cross in Louhans (Saône-et-Loire) in 1819 with garbage.[92] During the mission of Nemours in 1820, Jacques Canault, who hauled sacks of grain at the market, caused a scandal by entering the church of Nemours when a priest was speaking, shouting insults at his wife, and proclaiming loudly that he had not wanted her to be around people like the missionaries. He finally grabbed and struck his wife, dragging her out of the church.[93]

After the July Revolution, mission crosses became irresistible targets of the opponents of the Bourbons, and some of them went tumbling down.[94] In Bourges, an elaborate mission cross standing about twenty feet in height, capped by a crown of thorns, had been erected on the place St. Ursin in 1817. On the night of November 1–2, 1830, someone knocked the cross to the ground. Several days before Christmas, the faithful carried the cross into the cathedral, placing it behind the altar to the right of the entrance to the crypt, where it still stands.[95]

Liberty trees, planted during the French Revolution and after the July Revolution and that of 1848, carried very different political allegiances into public space. In Domme (Dordogne), the municipality planted a liberty tree on September 10, 1830, to commemorate the fall of the Bourbons. To workers, however, the liberty tree took on a different meaning, as they ran through the streets in September shouting against the rich and the "brigands," that is, those they identified with the Bourbons. Two days later, "workers and artisans" planted another tree in honor of a popular local lawyer, Vielmont, who had been elected to be an officer of the newly constituted national guard. The workers' tree, estimated (and probably exaggerated) at 100 feet in height, topped by a *coq romain* and a tricolor banner, towered over its more modest predecessor. Someone baptized the tree "the May tree of the poor," although it celebrated "Louis-Philippe 1er," liberty, and public order. But the second tree quickly drew the opposition of some of the bourgeoisie of Domme, who resented Vielmont's popularity. With the trial of four men arrested, presumably for denouncing the rich, defended in court by Vielmont, the subprefect ordered both trees felled in the interest of public order. In the early years of the July Monarchy, Domme remained divided between the "party of the rich" and the "party of the poor."[96] While representing each government for which they served, CPs often stood right in between.

Public Space, Popular Justice

If mission crosses represented for liberals the appropriation of public space by the Church, closely identified with the Bourbon Restoration, by charivaris ordinary folk occupied pubic space to express their disapproval of what they considered violations of the way they thought things should and had always been done. Here, too, we see how "early modern" the first half of the nineteenth century remained. The confrontation between ordinary people and police was another dimension of the struggle for the streets of cities and towns: the right to assemble, to participate in a charivari, to disguise oneself and carry out a masquerade, to form a *cortège* during the Carnival season, to sing and dance. CPs thus watched over popular festivity—that which was part official festivals and holidays, where each event or sequence was programmed carefully in advance, and those more spontaneous in character.[97]

With their "rough music," charivaris mocked ordinary people whose "transgressions" offended notions of popular justice: the widow who married sooner than was considered acceptable, or who remarried at all, as in the case of a widow in Longwy in 1829 who had just married a policeman; the young woman who married someone from another village, or another quartier; the groom who failed to pay suitable "tribute"—often wine—to other males his age; and, in at least one case, someone who wed a Protestant.[98] Charivaris thus represent another side of "public scandal." As Arlette Farge has noted, "scandal and public order are enemies," and to the police of eighteenth-century Paris, "creating a scandal was sufficient reason for the police to intervene."[99] Yet ordinary people held that a violation of the notion of popular justice—the ways things ought to be done—was in itself a public scandal: The charivari would set things right again.

In the very small town of Bourganeuf (Creuse) during the July Monarchy, a farmer died in an accident. Because he had not had his marriage to his cousin blessed by the Church, the priest refused to bury him. His friends left the body outside the door of the church all night in protest. The next morning, a crowd gathered outside the door of the church and carried the body into the church, and then to the cemetery. A charivari was then "offered" to the priest, before it was disbanded by the arrival of authorities. The next day, a crowd returned to undertake a noisy charivari to the priest's sister, who had urged the curé to stand firm and not bury the dead farmer.[100]

In the Midi, the Hérault was a *pays privilégié* of the charivari (*pailhade* or *paillade*). During Carnival in 1819, a tanner called Miquel who lived in one of the faubourgs of Béziers complained bitterly that his enemies were saying that he was having domestic problems. This brought on him "shame and dishonor": "This orgy . . . known as a *pailhade* . . . is for my entire family the cause of tears and a subject of deathly shame." "Infamous" couplets had been composed, presenting before all the neighborhood (indeed all Béziers) his wife as unfaithful; the "shameful spectacle" moved in a calculated fashion from street to street, after having heaped abuse on its victims before their residence: "The man and his wife were disgracefully played by these vile actors. They fall back on irony, derision and insult and this abominable spectacle had no other goal than to dishonor an honest family by representing a woman as unfaithful, and a husband as barbaric and cruel; is it permitted to divert the public at the cost of the tears and desolation of a virtuous person?" Miquel's explanation was that the previous year he had refused to participate in a charivari, and now his enemies wanted to take their revenge. He also lamented that "religion is losing its authority on hearts," the kind of statement intended to win support of a prefect of the early Restoration period. The prefect issued a decree banning "gatherings known under the name of a pailhade, or charivari," and "songs that the public understands are directed at an individual or at a family . . . and masked gatherings that go through town at night or during the day." Official permission had to be obtained for any roll of drums, used to summon participants. In any case, the prefect did not believe his not terribly believable story: "Were it true, public moral standards would oppose such scenes." The truth had a way of getting around.[101]

In Hautes-Pyrénées, the charivari (or "chaglivari"), or "brenade," as it was occasionally called when accompanied by physical humiliation, seemed a way of life in the 1820s and 1830s. Townspeople and villagers alike banged on pots and pans and shouted outside the window of a schoolteacher who had insulted the people of Madiran by bragging that he was stronger than any of them (some residents complained that this particular charivari frightened the animals). It could even be a dangerous one, as twice in the 1820s persons standing among the crowd "offering" a charivari or its equivalent were shot to death by a furious target for their "rough music." In 1837, a charivari motivated by a woman's "scandalous conduct" led to a man being stabbed to death in Langres with a soldier's bayonet.[102] Yet such violence was fairly rare. Moreover, the police often tolerated charivaris to avoid possibly more serious disturbances that could rapidly take on political overtones.

The first years of the July Monarchy brought the politicization of the charivari.[103] The sense of popular justice infused the charivari with republican notions of liberty, fraternity, equality, targeting Orleanist administrators, magistrates, and deputies—and Legitimist deputies as well. Protests against the ineligibility of a liberal from election as officer in the national guard of Épinal because he lived in Forges, a commune just outside town, led to a charivari mocking an influential local notary popularly believed to have orchestrated this particular ruling. The charivari led to a demonstration that "took on a serious character. Ordinary people mixed in with children," suspicion that mysterious "leaders" were orchestrating events—"a tall man with a mustache," "several men, I have been assured, were led into cabarets and received money there," the prefect's implication being that only such leadership or the handing out of money could lead ordinary people to take an interest in elite political issues, and "scenes of disorder such that the town of Épinal have never provided an example since the most critical times of the Revolution," as insults and then rocks cascaded against the house of the notary. The CP could do nothing against such a crowd. Troops put an end to the noisy evening.[104]

In Blois, police attempts to prevent a traditional charivari in 1834 quickly became a political incident. On January 20, shouts of "Down with the *juste milieu!*" echoed in the theater, followed by the almost inevitable "Long live the Republic!" and "licentious" shouts here and there. Two days later, a charivari began in protest of "an immoral act attributed to an inhabitant" of a particular quartier. When the police tried to stop it, a crowd gathered in protest. They returned a second night, when the editor of *Le Constitutionnel de Loir-et-Cher* told those assembled, "You are French, you are free to undertake a legitimate charivari."[105] CPs were thus caught between the stern voice of the authorities they served and popular tradition. They frequently were forced to bend to the latter.

The charivari merged easily with and became almost indistinguishable from—if musical instruments were present—"seditious serenades," in which republican songs were sung either in front of the residence of an unpopular deputy or official or simply as an act of protest in the streets. In Rouen in 1820, well over a thousand people turned out for a serenade in honor of the liberal Lafitte, defying the mayor's warning against crowds, including workers, forming on the public way, "under the pretext of serenades given in different quartiers."[106]

We jump ahead to 1851 and across the sea to the Corsican town of Sartène. There, the CP himself became a target of popular derision. Revelers gathered beneath his window to offer a mocking serenade that he obviously did not want to hear. Two warnings moved them away. But when they reached a nearby square, the serenade was transformed into a "bad charivari." The CP awakened four gendarmes, summoning them to meet him at the place. Several of the revelers were soldiers, who fled into a nearby shop, whose owner not only did not turn them over to authorities but offered them rum and then tried to shut the door on the CP, announcing, "I am at home, and I have the right to do what I want." Confronted with force, the storekeeper grabbed "a sharp weapon" before a gendarme disarmed him and hauled him away. The CP stood accused of threatening the revelers with a rifle, and then offering chestnuts and two bottles of wine if they would stop the noise![107]

The masquerade, like the charivari, was easily adapted to political protest. Carnival offered a perfect setting for charivaris, which, as the normal festivities themselves, provided authorities with opportunity, as the prefect of the Hautes-Pyrénées put it in 1822, "to gauge the popular mood."[108] Thus periodically authorities put forth decrees, which were conspicuously posted or announced by town criers, setting limits to Carnival revelry, forbidding anyone masked or disguised to carry a weapon, and in a general way any disguises or behavior that could "trouble public order [or] in any way affront decency and public morality."[109] Those masked or in other ways disguised could not be armed, "nor disguise themselves in religious robes of a nature to outrage decency or morals, or be seditious or trouble public order, could not sing any song while disguised, and had to walk very slowly."[110]

In Draguignan (Var) during Carnival season, 1826, a number of young artisans got up on a wagon and, preceded by three musicians on horses, performed a masquerade on behalf of those known locally as the "chevaliers des éteignoirs." Each "actor" in this dramatic procession wore a long robe of black silk, "sprinkled with pieces of white paper, shaped in the form of an éteignoir," and a pointed hat of velvet, while carrying a long object on which were hung two éteignoirs. They stopped several times in town, at which they "received" into their order those whom the procureur général designated as "the most celebrated writers who have defended the throne with so much courage and talent." The names of Louis de Bonald and several other major figures of conservative Restoration ideology could be identified in the display from anagrams. At each stop, the "commanders" or the "chevaliers" of this "order," who had "shown respect for the old doctrines and demonstrated their zeal for the maintenance of conservative prejudices" extinguished candles representing "the lights of the century." At one stopping point, the "commander" proclaimed his pride in the efforts of his chevaliers warring on the century of light, reminding them of "this focal points that the enlightened call the Constitutional Charter, and that is threatened by extinction at all price." The organizer of this spectacle in public space, Astier, a young barber, was fortunate to escape with a month in prison and a fine.[111]

The Second Republic brought more determined police efforts to clear political masquerades from the streets. In Narbonne during Carnival in the politicized year of 1849, men

> disguised went through the streets dressed as those targeted for ridicule and contempt, (including) magistrates and the President of the Republic. One of the actors wore a gray frock coat, a small, three-pointed hat, cocked hat, so as to imitate the clothes worn by the Emperor Napoleon. He was astride a donkey . . . one could read in large letters: Boulogne and Strasbourg (the sites of Louis Napoleon's two pathetic attempts to enter France and find support during the July Monarchy). This person assumed the most grotesque poses.

At the same time, a "troop" of masked men carried a mannequin dressed as a cavalryman in the national guard, representing the "elite" of Narbonne. The revelers then decapitated the mannequin and tossed it into the river.[112] In the Midi, popular dances, notably the *farandole,* took on the character of political defiance in the face of repression orchestrated from Paris.[113] More than any other period we are considering, it was during the Second Republic that the minister of the interior and the prefects pushed CPs toward the maintenance of perfect order in the streets, at least in trying to end political demonstrations.

Suspects

In all three regimes, political surveillance constituted the essence of haute police, defined in 1841 as "everything related to the security of the king and of the state and also all related to public spirit, opinions manifested, news that circulates as it arrives, and the conduct of men known to be opposed to the government," including any kind of political offenses.[114] Different from attempts to control public space through the routine policing of potentially turbulent public spaces, this political police work waxed and waned with the periods of highly charged political opposition. Political policing targeted relatively well-educated and sometimes well-heeled people suspected of organizing opposition or even conspiring against the regime. This was particularly true during the Restoration; however, during the July Monarchy and Second Republic, political dissidence and social protest increasingly converged, with the emergence of workers as contenders for political power against the background of first republicanism and then democratic socialism. If during grain riots that occurred in many regions in 1817, administrative authorities and policeman did not often seek political conspirators, during the July Monarchy this was no longer the case.

Political policing was perhaps summarized by the comment of the mayor of Dax (Landes) in September 1833 on the visit of the editor of a republican newspaper: "The eye of the police is on him." A concert put on by republicans attracted police attention; in the wake of the Polish insurrection against Russian rule, Poles would be admitted for free and everyone else would pay 1.50 francs. One of the organizers confronted the policeman, telling him that he would have to pay to get in, adding in a "a dry and menacing tone" that he was unworthy to appear in such company.[115]

Individual demonstrations of political opposition included "seditious" shouts and songs in streets and other public places. Those who shouted or sang provocatively could simply disappear quickly into the night, distant steps when the CP or his agent approached on rounds. Only gradually did gas lighting come to provincial cities and towns, in Clermont by 1840 but not until eight years later in Aurillac, Mende, and Moulins. Even the most assiduous policeman who had been at his post for some years could not possibly know everyone's voice, even in a small town. In 1829, the mayor of Valence complained that the CP had failed to identify a man who for six weeks had accompanied his seditious songs, some written by the poet Béranger, with a guitar, "insulting all of the kings on the earth." Because he was from Valence, he drew only a warning, as did the proprietor of a café who profited from the singer's popularity with his clients.[116]

Likewise, "seditious" *placards* scrawled and left in a public place overnight could attract a crowd in the morning, therefore posing at least a hypothetical threat to public order. Police tore down a very unoriginal sign left overnight in 1823 in Montmédy (Ardennes), between the upper and lower parts of town, "House for sale, priest to be hung!" denouncing the Bourbons and praising Napoleon.[117] When the municipal council of Sarlat opened *ateliers de charité* in spring 1831, the CP came on threatening posters scrawled by hand at daybreak on two successive mornings: "A salary or death!" read the first; on the second, a guillotine had been skillfully drawn, complete with a severed head resting on the scaffold. Therefore, the experienced instinct of authorities was to look for a painter as a possible suspect.[118]

The 1820s and 1830s brought a revolution in print culture, one with increasing political ramifications. CPs had to know the laws and ordinances on covering the production and sale of books and other printed matter.[119] The police took on further responsibility for the policing of lithographs—"engravings and lithographs act immediately on the popular imagination"—deemed offensive to "public decency and propriety." Common dissident caricatures of the rotund King Louis Philippe as an oversized pear were not the monopoly of Philipon and Daumier in Paris: Early in the July Monarchy, authorities in Alençon came across a poster on which was scrawled a drawing in 1833 with the caption, "Triumphal entry of the rainbow of pears."[120] When Alibaud attempted to assassinate Louis Philippe in 1836, the CP of Bar-le-Duc searched bookstores looking for portraits of the former rumored to be there.[121]

Small political symbols took up a disproportionate amount of the time of CPs. In the first years of the Restoration, the hunt for what the minister of general police called "these sad monuments of adulation that should all be gone"—images and symbols of the ex-emperor—assumed priority. In Orléans in 1816 there still could be found "perhaps unintentionally, but very generally found in all cabarets, inns, prints, and unfortunate images representing Bonaparte, Marie-Louise, and the King of Rome." The minister of the interior authorized the municipal council to burn publicly such images.[122]

Much of the weight of this obsessive political surveillance fell on the CPs. In 1822, the prefect of the Rhône reminded Lyon's commissaires that they were "to have a profound knowledge of the principal inhabitants of your district, being informed as to their opinions, their character, and the extent to which they can be influenced; as a result, you will know in advance any hostile projects before they can be begun." He asked the police to begin a secret register of the city's principal inhabitants, and to write down their observations on their political opinions and conduct, while at the same time insisting that the "troublemakers" were, in general, outsiders, "thus it is outsiders [*étrangers*] you should consider with open eyes." Yet it would be an exaggeration to claim that the police really believed they could impose perfect order on Lyonnais neighborhoods. The prefect also made clear that he would not tolerate "inquisitionary measures," and that all citizens had the right to the liberty and security and that by efficiency and fairness, the CP would acquire "the only price worthy of an honest man, esteem and public respect."[123]

Four years later, the prefect again ordered each CP in Lyon to provide detailed information on his district. For example, in the arrondissement of Palais des arts, Paulin complained that the merchants "could not be trusted and lack religion," and the clerks "profess detestable principles." As for the workers, they were, like workers elsewhere in France, "machines put in motion by those who employ them." The workers would follow "direction" should it come from political opponents of the government. The "least spark" could unleash the "volcano." Around the place des Terreaux and the place de la Croix-Rousse, Vaché assessed that although the silk workers ("of somewhat limited intelligence") were not particularly interested in politics, and workers from outside Lyon were to be feared, including "individuals whose means of existence are not certain." The district of the Halle aux blés in the heart of the Presqu'ile included St. Nizier, Cordeliers, and the commercial rue Mercière. Its population of 25,000 stood as a center of religious piety in Lyon. Thus, one of the principal preoccupations noted by CP Delesgallery in the district was infractions of the law against Sunday work. The district of Métropole, too, may have seemed a center of religious observance centered on the Cathedral of St. Jean, but the CP assigned to the district complained that the policemen were "dragged in the mud" in the district, held without respect, and seen as little more than a simple agent, including by a certain class of people "with whom one should not trifle."[124]

Prefects routinely ordered CPs to be on the lookout for and to report on political travelers believed to be firming up links between political opponents. CPs or their agents thus greeted coaches, boats, and, increasingly during the July Monarchy, trains, as well as keeping alert for outsiders when making their nightly rounds of cafés or checking the registers of innkeepers. The lookout around Christmas, 1822, for "three English radicals" (called Mitchell, Metlack, and Adamson, the latter comically misspelled) in the Hautes-Pyrénées would have been obviously made easier by the fact that each spoke English or at best French with an accent that quickly revealed "un rostbif," although with the development of spas in the Hautes-Pyrénées, English visitors were becoming considerably more common. In any case, the police had descriptions of the three around Christmas 1822: "The first is a very handsome man, the second fat, and the third, small and thin."[125] Authorities could hold anyone deemed suspicious for up to twenty days, and, if what information could be collected in the interim was damaging, they could be turned over to the courts as vagabonds.[126]

We now follow with a CP two pairs of St. Simonian workers who turned up in Angers in March 1833. The first men arrived by steamboat and walked to the house of a certain M. Hock, with whom they stayed. When they left Hock's residence to sing several hymns outside, they attracted more derision than sympathy, despite the fact that one of them sang well. The next day they strolled through town in their bizarre outfits, explaining on behalf of "proletarians, that is, men who live from day to day working with their hands . . . the political, fundamental doctrine of our religion is: each according to his capacity and each according to his works." After dining with a group of about a dozen young sympathizers, they left for Saumur, after having been interrogated by the CP, leaving behind copies of St. Simonian songs espousing the equality of women.[127] Their visit began a flurry of correspondence as authorities compiled a list of St. Simonians in the Loire Valley and the CPs increased their surveillance of coaches and river boats docking on the Loire River.

The next month, two more St. Simonians arrived in Angers: J. Biard, a twenty-five-year-old Parisian who announced his occupation as "a printer and an apostle of Saint-Simonianism," was traveling with Ferdinand Deligne, an eighteen-year-old journeyman shoemaker. Arrested for troubling public order (by wearing a St. Simonian costume in public), Biard was interrogated by a judge in Angers, before whom he denied persistent rumors (which had accompanied their predecessors) that he and his followers intended to undercut workers' wages by working for less or that they referred to those "who possess" as "masters," which could bring them prosecution for "exciting one class of citizens against another." Biard and Deligne also left for Saumur, amid mocking whistles via the faubourg St. Michel, under the close scrutiny of the police.[128]

Signalements, or descriptions of suspects sent around to prefectures and then on to virtually all towns, assisted the police in an age before photographs were used for such purposes. The signalement of the infamous royalist bandit killer Graffaud dit Quatre Taillons stands for many, even if he was wanted for considerably more heinous crimes than virtually anyone. A folk hero to many Catholic villagers in the Gard but feared and hated like the plague by Protestants, his description turned up everywhere in the southeast following the fall of the Bourbons in July 1830. His days were numbered. Quatre Taillons was forty-eight years of age, hardly an imposing physical presence at barely five feet tall with short, blond hair, "chestnut colored eyebrows and beard, ordinary forehead, blue eyes that are set back, well-shaped nose, average mouth, round chin, freckled face, gray sideburns, very deep complexion, smallpox marks," with traces of contusions on his face and hands. The detail in these written descriptions is impressive. Quatre Taillons's face seemed in some places darker than others, his skin noticeably wrinkled beneath his eyes, and scrape or burn marks on his left hand. He usually wore a felt hat and carried a canvas sack with the few clothes he owned and could carry with him. The police carefully checked auberges and "places of *débauche*" looking for him and spoke with public drivers, but they did not have much hope of finding help from "the rabble who often paralyze the action of the police, there are many of them, in general poor, and they accept no responsibility for anything." In November 1830, gendarmes found Quatre Taillons sleeping in a field outside a Catholic village in the Gard near the Rhône and beat him to death.[129]

In the early 1820s, and not for the last time, political refugees poured into France from Spain, arriving in Toulouse, Bordeaux, and other places without any papers at all. A decade later came a stream of refugees from Poland following the 1831 insurrection there, passing through Lorraine, many heading for Paris. From Piedmont, many refugees found their way to Lyon.[130] In those times, such refugees drew special police surveillance, particularly because the political causes with which they were identified earned the support of liberals and republicans in France. Cartons of their dossiers await historians. Most of the forty-one foreigners who lived in Poitiers in 1836 were Polish refugees, all of whom seemed to be republicans. Although many had little money, most seemed to live well enough, sometimes seen in cafés and the theater, leaving the author of an anonymous denunciation to suggest that they were perhaps financed by a secret republican political committee in Paris. In 1835, fifty-five foreign refugees lived in Troyes, forty-nine of them Polish, five Spanish, and one Swiss from Neuchâtel.[131] In Châteauroux, "mauvais sujets" who turn up in a police report included two Italians who hung around cafés, asking for help. They had passports in order for the trek from Périgueux to Paris, so the police had to watch them until they moved on.[132]

We have seen before that CPs were responsible for surveillance of ex-convicts who were allowed to take up residency in a certain city or town. Haute police included the surveillance of individuals who had been convicted of political offenses, most of whom had already served at least some time in jail. Assigned to reside in a certain town, they were to check in regularly with the police, or the mayor, rather like parole in the United States. Among those people who figured on any list of those subject to police surveillance were had been convicted for some sort of political activity. Mont-de-Marsan was hardly a hot spot of political intrigue, but in 1839 there were four such people to watch: Two had been convicted of Legitimist intrigue; the other two were widows whose husbands had been hostile to the Restoration and, not that long after the Duchesse de Berri's ill-fated attempt to launch another civil war in the west, seemed to merit close attention.[133]

In Tours in the early 1820s, commissaire Delisle kept track of a certain Vizier, who had spent a month in jail somewhere because of his "unfortunate religious and political opinions." When he left for Paris with his wife and young son but without a proper passport "following his habit," his reputation followed him to the capital, whose police were advised that he should be watched as someone "vicious and capable of aiding the enemies of the government. He has some education," and might adversely influence the young. Vizier seemed no minor political hack: He had penned verses and sent them to Benjamin Constant, from whom he had received a letter of congratulations. Delisle was even able to provide the address where Vizier had worked in 1810 in Paris, sending along a description of the young (age twenty-one to twenty-six) thin, pale man, "with eyes fixed, throwing out saliva as he speaks . . . his wife is small, ordinary looking, and speaks poorly." Delisle was tough, extending liberals no quarter. When an ex-priest and former Jacobin called Vidal living in the region of Tours committed suicide by throwing himself into the Loire, the CP claimed that the former priest had taken his life because of the "grief that he suffers in seeing the monarchy soon immune from any attack." And on the news of another suicide by another former priest, this one married and a friend of the above, Delisle's comment was, "one revolutionary less."[134]

In 1833 came "revelations" of a plot told to the police in the Sarthe by a boot maker. The story was grand and predictable: Sometime within a month, Sartois nobles would lead an insurrection to restore the Bourbon monarchy. The man had been tipped off by a young man called Corbin, whom the artisan had engaged to help him. Corbin, the son of a laundress, related that after having been taken by a marquis to the Grand Hôtel de l'Europe in Le Mans, several nobles for whom his mother worked proposed that he go to Paris "to conspire." They assured him that an army of 80,000 devoted and courageous men stood ready to march to restore the Bourbon monarchy.

One of the CPs in Le Mans knew of Corbin, who had worked for a shoemaker in the parish of St. Julien. Corbin had an unfavorable reputation in his neighborhood, suspected "of being attached to a shameful vice." Moreover, the young man seemed to have left his umbrella on one of the public promenades of Le Mans, where homosexuals met in near anonymity. The young man's forgetfulness seemed to confirm what had been suspected, and he had left town in shame. It was believed that he had gone to Paris, although it could not be verified if he had departed with "a prominent personage of the region," the supposed senior partner in Carlist plots. Corbin's family had a good reputation, with no evidence that they were embroiled with chouannerie. As for Corbin, he was a simple lad, a good worker: "The only reproach against him is the pederasty, to which he is addicted, which has brought upon him the hatred of his friends and the chastisements of his mother, knowing the kind of people whom he sees."[135] So much for a plot. Yet CPs had to be ready during politically contentious times to follow up every lead and every story, no matter how improbable.

Thus the police in 1826 took Pierre-Alexandre Meurice seriously. The CP of Issoudun (Indre) arrested him in 1826 for "violence and seditious outbursts" for which he stood accused in the nearby village of St. Gilles. He had walked all the way from Perpignan and claimed to be heading to Abbeville in the Somme, carrying his passport marked for that journey and thirty centimes he had managed to collect in assistance from the mayors who had taken pity on him along the way. Stopping in an auberge, Meurice ordered a half bottle of wine and some bread, paying his bill. He then engaged the people sitting at the next table in conversation. Emboldened by the wine, he began to intone "on the miseries of the time," blaming the woes of commerce on Charles X, insisting that workers could barely survive, whereas under Napoleon everyone had been happy. Meurice then claimed that he had served as an officer in the emperor's army, and recounted various exploits, asking his increasingly skeptical neighbors to shout "Long live the Emperor!" with him. When they refused, he grabbed the bottle and, in doing so, knocked over a glass. When the publican chided him, saying that a veteran of Bonaparte's army should behave more appropriately, Meurice hit the man with his cane, and then asked where the mayor lived, so that he could file a complaint against him! Finding only the deputy mayor's house, he excitedly related the insults he believed he had suffered at the cabaret and broke two panes of glass when the wife of the municipal official understandably slammed the door shut. At this point, passers-by grabbed and restrained Meurice until gendarmes arrived, at which point he challenged the deputy mayor to a duel, babbling that he had served as Lazare Carnot's secretary. Clearly Meurice was not in very good shape, but he was allowed to continue his trip to Picardy, given "his little intelligence and his demented state." The local authorities, of course, just wanted to get rid of him.

Meurice had not come to the region of Issoudun by accident. He had spent about ten years there, earning the reputation of being rather odd indeed. He was so dirty that "even people from the lowest class" would not go near him. His ravenous appetite gave rise not only to obesity but to a story that he ate twelve pounds of bread in a day. This self-styled man of letters claimed to have been in Paris at the outbreak of the Revolution before serving as secretary to General Kellermann (and not Carnot, as the story had changed). He spun wild tales of glory days as he stood in rags. The loss of a great deal of weight for lack of food revealed the hard times that carried him back to Issoudun. A succession of temporary jobs had followed: He worked as a copyist, peddled for a while selling sewing materials on a public square, and then selling goods in a store for a short time before leaving for Rouen in 1824, it was said, to be with his mother. A year later, he was back in Issoudun, but not for long, announcing that he was heading north to Picardy. Then he disappeared. Now, his arrest for sedition surprised even his critics, as when he had been in Issoudun he did not talk about politics, instead reassuring various creditors that he had earned some money. But those who knew him had noticed that "the misery that followed him had somewhat warped his ideas, and that it should be presumed that this led him to utter the seditious remarks that led to his arrest."[136] Meurice may have been a sad sack, but he was not really politically dangerous.

Those suspected of political intrigue could be expelled from town. Not everyone went quietly. Clément and Latour, two of Toulouse's CPs, arrested Jean-Chrysostôme Delmas in the Café François in July 1822, refusing to show him the warrant for his arrest. From the Ariège, Delmas had been a law student for seven years. The mayor, Baron de Bellegarde, ordered him to leave town, warning that if he failed to comply, gendarmes would take him away. Delmas had been among liberals accused of causing commotion at the theater, a young man "known for his bad opinions, his violent character, and his presence in every place where there is disorder." Three of his friends had taken the hint and left Toulouse. Now the two policemen hauled the young student off to jail. From his cell, Delmas dashed off a letter of protest, noting that article 114 of the Charter guaranteed "individual liberty." He also expressed his fear of being humiliated if gendarmes escorted him back to his village, "exposed to the execrations of people who will not be able to know the cause of my detention." Gendarmes came to get him at five in the morning on July 22. His humiliation was complete: "Attached to the same chain as two criminals also being led away. In this state, I crossed the Place du Capitole, the rues des Balances, du Pont, etc.," and then was passed from one gendarme brigade to the next until he was deposited in Mongaillard. He published his angry letters of protest to the mayor and the prosecutor general about the incident. Delmas was expelled from law school and two years later left for Paris.[137]

The archives are full of rich reports on political policing. Such reports have been the stuff of social and political history for the past several decades. They have told us much about the ongoing centralization of state authority; the determination, organization, and resilience of the political opponents of each regime; and now a good deal about policing during the first half of the French nineteenth century. Here again, we see striking continuities with the Ancien Régime, including the preoccupation with the alleged role of political dissidents coming from the outside in search of allies—an important part of haute police—and concern that an incident in a public space (market, octroi, theater) might swell into a demonstration or a riot. Yet as in the Ancien Régime, political policing was but one of the duties of the CPs, having most often relatively little impact on their daily routines.

5

SITUATIONS IRRÉGULIÈRES:
THE COMINGS AND GOINGS
OF ORDINARY PEOPLE

On July 18, 1847, a commissaire de police led three people out of Strasbourg after they had been arrested for begging. They had entered town by the Porte-de-Pierre and begun to beg. One of the *mendiants* was Jean Jung, a fifteen-year-old with a wooden leg. He had been born in a village in the Palatinate. With him was Michel Fischer, who was the same age. He was carrying a small child, his three-year-old brother. Who knows what the CP thought as he sent them on their way? From his point of view, the three were outsiders, not from Strasbourg, and they had to go.[1]

In this chapter we will focus on the policing of outsiders in French provincial cities and towns. We will have the chance to meet some of the travelers, itinerant workers and peddlers, vagabonds and beggars who were the focus of considerable police attention. The effort of the state through its police to regulate geographic mobility during the first half of the nineteenth century reflected important continuities with the Ancien Régime. In the eighteenth century, the state had become increasingly involved in the policing of beggars, vagabonds, and others "who could not be vouched for," that is, *gens sans aveu,* who could offer no evidence of their good character and legal standing.[2] Until the 1720s, the monarchy conceived of its proper role as legislator, issuing laws against begging and vagrancy that local authorities were directed to carry out. This traditional practice gave way in the eighteenth century to increased involvement of the state in matters of enforcement. However, the timeless practice was to chase outsiders away, enforced by the maréchaussée (predecessors of the gendarmerie). During the period 1724–33, the state launched a new campaign for suppressing *mendicité* and for the first time provided some of the financing needed to intern beggars in local *hôpitaux généraux* that would take in not only the local poor but outsiders as well. Although the practice of interning beggars had been established in the seventeenth century, this campaign represented the first kingdom-wide effort, a "great confinement" or "great roundup" of the wandering, begging poor on a national scale. When the state withdrew its financial support in 1733, the program soon collapsed, as local authorities returned to the traditional practice of reserving hôpitaux for indigent paupers. The year 1764 brought a second, more energetic attempt by the royal state to reduce the problem. The crown (through the Controller General), ordered the construction of *dépôts de mendicité* and, directed by the intendants, a second "roundup" followed that focused squarely on employable beggars and vagabonds, in this case the mobile poor considered fit for work. The maréchaussée, reformed and expanded, were empowered to pass summary judgments on those they arrested, circumventing normal criminal procedure, sending them to the dépôts, which municipal authorities could not do. By the 1760s, and in part as a result of this second, more forceful state intervention, the practice of carrying passports or similar identification became widespread among common travelers who wished to avoid arrest and possible detention. Those who could not produce papers were presumed guilty of vagrancy and of possibly being dangerous. Passports already made it easier to identify those considered marginal.

Although no law defined begging or simple vagrancy as a crime, the presumptions inherent in summary judgments had the effect of criminalizing vagrancy, even though local inhabitants continued to tolerate their neighbors who occasionally begged. The 1760s in particular witnessed the increased criminalization of vagrancy. This continued to be the case during the first half of the nineteenth century.[3]

In his much appreciated but controversial *Peasants into Frenchmen,* Eugen Weber quotes a contemporary about nineteenth-century France, "until recently, no one left his native town. . . . Today [after the railway] no one stays put."[4] Of the former, he could not have been more wrong. French roads had always been alive with people on the move. However, as in the Ancien Régime, the upper classes (who could basically move about as they pleased) remained suspicious of geographic mobility in itself, of seasonal migrants and other workers on the move, and particularly of vagrants, who invariably chose cities and towns as their destinations. The response of the police to beggars, in particular, should help us assess to what extent the former aimed at perfect order in the city. Moreover, we will want to see if significant differences existed in the way they treated "outsiders" and people known to be from town.

French police could (and still can) demand that anyone present their papers at any time, for whatever reason. All adults in France had to be in possession of a passport, which was valid for a year, to travel beyond the limits of their département. (This obligation had been created on May 25, 1792, and reaffirmed October 2, 1795.) In principle no person could leave any commune without a passport, given by the mayor, for which one had to pay several francs, unless it was a passport for someone indigent. All those arriving to stay for any period in a town had to present him- or herself to the mayor within twenty-four hours of arrival. Anyone arrested without a valid passport could be held for twenty days; if no information could be obtained that placed them in something of an honorable light, he or she could be presumed to be a vagabond.[5] Yet to be sure, travelers who had upper class written all over them no doubt could in most cases continue to move about as they pleased, without any authorities ever demanding to see their passport.

CPs inspected passports, making sure that plebeian travelers with a passport marked with a specific itinerary by authorities followed the appropriate route.[6] Passports provided specific details about those who carried them. In 1832, the mayor of Angoulême gave a passport to Jacques Renaud, twenty-one years of age, noting that although he had been in the seminary there, he would not be wearing ecclesiastical garb, as he had left the order.[7] Yet particularly during hard times, streams of poor people arrived carrying their passports, or a simple *permis de séjour* given them by the mayor of their own communes. Three such people, among so very many, who turned up in Bordeaux "cannot really justify their presence in the capital of Gironde: one is a laborer, the second a peddler, without merchandise and without the appropriate license, a third without trade or occupation, etc." The "real reason" they were in Bordeaux was the hope of survival by begging.[8]

The destitute, however, were not the only ones stopped far from home, traveling in an "irregular situation." For example, in Aix in 1826, police arrested a man who could produce no papers, who appeared to have been "well brought up." Taken off to jail, he finally said he was Thomas Jacquin, a *commis négociant* from Metz, the son of a tax official. Asked about why he was traveling without papers, he replied, mysteriously enough, "that he wanted to atone for the bad things of which he had been guilty." Yet judicial authorities could not find any reason to hold him longer and ordered him freed. Claiming he wanted to see his parents, he left Aix with a passport with an obligatory route back to the Moselle, receiving a small sum to help him along the way.[9]

Before photographs had become part of policing during the first decades of the Third Republic, descriptions (*signalements*) of those to be arrested or watched had to do. Based on verbal descriptions, specific physical features that were readily identifiable and stood out became terribly important. Height, eye color, shape of face and chin, noticeable scars (the ravages of smallpox, injuries, knife slashes), limps, lisps, accents, even clothing, and nicknames—Le Berrichon, Nez-plat, and so on—could add up to a picture. Police had at least something to go on in 1831 as they looked for Claude Didier, called Jean, a ribbonmaker, suspected of having murdered Jeanne Chevalier of St. Etienne. Born in 1802, Didier limped because of a fracture that had never properly healed because he was always on the move.[10] "Very white and well-arranged teeth" made the poacher Claude Montcharmont stand out in a century of awful teeth, as CPs and gendarmes searched for him in 1851 in the Saône-et-Loire after he had killed two gendarmes and a rural guard who had come to arrest him.[11]

Ordinary Travelers

Suspicion of *étrangers*—that is, anyone from the outside—remained endemic but was more apt to characterize higher authorities and elites than the police themselves, who generally knew what kind of people to expect to arrive and when. Watching and sometimes furnishing detailed information on every voyager who arrived in town was inevitably a daunting task. Thus, the prefect of the Deux-Sèvres complained in 1825 to the gendarmerie that he was not receiving daily information about travelers and was reminded that it was the responsibility of his CPs to furnish such information.[12] Early in the July Monarchy, two CPs in the Ain responsible for towns standing between Geneva and Lyon complained that they could not properly survey an impossible number of travelers.[13]

Commissaires de police (or in places their agents) were responsible for obtaining from innkeepers and other lodgers, boatmen, and coachmen the number, names, and occupations of those arriving in town.[14] This was easier said than done, however, because innkeepers notoriously kept bad records (perhaps sometimes with reason) and paid little attention to ensure that their lodgers had proper papers. When in 1818, gendarmes were on the lookout for *malfaiteurs* in the Isère, believed to be moving across the Rhône, the CP promised to help in the search for them by carefully checking the auberges and cabarets of Voiron, as well as watching all étrangers and peddlers. The mayor maintained a ban on the lodging of all "beggars, vagabonds, and gens sans aveu," hoping against hope that more decrees would prevent them from finding "asylum, as they are obliged to wander, or else to sleep in shops or ships, where they are easily arrested by the night guards or the other patrols that cover the town." After the cafés and cabarets closed at night, anyone on the streets could be considered suspect.[15]

In 1817 the prefect of Saône-et-Loire complained that authorities in Chalon and Mâcon had been lax in monitoring the registers of hotels and inns. The mayor of the latter town replied indignantly that the police and gendarmes checked the registers and the passports of guests every day.[16] Yet when in 1822 the deputy mayor of La Riche, just outside Tours, went with the rural guard in search of two "mauvais sujets" and asked to see the register of a lodger, then found that there were inscriptions only every fifteen days or so, "I reminded them that in fifteen days a person can travel across all of France."[17] In 1826, the registers of some auberges and other lodging places "often included irrelevant or ridiculous notes, often insulting to individuals or to the government."[18] The mayor of Lyon complained in 1833 that the register kept by lodgers who ran the scores of garnis frequently included illegible names, or with first names and age omitted, or that several times the first name of the guest had been entered first. How could one even guess as to how many people had left Lyon? A recent patrol had arrested fifteen people, demonstrating that lodgers were being remiss. Five Poles had been inscribed on a single line on one register, presumably also sharing the same room.[19]

The night of April 7/8, 1830, twelve travelers officially stayed over in Épinal—that is, they were registered as being there. Seven were wagon drivers, four claimed to be merchants, the twelfth was a barrel-maker. One was from Paris, another from the Nord; the others had come from adjacent or nearby départements: four from the Haute-Saône, two from the Moselle, two from the Meurthe, and one each from the Jura and the Haute-Marne.[20] In Brittany, Vannes usually had fewer than ten people passing through, at least those known to police (nine on the last day of January 1848—two manufacturers of paper, a banker, a property owner, tinsmith, salesman, a state land inspector, a soldier, and a lawyer), seven on July 8, and eight on August 25.[21] The four hotels of Moulins, standing on a major road, divided up nine clients, most of whom were merchants of some kind, on the night of February 6, 1839. Nineteen travelers stayed in Altkirch's four hotels on one day in August 1826.[22] In Tours, a much larger town standing at the intersection of major routes, 260 people stayed more than twenty-four hours in an auberge or hotel in November and 222 on one night in December 1831.[23]

The police were quick to distinguish between well-heeled travelers who arrived by public or private transport, whether coach or ship (in the case of river towns and seaports), and ordinary people who usually arrived on foot, carrying what they had with them.[24] Between July 30 and August 5, 1836, the CP of Châtellerault (Vienne) stamped fifteen passports and handed out six. Of the latter, four went to residents of the town, including a former sailor traveling to Nantes, perhaps in search of work, a *rentière* going to Metz, a wholesale merchant off to La Rochelle, and a tailor on his way to Tours; during the last week in December of the same year, he stamped twelve and gave out two (a hairdresser off to try his luck in Paris, and a sailor heading for Nantes). Against such a list of relatively well-heeled travelers, their papers perfectly in order, one has to contrast the 108 indigent travelers who passed through Châtellerault between January 1 and May 12, 1836, to whom 118.20 francs were given in aid, slightly more than a single franc for each.[25]

Few workers could afford a hotel or an inn, and most arriving in town took lodging in garnis, rooming houses. In hard times, the number of outsiders without work simply overwhelmed the ability of police to keep track of them. Yet they did the best they could: During the period May 1–20, 1826, 275 workers arrived and 163 left, adding 112 more workers to Mulhouse during this short period.[26] The CP for the district of the hôtel de ville in Lyon reported in February 1823 that his district seemed full of such workers, hanging around cabarets during the day. On his rounds at eleven at night—closing hour—he noted that many of them had "imperial" mustaches, including hair below the lower lip, which might be taken either as a sign of rallying to the Restoration or of resistance. Not very helpful, but another police report from the same arrondissement reported that all of these *ouvriers étrangers* were behaving themselves and carried proper papers.[27]

However, obviously many (if not most) people who arrived in any town could afford neither the relative luxury of coming by coach or boat or of staying in an inn or hotel. They were thus like the tens, hundreds, or in the case of Paris, thousands of individuals who were not counted by census-takers because they lived nowhere.[28]

On the Move: Itinerant Workers, Peddlers, Vagabonds, and Fearsome Bands of Thieves

The comings and goings of some ordinary people lacked predictability, which made such mobility worrisome. Public and police attention increasingly focused on outsiders believed to have come to town to stir up trouble. The geographically mobile became closely identified with the "dangerous classes." Let's listen to the prefect of the Rhône at the beginning of 1827: "The ancient and true population of Lyon is sincerely and solidly attached to religion and good order. The deplorable scenes that have been occasionally seen in Lyon can only be attributed to a mobile population, composed of outsiders, idle and *sans aveu*, who pour into this great city."[29]

Not only abject poverty but also calendar dictated much of the comings and goings of ordinary poor people, some of whose travels were quite predictable and thus not feared. While seasonal migrations from the Limousin, the Pyrénées, and the Alps are well known to historians, other, more modest temporary movements of population were also regularly anticipated by local police. To take one example from many, wagon drivers wearing blue smocks leading as many six four-wheeled wagons, each pulled by a single horse, could in many places immediately be identified as being from the Franche-Comté.[30]

Economic crisis, whether in the long or short term, propelled workers onto the road: Many carried passports eagerly given by their village mayors. When they returned home after another season in the city, seasonal migrants brought considerable changes to their home villages, not the least of which was a knowledge of French; "thanks to seasonal migrants French is understood everywhere here," noted the officer surveying the Creuse in 1844, whereas French was almost entirely unknown in nearby Treignac, which had few or no seasonal migrants.[31] In the mountainous Auvergne, the subprefect of Riom (Puy-de-Dôme) issued 957 passports to local people walking to work in distant places in 1818, 875 in 1819, and 1,148 in 1820 (many wearing parts of old military uniforms, a reminder of what was the consummate national institution, making it more difficult to identify them as being from a particular region). After all, the Auvergnat département of the Puy-de-Dôme, like its neighbor the Cantal, was a major departure point for seasonal migration, including building workers, pit sawyers, and peddlers. At least 8,000 to 9,000 seasonal migrants left each year, most in the spring, returning late in the fall.[32]

Departmental and municipal authorities could prevent ordinary people from leaving for regions and towns where it was believed they would simply add to the number of the destitute poor. Indeed, it has been contended that the main goal of the entire system of livrets and passports was to limit the numbers of people heading to cities and towns.[33]

In 1818 the prefect of the Vosges noted that authorities in his département were vigilant in policing requests by the "class of ordinary workers"—that is, unskilled—to travel to the capital. They had authorization to go to Paris only if they could somehow demonstrate that their trade provided them with "the means of existence." The minister of the interior wrote the prefect of the Meuse on May 29, 1830, that various people from Stainville had asked for information on "the chances of success emigrating to America," and requested help in getting there. His response was unequivocal. They were to be told that "the majority of Europeans who, based on fanciful hopes, have recently embarked for the new world, have found upon arriving only misery and total rejection and that the small number of those who have survived illnesses that are the inevitable result of a change in climate, along with fatigue and all sorts of deprivations, can consider themselves the lucky ones if they could procure the means to return home again." However, the police could not stop them from this "hazardous enterprise" if they could find a way of getting to America.[34]

Each year hundreds if not thousands of workers managed to get to Paris, in the hope of finding work. Countless rural mayors were only too happy to provide proper papers for the poor, knowing that their departure might subtract from those dependent on charity. A "multitude" of "indigent travelers, carrying various authorizations" could be found on the roads, particularly in the worst of times, when the harvest had failed.[35] In the desire to expedite the departure of someone who was obviously both down-and-out and unknown, mayors could provide *secours de route,* small sums of charitable assistance sometimes specified on the passport, so that the impoverished traveler could at least get to the next stop. Thus Madame Devildon, née Sarah Clinton, received a "certificate of indigence" in 1831 in Niort because of the "notoriety of the extremely difficult position of this woman."[36]

Workers walking from Luxembourg and from parts of Lorraine could be expected to pass through towns in the Meuse every February. During one week in February 1823, 600 such workers traveled through Verdun in the Meuse, 150 on a single day, counted by a police agent posted at the gates of the city to watch them. "Only" 50 turned up the next day—a good many, to be sure, but nowhere near the figure of 4,000 workers, most from Lorraine, reported traveling through the Moselle, followed by a contingent from Luxembourg. But whereas the previous year there had been enough work for them in the capital, in 1823 officials had been told to try to discourage such migration. In that year in the Moselle, no more passports were being given for travel to Paris. In Verdun, which some of the seasonal migrants tried to avoid for fear of being sent back by the police, the mayor refused to hand out passports for Paris to a group of ten Luxembourgeois day laborers, all from the same commune, Kagl or Grand-Charage (had they been able to demonstrate that they had artisanal status, they might have been allowed to proceed). Their passports were stamped for a return to Luxembourg. Yet as the prefect of the Meuse pointed out, they could not really be stopped if their passports were in order, as was indeed the case with almost all of those who had left the Moselle in search of work, hoping to be hired to dig the canals being extended north of Paris. If the minister of the interior seemed surprised by the extraordinary number of workers heading to Paris, in the Meuse it surprised no one. The task of the police in each town remained to observe what seemed normal, report on what was unusual, and to enforce as best they could whatever directives had come from Paris or from the prefecture.[37]

Each workers had to have his livret in order, "signed and authenticated at no cost by a commissaire de police" (or in certain places an agent). The livret had been first established in 1781, and maintained through the Revolution, Restoration, and Empire, surviving until 1890. Any worker traveling without a livret could be arrested as a vagabond.[38] When in 1825 Norman spinners who had been involved in certain "disorders" in Rouen were thought to be on their way to Alsace in search of work, word followed that their papers, including their livrets, should be checked, with particular attention to their birthplace and where they had previously worked.[39]

Vagabonds remained part of the rich texture of urban life. Jean Brunet was arrested in Moissac (Tarn-et-Garonne) in 1822. He had spent three months in Lyon, jailed on the same charge, despite indignantly claiming that he had worked in the port of Nantes until 1821. On his release, he obtained fifteen centimes and a passport with an obligatory itinerary for Lesparre in the Gironde, where he also insisted he had worked before. But instead Brunet "had wandered here and there, begging and remaining a vagabond," and he had "lost" his passport. After his latest arrest, gendarmes took him to Nantes. In his interrogation, he claimed that he had indeed intended to go to Nantes (though Moissac was not exactly on the route) but did not know anyone there, even though he had been born there. He then related two stints in the army, between which he had worked in the port and at the Hôtel Dieu. But then he tripped over his story that he had been lanced while serving in a colonial batallion, finally admitting that he had been somehow wounded by a sword in the barracks. Moreover, his presence in the places in which he claimed to have worked could not be verified. When asked to explain how he had survived for all these years, he replied, "I traveled through different departments with an indigent's passport." This was true enough, and in this Jean Brunet was hardly alone.[40]

Jacques Marcou, thirty-one years of age and an itinerant farm laborer, was arrested in Port-Vendres (Pyrénées-Orientales). When asked why he had no passport, he replied that he had lost it in Spain, somewhere between Bascara and Figueras. He had arrived in Lisbon working as a deckhand on the ship of an American merchant. One day, "having again my feet on the ground . . . while drinking considerably I noticed while on the beach one day that the ship *Larose* had left port," and with it, unfortunately, his work. The French *consulat* provided him with a passport that would allow him to return to Montpellier, his birthplace. He took a ship to Barcelona, and then walked the hundred miles to Port Vendres. The commissaire pushed his questioning. Marcou stuck to his guns, denying being a deserter, although he admitted having taken several names along his route. When it became clear that gendarmes would be taking him back to Montpellier, he suddenly claimed that he had been born in the Charentes, in St. Jean d'Angély, much further away. When asked if he had ever been arrested as a vagabond, he replied, "I am not a vagabond." And he was not.[41]

In February 1851, the CP of Voiron (Isère) arrested Louis Croisier. He carried with him in a time of great political repression "a satire on the rich," a popular almanac, and several other manuscripts, poems, and songs that he hoped to sell. He was jailed. Still, Croisier impressed local authorities, one of whom concluded that he "had enough talent to get out of the deplorable situation in which he finds himself, unless he is happy living in misery as a vagabond." Suspected at first of being either a socialist or Legitimist agent, his sad physical appearance seemed to his interlocutors to offer a sharp contrast with the quality of the poems and other writing that he carried with him, which he proudly insisted he had composed himself. But what he had written seemed harmless enough. He could be faulted only for having left home traveling with a passport not in proper order, and after having received secours de route in Lyon he had continued on his way. He was sent back to Villefranche-sur-Saône, though he probably did not stay there very long.[42]

Geneviève Brodet, confidence woman and thief, did more than just survive on the road for some years. She did very well, in part because her upper-class airs and the stories she spun protected her from suspicion, at least up to a point. Released from jail in St. Flour in March 1814, claiming that she had been "a prisoner of state," and destitute, the seventy-five-year-old lady's claim that she was a nun in the order of the Visitation drew the patronage of several wealthy ladies. Her passport allows us to view her prominent nose, small chin, black eyes, and ashen complexion, "a tic in the right eye, quite small, with her head constantly resting on her left shoulder." In St. Flour, she continued to frequent "the most distinguished families," while regularly taking the sacraments in church. No fool during the Restoration, "she appeared to be a zealous apostle of the royal family," describing how she had been a victim of her devotion to the Bourbons, stories that contributed no small amount to her being hosted at the best tables in St. Flour. Late in the fall, she took off for Troyes, her place of birth, claiming that she wanted to see her sister and sell what she owned there. She returned at the end of spring. In July, she was off again, to Mende, she said, to thank the ladies who had been good to her while she had languished in jail (also) there. In Mende, her behavior abruptly changed. Gone was humble misery: She took lodgings and meals at the best *traiteur,* then left Mende without paying. Returning to St. Flour in September 1816, she stopped seeing her previous benefactors, instead taking a room in the house of a poor woman. Then she left again, she said, to see her sister in Clermont (slipping up on the supposed location of her sibling), leaving behind debts. The next year she started up again in the village of Guillon in the Yonne. There, while taking communion every day in church (despite not having gone to confession first, which "surprised" the local faithful), she teamed up with a "visionary" called Perrault, who claimed to be inspired directly by the Angel Gabriel. She was arrested in Avallon for vagabondage and, not surprisingly, theft, now claiming while affecting "an extraordinary piety" that she had been a nun in a convent in Châlons-sur-Marne and that she had been imprisoned for her religiosity and political opinions in 1793 and then later on the Ile-de-Ré. However, "bizarrely enough, she could remember none of the names of the concierges of these two prisons." After a few months in jail and despite being subject to official surveillance for a period after that, she may well have started up the game she knew how to play so well again at age seventy-eight.[43]

The key to not being sent back to one's village or escorted to the frontier as a vagabond, in the case of someone not French, was having someone in town who could vouch for his character and prospects in life and whose social status by association raised the person sitting in front of police interrogators above the rank of the down and out. Outsiders, of course, were far more likely to be tolerated, and thus to have some social or informal right to stay, if they worked or at least had some prospect of working. When the police arrested Jean-Louis Lonchant, a twenty-one-year-old Swiss, in a *maison de débauche* in Lyon in 1822, he claimed to work for a traiteur. Without papers, he said he was awaiting his passport to be stamped in Paris, his last major stop. Without proper papers, a place to stay, or any money, the mayor ordered the gendarmerie to take him to the Swiss frontier. However, the traiteur for whom the young man had worked vouched for him, calling his "integrity beyond reproach." Moreover, a merchant stepped forward to say that he had paid Lonchant's way to Lyon, after having promised him a job, but that he had hired someone else when it took him longer to reach the city than had been anticipated. By order of the prefect, Lonchant was let go to get on in Lyon as best he could.[44]

Of course it was relatively easy for someone traveling without a passport to disappear from view. Joseph Guédon had a reason to lie low in the Meuse, for he was wanted for a murder committed in neighboring Meurthe. Guédon carried only a certificate of good conduct, which the mayor of his commune had provided, probably just to get rid of him. But he thus could present neither a passport nor the required worker's livret. In Bar-le-Duc, he had been taken on as an apprentice spinner, but his "ignorance" was such that he had been unable to do any work at all. The master had acted in good faith, but the mayor informed him that no one should be admitted to a workshop who did not have a passport, "the only document that can serve to establish an individual's identity."[45]

In Ardèche in 1827, a certain Joseph, or Jean dit l'Américain, traveling under the name of Jean-Baptiste Bosq, a *marchand colporteur*, was arrested in Aubenas with a passport that had been stamped in Grenoble for a trip to Tournon on the Rhône. On the day of a fair, when he knew that the mairie would be crowded, he went to get his passport stamped and was arrested shortly thereafter. He had managed to get through Villeneuve-de-Berg with only part of a passport and left for Valence. But the strange route he had taken to Valence raised suspicions.[46]

Poor women traveling alone sometimes faced official assumption, explicit or implicit, that they were prostitutes. Some were. Marie Imbault, who gave her profession as "dressmaker," traveled in 1831 from the Indre-et-Loire along the valley of the Loire with a passport that would allow her to visit her uncle in Saumur. Born in the nearby Loir-et-Cher, she was twenty years of age and illiterate. She carried proudly some sort of favorable testimony from two residents of her village, attesting to her honesty. An accompanying letter asked the civilian and military authorities to permit her to "circulate freely." But having attracted unfavorable public attention, she was arrested as a prostitute, a camp follower in this case of the 41st infantry, and jailed. Virtually everywhere, variations on the same orders rang out: "Idleness being the occasion of crimes and offenses, individuals known to be idle and without resources should be watched by the police, who have the right to demand that they prove their means of existence."[47]

One of Lyon's CPs arrested Antoinette Decolte, twenty-five years of age, while making his rounds in 1829. She claimed to be a spinner but admitted to being without a home since leaving her Auvergnat village near Ambert nine months earlier. What had she done in the meantime? She had spent eight of the nine months in jail for not having papers. Since being freed, she claimed to have worked for a shoemaker. The police did not believe her, because otherwise why would she have been standing on the rue La Croix attracting the looks of passers-by? To this she simply replied, "I have nothing more to say to you."[48]

Mentally deficient people turned up frequently on the road. In March 1830, the prefect of the Pyrénées-Orientales sent a letter to Privas describing a man who had been arrested in Perpignan and was thought to have lived in Largentière (Ardèche). Appearing to be in his thirties with "with a scar along side his left eye, missing several upper teeth, with pants and a jacket of grey cloth, and an old round hat," the man appeared to be in a permanent state of madness, or at least pretended convincingly to be. From his ramblings, he seemed to be a certain "Bouquet," another *enfant de troupe,* who said he had neither a first name nor a home. He turned out be Pierre Pugnère of the village of Montréal, above Largentière, an *aliéné* condemned by the tribunal a month earlier. He had been arrested in 1828 in Montauban, where he called himself Giberne, before hitting the road again. Gendarmes returned him to his parents in Montréal, where the mayor identified him.[49] Not far from Largentière, police arrested Antoine Faure in Montélimar in 1837. "Insane," he claimed to be from "St. Barthélemy d'Auvergne." After spending fifteen days in jail, he was escorted to the Puy-de-Dôme, apparently before it was discovered that there is no such village.[50]

The law of July 23, 1791, seemed clear on the matter, at least as interpreted by the ministry of the interior: "Whenever a person in a demented state appears on the public way, and when he compromises by acts of fury public security, the first obligation of the municipal authorities should be to have him arrested and provisionally placed in a safe place, where he could not possibly do any damage."[51]

Was someone down and out who loudly said something considered outrageous, threatening, or seditious "malevolent" or simply mentally disturbed? For example, a stranger passing through Bar-le-Duc in 1822 claimed to be the Dauphin, the son of Louis XVI, among "many other absurd and seditious" ramblings. He was Claude Cottez, and his clothes and sabots revealed his peasant origins in Jura. He was known in the Marne, too, for making similar statements and for threatening an innkeeper who had turned him away, telling her that she had best repent, because war was coming and her house would be burned.[52]

For about a fortnight in August 1819, passers-by in Villefranche-sur-Saône were treated to a pathetic spectacle. A mentally ill man called Cousin had turned up. He quickly became "a toy of the multitude, who dressed him grotesquely as a woman and let him run about in the streets, followed by children who force a thousand humiliations on him. Such a spectacle is appalling for humanity." To put an end to this, the police arrested the man, lodged him in the insalubrious jail (which was technically illegal, as he had not been charged with anything), and soon had him returned to his village.[53]

Bands of thieves accentuated the fear of the mobile poor. Any spate of thefts in any town inevitably gave rise to the public perception that bands of thieves were operating, another type of seasonal work. Such bands had terrorized many regions during the Ancien Régime and the Revolution, particularly the Directory, the most notorious among them including *la bande juive* that operated late in the eighteenth century, the beggar bands of the Beauce, and their counterparts in Brittany. Restoration gendarmes had largely succeeded in eliminating bands that terrorized some parts of the country (although as in Britain some of them enjoyed the reputation of being "anti-heroes").[54]

Yet bands of thieves still surfaced from time to time. Nine armed men seized 27,400 francs in pieces of silver worth 6 francs near the village of Durtal (Maine-et-Loire) in 1834.[55] A band of *filous* turned up in October 1833 at the annual fair in Yssingeaux (Haute-Loire). They were arrested as vagabonds, although their passports listed their occupations as "merchants." The band exhibited exceptional organization, carrying a "Tableau statistique de toutes les foires de France," a road map of France, and an *Almanach de France,* in short, some of the tools of the trade of a band on the run that preyed on fairs and markets.[56]

Waves of thefts led to speculation that a band of thieves was operating in the region, as in the case of a series of attacks on the roads outside of Lyon in 1834 and in the city itself. The prefect ordered searches of several villages, using four CPs from Lyon. He believed that a number of arrests would serve to dislodge criminals hiding in the region, who would either be arrested or leave the area; in either case, they would no longer be his problem.[57]

Foreigners, who were easy to blame for almost anything, swelled the ranks of some such bands consisted of foreigners. One such band operated in Auvergne in 1820. A list of some members of the band included thirty-eight people, all apparently ex-convicts. A certain Bruno, believed to be French and fifty-five years of age, led the band. He stood barely five feet tall and carried a large cane, wrapped toward its top in animal skin, like that of a butcher. His hair was gray, his face round, and he wore a *carmagnole* of green cloth and blue cotton pants. Known to the others in his band as "le Maquignon" (almost certainly in the sense of the trickster, not a trader of cattle or horses), he spoke with a marked Provençal accent and was believed to be from Avignon. This made sense, as the band had worked the fair in Beaucaire, as well as those of Nîmes and Bagnols-sur-Cèze. Adding to the Provençal composition of the band was the corpulent François Maréchal, "le Provençal," whose clothes at first view offered an image of respectability. His colleagues included "le petit Provençal," eighteen years old, stocky, and short but known to be a "a good shot, capable of killing." His specialized in stealing watches and handkerchiefs. The Italian Sommarviolte sported a diamond pin and a watch with a chain of gold. Pallas, another Italian, was missing many if not most of his teeth and could be recognized also by his hunting jacket of dirty gray cloth and striped blue pants. Although some band members traveled with their wives, several women were full-fledged members of the band. These included *"la femme Pascal,* thin, her faced burned by the sun," whose husband was an ex-convict living under surveillance in Embrun high in the Alps, and a young pregnant woman from the region of Toulouse, where she had served five years in prison. Other members of this international aggregate included Gandoffy or Gandolff dit *le cuisinier,* a corpulent Piedmontese of forty years age, somewhat elegantly dressed in a green coat and black waistcoat, traveling with his wife in a wagon carrying cloth that could be sold or could serve as a pretext to have come to market. Other members included a certain Quatre-Guet (the report brilliantly added, "we do not think that Quatre-Guet is his real name"), Fifi *dite* Quatreguet, his companion, Joanny, an Italian thirty-two years of age, "marked by smallpox, indeed a shabby figure," wearing "a very large sack" clothes, accompanied by his wife and twelve-year-old daughter, Morel, who had run a cabaret in Brotteaux for a short time and told people that he was a police agent before joining the band, and, finally, a certain Favache, forty-eight or fifty years of age, "fat and dressed like a peasant."[58]

Rumors in 1843 had a bande juive operating in Alsace and Lorraine. It appeared to be based in Switzerland and nearby German states, returning to France "to escape the laws there."[59] There were also "Spanish" or "Catalan" bands—gypsies, the ultimate outsiders. In 1817, seven Catalans suspected in Angoulême and claiming to be mule merchants, stood accused of tricking the gullible, deftly and with lightning speed exchanging money when asking for change, and then disappearing quickly into the crowd.[60] Here the "outsiders"—in a sense, "the other"—against whom the police were responsible for protecting were not only foreigners but "exotic" ones at that.

Beggars

Beggars were omnipresent in the urban landscape in French cities during the nineteenth century, particularly during the first half, because cyclical harvest failures brought enormous hardship. Through every town a veritable procession of destitute people passed, old and young, crippled and healthy. It was not only Paris, Lyon, Marseille, Bordeaux, Toulouse, and Rouen that seemed overwhelmed, but much smaller towns, as well as mere bourgs. Villages of course also had beggars, both those familiar to other residents because they lived there or those passing through, their presence anything but reassuring because they were not known, and therefore suspect. Although part of urban life, beggars stood to many as a symbol of urban disorder, pure and simple.

Harvest failures thus quickly swelled the number of beggars, whether they were the local downtrodden or outsiders arriving from the countryside or other towns to try their luck at surviving in a new place. Local officials estimated the number of poor in Aurillac during the winter of 1828–29 at 1,500 and predicted that the figure might well double during the coming winter. Everywhere it was the same story. The police tolerated beggars, but most of the time such toleration was restricted to those known to be from town.[61] Mendiants étrangers were required to carry their passports with them, on which at least their place of birth had to be marked (but not, obviously, a place of residence for many). Instructions in 1817 from the ministry of the interior reminded mayors that they should know the people under their jurisdiction, rich and poor, and that the law of July

22, 1791, required them to keep a register on which information about the poor was to be entered.[62] Outsiders could face the full brunt of the law.

Travelers not carrying a valid passport (including an appropriate stamp permitting travel in France) were in principle to be led to a municipal official to be interrogated and arrested. They could be held until their legal residence could be determined, and then escorted "from brigade to brigade" by gendarmes until reaching what had once passed for home.[63] After twenty days, anyone in that infamous French situation—*une situation irrégulière*—could be held as a vagabond. Yet the reality could at times be different. The arrival of destitute *compagnards* who came to beg in towns was sometimes tolerated. When the CP of Voiron interrogated eight people from the Ain in a cabaret, not one had a passport. But as none had done anything "reprehensible" such as begging, he simply let them go.[64] In any case, local authorities believed that the force of law should fall on the able-bodied, who were able to work—when work could be found. No law ordered that gendarmes or the police were obliged to turn over those traveling without passports to the judicial branch. They could simply be sent away, in the hope that they would not return.[65]

Records for Poitiers provide some idea of the numbers of passports given to indigent travelers: 1,497 during the period 1834 to 1848, highest in 1835 (139), 1837 (113), and more predictably, 1847 (128) and 1848 (230). Police listed a profession for most people, allowing each to claim a certain dignity, even if their plight indicated that their one-time trade of shoemaker or—more common—seamstress or day laborer was something of an illusion of hope. Notes by mayors or even prefects sometimes indicate the reason for the bestowal of a passport, given "given his extreme misery," or "following the request of the local authority, as no charges have been filed."[66]

The face of gnawing poverty and sometimes heroic resiliency and survival was everywhere, particularly during those classic years of high prices and hard times, 1817–18, 1826–28, 1840–41, and 1846–47, when the numbers of the wandering poor on the road peaked. In 1828, prefects all over France had reason to be pessimistic. From the Nord came the estimate of 150,000 people "in misery . . . we thus find more beggars in towns and in the countryside, and the offices of charitable associations cannot distribute more than five francs each year to each indigent person." In the Sarthe, "men armed with pitchforks have demanded alms with threats at the door of isolated houses." In the Ardennes, "misery is great in Sedan, because so many workers have been let go because of the stagnation of the manufactures."[67] The seasonality of many menial tasks and economic crisis could suddenly deprive workers of resources. In November 1831, the mayor of Palais on Belle-Isle reported in near panic that all the workers who had been employed repairing his town's lighthouse, docks, and bridge had just been let go. Without income and therefore without bread, they had come to ask for work. The mayor had only a few temporary jobs to offer. However, the unemployed could not simply walk off the island and try their luck somewhere else.[68]

The resources of Sociétés de bienfaisance, where they existed, fell far short of being able to help very many people among the poor. In Strasbourg, a Society for the Extinction of Begging had been founded in 1830, followed by a smaller association for the patronage of young former convicts. Strasbourg's hospice had 600 beds, but about 900 people were counted there each day. In the hope of "moralizing" the poor, the mayor provided some of them with rough work on the edge of the city, and established in the interest of "some tormented lives" a "house of refuge" with 137 beds, almost all of which were always full of those regularly on the streets (75 men and 41 women at the time of a report in 1847). In addition, Catholics, Protestants, and Jews organized charity for those of their respective confessions but concentrated their efforts on those from Strasbourg. The city's population of poor in 1850 seemed to be about 9,000 people, one-tenth of whom were "permanently" poor. The Société de bienfaisance distributed about 25,000 kilograms of bread each year.

Yet the begging poor from Strasbourg alone overwhelmed available resources. Pierre Feld, who had moved from the village of Wingen, was fifty-two years of age in 1843 at the time of his seventh arrest in Strasbourg for begging— "not for forty years had he had a home, family, or friends." In 1847, police arrested 221 people for begging or vagabondage in the northern canton alone. On February 22, the catch included a Piedmontese deserter, a seventy-three-year-old beggar and vagabond who insisted that he was a day laborer, "illegitimate," born in Strasbourg and eight years of age, and a woman from Sarreguemines, who traveled with her nine-year-old daughter.[69]

It was the same in virtually every town, although the number of beggars varied with the season, harvest, and economy. In Cahors, when the weather was good and workers had employment, "the only beggars one sees are crippled or in other ways infirm, children, or old people, some of the latter reduced to misery by poor conduct, laziness, or debauche."[70] Chartres was relatively favored. The mounting expenses of its well-organized charity office during the Restoration reflected the growing crisis: From 5,563 francs expended in 1820, the cost of taking care of what poor could be accommodated rose to 19,979 francs in 1829. It distributed assistance in the town's neighborhood, helping about 900 needy people each year. Chartres also benefited from a hospice for the sick, in which about ninety people received some sort of help every day, and another institution housing the elderly and orphans; run by two nuns, it had 134 living there in 1830. In addition, a smaller institution cared for eight blind people. Moreover a Société de charité maternelle had recently been started up with the help of Madame la Dauphine.[71] In the spring of 1848, full of hope but also hard times, in the Côtes-du-Nord, Guingamp had a well-organized Bureau de bienfaisance, its goal to "reduce the misery of the working population of the town." Drawing on passing the hat and profits from lottery drawings, it provided some services to the destitute of the small Breton town. But Guingamp had 40,000 to 50,000 francs in debts, and no lamps, no slaughterhouse, no covered market, and no town hall, so that "virtually everything remains to be done." The winter of 1849 approached, with few funds left at the Bureau de bienfaisance, and little hope for the destitute of the region.[72] It was like that.

Periodically prefects and mayors posted notices, particularly at the gates of towns, warning beggars "and gens sans aveu, those who have no fixed residence nor means of subsistence, and who exercise habitually no trade nor occupation," that they risked six months in jail, and then incarceration in a dépôt de mendicité. More severe penalties existed for trespassing, carrying arms, or making any kind of threat. Prefects and subprefects could provide passports with obligatory itineraries to those found begging; if they complied, the poor could receive fifteen centimes per league traveled to get them back to their villages. If they failed to follow the itinerary, they could be arrested and jailed.[73] In the event that they strayed off the route which they were to take, they lost the right to *secours de route* and could be arrested as a vagabond. Particularly severe sanctions stood ready to punish beggars traveling in groups (if not traveling as a family) because of the fear of intimidation and violence.

The Genoese known as "Batti-berbe," who traveled through the Nord in 1817,[74] or "espagnols"—which usually meant gypsies in the Midi—were feared outsiders. The mayor ordered the police to launch a campaign against all "outsiders" begging in Béziers in 1816, who were to be sent packing. Those from town were subsequently to wear iron plaques identifying each as a "beggar of the town of Béziers."[75]

In February 1819, the newly appointed prefect of the Saône-et-Loire, Alexandre Feutrier, arrived to take up his post. "Upon my arrival in Mâcon," then a town of about 10,000 people, "I was struck by seeing hundreds of children who ran through the public places, filled up the streets, bothering and insulting passers-by, and participating in all the disorders that follow idleness. Groups of beggars demanded money, sometimes with insolence." When gendarmes arrested and escorted them to the villages in the vicinity from which they had come, they simply returned to town. A little more than a year later, the same prefect claimed to have made Mâcon "a new town" by establishing a bureau de bienfaisance and "regularizing" begging and by keeping lists of "acceptable" beggars—those from Mâcon with physical disabilities, illness, age, or other infirmities that kept them from working.[76] Yet he could have had no illusions about such solutions being anything more than temporary.

Periodic surveys by mayors provide some idea of the approximate number of beggars found in French towns. In 1840 (a hard year, another harvest failure), in Saône-et-Loire, police estimated the number of beggars in Charolles (population 3,226) at 70 to 90 in Mâcon (11,994), 40 to 50 in Cluny (4,255), 70 in Tournus (5,407), 25 in Louhans (3,674), and in Chalon (12,400 inhabitants), where the subprefect called begging a "social calamity," 200 people begged for their living.[77] In 1850, the prefect assessed the number of beggars in Auch to be "about, as most everywhere, about 1/18 of the population, about 500 of the 9,099 people living here." Of those, four-fifths lacked any resources, despite some occasional help from the charitable organization there. If those "outsiders" were sent out of town, the prefect estimated that the number of beggars would fall to 150–200, still a considerable, visible presence. In 1850, everywhere the situation seemed out of control, in the countryside as well as in towns. Precise statistics came from the Isère: 1,795 people begged, including 627 men, 609 women, and 564 children. Of these, 1,085 were considred "invalide," that is, beggars without physical impairment who presumably could work (if someone offered them work), and 843 were considered "valide."[78]

In 1831, the prefect of Morbihan estimated that about 5,000 people in his département could not survive without public charity, that is, about one-eighty-fifth of the population. He faulted the weak development of agriculture, which he managed to blame on their lack of education because the peasants spoke Breton. Of these 5,000 people, about 2,000 begged to survive, 1/200 of the population, or 40 percent of the indigent population. He blamed this large number on "the carefree attitude so natural to people here and the ease by which they receive help from public charity."[79]

Certain regions—Brittany was one—were well known for having many beggars. Others were not, including the Hautes-Alpes. Did the bitter cold weather of the Alps discourage begging? Or did the kind of pride noted at the beginning of the twentieth century by Emilie Carles in the village of Val-de-Prés make begging unthinkable?[80] The population of Embrun stood at about 3,200 during the Restoration. Of these, about 200 were described as being "poor," but, at least in 1822, none were known to beg. In Briançon, the town with the highest altitude in Europe, there were about 300 "poor," but no known beggars.[81]

The police were particularly strict with beggars faking devastating injuries or horrible illnesses, rather like those Parisian beggars who had for centuries retreated to the "cour des miracles," where their terrible wounds and infirmities disappeared after their time on the street each day was done. In 1821, the mayor of Troyes complained about "crippled or maimed beggars who are afflicted by monstrous deformities" who could be found on the public way. Almost every day, two beggars, the twenty- and twenty-three-year-old sons of a widow from the nearby village of St. André-les-Vergers, turned up with a chair to beg near the Porte Belfroy. "Both of repulsive appearance," they were said to have been the cause of several accidents by people horrified at their mien. The mayor of St. André-les-Vergers was to order them to stay home.[82] In Lyon in 1822 a CP arrested Jacques Navet-Vignat, a fifty-six-year-old Piedmontese who claimed to be a miner, "for having taken advantage of the public's gullibility by faking infirmities and thus obtaining money by such trickery." Gendarmes escorted him to the frontier.[83]

The dépôts de mendicité in which beggars were incarcerated at times seemed a solution. In an undated report from the early 1840s, the prefect of the Saône-et-Loire expressed the opinion that the ban on begging and the presence of the dépôt de mendicité had brought "the immediate disappearance of a throng of gens sans aveu . . . passers-by are no longer assailed." However, the prefect of Nièvre had it right in 1818 when he correctly assessed that the dépôts were really only an "illusory solution," particularly because many destitute people, instead of trying to avoid being sent to such an institution, wanted to be sent there, where at least they would be fed something every day.[84] For example, Nicolas Baudot, who lived in Trois-Fontaines (Marne), described in 1816 to the subprefect in

Reims "the unfortunate situation in which I find myself, having completely lost my sight." He owned only a tiny house, "of which its value, and beyond, is mortgaged." His wife was sixty-eight years of age, "bent over, under the weight of the years and of infirmities." They had six grown children, but each was as poor as the parents who had brought them into the world, thus unable to provide for them. He asked the prefect for "justice," to be placed in a dépôt de mendicité: "If not, the only thing left for me is undoubtedly to die of hunger." The mayor of Trois-Fontaines confirmed with his signature this wrenching account of poverty and decline.[85]

However, most départements did not have dépôts de mendicité. The Aisne had one in Montreuil-sous-Aisne near the hilltop cathedral town of Laon; it had 500 beds in 1826, 360 of which were in use in 1825, one-fifth of them for children. And in the Loiret a dépôt opened up in Beaugency in 1840, a year after begging had been banned in the département, the goal to "moralize" beggars with work. That located in the village of Gorze in the Moselle was swamped by beggars sent by neighboring départements. In Blois, the small dépôt de mendicité had in 1847 been transferred to the building that housed the Hôtel Dieu. However, the dépôt de mendicité in the Gironde, established during the Empire, had been closed because it had proven too expensive to maintain.[86] That of Chalon, created in 1837, shut its doors a year later.[87]

The police, to repeat, were to take "outsiders" to city gates, foreigners to the nearest frontier. "I sent out of town a large number of beggars," reported casually one of the commissaires of Tours in his weekly report in October 1822.[88] In Poitiers in 1850, the CPs arrested beggars not from town, gave them something to eat, and lodged them for the night, escorting them to the edge of town the next mornings.[89] One of Grenoble's commissaires included, in April 1848, among his daily duties compiling a list of people who appeared suspect, "whether for lack of means of existence, or for any other reason. I take care to consider each case with scrupulous attention, and then to kick them out of town. No day goes by without such people turning up, or whom the agents bring to me, some here under the pretext of looking for work, others simply because they were found begging." He would give bread to some, but then have an agent escort them outside Grenoble "to get them to go on their way." He took away the passports of others, found them lodgings for the night, and the next day had them escorted out of town. But if they came back, he would put them at the disposition of the mayor, who could order their arrest and requisition gendarmes to have them escorted back to their country. But because Grenoble no longer had town walls, it was easy for those recently expelled to slip back into town.[90]

Even within the range of the unfriendly, the reception that the down and almost out received therefore varied considerably. In May 1828, a period of particular hardship, the prefect of the Eure decided that in view of the large number of beggars wandering through his jurisdiction, in addition to a valid passport, any newcomer who could not demonstrate some means of existence had to have a certificate of *bonne vie et moeurs* given by authorities in the last place they had resided. If not, any mayor could order the person to leave within twenty-four hours or face arrest. Eustache and Pierre Colombat, two Savoyard siblings seventeen and eleven years of age, had only as papers a "certificat" given by the mayor of their village. They were arrested as beggars in 1822 in Lyon. The oldest was blind. They were passed from gendarmerie brigade to brigade, returned to Savoy, forbidden to return to Lyon.[91] Of course, some mayors, particularly those of small towns and villages, continued to provide even some troublesome beggars with such certificates so that they would leave and their minor problem would then become that of someone else.[92]

A report by one of the CPs of Troyes allows us to meet the two people he arrested for begging one day. Jeanne Feriot, from near Vesoul (Haute-Saône), had arrived in town earlier that month with her husband, a day laborer, and their two children, six and nine years of age. Her husband had found some work for about a month and then returned home, hoping to find a temporary job in the vineyards and promising to send for them once he had work. In Troyes, Jeanne Feriot had no luck looking for factory work as a spinner. Thus she had been forced to beg to survive, along with her two children, who sat with her in the police office. Nicolas Petit, twenty years of age, was from a village in Burgundy, the son of *vignerons*. He had been in Troyes for a fortnight, sleeping in the barn of a farmer on the edge of town. He had no money and begged to have something to eat; he quickly added that he had "always done so with decency," knowing that any kind of threat could bring a stiff jail sentence. His only hope was a distant relative who was a builder who had given him some bread had promised that he would try to help him find charity and perhaps also something to cure a skin disease he had had for about three years.[93] On one day in February 1834, the jail in Nantes had just one occupant: an eighty-two-year-old day laborer, arrested for begging.[94]

Jean Léonard, who thought he had been born in 1767 or 1768, had a remarkable career as a vagabond, demonstrating not inconsiderable abilities of resilience. He was born in the village of Dommarien (Haute-Marne), south of Langres, although apparently not in dire poverty. Despite his claims that he had worked as a surgeon—though this was not then an occupation of great prestige—in Chassigny a few kilometers away, he seems to have been arrested for begging as early as 1808. He was assigned residence in his village, but had left without authorization. What was he to do there, with no relatives and finding no one who would lodge him, because he had no money? Léonard owned only resourcefulness, audacity, and the ability to read and write. For a time, he found work in Napoleon's army, where surgeons were always in great demand, and where the tools of his trade, such as they were, would be provided him. However, he got himself in some trouble and ended up in irons. After being allowed to leave "under the surveillance of la Haute Police," he was arrested in 1810 and 1811 in the Aube and sent to prison in Clairvaux, and then in Chaumont, where he had most recently lived in 1798. His incarceration was a source of great anguish to his parents, who were known to the subprefect. Other arrests followed, in Montluçon in 1815 and Troyes in 1816, and for a time he was placed under legal surveillance in the Côte d'or.

But where was Léonard to be assigned residence? His aged parents, who lived in Chaumont, had given up on him. Moreover, he was no spring chicken; outside of the army, he could not start up again as a surgeon because he did not have the proper tools. For the past twelve years, he had "done virtually nothing," except for the years spent in the galleys. From jail, again, in Chaumont in 1817, from which he tried to obtain his transfer to spare themselves further embarrassment, Léonard wrote three relatively elegantly constructed letters to the prefect of the Haute Marne asking for help. He knew somebody, or his family knew somebody—a certain Humblot—who lived in Bussières in the distant Puy-de-Dôme, and who could vouch for him (as his parents apparently would no longer do) and insisted that although his youth had been somewhat turbulent, he had never done anything "harmful to society." Léonard even penned a poem from prison in honor of King Louis XVIII, to whom he wanted to express "his sincerity."

By order of the prefect of the Haute-Marne, Léonard was freed in September 1817. He now sought, logically enough, employment in its prison, whose concierge now knew him well and could vouch for his conduct. But apparently the position never came through, as two years later he was arrested again as a vagabond traveling without a passport near Poitiers and returned to prison in Chaumont—the last thing his often humiliated parents wanted. At the prison, he found some work that earned him enough to supplement convict food. He asked to be allowed to go to the village of Prauthoy, claiming that he had a relative there who could help. But the only Léonard there was an elderly man who did not remember him, and his request to be assigned residence was turned down.

Freed again, he was arrested again for begging and imprisoned. But in March 1822, he was given the job of guard in the dépôt de mendicité in St. Dizier, where he kept track of the mentally ill. He did a good job, asking only that he be given the dignity of being differentiated from those he was to watch. He asked for a half bottle of wine a day, that he be allowed to eat with the domestics (not with those he watched), sleep in an office "near the prisoners, but so that he would not be confused with them," and be given clothes. The administrators awarded him a bonus of ten francs a month. But after a year of work, in March 1823, he walked out of the dépôt and was arrested not long afterward in Tours, where he explained that "his intention was to find work as a nurse in the hospital of the army in Spain," this at the time of the French invasion to assist in the crushing of Spanish liberals.

We lose all trace of Léonard for six years. We know that in March 1829 he was freed from jail in Loches (Indre-et-Loire) and was sent to Langres, where he was to be under legal surveillance. He never arrived, his resourcefulness and hope at an end. A traveler found his body in a stream, between the villages of Mâatz and Grandchamp, "his obligatory itinerary which was to be exchanged for the certificate of liberation from jail on the edge of the water, torn into very small pieces."[95]

Françoise Raboteau was arrested in Tours on February 20, 1823, accused of vagabondage. Born in nearby Saumur, she was forty years of age. CP Delisle interrogated the woman, asking from where she had come. Her replies were evasive: "I was in Blois, and I was in Amboise, and a little further; I went on these trips to enjoy myself." Asked where her belongings were, besides what she was wearing, she replied, "I don't have any, not even a bag, nor a shirt. I sold everything." She had spent these meager profits traveling, buying enough food to get by in the "economy of makeshifts." She had nothing left. Françoise Raboteau could not specify to whom and when she had sold her clothes. She then became very agitated, repeating repeated several times, "I didn't do anything bad," but refused to say what she had been doing for the past five months. She signed the copy of her interrogation with an X.[96]

Poor families and particularly impoverished women traveling with children found that begging together was literally the only way of keeping their family together. If one or more members of a family went off on their own, the chances were overwhelming that they would never see each other again. In the spring of 1821, the mayor of Moulins (Allier) provided Joséphine Canalyse and her three young children a letter that asked civil and military authorities to allow her to travel freely and to provide transportation and secours de route as she searched for her husband, thought to be in Valenciennes. Her passport contains the signatures or stamps of six prefects or other officials who had examined it along her way. These indicated that compassion, at least briefly, held the upper hand, although whether she ever found her husband again we cannot say. The odds were certainly stacked against her.[97] A circular from the minister of the interior in 1826 warned that "saltimbanques, street-entertainers, conjurers," who "without being precisely in the class of beggars and vagabonds, have only precarious means of existence." Some traveled with children, "some of whom had been entrusted to them, but more often have been taken from their parents." The police were to establish the identity and relationship of the children to those with whom they traveled and worked.[98]

Many young children on their own survived by begging. The tribunal in Tours acquitted "*le Sieur* [*sic*] Antoine Roche, ten years of age" of begging, but the prosecuting attorney admitted that it would be difficult for "this unfortunate child" to return to his original home in distant Puy-de-Dôme alone (and return to what?) and asked that the gendarmerie assure his transport; the boy would be handed over from brigade to brigade until deposited unceremoniously near Issoire, a world away.[99] When a CP arrested a young deaf mute of about sixteen years of age in the Indre-et-Loire in 1841, he managed to convey that he was from Amboise. When no one could be found there who knew the boy, he was placed in the hospital of Tours. There, nuns looked after him, noting, "He gives signs of much intelligence and seems to have all his faculties." But who was to pay for his care? Local authorities implored the prefect of the Loir-et-Cher to intensify their search for the boy's family, sending along his description: 1.29 meters in height, gray eyes, brown hair, "dressed in a ragged shirt of blue cotton, a blue and white jacket of fustian, and pants of rough white cloths." His very hard life almost certainly went on without the help of relatives.[100]

What can one do except weep when hearing the story of Jacques Coste, a ten-year-old-boy found crying on a road near Châtellerault in 1835? When asked what the matter was, he replied that he did not know where he was going, that his mother had died eight days earlier, his father three years earlier. He knew of no other relatives. Taken to the house of the mayor of the village of Migné southeast of Châteauroux, he related that his father, a day laborer, had lived in Ruffec (Charente), and that after his mother's death, their furniture had been sold to pay debts, and he had no reason to stay there. The gendarmerie took the boy to the hospital in Poitiers; the concierge of the prefecture hired him to run errands. However, the prefect wrote his counterpart in the Charente for verification of the boy's story, and no such family had been known in Ruffec. Had he made up the story? It does not make any difference. The fact remained that he was traveling alone at age ten. An administrative note attached to his small dossier indicated that he was to be returned to the Charente, and that the département would be asking for reimbursement for his short stay in the hospital.[101]

Alphonse, a young boy with a tattoo on each arm, was arrested in Nevers in 1822 and again three years later. Interrogated, he could not "precisely" given his age, but "according to what he had been told" believed that he was about thirteen years old, but had no idea where he had been born and had no trade. After being abandoned in Lyon at the age of two or three on a quai of the Rhône by his single mother, he had the good fortune to be taken in by a soldier whom he came to call his father, baptized with some sort of countess as a godmother, with her son, who was also in the army, as godfather. His adoptive father took him with him to posts in Besançon, Lunéville, Poitiers, and then Nantes, before leaving the army to become a gendarme. At that point, he gave the boy to a brigadier named François, who took him to Nantes, then to Poitiers. Alphonse was asleep when the troops left again and did not follow them, returning to Nantes where he was arrested, before being brought back by gendarmes to Lyon. He then left for Poitiers, but stopped in Nevers, where he found a job working in the kitchen of the garrison there. Limoges, Poitiers, and then Nevers, where he was arrested without papers, were his next stops. Gendarmes took him to Lyon, where he was imprisoned until his countess godmother came to obtain his release. Then he remained for some time, before going "from one barracks to another in order to make ends meet." But he left again, still hoping to find the seventeenth regiment, that of the François who had been good to him. In Nevers, a woman for whom he had worked in the canteen recognized him and took him in, but he was also recognized by the same CP who had hauled him in the previous trip and arrested again for lack of papers. Gendarmes returned him to Lyon again. From prison he promised that he would behave himself, assuring authorities that he worked hard and that anyone for whom he worked would be pleased. He was freed in October 1825. His "father" was in Martinique, and the only hope of this amazingly resourceful boy was to continue with what he knew, following the army and eating what soldiers wished to give him.[102]

Public letter writers helped the itinerant begging poor find a voice that has entered the historical record. A public writer penned seventy-five-year-old Marie Bocognano's sad story to the prefect of Corsica in 1827. She asked for his assistance, describing her poverty and infirmities, including a withered right arm that prevented her from any kind of work. She had two little nephews to feed; they had been abandoned by their parents. The prefect ordered the police to check into her story. The CP discovered that she had three married sons, all workers at the port, who could have been able to help her.[103]

Thus for tens of thousands of poor people, old and young, begging in the streets and public places of France's urban world offered the only hope of survival. Some did not make it. On their rounds during winter mornings, police came on miserable beggars who had not survived another frozen night without shelter. In Tours on the morning of February 8, 1830, a policeman found François Aubry, an elderly man somewhere in his seventies from the nearby village of Cleré, in a ditch, freezing and absolutely exhausted. He carried him to a nearby house, but Aubry died a few minutes later.[104]

The periodic measures taken by prefects and/or mayors to discourage beggars and begging simply shifted them from one region or one city to another, or from city and town into the faubourgs, suburbs, or surrounding villages. In August 1843, the commissaire central of Lille assessed the results of a municipal campaign to chase away beggars. The latter, including some afflicted with awful physical infirmities, as well as Belgian women and children come to beg and some small Savoyards, had been forced into the faubourgs or surrounding villages, particularly Fives and Wazemmes. The begging poor had to have somewhere to go.[105]

The hopeful beginnings of the Second Republic in the spring of 1848 focused some sympathetic attention on the problem of the destitute. The subprefect of Remiremont (Vosges) expressed his hope that in the newly reborn era of fraternity, thanks to "Christianity in action," the poor would no longer be abandoned to the "uncertainties of individual charity." However, most towns had no means for coping with such misery, "a veritable cholera even more heart-breaking than the Asiatic cholera because it takes lives so slowly." He sent along a letter he had received from a bed-ridden poor old woman of sixty-eight years, who seemed on the verge of starving to death. The mayor had allocated her five francs a month, until the funds of the bureau de bienfaisance ran out. Now, she wrote (or someone wrote for her) to ask respectfully for the prefect's assistance: "I have been abandoned by everybody."[106]

One might be tempted to take the growing obsession with sweeping before shops, apartment buildings, and houses and apply it to the policing of those considered "unwanted" or "dirty," les marginaux increasingly identified with crime by the upper classes. Yet it is too simplistic to claim that the police tried to impose perfect order on the streets that they patrolled. CPs often evidenced sympathy for the wandering, begging poor—even some outsiders—who occupied no small amount of their time, even as they applied laws and ordinances intended to force them from town. In any case, insiders retained a considerable advantage. The CPs focused their attention on outsiders. But even period campaigns against marginaux, particularly beggars, could obtain only limited and temporary success, as authorities defined it, at best. The wandering, begging poor, imposing in number, remained part of the texture of urban life, their situations fragile and ever vulnerable, despite impressive resourcefulness, to the vicissitudes of the economy, circumstances, and simple bad luck.

6

POLICING THE DAILY LIVES OF LOCAL PEOPLE

During the evening of October 12, 1848, CP Roussin was on patrol in Tours near the railway station when he came on a woman, Madame Lescalvert, standing on the sidewalk, across from the Café l'univers. Suspecting her of being a prostitute, he first asked her either to "move along" or return home, or else she could be arrested for having violated regulations on prostitution. When the woman replied with hostility and in an "arrogant" and "familiar" tone, he ordered her to follow him to the bureau de police. To Roussin, "she really had the physiognomy of an eye-catcher, and the quartier was infested with prostitutes." He had simply "tried to put an end to this disorder." As dispute heated up, a certain Joseph Huot appeared, claiming indignantly to be the husband of the woman. But commissaire Roussin knew Huot's own wife, and she was not the woman who had loitered near the café.

In the meantime, about eighty people had gathered around, most of them blacksmiths from the railway works whose day was finally done, described by Roussin as "frenzied workers." Several recognized the woman as the spouse of Lescalvert, one of their workmates. This led Huot to proclaim even more insistently the woman's innocence, while insulting the policeman. The fact that she was married did not necessarily mean that Madame Lescalvert was not a prostitute trying to make "sa fin du mois" (money to pay debts due at the end of the month), but it made it even more likely that the woman was waiting for her husband to return from work. Indeed M. Lescalvert arrived, as the workers rudely and grossly castigated the policeman, ripping away his sash of authority, while calling him a "big pig." Roussin took refuge in a nearby baker's house, while Lescalvert took his wife home. Huot shouted that the policeman should be killed.

Roussin should probably have let things go, but he did not. After the crowd had begun to disperse, he emerged from the house, found some gendarmes, and led them to the home of the Lescalverts to determine if their conduct appeared "regular," or if his suspicions had been well founded. But Lescalvert had no intention of permitting Roussin and the gendarmes to enter his home. As Huot continued to incite the workers to support him, Roussin backed off. But before leaving, he ordered la femme Lescalvert to come to his office the next morning to identify some of those men who had earlier insulted him. Then he arrested Huot on charges of obstructing authority with violence and inciting a riot, hauling him off to spend the night in "the violin," that evocative contemporary description of jail.

Early the next morning found the Lescalverts and several of the workers waiting at the office of the prosecutor, where they denounced Roussin in no uncertain terms. The prosecutor then sharply criticized the commissaire for imprudent judgment. Political tensions ran high in the wake of the June Days. The magistrate then tried to convince Madame Lescalvert that Roussin's poor handling of the situation stemmed from his inexperience and from "a default of character." Huot, now out of jail, seemed satisfied, but Madame Lescalvert was not. Knowing how to use the system, she demanded that her case be brought before a tribunal. The prosecutor recommended that Roussin be transferred to another town. Several days later, the Lescalverts accepted Roussin's apology, and Madame Lescalvert withdrew her complaint. Roussin was the loser in all of this, for having let a minor incident take on considerably greater importance.[1]

Most commissaires de police never encountered a riot or a demonstration. The relative turbulence of Paris and Lyon was not duplicated in most cities and towns, despite the obsession of elites with the possibilities of social upheaval. Moreover, serious crime was not a regular part of daily urban life, at least in provincial France outside of the largest cities, and thus not usually the main task of most CPs. What, then, did police do in provincial urban settings? They carried out routine tasks involving public hygiene, keeping streets clear of traffic, watching the market, and verifying the registers of hotel- and innkeepers. They policed petty crime, including prostitution and gambling, in the towns or districts for which they were responsible. And, as needed and when possible, they intervened in disputes between neighbors, compagnons, civilians and soldiers, within families. The hour of the day and the calendar more often than not determined their very long workdays. Normally, there was a certain predictability to much of it. Thus CPs continued to serve local communities in their largely peaceful routines, even if, as we shall see elsewhere, their role as representatives of the state and particularly the prefect could suddenly alter the focus of their attention.

In the eighteenth century, the police had tended to leave the streets to ordinary people, yet attempted to clear public spaces of those perceived as outsiders if they were *marginaux*. During the period we are considering, did CPs try to make the streets something of an extension of bourgeois apartments, the exclusive domain of the privileged?[2] Michel Foucault argues that "the existence of crime played a functional social role" in the expansion of policing over time, "not only as a crucial justification for the police in seeking to increase their own authority, but more widely for the capitalist industrial state in its attempts to underwrite the social order by expanding its regulation of social life, and its powers to 'discipline and punish' the working class." In response to the draconian law on cafés proposed by the "party of order" in 1851, Victor Hennequin, a Fourierist journalist, defended cafés by evoking the right to assemble (which had already been seriously undermined by legislation against "clubs" and other aspects of police repression) and "the inviolability of domicile." One historian argues that Hennequin's spirited defense "anticipat(ed) Michel Foucault's theories in *Discipline and Punish*," by claiming "that the ultimate goal of the bourgeoisie was to impose the cellular system of surveillance found in prisons on the entire nation."[3] We can see Foucault's influence in a recent thesis on relations between *pouvoir* and elites, and ordinary people in Lyon:

> Nineteenth-century elites, despite changes in government, appropriated this ideal theory and sought to apply it. To institute it in real life, influence urban forms and control men, they used the police, of whom they took care to rationalize its organization across the decades. For the authorities, to discipline and punish deeds and gestures—thus *les esprits*—of each person was primary, but the weight of the initial project had as a consequence a difficult application.[4]

In sharp contrast, Jennifer Davis argues that such views fail "to recognize that there were crucial constraints upon the police, throughout this period, which have been at least as important in shaping their practices as were the unprecedented powers they acquired during this same time." Writing of the second half of the century, she notes that the police "concentrated their attention on marginal social groups who already fit popular stereotypes of the potential criminals. . . . this was the urban casual poor."[5] A scholar of nineteenth-century Lyon has emphasized the extension of the system of *quadrillage* or *îlotage*, 1800–80, as an attempt by the police, in response to official and elite pressure, to impose perfect order on France's second city. He argues that police "surveillance involved a triple process: locate individuals, classify them, and keep them in their place."[6]

Crime

Crime remained part of the image and reality of urban life, but not to the extent elite contemporaries imagined. Crime statistics began to be published in France in 1825. This in itself probably increased upper-class preoccupation with the threat to order posed by "the dangerous and laboring classes," the two essentially conflated. Henri Frégier's description of criminals sums up contemporary fears, subsequently marshaled by the historian of Paris, Louis Chevalier: "In addition to the wealthy classes, the labouring classes and the poor classes, the big towns also contain the dangerous classes. Idleness, gaming, vagabondage, prostitution and misery ceaselessly swell the number of those whom the police watch, and for whom justice waits. They live in their own particular districts; they have a language, habits, disorderliness, a life which is their own."[7] In his memoirs, Louis Canler, policeman in Paris during the July Monarchy and the Second Republic, reviewed various types of crime in the capital. With the kind of precision embodied in Julien Alletz's dictionary of policing, Canler titled his chapter on theft: "The thieves by categories, their auxiliaries, and la police de sûreté." He assumed that "it is unfortunately too clear that there existed in among the dregs [les bas-fonds] of the population of the capital a world of scoundrels who constantly live outside the law."[8] Claude Châtelard, who has studied crime in the nineteenth-century Stéphanois, concludes that during the period under consideration, an increase in crimes and delinquence set loose "panic, creating a psychosis revealing grave troubles in a society's existence."[9]

Frégier and Canler, to be sure, were considering Paris, whereas Châtelard's work focuses on St. Etienne, France's fast-growing city during the first half of the nineteenth century. However, leaving aside the question of whether the images of such large, burgeoning places corresponded to social reality, what about most of France's cities and towns?

With begging, thefts represented the most prevalent "crimes" that concerned CPs in large cities as in small towns. Crime was increasingly against property and not persons, a transition that had already been under way in the eighteenth century. The military officer undertaking a reconnaissance militaire in La Rochelle in 1843 noted that of 100 crimes, 58 involved thefts.[10]

Cold weather increased thefts, many of which were blamed on beggars, for example from small cashboxes destined to the poor inside cathedrals and churches. In Tours, Cazeaux père believed that tough times put former convicts who could not find work in the position of having to steal to survive: "Most of them have no home, no place to go, no family, no friends, no property, no income, everthing is finished for them." Those who had chosen Tours as their legal residence and who were to report to the police periodically, turned up in the mayor's office, where they received "a carte de sécurité or authorization to enter a hospital, on which is inscribed in large letters, UNDER SURVEILLANCE!" Because "lodgers don't want anything to do with them, nor any longer does the hospice, so they wander unhappily in the streets." Finally, with nowhere to go, they would leave Tours, "by any gate, all roads are the same to them, they wander in the countryside," until arrested for begging and brought back to Tours to face a judge. By that time, even jail bread seemed fine. Cazeaux's solution for such thieves was to establish a workhouse, "which would save them from harm, and society would gain considerably."[11]

Pickpockets lurked at events that drew crowds.[12] No reported thefts had occurred in Troyes for about three weeks in late 1819. Suddenly, teams of pickpockets turned up in the market. The CP searched the rooms of lodgers. As for the mayor, he associated the spate of thefts with the arrival of "singers, traveling musicians, tooth-pullers, marionneteurs," blaming outsiders as one did.[13] In Metz during the winter of 1842–43, there were so many thefts (to say nothing of the murder of a banker) that worried citizens imagined a plot against the town by "an association of criminals from the capital."[14] When thefts rose by a third in Marseille in 1848, the CPs stood accused of being lax.[15] In larger cities thieves used "false keys," and most thefts occurred when no one was home.

Yet one should not exaggerate crime in French towns at this time. Daily police reports in many towns leave one with the impression that French provincial cities and towns were surprisingly free from crime. Long periods of time could pass without any crimes at all. In 1819, Auch suffered "none of those crimes from which society so often suffers has been noted to the administration." There during the first two months of 1832, not a single event of interest to the police or arrest occurred. March brought only thefts committed by Jaquette Forgues, *fille de mauvaise vie* (when she was arrested she described herself as a "day laborer"), and a theft from a shop by Louis Alem, a farmhand, who had lived in Auch for only several months, were the only reported crimes in three months. The subsequent arrest of a music teacher from the Moselle for traveling without a passport (he was subsequently freed when a letter from the prefect of Hautes-Pyrénées offered a reasonable explanation for his presence), some laundry stolen in June, and grapes stolen before the harvest in September represented the only other "disruptions" of public order in the capital and cathedral town of the Gers during the entire year.[16]

In Grenoble only one theft was reported during May 1823, and none at all the following month.[17] Melun was close enough to Paris to attract pickpockets from the capital who worked its markets and fairs. Yet in 1821, week after week passed during which commissaires had very little indeed to report, absolutely nothing one week ("Nothing occurred in Melun during the past week that merits the attention of the prefect," the only mention of anything out of the usual being a woman who "fell into the fit of madness to which she is subject and which makes her dangerous"). During most weeks, the only news was no news, or very little: a petty theft or two, a merchant cheating on weights and measures, drunks shouting in the streets after the cabarets finally closed down, or after *fêtes* ended, careless residents on the upper floors of buildings tossing out "water" carelessly into the street below, arrests for begging. The CP in Melun in 1821 caught the thirteen-year-old son of a postal employee in Paris, who had run away from home—rather like the famous St. Just—with "silverware and a silver cup."[18] Intriguing arrests were few, but include that of a bear trainer, suspected of theft, who turned out to have with him thousands of francs in gold, and of "Marie-Jeanne Gobert, 60 years of age, because she is demented because of an excess of religious devotion."[19]

In the entire arrondissement of Mirecourt in the Vosges, only thirty thefts were reported in the first five months of 1819. In Neufchâteau, over the course of twelve months in 1821–22, one theft of any importance came to police attention.[20] In Bourgoin (Isère), the list of his activities provided by the CP for June 1817 listed only procès-verbaux for a theft from a cabaretier, one case of "bad treatment," two bakers cheating on weights, one arrest for making too much noise at night, and a fruitless search for suspected "plotters" against the Restoration, the kind of exercise that must have led to quiet murmurs of "oh, no, here we go again."[21] In the canton of Dunkerque, "no crime nor offense" were reported during the last half of December 1845.[22] Such cheering news would not have reassured a wholesale merchant in Le Havre in 1824, who lost the staggering sum of 127,000 francs to an acrobatic thief who climbed a wall and managed to get into his house.[23]

Regular reports also for Tours in 1824 give a fairly good idea of the major preoccupations of the commissaires there: the murder of a young woman who ran a bar, a crime for which two soldiers were suspected; the arrest of a man for taking off his pants in front of forty to fifty people; a self-proclaimed "knight of industry" who was evicted from town after duping locals; the theft of money from a drawer in a bureau de tabac, the suspect a longshoreman with a long criminal record ("whom I am very happy to purge from our town"); the arrest of a woman who had asked for a passport in Tours, after having been refused one in her village, and whose vague answers about the whereabouts of her nine-year-old girl raised suspicions that the latter had met an awful fate, the case passed on to the prosecuting attorney; the arrest of a man and then a woman for theft and vagabondage; several complaints about soldiers firing their guns randomly on the street; and reports or rumors that "six very clever thieves" were rumored to be on the way to Tours.[24]

Cazeaux père reported that thefts represented a small part of his various duties in Tours in December 1830: There had been just four of them. Most of his time was taken up by giving poor people passes that would admit them to a hospital; answering various minor complaints about neighbors, the state of roads, and so on; and providing information requested by higher authorities. Crimes and attempted crimes were few and far between.[25]

"Outsiders [étrangers]" were often automatically suspected of thefts, sometimes with good reason.[26] The polished professional thief called Lefèvre was arrested in Nîmes after a struggle. "One of the most adroit and shrewd thieves in all of France," Lefèvre, with four aliases, was wanted for five crimes. He had worked Nîmes during Carnival season, 1842; what better time than to perform his métier among the masked? When several thefts occurred in Privas in 1827, police suspected a certain Antoine Esteinel, twenty-eight, a farmer from Châteauneuf-sur-Rhône, and arrested him. Living on the edge of Privas for several years, he was wanted for having skipped out on military service, although he denied ever having been called into the army. Police suspected that the birth certificate that he carried with him was that of his brother (but how was one to locate his brother?).[27]

Many and sometimes most thefts and indeed other crimes were solved. In Richard Cobb's view, "one should not underestimate the French police—a mistake that many of their habitual customers made, ending up with the *chaîne* as a result—for they were, on most occasions, a few steps ahead of professional crime."[28] The world that Cobb has so beautifully described for the Ancien Régime, Revolution, and First Empire lived on until at least midcentury.

CPs sometimes operated on the principle of "la clameur publique"—the word on the street—in identifying suspects, although the cases against them had to be proven before the appropriate tribunal or court. In Tours late in 1831, this was enough to get a locksmith arrested on suspicion of having "committed several indecencies," and a day laborer named Pierre Pianno was arrested at the barrière for a theft of 145 francs, which he had with him. In Épinal in 1833, amid a wave of spring thefts, "public rumor" led police to the house of a wheelwright and his wife, where goods taken in a number of thefts were found.[29] In small towns, it was not difficult to identify habitual violators of the public peace, as in Briançon in 1818, when four drunks were making noise late at night, and it proved easy to identify them, "the four individuals being known in town," but in this case they were spared from arrest by their notoriety and the fact that their misdeed was hardly very serious.[30]

Those suspected of theft often were sometimes identified with remarkable speed, for example, when thieves attempted to sell a horse at a price that seemed far below fair value. In Besançon, all eight reported thefts in February 1838 led to arrests. That town's sometimes turbulent rue Battant was well known for its brawls but also as a place where stolen property ended up. Thus the police knew exactly where to go, in which cabarets to inquire, and which prostitutes might provide information on certain clients.[31]

Letters of denunciation sometimes pointed in the right direction but most often were not very helpful. An anonymous letter penned in Poitiers on the last day of 1850 provided police with a list of those its author believed were "our principal thieves who do not dare do their work in town," preferring the faubourgs. The list included a shoemaker, an unemployed man, a plasterer, a rabbit skins merchant, two men living in a rooming house about whom nothing else was known, the nephew of the owner of the same rooming house, and a for-mer *cuirassier*, names provided, all, of course, with absolutely no proof.[32]

In Bordeaux, many of the duties of CPs focused on the port and Gironde estu-ary, where many people drowned or committed suicide by throwing themselves into the water.[33] The summary of reported crimes for 1822 seems most notewor-thy for the number of drownings (seventeen) and other accidental deaths (twenty-three); reported crimes seem remarkably few for a city of such size: one infanticide, two attempted murders, eleven thefts, one rape, two attempted rapes, two duels, one case of attempted arson, one brawl, and one political crime. Among the twelve suicides and four attempted suicides in Bordeaux were a young girl who despaired when she discovered that she was pregnant, a woman who had lost money confided to her, "business gone badly," and a cavalary officer who left a note asking his father to pay his debts. The political offense amounted only to the discovery of "an abominable song, called the 'national song,' left on several streets and in a hatmaker's shop, where they were intentionally left."[34]

Four years later, there were few reported crimes in Bordeaux "and almost all of their authors have been arrested and turned over to justice," a result apparently achieved by replacing some of the more "indulgent'" police agents. The harsh win-ter of 1829–30 brought "a group of people who carried out some acts of disorder" on the outskirts of the city, cutting down trees for firewood and stealing clothes, di-viding them up, and returning to Bordeaux. Spring brought thefts in most quartiers of the city, most by a band of about twelve children working under the di-rection of a convict and with the help of "false keys." Most of the young thieves were from Bordeaux, and all were arrested, charged with more than 100 thefts.[35]

Indeed, one is again struck by the sheer routine of police operations. In 1818, Vienne's CP provided a diary of his operations during the month of April. These included the monitoring of bankers and prostitutes, nine cases of "errors" made by merchants selling at the market by weight and measures, the recovery of material stolen from a rope-maker, a procès-verbal for making too much noise, the seizure of a statue of Bonaparte, a procès-verbal given to a shoemaker who employed a foreigner without reporting this fact to the police, the discovery of a tricolor flag attached to a tree and a seditious song, and the arrest of a single thief.[36] In Avignon, several years of systematic reports during the middle years of the Restoration reveal the occasional reported thefts, but rarely more than one or two a month, occasional suicides, various swindles large and small, endemic brawls among river workers, and many drownings in the swirling waters of the Rhône. During three years (1823, 1826, and 1827) the only major events included the shocking suicide of a recently ordained priest; the arrest of three men (one of whom wore the *légion d'honneur*) who had robbed a merchant; a disorder occurred when the "lutteur de Marseille" did not appear as advertised to perform, and the angry audience tore the place apart and assailed the police; and the arrest of a priest from the Var traveling with a girl whom he tried to pass off as his younger sister. These events were enough to keep people talking for a while but did not really threaten "public order."[37]

The police blotter, of course, runs much longer in Lyon. France's second-largest city suffered waves of thefts, for example during the difficult winter of 1817–18. The national guard undertook ten patrols each night, accompanied by sergents de ville. Gendarmes also patrolled along the quais of the Saône and the Rhône Rivers, the place des Jacobins, and the quartiers of Bellecour and Perrache, Celestins, and the faubourg of Vaise. Yet Lyon remained something of a paradise for thieves. Not only could the police and various patrols not be everywhere, but the labyrinth of *traboules,* passageways intended to keep silk dry as it was being transported, offered protection to those with some reason not to be readily seen (as they did later during the Resistance in World War II).[38] Night posts helped. Thus CP Rousset protested in 1822 the suppression of that on the quai of the Rhône at the corner of the rue Gentil, leaving no night post between the Pont de la Guillotière and the hôtel de ville. Moreover, that on Sunday and Monday nights at the entry of the quai Villeroy was often abandoned long before daybreak.[39]

Reports for the first months of 1831 evoke a parade of investigations of theft, and arrests of vagabonds and beggars. During one twenty-four-hour period in April, police made thirty-four arrests, of whom sixteen were freed. Those jailed included six people found sleeping outside or in boats, five beggars, three without proper papers, and one prostitute. The next day, police made twenty-two arrests, fifteen for involvement in a brawl with soldiers. Arrests sometimes reflected the police emphasis of the day. Of twenty-six arrests another day in April, fourteen were prostitutes, presumably for not having turned up for their medical inspection. Thus, arrests could vary from day to day. There were six and nine arrests over a two-day period in early May. Later that month, seventeen were arrested during one twenty-four-hour-period, and fifty procès-verbaux of various kinds were issued. Those arrested were charged with brawling, swindling, theft, vagabondage, assault, and not having proper papers.[40]

Everywhere drinking bouts and drunks occupied inordinate police attention; procès-verbaux for *tapage nocturne* leap out of virtually every list of police arrests. To be sure, regional differences remained considerable. In large cities and in the Nord, in particular, drunkenness seemed endemic, whereas in Narbonne, it would be "an unknown vice, even among the lower classes," which was still the case later in the century, while much of the rest of France seemed to be drinking itself into oblivion.[41] Drink loosened tongues, leading to arrests for ill-timed political outbursts. For example, in Niort in 1824, Charles Tardineau, saltambanque and self-proclaimed dancing teacher, was having a drink in a cabaret, where he "heaped insults on priests and vicars, saying that they were all pigs and rabble and that he had what was necessary to take care of them, while pretending to take aim at them with his cane, proclaiming that if everyone was like him, the white flag [of the Bourbons] would soon be taken down."[42]

Drunkenness could bring terrible tragedies. In January 1843, a woman was horribly burned in a fire in Tours that broke out when she was drunk. The doctor summoned by neighbors and the police said that nothing could be done for her, and he called a priest to the house. The latter asked that she be taken to the hospice of La Riche, but was told that there were no beds available, nor were there any in the hospital of Tours. She died without receiving any care.[43]

The daily routines of policing were often surprisingly free of violence, aside from fights between workers and occasional domestic violence. In 1832, no murders occurred in the départements of the Sarthe and Maine-et-Loire, but there were four in the Mayenne. Many of these were "crimes of passion," including that of the wife killed by the husband's former lover by stabbing her twenty-one times in April 1845 in Le Mans.[44] In the Haute-Loire, several murders occurred early in the July Monarchy, but these were family affairs, as in the case of the death of Madame André Guilhot dit Chazot: "Public rumor" suspected her husband, who seemed fully capable of carrying out such an awful act. In the case of the murder of a member of the municipal council of Brioude, public attention focused on several people noted as having something to gain from the man's death, and his niece's spouse was soon arrested.[45] Some of the most violent crimes occurred beyond the reach of the CPs. Before daybreak on August 31, 1832, a pistol shot point-blank to the head on a path near Poitiers killed Charles Cartier, day laborer, as he headed to work in the countryside. The gun that took his life was found, and then the suspected murderer, his son-in-law.[46] Duels, some of which took lives, were illegal, and most often took place on the edge of town.

St. Etienne, which grew faster than any other city in France during the first half of the century, had, as discussed previously, a reputation for being a particularly turbulent place, in part because of the massive concentration of "outsiders." Mariette Trinité and Elisabeth Many were arrested in November 1828 for vagrancy and prostitution. The former, an *enfant naturel* from the hospice in Montbrison, had been arrested several times, each time taken back to what passed for home, "from which she returns each time to deliver herself to debauchery." She was "incorrigible," but not dangerous.[47] When arrested for vagrancy in 1833, François Dubois held an indigent's passport given him in the Loir-et-Cher, with a mandatory route for St. Etienne, where he said he had been born. He claimed to have been a cabinetmaker and a soldier, but he had no papers proving either. Moreover, there was no record of his having been baptized in St. Etienne. Even more damaging, three witnesses identified him as François Jolibois, who had spent three years in prison in Toulon. He was sent on his way. So was a convicted vagabond, François Bernard, a caster who carried a passport and some change given him by a mayor eager to get rid of him. Finding no work in St. Etienne, he received a passport with an obligatory itinerary for Vienne, where he again looked for work. Another outsider, not dangerous, only very poor.[48]

Likewise, André Comarmond, age fifty-eight, had left his village of Pollionnay (Rhône). Two weeks later, the police arrested him in St. Étienne in 1828 for vagabondage. His story was that he had been stopped in St. Chamond, where he had worked in his état as a tailor. He had not asked the mayor of that town for a passport because he did not believe it necessary, as he had worked in St. Étienne before. But the CP thought that his scruffy appearance did not suggest even the modest status of a tailor. The police knew how to recognize people who worked and in what trades. Moreover, the CP did not believe Comarmond's claim that it was "misfortune reduced me to this," that he had been sick for a long time. Not having a livret or a passport left Comarmond in the uncomfortable status of being considered a vagabond. Indeed, the master tailor who had once employed him in St. Chamond said it had been three years since he had seen him, although he had had no reason to complain about his work.[49]

It was no easy job keeping track of all of the people arriving in St. Étienne, but the police seemed able to get all lodgers to keep the required register of their guests. Those outsiders who could not justify their stay were sent on their way, particularly if they begged.[50] The passport system worked surprisingly well. Moreover, accents served as a form of identity that could give one away; so could hands with (or in some cases without) calluses or colored by fabric dye.

Drunkenness seemed endemic in the growing industrial city. On April 8, 1849, the police found the body of Claude Javelle, a deaf-mute, dead "following an excess of drunkenness. Next to his body, seated in a chair, her head resting against the chimney and in a state of complete drunkenness was his wife. Never a more disgusting scene has been seen." As the CP for the southern district reported on October 22, 1849, "Every day my office is encumbered with complaints of husbands against their wives and wives against their husbands, all due to debauchery and drunkenness." The police reported on November 12, 1849, that all was calm in St. Étienne, "besides these scenes of drunkenness which occur so often and which are tending to increase . . . Except for a great number of drunks, the town was calm last night."[51]

More often, the police reported signs of the gnawing poverty and grim deaths that befell ordinary people, such as a man in his eighties, born in the Haute-Loire, as were so many in St. Étienne, found frozen to death in his bed during the harsh winter of 1840.[52] Thefts occurred almost every day, but this is hardly surprising in a town that now had 70,000 inhabitants. Between February 2 and 19, 1841, nine people were arrested for five thefts (of jewelry, purse and its contents, silver, some silk, and what must have been a small machine from a caster), one man was arrested for rape, and there was an attempted theft in nearby woods.[53]

In 1842, there were 79 misdemeanors and 17 crimes in St. Étienne against property, 43 misdemeanors and 6 crimes against persons and against "morality," and 52 misdemeanors, for a total of 174 misdemeanors and 23 crimes, less than 1 misdemeanor every two days and about one crime every sixteen days. This, again, was in the fastest-growing city in France. Elite Stéphanois imagined they had more to fear than they did.[54] In the meantime, St. Étienne's CPs were privileged viewers of and participants in the growth of France's Manchester. And, at the same time, their work reflected the obsession with political policing that characterized each of the three regimes, suggesting considerable continuity even in a time of great social and political change. During strikes, for example those of 1833, the attention of the police was focused (as ordered from above) on the growth of republicanism in St. Étienne and above all of suspected links with militants in Lyon.

In such moments of national political crisis, the routines of daily policing had to give way to orders from Paris. But in most cities and towns in most times, the routines of daily policing remained quite the same, while contributing to the emerging self-image of the CP. With that in mind, we turn to examine some of the other principle focuses for policing.

Policing the Expected: Prostitution and Illegal Gambling

The police generally tolerated prostitutes, unless they were found to have venereal disease or caused scandal on public space, because like the CPs, prostitutes were part of urban life. In Paris, certain commissaires were assigned specifically to police the storied profession, but in the provinces the policing of prostitution was part of the daily routine. As in the case of beggars, insiders were favored and more likely to be tolerated.[55]

The line between toleration and intervention, however, was thin and depended on the extent that public space and order were troubled by the commotion that invariably surrounded *maisons de tolérance*. Police were most apt to intervene when "public order" was disrupted,[56] and disputes poured out into the street, turning into brawls. By the law of July 19–22, 1791, CPs could enter brothels in the interest of public order to ensure, for example, that such houses were properly lit. For example, in Vesoul in 1829, complaints denounced three woman of "ill repute" seen fighting. They had been tolerated as long as they worked as weavers, but most of the time they delivered themselves to "dissipation and debauchery," working out of a common cabaret that had recently opened. Following a bloody fight, authorities expelled one of the women; gendarmes returned her to Nevers.[57] In Privas, the minuscule prefecture of Ardèche, CP Madier in 1827 had to intervene on several occasions at a maison de tolérance, once arresting a prostitute who had entertained a Swiss guard rather noisily. The prostitute's husband then claimed the policeman had threatened him. Witnesses included two sisters who worked as prostitutes, a shoemaker named Fix, known as "No Regrets," a neighbor of some means, and a young woman who worked at the prefecture. Several months later, several extremely young "libertines" troubled public order before being arrested, and inspected by a doctor, who found that both had venereal disease. CP Madier had little else to keep him busy in Privas: several thefts, news of occasional travelers robbed on the route over the Col d'Escrinet from Aubenas, problems with revelers making too much noise at night, procès-verbaux for failing to sweep in front of one's house or store and handed out to someone who let a pig run free in the street.[58]

Prostitutes set up shop wherever they could, many ignoring the obligatory humiliating medical checkups (*visites sanitaires*). In Nantes, among other towns, *femmes publiques* were banned from cafés or promenades; it was the daunting task of CPs to enforce this regulation. In some places, the poorest and most miserable of the prostitutes worked on the edge of town, selling their services in fields, bushes, and forests, as much as possible beyond police control.[59]

The mayor of Lille in 1827 closed several brothels on a single street, the rue de la Nef (and thus close to a church) but allowed one to remain open. In response to a petition by neighbors asking that that one, too, be closed, he replied that the house stood a sufficient distance from the other houses, assuring the other residents of the street that the police would continue to take "every precaution to avoid complaints and to prevent abuses."[60] In Poitiers, several teachers thanked the mayor for having closed several brothels, while providing a list of several that remained open, one located conveniently just below an army barracks.[61]

We get at least some idea of the imposing numbers of prostitutes in large cities from the number of them sent to the hospice of Antiquaille in Lyon during a six-year period during the July Monarchy (remembering, of course, that many hundreds did not turn up in that hospice): The number jumped from 220 in 1823 to 288 the following year, then reaching 493 in 1826 and again 1828.[62] A Lyon police report from 1833 insisted that the number of prostitutes varied constantly in the city (declared and clandestine), but that about 325–50 women showed up for their health checkup, obligatory as of 1813, for which in principle they were to pay three francs a month (although they could not be forced to pay what they did not have).[63]

In 1816, Riom, a town of about 10,000 people, counted only 10 prostitutes, but these were only those women declaring prostitution to be their trade; Clermont-Ferrand, much bigger, at the same time had 110 prostitutes "of whom we are aware," including relatively young girls.[64] Blois counted forty-five prostitutes in the Restoration. All but two were from town, which afforded them a certain toleration, if they were relatively discrete as they worked the square that was the center of their professional lives. Early in the July Monarchy, to nobody's surprise, an epidemic of venereal disease cases swept the garrison. Young women who had arrived from up river in Orléans were blamed, spending all night "in isolated pathways were they are involved with soldiers and young workers." And from the brothels prostitutes "provoked" young men, "they expose themselves half-nude in their doorways, beckoning passers-by in the most indecent ways," not far from a school.[65] In 1819, about forty to forty-five prostitutes worked in Cahors, a staggeringly large number considering the small size of the town. Of these, ten to fifteen women or girls usually had VD at any time. That year, the conseil général of the Lot voted funds to provide a regular place of inspection of prostitutes. However, the sisters at the hospice refused to take in any woman so infected. The prefect's strategy was each year to have two or three of the most notorious sent out of town, presumably back to the communes of their origins. La fille Bourdet was among those arrested that year. She had been in Cahors for four or five years before being returned on the prefect's orders to her home in Gourdon. She stayed some time with her parents, finding work as a domestic servant. But soon after she returned to Cahors and the only work she really knew.[66]

"Outsiders" dodged CPs as best they could in times of crackdowns. Marguérite Faitrise, twenty-five, had left her home in the Puy-de-Dôme for Montbrison, where she prostituted herself. Forced home by her mother, she returned to Montbrison, married, and then left her husband. She then infected several soldiers with VD, as well as, sadly, somehow, her two-year-old niece. She was reduced to begging. Arrested by a CP and imprisoned, we lose sight of her in 1840.[67] In Besançon in July 1833, the police came on a deaf-mute girl from the Pas-de-Calais. She was able to communicate that she had been forced to come to Besançon, presumably for prostitution, by someone who took her money and then abandoned her, and that she had a brother who was a cabinetmaker in Paris. She was placed in a school for the deaf, but she escaped. There was little that could be done.[68]

The prefect of the Hautes-Alpes had it right when in 1820 he noted that the people of his département manifested "indulgence for delinquents and others guilty of offenses when they are from here."[69] But not for outsiders. In 1817, at least three women were led away from Bar-le-Duc. Gendarmes returned Victoire Simon to Verdun after she had been arrested without papers, living "a dissolute life." The mayor of Verdun was to ensure that she never returned to Bar-le-Duc. Easier said than done. The "libertine" Ursule Rigeubach was escorted back to the Bas-Rhin, and Louise Tourbier, accused of "débauche," led home to Laon with an indigent's passport.[70] Gabrielle Michaud, a twenty-seven-year-old Savoyarde, was arrested and imprisoned because she worked as a prostitute "of the lowest class, bringing together all of the faults of her horrible profession." She was ordered taken to the Swiss frontier. But she would be back. And so would Henriette Ennemond, from Geneva, who showed up to be treated for VD, but was taken to the frontier when the mayor decided that it would be a shame to spend money on a foreigner.[71] When the mayor of Poitiers in 1846 wanted to purge the town of two young girls, both minors, whose conduct could best be described as "irregular," he requested a passport and secours de route for Amélie, who was six months pregnant, and Sophie, both of whom had been employed as chambermaids, who both were to be sent home to Guéret.[72] Here, again, being local or being an outsider was the issue.

The plight of Mariette Masson in 1822 reveals the stigma that could follow a prostitute, again, particularly an outsider. The young woman was arrested by one of Lyon's commissaires as a vagabond because she had no papers. But instead of taking her to judicial authorities, as required by law, the policeman took her to jail, without a procès-verbal, and a deputy mayor simply drew up and signed a *mandat de dépôt*. Masson clamed that she did not know that she needed a passport to go to Lyon and that the wife of her employer, for whom she had worked for three months, had asked her to go see her sister, a woman called Saunier, who happened to run a maison de tolérance, to ask for news of her father, an old, infirm man. She had been arrested while going into the maison Saunier, but claimed that she did not know the reputation of the establishment. It sounded highly unlikely, but the code pénal did not give the CP the right to treat her as a prostitute without a proper procès-verbal. Indignant, the woman provided a list of people, including some merchant manufacturers in the silk industry, who could vouch for her, and she was freed. Yet Mariette had for some time been on the list of registered prostitutes and had gone through the routine medical visits. However, a year earlier, she had asked for her removal from this list, having "appeared to have left a more regular life," even if her conduct was "not without reproach." For nine months, she had not worked, and her last employer had heard nothing about her for some time. Mariette stood firm, insisting that others could vouch for the fact that she was "neither naughty, nor a thief." Many women drifted in and out of prostitution, some "pour faire leur fin du mois." Was this the case of Mariette? Quite possibly, but the fact remained that she had not deserved to be treated in a high-handed and illegal way, even if she was not from Lyon.[73]

CPs treated prostitutes with at least some dignity if they were part of the community. Demoiselle Michin, long a resident of Caen, died late in 1815. Her demise saddened her colleagues and probably some of her clients as well. Six of her colleagues carried her body to the cemetery, but the priest of the church of St. Jean refused to bury the prostitute and had locked the church. The women then left with the body, accompanied by a large number of people, loudly denouncing the priest. As a prostitute urged the crowd to break it open, the CP for the district arrived and convinced the priest to open the door. As often in disputes, the CP arranged a compromise: If the prostitutes would renounce the right to carry the body, the clergy would do so. Despite the refusal of any of the three priests who carried the body to the cemetery to bless it, and despite the insistence of someone present that an unblessed body could not be buried, the Demoiselle Michin was finally laid to rest, mourned if unblessed.[74]

CPs also had to be very sure with whom they were dealing when they accused someone of being a prostitute. In this sense, the commissaire can be seen as embodying the principle of neighborhood policing.[75] In Lille, CP Longhaie had to pay 100 francs to the *époux* Galand in 1845. The police had been searching for a prostitute suspected of passing VD to the garrison. Longhaie came on the femme Galand, who worked as a servant, and, seeing that she had a spot on her face, and without interrogating the woman, he forced her to an inspection by a doctor, a "shameful visit" that angered the prefect and eventually cost the policeman about a month's salary. The procureur asked that Longhaie be sent elsewhere, because his presence could only bring the police "disrespect and embarrassment."[76] Likewise, poor judgment—"his habitual casualness"—cost Jules César Vanbambecke his post in 1843 after only a year in Nevers when a cabinetmaker threatened a lawsuit because the CP had mistakenly decided that the artisan's house was a brothel.[77]

Gambling, like prostitution, remained part of urban life. From Confolens (Charente) in 1843 came a policeman's lament that nothing could put an end to it. The same year in Troyes, clandestine gambling went on in auberges and the backrooms of cafés (where gambling was illegal), before and after the prefect issued an ordinance banning gambling.[78] Gambling was absolutely endemic in Montauban. There CP Jacques Bellier received bonuses in 1833 and 1834 for his persistence in his battle against illegal gambling and an additional small sum in 1838.[79] When his colleague Quentin Mairel tried to shut down a game in 1836, seizing cards and money in a café, the game later continued with new cards and with thirty participants, including professional gamblers. Mairel returned a few days later, sporting his sash of authority, but was "maltraité" and insulted. This led to the arrest of a man and a trial, but even his own agent refused to recognize his own signature from a previous procès-verbal. The acquitted man celebrated his triumph in a nearby café with seven men who had appeared as witnesses. Mairel complained bitterly about having to work "among a population of a unique, exceptional character," where the police served as "scapegoats whose sad, precarious and humiliating position is well worth interest and pity." The mayor offered no direction and the agents were exposed to insults from the population.[80]

Policing the Expected: Compagnons

The comings and goings of compagnons were a fact of urban life, particularly in towns that were along the route of the Tour de France, including the stops at which the artisans perfected their skills and brawled with their rivals. The police knew more or less what to expect. These artisans directed their organized fury at their rivals, not at authorities (unless they believed that the police had overreacted). In March 1818, the mayor of Bordeaux encountered in the streets "a convoy of several masons and stonecutters, pompously sporting all of the signs of their old compagnonnage, accompanying the body of one of their comrades to its tomb." Here, clearly, it was organization, the solidarity of the compagnons, and not disorganization that preoccupied police. Only respect for the deceased prevented him from trying to put an end to the procession, a move that would almost inevitably have led to resistance and public scandal. After the funeral ended, the police arrested two workers "whose hats were decorated with ribbons," symbols that were illegal by virtue of the Le Chapelier law during the Revolution. Sending along a report to the procureur, despite the fact that the artisans presented the earlier authorization they had received, the mayor asked the magistrate to set an example for "the many compagnons who already appear ready to take to the streets and public places in order to recommence their murderous fights and to alarm the entire town." Armed with some of the tools of their trade, a number of *ouvriers menuisiers* of the Devoir attacked two other workers in an auberge. The police arrived quickly, arresting four young workers. Following several more arrests, the mayor promised a crackdown.[81] As for the prefect, he understood "how difficult it is to destroy the confraternities, which have survived the Revolution" (which brought the formal interdiction of workers' associations and strikes). He therefore asked the mayor to draw up a list of workers' associations, including the compagnnonages, their leaders, place of meetings, and "troublemakers." However, in July, the cabinetmakers were at it again, carrying their fighting to the edge of Bordeaux to avoid the police.[82]

Tours was a center of the compagnnonage and of their strikes. In August 1825, compagnons put "off limits" a manufacturer and merchant of hats called Braut, sending to other towns notice of this action. Except for two married men, all those working for Braut quit, work undone. The *ouvriers chapeliers* announced a list of other workshops also put on the index, including dire but surely exaggerated warnings, such as "boycott forever! Death to anyone who works there!" About the same time, a certain François Danay dit *l'écrase renard,* from the tough faubourg of St. Symphorien across the Loire and not a man to take lightly, threatened other carpenters if they continued to work for a certain entrepreneur.[83] The next year brought a pitched battle between bakers and other workers in a cabaret in March; "in the darkness, bottles, glasses, stools, everything was smashed."[84]

Down the Loire, compagnons also drew unfailing police attention in Nantes. A certain "Rivière," nephew of a local priest "and brought up by him with a love for the august dynasty of our kings," wanted to be a police spy. At the end of 1824, a year that had brought meetings and a major strike by *cordiers,* he sent an unsolicited letter to the prefect providing information on bloody rivalries between compagnons in Nantes. This letter came at a time that the municipal administration was trying to "destroy"—in the mayor's words—the compagnonnage by, among other measures, banning their "distinctive marks." Rivière reported that a worker who lost a fight with a rival was escorted proudly out of town by his compagnons, even if they lost a day of work doing so, and that compagnons were welcomed to town with three francs; he also provided information on the funds kept in the mother house in Nantes used to support striking artisans, exactly the kind of thing authorities wanted to know. He blithely suggested that authorities encourage the formation of a Société de bienfaisance that would undercut the influence of the compagnnonages.[85]

Throughout the July Monarchy, the activities of Nantes workers, particularly those of Ville-en-Bois, which had its own CP, preoccupied the police of that town. In 1836, the Loire port was rocked by "agitation" among workers (including masons and weavers) who refused to work for their employers. In mid-September, some 1,800 workers refused to work, and a pitched battle against gendarmes and national guardsmen followed. Nantes's CPs were simply overwhelmed, complaining bitterly about their "apathetic and incapable" agents who failed to adequately assist them. When the municipality put forth its "Organisation du corps des sergents de ville" in November 1847, it noted that the duties of the police would remain the same, with one significant difference that had the policing of compagnons in mind. Henceforth, workers could not without authorization gather together and march together "on the public way, nor appear in public with the ordinary marks of the compagnonnage."[86] This was more easily said than done. CPs submitted innumerable detailed, informed reports on the compagnons, their rivalries, brawls, leisure activities, organizations, strikes, and movements in and out of Nantes, above all, in 1845.[87]

Avignon witnessed ferocious, even legendary brawls between rival groups of compagnons (*dévorants, gavots, indépendants, révoltés,* and others). There, too, a municipal ban on compagnons wearing any signs of their affiliations in public, including carrying the canes and sticks that they often used to bash each other, came in 1820.[88] When the compagnons du Devoir arrived in town, the commissaire claimed that he could tell by their body language if they planned "to attack other compagnons from other trades. They marched together in silence." The commissaire had his agent follow them everywhere and, although in this particular instance in 1823 three were armed with large clubs, no arrests were made. Here, again, authorities feared that such a move would lead to more trouble than the modest show of force was worth. The numbers of compagnons (including a Hungarian shoemaker) brawling could be imposing, as in the case of the estimated forty men who attacked a cabaret, damaging the billiards table, because eight glaziers or locksmiths—the CP was not sure which—were about to have a meal there. Three workers were hurt in the melee that followed. In 1837 a compagnon died in a fight. In 1846, police and gendarmes were able to prevent the compagnons of stonecutters, celebrating their fête, from going to the viaduct of the Durance to attack rival compagnons in the same profession, as the "wolves, that they want to eat."[89]

Yet the battles between compagnons were long-standing, even predictable, again suggesting considerable continuity with the Ancien Régime, and they posed only a temporary threat to public order. To repeat, compagnons battled each other, not the state.[90] Moreover, by the very nature of the Tour de France, most compagnons would be moving on. Likewise, battles between *portefaix* from Mâcon and the small bourg of St. Laurent across the Saône River, and between the bargemen and dock workers of Arc and those of the larger town of Gray, much further up the Saône, posed only minor, again predictable disruptions.[91]

Brawling Soldiers and Sailors
and Watching *Forçats libérés*

Compagnons were not the only chronic brawlers who occupied police attention. In garrison towns and ports, townsmen and soldiers, civilians and sailors, and soldiers and seamen frequently came to blows in and around cafés, cabarets, brothels, and streets. In Melun in 1824, a quarrel between three officers and a tailor over a prostitute led to a challenge to a duel. By the next morning, the tailor had decided not to duel. For his good sense, his three newly acquired enemies beat him to a pulp. And so trouble was foreseen for the next dance. Predictably, an officer insulted a civilian and the police, as well, leading the commissaire to end the dance. A melee followed: Soldiers wounded three people with their swords and threats followed, which by this time had to be taken very seriously. The situation was not helped by the appearance of an aggressive sign addressed "To the Royal Hussars, who do not have the courage to defend France . . . but instead show their valor by slitting the throats of their brothers."[92]

In 1823 in Le Havre, a sailor from Cherbourg was killed in one such brawl, this one pitting soldiers and sailors against "the worst" men of the rough port. During the mid-1820s, a regulation in Le Havre forbade "foreign sailors"—that is, not from Le Havre—from being on the streets after 10:30, or they would be subject to a whopping fine of six francs. In the early July Monarchy the mayor had to post a special ordinance making it obligatory for sailors to bring their papers to the town hall. Police surveillance increased and three months in jail was promised to sailors who failed to comply or resisted civil authority.[93]

CPs also had to keep an eye on former convicts (some 40,000 in 1835) assigned residence in their town (they were forbidden during the July Monarchy from living in Paris, Lyon, Bordeaux, Lille, Strasbourg, Nantes, Brest, Toulon, Rochefort, Lorient, and Cherbourg). In 1817 in the Oise, there was one *forçat libéré* for every 4,000 people, a "plague" (albeit seemingly rather a small one) in the eyes of the prefect. Relatively large towns could have a fairly large number of ex-convicts subject to surveillance. Troyes had 122 ex-convicts in residence in 1835, and locals insisted that thefts had increased with their number. The prefect requested funds to pay secret police to penetrate their milieu. In 1842, fifty-four people were subject to police surveillance in Tours. Of these, forty-four were living in town, five in the hospice, and one in the jail, while four lived beyond the octroi in the faubourgs, including one described as "wandering in the countryside."[94]

Drinking Places

Most police attention to cafés and cabarets was not primarily directed at political opponents but rather at maintaining public order. Notable exceptions, of course, were periods of particularly intense political surveillance, notably at the time of the Carbonari plots and other alleged conspiracies, 1820–21, the first and last years of the July Monarchy, and during the "chasse aux rouges" during the Second Republic.[95] In ordinary times, drunks usually preoccupied the police only when they spilled out into the street, made noise, and generated disturbances.[96] No law yet forbade a cafetier or cabaretier from serving drunk men and women or, for that matter, children, and a law against public drunkenness would have to await 1873.[97] Yet it was essential for CPs to get to know each débit de boisson and to get to know its clientele in his particular district or town.[98]

CPs were to enforce the times of closure of drinking places, usually 11 P.M. in the summer and 10 P.M. in the winter. In 1828, a petition of seventy-five residents of Valence asked the prefect to order that cafés close at ten at night all year long. Their reasoning was that such places at that time attracted only "workers and compagnons." If the bells sounded at eleven, the night's work of the police in Valence only then began. The result of the extra drinking, they argued, was increased cost for charitable institutions and increased misery for those spending all of their money drinking. The petitioners claimed that only about 20 people among the 10,000 residents would oppose such a measure. A priest had orchestrated the petition, and most of those who signed belonged to a religious association he directed. Those signing had a place to go at night, but they would, as the mayor noted, coolly deny others the same right.[99] In the Croix-Rousse overlooking Lyon, the mayor in 1850 shared the opinion that cafés should be allowed to remain open until eleven in the summer, as many workers ordinarily went into the countryside on Sunday and Monday to take advantage of nice weather. On their return, most stopped at least briefly in the cafés, and "it would perhaps be too severe to deprive them of this pleasure." Moreover, both the interests of the owners of cabarets and cafés and of the tax office of the octroi argued in favor of remaining open an extra hour.[100] Sundays and feast days necessitated the closing of public establishments. During the Restoration, cafés and cabarets were in principle to be closed during Mass (and vespers, as well). Thus the prefect of the Rhône in 1817 asked the mayor of Belleville to use his influence to achieve this with the "restoration of public morality" in mind.[101]

"Routine" Municipal Tasks

One of the manuals written for CPs at the beginning of the 1850s reminded each policeman that "while 'studying incessantly the trends of the social economy,' he must at any time be able to descend from such heights to the details of traffic control, public lighting, street-cleaning, and practical politics."[102] Such mundane duties occupied a considerable part of the work of the police. Since his arrival in Aubenas, reported the CP of that small hilltop town in 1849, "I have recognized four abuses that must be eliminated: the dirty condition of the streets, untimely discharges from windows, songs and noise at night, and the proper closing of public establishments." He boasted that he had brought a great improvement in these four matters. Each day someone hired by the mayor goes through the streets ringing a bell to remind residents of their obligation to sweep in front of their houses . . . songs and disruptions at night have completely disappeared, and as for the closing of public establishments, I have taken almost all the publicans, or at least the most recalcitrant, before the tribunal, and had them condemned to various fines. I now have reason to believe that these places will close at ten at night, as they should.[103]

Each morning, sweeping before houses in cities and towns was to be completed by 8 A.M., so that the removal of trash could begin an hour later. However, one of the CPs in Montauban estimated that for reasons of absence, illness, or negligence, about one in twenty-five propriétaires failed to comply, and the number of wagons used for hailing waste was inadequate, such that virtually every day the task was not completed until late in the afternoon, if at all. He suggested that unemployed workers be paid with small sums provided by the owners to do the sweeping, which might reduce or even end begging, freeing the police from chasing down those who failed to fulfill their responsibilities (who could be assessed a fine of four or five francs).[104] When the CP of Gap noted in his report to the prefect that the streets were clean, the prefect angrily retorted "that it is notorious that they serve as public latrines for an infinite number of citizens." If the police were doing their duty, he added, those "individuals used to these infamous practices" would receive procès-verbaux.[105] And during years of cholera—1832 and 1849—mayors communicated to CPs a sense of urgency that they pay special attention to enforcing laws and ordinances relative to public health.[106]

To be sure, more than mud could encumber the public way. Commissaires often came on dead dogs who had been poisoned. In Vesoul, a municipal ordinance in 1819 reminded inhabitants not to toss dead animals into the streets. Canine corpses littered ditches in La Rochelle in 1842 before those with the contract to take away garbage came to gather them up.[107]

Particular Urban Challenges

Some towns posed special challenges to their CPs, for example, those stemming from the nature of their topography or the structure of manufacturing work in and around them. For example, Poitiers, Angoulême, St. Claude, and Béziers, among many other towns, offered imposing hills that had to be climbed time after time. The small town of Muret, in the southern shadow of Toulouse, included the hamlets of Ox and Estantens, both so far away from the nucleated town that inspectors—here the equivalent of agents—had to be appointed to look after each. Many towns of even modest size were centers of considerable industrial production in the countryside, with villages integrated into urban life through networks of merchant manufacturing, merchants and workers coming and going all of the time. In the Nord, Le Cateau had 950 workers in 1820, but another 5,000 labored in surrounding villages, typifying French industrialization in the first half of the nineteenth century.[108] In the mountainous Jura, St. Claude had only a population of 5,533 in 1827, but thousands of workers labored in nearby villages making pipes, combs, and other wood items and working precious stones sent from Paris; there were few houses from which the sounds of hammers could not be heard. These workers, a common sight in town, in some ways swelled the population of St. Claude.[109]

Étampes, with a population of 7,600 in 1826, was difficult to police because it stretched along the road from Paris to Orléans, almost a league in length, with another long route crossing it at a right angle. A *ville ouverte,* it was surrounded by gardens. Many thefts in Étampes generated complaints that its CP was negligent. Jean-Charles Savouret defended himself, pointing out that he had brought the authors of eleven thefts to justice. The houses and gardens on the edge of town offered an irresistible target for thieves, some of whom carried ladders with them. He had to defend himself against anonymous denunciations. In any case, the policeman could not be everywhere at once, especially at sixty-six years of age.[110]

In Poitiers, it was students who kept the police on their toes: "No night goes by without the students organizing their farces; the night before last it was the sign of a hat maker on the rue des cordeliers that flew away." In 1825 when someone posted a letter hostile to the government at the theater during the night, the search for its author was complicated by the presence of so many students, who could, in principle, write relatively polished prose.[111] Their counterparts in Toulouse also claimed police attention. In 1817 several incidents occurred at the theater, involving as many as fifty students: The minister of the interior noted that "without doubt authorities should be indulgent with the carelessness of youth," but a recent example of open resistance to the police was unacceptable. The mayor thus refused the students' request to open a dance hall, noting that "parents who sent their children to our town have counted on our paternal surveillance," which, from the point of view of authorities, included the police.[112]

Police work could confirm the particular and sometimes damning reputations of towns. In 1820, CP Abel offered his impressions of the difficulties that would await anyone brought from the outside to serve in Clermont: "The population of this town, pressed against the mountains, is made up of mountain people for the most part, poor, ignorant, and jealous . . . life goes on in the narrow circle of local habits and shared sensations, not worth very much. Because the region is compact, each person thinks himself the center. Thus the Clermontais live for themselves . . . and reject outsiders with horror."[113] No town could have had a worse local reputation than the small Norman town of Vire. With a population of 7,339, the officer carrying out a military survey in 1839 had little good to report about Vire and its "depraved" morals: "Knock on a landmark in Vire and either a usurer, or a prostitute, or a sodomite will pop out." During the previous year, twelve people had been incarcerated for the latter; and "every day the court in Vire hears accusations of usury, and even priests are not exempt."[114]

The situation of Mediterranean towns whose populations were swelling with the arrival of immigrants from the Midi, Corsica, and the Italian states convinced some of their policemen that they faced daunting challenges. The "Observations on the administration of the Police in the town of Toulon," penned by CP Dupont nine months after his arrival at his post, expressed his considered view that the growing port city had followed the example of Marseille by becoming "the refuge for corruption in the south of France and in the states of the Kingdom of Sardinia." With so much prostitution and gambling, two CPs were not enough. There were not enough agents to report various crimes and offenses. These *appariteurs*, who served "by divine right" as secretaries to the CPs, sometimes came to work in the morning and turned loose prostitutes arrested overnight, or, if the mood struck them, left them in the small cell without food or water. There was more behind Dupont's "Observations" than a desire to contribute to better policing in the rough port city. He had just been fired.[115]

Corsican towns offered the challenge of long-standing family rivalries that could quickly bring out stiletto knives. Brawls between groups of rival young men surged frequently; particularly bloody were those fought over "women of captivating passion and voluptuousness." In Bastia, hatred between residents of Terrenoux and Terrevechia, the high and low towns of the northern Corsican city, generated considerable bloodshed.[116] In addition, smuggling, made endemic by need and profitable by the long and essentially unpoliced coastline, weighed heavily on the beleaguered CPs.[117]

In Sartène during the early July Monarchy, le Borgo, a faubourg, and Santa Anna were virtually at war, with gunfire echoing at night, at least until the two neighborhoods signed a peace treaty in the church of Sainte-Maria.[118] In Ajaccio, the commissaire complained in 1832 that the enforcement of the ban against prohibited weapons would be easier if regular patrols could be organized between 8 P.M. and midnight "to search all men found in wine caves, cheap joints, cafés, etc."[119] Yet fights (some of which followed gambling disputes and many of which invariably attracted crowds), shootings, and stabbings by flashing stilettos, remained far more common than on the mainland.[120]

CP Étienne Martinette, a Corsican, bounced back and forth between Bastia and Ajaccio, his home. In 1814, he had been obliged to flee his island, where he had served as a commander of the national guard and where his family had purchased *biens nationaux* during the Revolution. Like Napoleon, he moved to Elba, and then to the Italian peninsula before returning to Corsica in 1823. But after the Revolution of 1830 made possible his appointment as CP the following year, he brought to court various "anarchists and Legitimists," earning the eternal hatred of their families. After arresting a dangerous bandit, Jules Rozzi de Canale, he foolishly called the latter's brothers cowards, not a smart move in Corsica. He barely escaped a promised attempt to kill him. Appointment in 1836 to Hyères probably saved his life. From Antibes, to which he was soon transferred, he complained that even off the island he was harassed not by vengeance-minded brothers but by virtually every Corsican passing through asking for loans. He complied, not having "the courage to refuse his compatriots," although he earned only 1,000 francs a year, out of which he had to pay his office expenses. And so Martinette asked to be transferred elsewhere in the Midi, or to Algiers.[121]

Any newly arriving CP in Corsica (or for that matter anywhere else) would have to take a crash course in knowing the quartiers and neighborhoods and which ones did not get along. One can imagine the challenges of being the first CP in a Corsican town. Moreover, bad blood between neighborhoods was hardly limited to Corsica. The police in Narbonne, an *agro-ville* with 10,258 inhabitants in 1825, and a crucial strategic point standing at the intersection of the road to Spain and that from Toulouse, would have to quickly learn the division of the town into *îlots,* just as police in towns in the Nord would have to get to know very quickly organization into *corons.*

Les choses de la vie: The Unexpected

The routines of daily policing brought encounters with the tragedy of suicide. In Beauvais in 1835, those taking their own lives included a house painter and a window maker, neither able to earn a living; a domestic, Delphine Bourgeonnier, "mentally ill and suffering a horrible illness for the last few days"; and a potter, a *faubourien* who hanged himself because of domestic problems, mental illness, and alcoholism; the latter two died on the same day in May.[122] Several examples from Tours speak for many, there and elsewhere. Early at dawn on the morning of October 7, 1843, the body of Eugénie Gauthier, twenty-five years of age, was pulled from the Loire. The policeman and the doctor who pronounced the young woman dead took the body back to her home on the rue Colbert. She had plunged into the river to kill herself. The young woman, "pious and very virtuous, but of weak mind and overly sensitive," was the oldest of eight children, mocked by siblings who, if neighbors were to be believed, received more affection than did their oldest sister from her mother and father. The night before, she had quarreled with her sisters over a nightcap, and stormed out of the house in anger. In vain, her parents had searched for her, worrying through the night, greeted at dawn by the CP with the body of their daughter.[123]

A CP in Tours officially recognized the death of an Italian-born glazier, thirty-three years of age, and an elderly man, a former wood merchant of some means. They lived together and decided to kill themselves. This they accomplished on New Year's Eve, using a coal stove to asphyxiate themselves. Days later, the putrefaction of their bodies attracted horrified attention, and someone notified the CP. The older man left a letter behind, detailing what he owed his landlord. The CP pieced together the story: The younger man "consented to the infamous passion of the old man, a well-known pederast" and, now facing contemptuous glances, they had decided to die together.[124]

In principle, the police were to attest to each death in his district or town.

However, as the mayor of Toulouse noted in 1829, there were not enough police to follow the letter of the law. Thus for some time the police had to limit themselves to taking the declarations of witnesses. Then, if anything struck them as abnormal or perhaps compromising public health, a CP would immediately go to the house of the defunct "to eliminate any doubts and undertake all necessary investigation."[125] Here, too, CPs had to be jacks of all trades. When the bishop of Bayonne in 1827 refused to allow the clergy of Bagnères to bury a former soldier who had lived in concubinage, the CP oversaw the inhumation.[126] The death of a former priest, who had married during the Revolution, caused a commotion in Louviers (Eure) when the priest refused to bury the man, despite the mayor's request. The priest and mayor argued bitterly in the church, because the former refused to allow the bells to be rung for the dead man. He also refused to permit the Brothers of Charity to accompany the casket to the cemetery, and so the former priest was buried by the mayor, the CP, and the rural guard.[127]

One can also multiply the case of the abandonment of poor baby Josephine by the thousands. Abandoned in Chartres at about nine in the evening on April 5, 1850, she was wrapped in a red wool blanket. On a ribbon attached to the baby, only the name "Josephine" could be read, her last name not provided for obvious reasons.[128] In April 1850, the CP for Dax surprised two men from nearby villages abandoning a newly born baby in front of the hospice at two in the morning. The infant was returned to the unwed mother in her village, where one of the men, a domestic, was certainly the father. Within the next week, five other infants were left at the door of Dax's principal charitable institution.[129] Somewhat older children, too, were sometimes abandoned, as in Niort, where a prostitute from St. Maixent abandoned her two offspring near the hospice in 1829.[130] Remarkably enough, in Poitiers, in 1826, several members of the same family tried to stuff a twenty-five-year-old woman into the *tour* at the Hôpital général for children. When that failed, they left her at the door, ringing the bell before their hurried departure. Auguste Melevier, "who since some time has lost her mind," was being abused by her husband and Moître dit Manceau, another dock worker.[131]

The CPs entered the secret world of abortion. In 1823, a CP in Besançon reported that a girl "had taken chemicals in order to precipitate an abortion," a potion provided by a local pharmacist.[132] Similarly, charges were filed against François Chevalier, officier de santé, in 1822 for infanticide. A "corrosive liquid" was found in his house, as well as the "murderous instrument" itself. Charges were brought against three women, including one who remained dangerously ill, from the Croix-Rousse. That same year, a suspected infanticide in Lyon led to an inquiry as to whether incest had been committed. Such a charge followed neighborly suspicions. A young woman who lived with her father and kept to herself had been taken to be pregnant and had not been seen since Christmas. This led her neighbors to assume that she had given birth. But word that she had lost a baby, for the second time, led to suspicion. Two neighbors demanded that authorities intervene "to bring to an end such horrible behavior by a father and his daughter," without, however, any proof.[133]

Missing Persons

Police were also asked to search for family members who had left other towns and then simply disappeared. Prefects and mayors passed on pathetic pleas, most scrawled badly or written by a public writer, asking for information on a missing relative thought to be somewhere in the vicinity. Thus, a father from the Charente-Inférieure wrote in 1826 (in the third person) that "the son of an esteemed resident of the town of Pons left home last January 12: Théodore Moreau, fifteen years-of-age, 1.32 meters tall, very blond hair, blue eyes, a very thick upper lip." He received back good (or at least mixed) news for the father: A note across the page indicated that he had been located, "in Montrouge, with the Jesuits."[134] The prefect of the Nord received a request two years later from la dame Jonval, who lived in Wazemmes, asking the police to learn "the present location of her husband," who had abandoned her more than sixteen years before. She believed him to be in Paris. Alas, the police of the capital reported that "Sr. Jonval is completely unknown in the various places his wife indicated he might be," as well as by the masters rumored to have employed her husband. That was more to go on than most CPs had in such circumstances.[135] Similarly, in 1829 the police in the Nord were asked to look out for the debtors or heirs of a widow, whose two brothers had emigrated from the Basses-Alpes and never returned. From the capital came the sad news to a family that Adolphe Coquari had died at the Hôtel Dieu.[136] The news was better, however surprising, when a certain Madame Duchâteau wrote to ask the subprefect of Cambrai to send her late husband's death certificate so that she could be admitted to the *hospice des vieillards* in Amiens. A brief investigation determined that the death certificate could not be found because her husband was not dead and that he lived in Cambrai, albeit "in the state of indigence."[137] Likewise, the CP in Bourg-en-Bresse in 1843 was looking for a saddle maker called Bayet, who had deserted his wife in 1810, leaving her with six children and a father now seventy-eight years of age. From Lyon came information that a man who ran a brothel had seen him with 600 francs, but this could not be confirmed, although a carriage driver said that he at one point had been waiting for him. This was not much to go on.[138]

In contrast, the mother of Alexandre-François Bonnard wanted nothing at all to do with her son. He had been trained as a silk worker in Lyon, where his mother, a widow, still lived, and was "favorably known" in her quartier. Bonnard, however, had become a "mauvais sujet" who had cost his mother what little money she had trying one trade after another, living "the life of a vagabond and libertine." Now in jail, he had been arrested sleeping in a boat and for causing public scandal. His mother wanted nothing more to do with him, asking "if it would not be possible to save them from a child who had dishonored her and her family."[139]

Until at least the mid-nineteenth century France remained a predominantly agrarian society. To be sure, large-scale industrialization had already made considerable inroads in burgeoning manufacturing towns. But alongside of this was the intensification of traditional forms of manufacturing, particularly rural or cottage industry and artisanal production. However impressive the growth of Paris, which reached over 1 million inhabitants in 1846—almost exactly the same five years later in the wake of the agricultural crisis that began that year and then the Revolution of 1848—and that of Lyon and Marseille, it was the rising populations of considerably smaller mid- and small-sized towns that drove French urbanization overall. In towns like Tours, Poitiers, Strasbourg, Narbonne, and Douai, the preoccupations of the police remained largely the same as in the last decades of the Ancien Régime, even as policing in Paris, Lyon, and perhaps St. Étienne may have foreshadowed the twentieth-century image of the policeman as eternal crime fighter. As we will observe in the next chapter, the waxing and waning of movements of political opposition on a national scale, but primarily centered in the capital, Lyon, Toulouse, and several other large cities, could bring sudden orders to CPs to concentrate on political policing that momentarily overwhelmed the routines of daily life. However, on the local level in most French cities and towns, for the most part policing went on as before, even as the commissaires themselves became more professionalized.

7

THE STATE'S VICTORY OVER
DEFIANT MUNICIPALITIES

After the allies restored the Bourbons to the throne, after the 100 Days, noble émigrés returned to find that Louis XVIII would not turn the clock back to 1789. The restored Bourbon monarchy left the centralized apparatus of the state honed by Napoleon essentially intact, rejecting the decentralization of administrative authority. The old provinces were not reestablished; France remained divided into départements, as it is to this day. The prefects, added to the centralized administrative structure in 1800, remained in their respective departmental capitals, with subprefects presiding over subprefectures. The magistrature and army had similar organization. The Restoration monarchy found the highly centralized administrative apparatus an effective instrument with which to monitor its political enemies, and fear of opposition and demonstrations was never far from their minds. This fact serves as important context for understanding the ultimate dependence of the commissaires de police on the state, and not the municipalities in which they served. Mayors in many cities resisted prefects' claims on the CPs. Nowhere was this battle fought with more intensity than in Lyon.

Octrois provided the bulk of municipal resources, but only two of every twelve centimes collected went to the commune, money they could use "only under the authority of the prefect and the minister of finance."[1] Municipal councils could allocate the expenditures from its annual budget—subject, of course, to official approval. Municipalities needed the authorization of the minister of the interior to borrow money, and such loans could take considerable time. Furthermore, the municipal council met only with the authorization of the prefect and even then often not more than once a month in cities and towns, and considerably less often in villages. The alignment of streets, their renaming, the transfer of property to or from the municipality, the construction of a slaughterhouse—in many towns the limit of urbanisme during the Restoration—all were subject to official sanction by a hierarchy of committees and, ultimately, the Conseil d'état. Minutes of municipal council meetings were subject to the approval of the prefect. Even when things went well, everything moved very slowly.

Following the withdrawal early in 1821 of a proposal that would have brought slight changes in administrative centralization, a circular of the ministry of the interior stated firmly that "the guardianship [*la tutelle*] of the communes belongs essentially to the government, and this remains one of the fundamental rules of the monarchy." In the words of historian Félix Ponteil, "The centralization of the state imposed itself even more harshly than ever."[2]

During the last years of the Restoration, state centralization drew increased criticism from liberals. An *Essai sur un nouveau mode d'organisation des administrations départementales et municipales présenté au gouvernment par un habitant de l'Yonne* (1828) denounced prefects as "viceroys who do not take care of their départements." During a debate on local administration in the Chamber in 1829, A. Delaborde attacked the "spirit of centralization" that had deprived France's communes of any autonomy during the Empire and Restoration.[3] That year, proponents of decentralization proposed two laws to the Chamber of Deputies. One considered the organization of communes, and the other espoused the creation of conseils généraux and *conseils d'arrondissement* that could provide local elites with more of a voice. Early in 1830, the minister of the interior asked his prefects for a report on "improvements for which the administration has been responsible since the beginning of the Restoration," including "the end of useless impediments in municipal government." The mayor of Châteaudun replied that mayors should have more control over communal resources, including the right to approve the municipal acquisition or sale of property, alluding to the "remnants of the despotic administration of the Empire," a clear reference to state centralization.[4] The failure of many municipalities to undertake even the most rudimentary improvements to enhance the quality of urban life in some places helped mobilize political opposition to the Restoration.[5]

Thus, for many civic-minded residents of towns, the Revolution of 1830 appeared as an event of liberation. By virtue of the law of March 21, 1831, the municipal council elected the mayor and his deputies (the number of whom were determined by the population of the city, as was the number of councilmen), although the ministry of the interior (through the king) continued to appoint mayors and deputy mayors in large towns. Municipalities, however, remained subject to the same administrative control as during the Restoration.[6]

A bitter dispute in Sarlat in 1832 illustrates the resentment in some municipalities to what seemed exaggerated state authority. Many people in Sarlat, as elsewhere, opposed resumption of the tax on drink. In the municipal elections of 1831, eligible electors returned a council that included strong republican representation. The council then opened its meetings to the public (and apparently had begun to do so before the July Revolution), allowing even townspeople who were not councilmen to make suggestions. The prefect thus annulled the procès-verbaux of the meetings of July 27 and August 8, 1832, because, in accordance with article twenty-eight of the law of March 21, 1831, they had no legal standing until they had been approved by "superior authority." The subprefect himself attended the next meeting and read aloud the prefect's letter of annulment. Most of the council walked out after the mayor deferred to the subprefect to preside over the meeting.[7]

The municipal council of Sarlat defied the prefect by admitting the public to its next meeting, referring to "our constitutional standards and the needs of the time."[8] Furthermore, the council provocatively elected a secretary to take the minutes of the meeting—Roux *aîné,* a local republican editor—instead of having the secretary of the town hall take notes. The prefect annulled this procès-verbal, too. The following meeting was also opened to the public, though it attracted few people. Now the council brazenly voted twenty votes to two to publicize future procès-verbaux. The prefect asked the minister of the interior to dissolve the council. But as the mayor pointed out, the dissolution of the council would merely serve to attract attention to the debate; another election would return essentially the same men.[9]

To the prefect, the municipality continued to "support the doctrines of excessive democracy." With "rabble clogging the meeting room," the municipal council now was little more than a political club. "Orators" directed their speeches to the people, "invoking their views and soliciting applause. And the people applauded, shouting like Robespierre's followers." Moreover, the people of Sarlat had greeted the subprefect with a charivari, "republican turbulence" comparable to that of 1793.[10] The prefect eventually bludgeoned the municipal council of Sarlat into submission with his authority.

Yet the concentration of power in the hands of the centralized state had its supporters, even outside of the bureaucracy in which the CPs were cogs. In 1833 or 1834, a published *Lettre d'un observateur administratif à un député sur l'administration intérieure et sur la législation qui la régit* sang the praises of the state centralization, its author contending that "it has been through centralization that France became what it is today, a homogeneous state where laws and government orders are executed with as much promptness as uniformity."[11]

Between Unequal Authorities

That CPs remained subject to three different authorities remained a chronic and, for some municipalities, vexing problem. Competing claims on the allegiance and time of the CP sometimes pitted judicial authorities against the municipality. The decree of January 13, 1819, placed the "commissaires de police . . . under the immediate authority of the mayors; it is through these officials that they correspond with the prefect, besides specific cases in which the latter asks for direct reports from them." In 1820, the minister of the interior complained that the police were often slow to pass on information about crimes and misdemeanors to the office of prosecutors, sometimes sending reports to the mayor. In some places, procès-verbaux seemed to be passed on to judicial authorities only when municipal authorities got around to it.[12]

The rivalry between mayors and prefects was frequent, bitter, and revealing. Unlike the prefects and subprefects, mayors were not bureaucrats and professionals, despite the fact that in large towns throughout this period they were appointed by the central government. Arguably a natural tension existed between unpaid mayors and salaried CPs. In Clermont in 1820, CP Abel enjoyed the full support of the prefect but not the mayor, and was relegated to an office outside of the mairie. When Abel went to see the mayor, he found only his deputy mayors, one of whom, a wealthy merchant, ran the police "as if it were his shop." The deputy mayor had, if Abel is to be believed, forced out his predecessor, who told him to find other "valets" if he wanted to interfere with the police. He apparently found them in the agents (who were, after all, hired by the municipality).

Abel portrayed himself as besieged by enemies and unprotected by municipal authorities. Two women had alleged that a certain Jean Roux had tormented the daughter of one of them, demanding up to 600 francs "in order to relieve souls suffering in Purgatory." Abel worried about charges of calumny and hesitated when the mayor told him to find two witnesses and draw up a procès-verbal. The mayor denounced him to the prefect. Then the mayor asked Abel to draw up a list of Clermont's forty prostitutes, but then, apparently after a change of heart, blamed Abel for the "abominable decision to reduce to despair forty people in the joyous profession, as well as their thousand admirers, and to snatch from the poor officiers de santé their revenue" (from the obligatory medical inspections). The battle went on. The prefect first warned Abel never to send any letter to Paris unless he had seen it. Soon Abel himself was writing from Paris, dismissed from his post in Clermont because he could please neither authority.[13]

In 1825, CP Morel in Roanne lost his job, accused of laxity and of being a Freemason. But there was more. The mayor did not want the CP to be involved in haute police. A former subprefect of Roanne had returned to a warm welcome from the town's liberals, and Morel was under pressure from the current subprefect to step up surveillance of liberals. The laws of January 27, 1836, and January 1, 1843, reaffirmed "that the commissaires de police are charged with all that concerns la haute police and thus state security, under the authority of the prefects and subprefects." In Grenoble, Debonnaire was suspended in 1823 after the mayor complained about him to the prefect. The latter admitted that the policeman had a "impetuous and emotional personality," complemented by "ignorance and incompetence." However, noting Debonnaire's excellent political principles, he asked for a new post for him. Had the shoe been on the other foot—had Debonnaire been insubordinate to the prefect—that would have marked the end of his career in the police.[14]

Nowhere was the battle over the police fought more passionately than in Lyon (see Fig. 3), pitting France's proud second city against the Paris-centered state. It is a story worth telling, because Lyon, with a "local political culture of self-government," arguably stood as the most difficult obstacle to the victory of the state over municipal claims to prerogatives in policing.[15] Moreover, the perceived threat of political opposition and indeed collective violence in Lyon helped shape the determination of the state to put an end to municipal pretensions, ones that evoked in some ways the Ancien Régime, to control the police.

The Second Restoration had hardly begun when in late 1816 the mayor of Lyon, Comte Jean Meallet de Fargues, began quarreling with Lyon's lieutenant général de police over turf. The issue was political surveillance.[16] From the point

FIGURE 3. View of Lyon during the July Monarchy. Courtesy of the Bibliothèque nationale de France.

of view of the lieutenant général, the mayor of Lyon "considered himself to be a petty sovereign able to do what he wants, including anything that has to do with the police. This is an abuse whose drawbacks are serious and destroys harmony within the government."[17]

In 1817 mayor de Fargues complained that the CPs were not carrying out his orders. Lyon seemed even more filthy than usual, its narrow streets encumbered by mud, sometimes completely blocked by wagons. Believing the supervision of street sweeping beneath them, Lyon's CPs spent most of their time sniffing out imaginary plots, leaving the policing of the city to their miserably paid agents. The municipal council was tired of this, and, in the interest of saving money, wanted to reduce the number of CPs from 9 to 6, although Lyon now had nearly 130,000 inhabitants and Marseille, a smaller city, had proportionally more police. In 1818, the council formally proposed reducing the number of commissaires to six, while increasing the number of agents to twelve, and asked that the state pay for half of the cost of the police.[18]

An increase in thefts the next year brought the issue of municipal prerogatives to the fore, as it would several times in subsequent years. The municipal council asked for funds to pay for secret police, because mouchards employed by the prefecture had achieved nothing. The municipality interpreted relevant laws as allowing communes to make use of their own resources as they saw fit and with unconcealed bitterness requested to reallocation of 6,000 francs. The sarcasm and rancor of the letter enraged the prefect. The prefect's deference to the mayor, which had already begun to erode, completely unraveled. The municipal council seemed to "make itself almost completely independent" of prefectoral authority. The prefect clearly stated what was and would remain the position of the state: "Policing is part of the general administration: mayors exercise it only under the authority of the prefects." Indeed, the minutes of the municipal council could make one doubt if "they came from a city of the kingdom, but rather were the work of the council of Geneva." The time had come to make the city of Lyon understand that it is "like the other communes of France, under the authority of the government." Couthon, member of the Committee of Public Safety during the Terror, could not have said it better. There is, to be sure, something wonderfully ironic about a French prefect during the Restoration insisting on the primacy of hierarchy manifest in a centralized state with the determination of a Jacobin during the French Revolution, when, following the Federalist Revolt, troops shot down Lyonnais in mass reprisals and brought a reign of terror to France's second city, which lost even the right to its name, becoming temporarily known as the "Town without a Name" (*Ville Affranchie*).[19]

Lyon's new mayor, Baron Pierre Rambaud, insisted that existing laws had placed the police under the authority of the municipalities, except in certain specific situations.[20] After all, the mayor appointed the agents without recourse to "superior authorities." Policemen named in Paris felt no obligation to serve the mairie well, because the mayor could not promote (or for that matter fire) them, and in any case, they could be transferred at any time. The CPs appeared to consider some of the duties required of them by the mayor as beneath their status, such as providing lists of the carriages and coaches in the city. When in 1820 the mayor had asked CP Michel Brirot why a certain woman had been arrested, he replied, "I have no idea—go ask my agent." The mayor was furious at the response of someone who was, after all, a direct and salaried agent of the municipality. The municipal council proposed to divide the CPs into two classes, the first at the disposition of "superior authorities" and the second under the exclusive orders of the municipality.

Mayor Rambaud also raised the question of whether the police should be chosen among Lyonnais or étrangers, the municipality forcefully insisting that only the former could serve Lyon properly.[21] The prefect and the ministry of the interior, however, insisted that insiders were more easily subject to "local influences or cliques." The municipal council of Lyon with irritating regularity expressed its view that it should be allowed to present candidates for the post of CP, repeatedly underscoring the fact that it paid the salaries and office expenses of the CPs. The implicit assumption was that the council's choices be honored, that the sums allocated for office expenses be left fully at the disposition of the mayor, and that the state contribute half of these expenses.[22]

Following the assassination of the Duc de Berri in February 1820, the ministry of the interior reminded prefects and subprefects that CPs should be made aware of the primary responsibility they had toward the ministries in Paris. In response, the municipal council of Lyon in July again expressed its unanimous opinion that all CPs be appointed on its recommendation and that all be Lyonnais. When Prefect de Lezay-Marnesia declared this deliberation null and void, the municipality simply resubmitted it.[23]

The abolition of the post of lieutenant de police in Lyon in January 1822 did nothing to end the conflict between the state and the municipality of Lyon over the police.[24] Baron Rambaud took responsibility over certain tasks of local policing for which the lieutenant had been responsible, including the stamping of passports for internal travel and *feuilles de route*. However, police de sûreté was placed even more clearly under the direct authority of the new prefect, Camille de Tournon-Simiane. He reminded the CPs of the primacy of preventing "mouvements populaires." A general secretary would supervise a new office of the police, to which a CP would be attached because of the great number of cases in which *police judiciaire* would be involved. Moreover, the mayor was ordered to send periodic reports to the prefect assessing the performance of the CPs and not the other way around.[25]

Following a decree in 1823 that formally attached the commissaires to the prefecture, their reports increasingly went directly and often exclusively to the prefect. Certainly Lyon's reputation as being a major "point of rendez-vous" for *factieux* who "consider Lyon to be the base for their sinister projects" contributed to the prefect's insistence that municipal police be ultimately responsible to him and that CPs of his choice be named.[26]

The war between competing authorities inevitably began to wear on the CPs. They objected to reproaches they received from the prefecture and annoying instructions to watch for "the arrival of such and such person considered suspicious by the government." Some of these missives took days to reach the police. For example, a letter sent May 29, 1823, asking for the surveillance of "le Sr *—" was redirected toward the police by the mairie on June 4, arriving only the next day. The municipality had no funds to pay for secret police ("to discover thieves, one must have thieves"), whereas the prefect complained that the "parsimoniousness of this municipal administration is not easy to overcome." The prefect found some funds to pay for several secret agents, who worked in the suburbs of Vaise, Croix-Rousse, and la Guillotière, beyond the jurisdiction of the Lyon police. But again, the goal was political policing, not the principal concern of Lyon's feisty municipality.[27]

The war went on. When in 1823 the prefect asked the municipality to allocate funds to pay for a ninth CP, as well as two more agents, the council echoed its insistence that the number be reduced to six, in accordance with its "former municipal independence." When the minister of the interior appointed the ninth CP, the mayor retaliated by letting two temporary agents go. The prefect wanted the police in Lyon to work "like a machine. . . . We need a first authority who can give uniform impetus to each of the cogs of this machine," that is, under the prefect.[28]

In the meantime, the mayor howled that the CPs still seemed to "scorn policing that concerns itself with trash in the streets, which appears to them to be below the dignity that comes with their judicial functions." The mayor had six inspectors assigned to Lyon's bridges, thoroughfares, and street-cleaning, but they were not enough. The prefect had his own ideas. He believed that five CPs could be assigned to municipal policing and six available for sûreté, as well as one charged with watching printers and bookstores and another to assist tax officials. At a minimum, proper policing required more agents, perhaps even a corps of *officiers de paix,* as in Paris. The municipality's cavalier attitude galled the prefect. The operations of haute police slowed noticeably since the office of lieutenant de police had been abolished, in part because the CPs still sent many reports to the mayor. The Rhône's chief official vowed to use all legal means to compel the stubborn municipal council to vote additional funds for six new agents, so that each of the nine CPs would have two agents with whom to work. The minister of the interior emphatically rejected the municipality's latest plan, again annulling the procès-verbaux of the council meeting.[29]

Prefect René de Brosses, who remained in charge until the Revolution of 1830, complained about a new wave of thefts. More than 100 thefts had occurred with the help of ladders, break-ins, or "false keys." Ex-convicts were required to show up at the bureau de sûreté every ten or fifteen days, but most moved frequently, without bothering to inform the police. Two mouchards had turned up nothing. The CPs had no regular place to meet with their agents. Moreover, some of the prefect's letters to the mayor with ideas for improving the police of Lyon went answered. The mayor had failed to account for how funds the ministry had made available to pay for secret police had been used. Some of the money provided by the ministry had gone to pay for beds for prisoners, dog poison, and small indemnities for those who saved victims from drowning in the swirling waters of the Rhône. The municipal council blamed the CPs for the increase in thefts, claiming that the policemen were rarely to be seen in the districts to which they had been assigned. The corps of *surveillants de nuit* (considered to be a *garde municipale* as of 1840) were of no use in preventing thefts or discovering the guilty, despite their military-like organization. Most were artisans, "fathers of families, who do everything they can to avoid becoming worn out, because they have to work the next day after their night service." In any case, thieves could hear the patrols coming and waited until they had passed before carrying out their misdeeds. The prefect recommended reducing the corps of surveillants to thirty salaried men, four of them responsible for leading military patrols through Lyon at night, as had been done in Marseille. But the central problem, in the prefect's view, continued to be organizational. He urged that the judicial and municipal functions of the police be combined in the interest of efficiency. The prefecture received little relevant information about the activities of the police. Indeed, the mayor appeared to be undertaking something of a slowdown, "all these delays are detrimental to public service."[30]

The advent of a new mayor, Jean de Lacroix-Laval, at first seemed to offer hope for a rapprochement.[31] However, the municipality still insisted on a plan of action that threatened to make Lyon "a state within a state." The CPs were subject to lengthy morning meetings, or "audiences," with the mayor, some lasting three hours, leaving little time for their work in their arrondissements and leaving them dependent on the mayor.[32] The commissaires de police of Lyon, overwhelmed by their various tasks, in 1828 presented their own position as tactfully as possible. They sarcastically expressed their resentment at being accused of "this self-styled spirit of independence which by a very misguided vanity would make us forget that we are only simple inspectors of mud and trash." Expressing confidence that current legislation protected them, they cited all of the relevant laws that had defined their legal attributions. They were well aware of the fact that they took oaths of allegiance to the state and thus to their administrative superiors, and not to the mayor. The CPs boldly (and undoubtedly with the realization that the ministry held all of the key cards) implied that the hôtel de ville was responsible for Lyon's policing problems, for which they stood accused.[33]

The council finally agreed in 1826 to request the appointment of two more CPs and divided Lyon into eleven arrondissements.[34] However, fifteen or even sixteen CPs were in principle required by law. Two years later, de Brosses asked that the police be given a locale for meetings and insisted that the municipality hire more people to clean the streets. The real issue remained the municipality's "claims that would not have been tolerated in a republic," the mayor rejecting "the necessary authority of the government." Lyon espoused "a certain spirit of independence" that seemed to seek "the privileges of the free cities of Germany or the rights of the republican cities of Switzerland or North America."[35] At the same time, a local history of Lyon described "our great city in tears, in the middle of its manufactures in ruin, along with its old liberal institutions." This discourse must be seen in the context of a general rebellion against "the centralization of political decisions and of literary and artistic life" by the elite of a city celebrated by a local writer as the "metropolis of the French provinces," "the center of provincial unity," and the "seat of the national moral truth."[36]

At least eight separate municipal council deliberations insisted that the bullying of the ministry of the interior had left CPs operating independently of the municipality that had hired them. The police now communicated directly with the prefect and judicial authorities without the mayor's participation in these exchanges. The commission on finances offered another version of the old municipal plan to divide the police into two groups, with four of Lyon's twelve CPs assigned to haute police, that is, to the prefecture, and eight to the mairie. Again, the deliberation insisted that the mayor name all twelve and that all of those employed in the service of Lyon be from the city. Again the prefect annulled the offending deliberation, as if it had never taken place.[37]

His desk cluttered with denunciations and explanations coming from Lyon, the minister of the interior decided that policing there seemed "in general entrusted to not very skilled hands." There had been several attacks on individuals, more thefts, and a murder at Fourvière that had never been reported through the proper channels. The growing quartier of Perrache seemed dangerous during the winter of 1828–29. Several people were attacked by thieves at night on the Chaussée Perrache, near the prison being constructed there. Three men jumped Claude Savigny at 8 P.M. on December 30, taking thirty-five francs and leaving him half-dead on a heap of sand. In the first week of January, several more serious attacks occurred at the same place. In one arrondissement, the perpetrators of 221 of 442 crimes and other offenses in 1829 remained undiscovered, and many acquittals had followed because the police had been unable to come up with sufficient proof. The prefect blamed the municipality for a lack of energy in stopping misdeeds attributed to workers not from town, and the mayor, in turn, blamed the prefect's usurpation of authority over the CPs, unhappily caught in the middle of the struggle.[38]

A newspaper article denounced the state of Lyon. Shopkeepers, housewives, and domestics left garbage in the streets, including ashes and soot, and even worse things were thrown carelessly from windows. Wheelbarrows and piles of building materials dotted the streets. In some streets, games of *quilles, boules, aux petits palets,* and other "dangerous games" went on, blocking passage until the players were willing to step briefly aside. Coaches, whose drivers invariably insisted that they were waiting for their masters, also made circulation difficult. Traffic jams made the commercial rue Mercière daunting and disagreeable. Moreover, those venturing out into the streets could hear lewd, insulting songs. Lyon was developing a reputation as "the dirtiest city in Europe." Part of the problem, to be sure, stemmed from its location. Hills prevented the winds from airing out the city (compounding the problem of fog, and the chimney smoke that plagued all towns). Apartments were built so high that sunshine rarely reached the street far below. The CPs were so busy that they simply did not have time to write up procès-verbaux so as to encourage compliance with ordinances intended to keep the city as clean as possible. Not long afterward, a newspaper asked rhetorically and provocatively: "In what other region would property-owners and renters let the entries, stairways and courtyards of their lodgings be transformed into virtual cesspools? Only in Lyon." It called on the municipality to establish floating latrines on the rivers, force residents to take proper care of garbage, and enforce the closing of *traboules*, the passageways that passed through the quartier St. Jean, as well as the Croix-Rousse, protecting silk from the elements.[39]

Mayor de Lacroix-Laval vigorously defended his municipality. "Misleading" accounts in the newspapers had convinced the population that the town had been infested by thieves. Three men arrested in September 1829 admitted more than eighty thefts in and around Lyon; some who had received stolen property had also been identified. Almost all other thefts had been solved, their perpetrators arrested, including some notorious *malfaiteurs* who had plagued other towns in the kingdom. A third of the money from a gigantic heist had been recovered and most of the masterminds jailed. Yet Lyon's traboules facilitated surreptitious, unseen movement, particularly at night, and required not only shrewd policemen but also alert and helpful residents. Furthermore, the separation of Lyon's suburbs from the city itself—La Guillotière lay across the Rhône in the département of the Ain—meant that those trying to elude the police of Lyon could simply slip out of the city through one of the gates or cross the bridge over the Rhône. Attention increasingly turned toward the urban periphery, "the refuse and the sewer of all the bad subjects from all the neighboring départements," whose auberges offered asylum for "all types of criminals, from small-time crooks to the greatest thieves and their auxiliaries."[40]

The commissaires were under the gun. They had handed out more *procès-verbaux*, 1,097 in 1826, 1,234 in 1827, and 1,274 in 1828; the number of these relating to the cleanliness of the streets had also risen (105 to 115 to 270 in 1828). These were only small steps in a large, dirty city. The mayor estimated that if each property owner or renter swept in front of their buildings, sixty men working with twenty-nine wagons could only remove a quarter of the mud and refuse (or snow in the winter) even working several days. More sweepers were needed in Lyon.[41]

The procureur général concluded that the CPs now all merited the confidence of the authorities, even if all were not of the same ability. Striking in his report was the attention paid not to political views but to competence and the amount of "respect" they merited in the districts they patrolled. Here, too, the upper reaches of the bureaucracy were applying standards that at least to some extent reflected the professionalization of the police, as they were to other more favored groups, such as judges.[42]

However, better cooperation and perhaps performance did not end conflict between city and state. On January 9, 1829, the municipal council again insisted that the twelve CPs be named at the request of the mayor, and that none of the police who were paid by the municipality (in other words, all of them) "could be employed in any service not related to municipal policing." In addition, the council voiced its indignation at the annulment of the deliberations of March 3 and July 17 the previous year. It came as no surprise to the council that, yet again the prefect annulled the deliberations.[43] Then in April 1830, the municipality claimed that because Lyon's population had suffered a slight decline, it wanted to reduce the number of CPs (and thus their budget). One CP had since 1824 been attached to the prefecture, with his responsibilities now largely concerned with policing Lyon's faubourgs, not Lyon itself. The prefect held his ground. Prefect de Brosses again asserted that the CPs were principally "the direct representatives of the government in the different localities into which they are sent."[44]

As Lyon's new CPs set out on their patrols wearing bright new tricolor sashes following the July Revolution of 1830, the old dispute at first lost some of its acrimony amid a wave of optimism that the Orleanist regime could be all things to all people. Predictably, the latest revolution brought a purge of the police: Only three of the CPs in activity in 1829 were in service two years later. Expecting the newly reconstituted national guard, which in principle had about 10,000 members, to perform regular service, the municipality reduced by more than half funds allocated for the surveillants de nuit, and the mayor later proposed to phase them out completely.[45] The new mayor of Lyon, Docteur Clément Gabriel Prunelle, himself established the post of commissaire central in September 1830, while evoking decentralization in his first pronouncement, one that seemed to evoke the return of "municipal rights" Lyon had maintained before 1789.[46]

In November 1831, the canuts—Lyon's silk workers—rose up in revolt. The national guard, consisting of the "elite" of citizens, joined troops in shooting down silk workers.[47] In response, the next month, Prunelle reversed the traditional argument put forward by Lyon's municipality, insisting that the city required more CPs, not fewer, thirteen instead of ten, and that the number of agents be doubled to forty-eight. Panicked by the insurrection that had bloodied the streets of Lyon, the municipal council, which had for years refused to allocate additional funds on the budget, voted a supplementary credit of 45,200 francs to pay the salaries of four more commissaires, twenty-four additional agents, and two mouchards.[48] Popular collective action had made the ministry of the interior's victory almost complete.

The brutal repression of the canuts clearly demonstrated the benefits of centralized policing to the municipality. Lyon's leaders shared the fears of the upper classes they represented, worrying about the workers' secret societies that were deeply rooted in Lyon, but above all in the suburb of the Croix-Rousse. Indeed the fear of insurrection contributed to the professionalization of the police: "The surveillance of workers" was now specified among the duties included under "sûreté." In December 1831 an ordinance carried the number of CPs in Lyon to fourteen, and during the next decade the number of agents increased from thirty-two to forty-eight.[49]

At the same time, proposals considered the incorporation of Lyon's three major suburbs: Vaise, La Guillotière, and the Croix-Rousse. Such an administrative change would in principle make the surveillance and policing of each easier. From nine forts, the left bank of the Rhône could be watched. A report by a *commission des intérêts publiques* to the municipal council in 1833 supported the idea of "la ville ouverte et expansionniste." The French state increasingly viewed the annexation of the faubourgs as possibly further reducing the autonomy of the contentious municipality. Pierre-Yves Saunier summarizes, "The explicit object of central power was to break the authority of a municipality that had become too powerful, and which could stand as an obstacle to national actions. The secular debate on the police of Lyon incarnated the veritable conflict over sovereignty by carrying the debate over the parameters of the use of public force." The problems of policing and fear of working-class insurrection from the threatening periphery, one accentuated by the social fear engendered in Lyon itself by the insurrections of 1831 and 1834, were now linked to arguments in favor of "uniting" the faubourgs with Lyon.[50] Prefect Adrien de Gasparin, who took over in 1831, was determined to annex Lyon's suburbs, in part to put an end to the pretensions of autonomy so often arrogantly put forward by the municipality. Yet at the moment, nothing came of the plan, in part because of opposition from the municipalities of the suburbs and the deputies of the Rhône.[51]

The second insurrection of the canuts occurred in April 1834. More than any other event in Lyon, the violence of the uprising (largely surpassed by the savagery of the repression) made it easier for Lyon's authorities to accept the preponderant role of the ministry of the interior and the prefect in policing. Moreover, the Law on Associations passed in the wake of the insurrection could not eliminate republican activity. The Mutualists, Voraces, and other secret societies among the silk workers drew particular police attention, as agents tried to infiltrate them as well as Masonic lodges and virtually every other potential source of organized opposition. The municipal administration seemed to accept the state playing a more forceful role than before. All of the CPs who policed Lyon's quartiers were to come to the prefect's office three times a week.[52] Lyon has aptly been described as "the first city in which the police brought completely under state control [*étatisée*]."[53]

Stormy debates over the issue of to whom the police owed their primary allegiance went on in other towns as well. Two months after the July Revolution, the new subprefect of Douai complained of the poorly defined and badly regulated attributions of the CP. The policeman "completely removed himself from the authority of the subprefect and appears no longer willing to accept any orders than those given by the municipality."[54] In the Marne in 1843, the prefect complained that the CPs of Reims were resisting his authority. They had not bothered to go to see the subprefect until ten days after his arrival in Reims, viewed as a particular affront in the largest subprefecture in France. Moreover, they had complained to the mayor that the subprefect did not have the authority to ask for such reports. The mayor seemed to be behind this resistance to prefectorial authority.[55]

An incident in Roubaix in 1842 generated reflections on the problem of competing authorities. In his first eight days at the post, the CP, Davion, had already handed out forty procès-verbaux. He had summoned Lemarque, a dealer in secondhand goods, to his office for failure to keep a register, an obligation to discourage trade in stolen goods. But the encounter between Lemarque and Davion had not gone well. Lemarque had kept his hat on, indeed, "his tone, his manners, his language . . . [and] his attitude were so insulting and provocative" that he let him stew in jail. Of twenty-seven dealers in secondhand goods living in town, he was the only one who refused to keep a register, but it was his lack of respect that angered the policeman. He had left Lemarque in jail for two hours without notifying the procureur. The man had lodged a complaint, insisting that his honor had been compromised by incarceration. The mayor believed that Davion had gone too far, and perhaps did not understand the *pays* in which he held his post: "The region is cold, its people calm . . . what counts for the municipal administration is that the region always remains calm, tranquil, under the supervision of a wise and prudent police." When the mayor complained, Davion's response gave the impression that the CP wanted to place himself outside of the municipality. The policeman evoked the conciliatory methods he had used in Douai, adding that he wanted a copy of his letter deposited in the archives, where it still lies.[56]

The aftermath of the Revolution of 1848 further accentuated the centralization of policing under the auspices of the ministry of the interior.[57] The primacy of political policing dominated the history of the Second Republic and its systematic destruction by the government of Louis Napoleon Bonaparte.[58] A letter of instruction penned by Jules Favre, minister of the interior, on November 13, 1848, provided the rationale for bringing the CPs even more directly under the authority of the central government:

> The government of the Republic cannot in this respect accept the erring ways of the monarchy. Under our new regime, the more the principle of elections is given free reign, the more central authority should retain in its hands the initiatives and impetus that our laws have left us. [Commissaires de police] fall under the jurisdiction of the government, as much as political police. It belongs to the government to name them, without any commitments made by mayors or other local officials in advance undercutting its action.[59]

Like Lyon in the early 1830s, the case of Strasbourg seemed to confirm the benefits of the continued centralization of policing during the Second Republic, at least to the repressive regime holding the reins of power in Paris. As we saw in chapter 1, the city's brief experiment with a commissaire central had ended in 1828. In 1849, the minister of the interior read reports that indicated that the police in Strasbourg simply allowed political gatherings to disperse on their own. The prefect of the Bas-Rhin asked for the creation of the post of commissaire central, which existed in Beaune, Angers, Avignon, and a many other towns. The municipal council would have to approve the allocations of funds for such a position, which would be directly responsible to the prefect. Strasbourg's police lacked neither energy nor intelligence. But here again, one of the costs of local familiarity—including speaking French and the German dialect—was that they knew too many people, compromising their objectivity.[60]

The experience of Stéphane Comte as commissaire central in Strasbourg, following his nomination in July 1849, demonstrates the success that an outsider with the patronage of the state could have in political policing. He brought experience in the same post in Nîmes, as difficult a post as one could find in France in view of the rivalry between Protestants and Catholics. There Comte had demonstrated "unusual resourcefulness." At first he found it tough going in Strasbourg, facing the natural jealousy and hostility of the four other CPs—one for each canton—over whom he now enjoyed some authority. Moreover, he drew a greater salary (1,800 francs plus another 200 francs in bonuses and 600 francs for office expenses). His new underlings were old-timers, having served in Strasbourg since 1830, 1838, 1840, and 1841, respectively. Moreover, Comte had authority in every commune in the Bas-Rhin, and he carried with him a copy of his appointment in case his authority was challenged. The municipal council was not happy about having to pay his salary, because his authority stemmed not from the council. In particular, Mayor Kartz resented him, as his appointment further placed policing under the authority of the prefect. He denounced Comte's appointment as illegal, "an encroachment by the central administration on the rights and prerogatives of municipal authority." One member thundered that in thirteen years on the council, he had never seen the council's will ignored so flagrantly. Comte did not even know German. The mayor threatened to request formally that the Conseil d'état annul the appointment. It was an old story in Strasbourg, with its old prerogatives under the Holy Roman Empire replacing Lyon's federalism with the image of itself as something of a Swiss republic or German city-state. But Strasbourg's mayor had no choice but to formally install Comte as commissaire central to "centralize and supervise the work of the other commissaires de police."

"I suffer cruelly," reported Comte after fifteen days on the job. He had faced "repeated humiliations, that I cannot accept indefinitely." The municipal council and mayor refused cooperation. Only one of his colleagues seemed to him of any merit. Despite the title of commissaire central, he had no agents to assist him; those he borrowed from other CPs were of no quality—"as soon as they are out of my sight, they disappear in a twinkle of an eye." By early November, he was being attacked personally in Le Démocrate, and agents were denounced as mouchards in the city's innumerable brasseries, which remained a special target of police surveillance in Strasbourg. In 1851, the prefect reported with confidence that although people continued to talk of politics, those conversations were now faithfully reported to him. The owners of brasseries that stayed open a minute past 11 P.M. were slapped with a procès-verbal. Perhaps encouraged by a reward from the prefect of 1,000 francs for good work, Comte seized Montagnard political pamphlets. Hated by the republican Left, Comte performed so well that he stayed on in Strasbourg until 1854, the right man in the right place for the repressive centralized Bonapartist state.[61]

In Reims, too, the appointment of a commissaire central seemed to be the answer for political policing. The Montagnards had considerable influence in Reims, particularly in the working-class faubourgs. Appointed in April 1850, the commissaire central was only to take the orders of the mayor so far as municipal policing was concerned. However, the CPs were to send their reports directly to the commissaire central, who would have authority in the entire arrondissement of Reims. The commissaire central was "particularly responsible for political policing and for haute police under the authority of the subprefect of Reims and the prefect of the Marne." The municipal council put forward tactfully stated objections, that it was "difficult" that the commissaire central had been specifically charged with political policing, but, not surprisingly, to no avail.[62]

Back in Lyon, the Second Republic brought a fundamental reorganization of the police. Under the direction of the prefect of the Rhône, police authority became even more centralized. In 1850, the minister of the interior established a special commission to study Lyon's administration, envisioning the possible annexation of the "gangrenous body of the suburbs."[63] Adopting the model of Paris, the law of June 19, 1851, created "the agglomeration of Lyon," which included Lyon, La Guillotière, the Croix-Rousse, Vaise, Caluire, Ouillins, and Ste. Foy, as well as Villeurbanne, Vaux, Bron, and Venissieux in the Isère, and, across the Rhône, Rillieux and Miribel in the Ain. The prefect of the Rhône would be responsible for policing in the communes of his département, although his authority in the communes of the Isère and the Ain would be limited to the policing of passports, prisons, begging, and vagabondage. Of twenty-two CPs, twelve were assigned to Lyon's quartiers, three to La Guillotière, two to the Croix-Rousse and Caluire, and one each attached to the exterior communes of Oullins-Ste. Foy, Vaise, Villeurbanne, and Rillieux, as well as to the prefecture itself. In addition, Lyon now boasted six agents principaux, upgraded in title to inspecteurs, one assigned to the prefecture; one each given responsibility for enforcing laws against prostitution, sûreté, hotels and inns, travelers and ships; and a sixth charged with overseeing the suburbs and the nearby communes in the Ain and Isère. Forty-eight other agents were assigned to assist the CPs responsible for Lyon's quartiers. Tellingly, these agents were no longer to be named by the municipality but instead by the prefect. Following the example of Paris, 303 sergents-de-ville also would be available, armed and subject to military-like discipline, uniformed, and required to undertake gymnastic exercises to maintain their readiness to patrol, particularly at night.[64]

On October 1, 1851, a commissaire extraordinaire, named by the minister of the interior, assumed authority over the police in Lyon and was attached to the prefecture. The name of the post itself revealed the importance the government of Louis Napoleon Bonaparte assigned to policing in Lyon. The mayor could barely conceal his sarcasm, expressing thanks that procès-verbaux for contraventions still left under his authority were being sent to him.[65] To this special commissaire, whose task would be to resolve conflicts of authority between the prefect and the mayor, he commented, "I fully understand that it is painful for the municipal administration to see itself deprived of the appointment of so many employees and of the influence that such power gives it." Indeed on December 11, 1851, nine days after the coup d'état, the minister of the interior noted that Lyon's mayor failed "to recognize the limits of his authority" by ignoring the law of June 19, 1851, and "continuing to claim rights over the police that have ceased to belong to him and which should alone belong" to the prefect. "It is essential," he insisted, "through energetic measures, to put an end to such intolerable pretensions and encroachments."[66]

The decree of March 24, 1852, annexed la Guillotière, the Croix-Rousse, and

Vaise to Lyon. With a population of 221,609, Lyon was divided into five arrondissements, giving each a mayor and two *adjoints*. This served, as Saunier has noted, to conquer France's second, stubborn city by dividing it. Lyon would no longer have a mayor, and remained without one until 1881 (with the exception of 1870–73). The fear of the faubourgs certainly contributed to the centralization of police authority in Lyon. A former prefect, a member of the 1850 commission, put it this way: "Make no mistake, the suburban populations of Lyon are out there, their eyes trained on Lyon as on a prey, ready for pillage."[67]

As Louis Napoleon Bonaparte "stressed his commitment to administrative centralization," the law of March 28, 1852, authorized his naming CPs in towns of more than 6,000 inhabitants. The commissaires were placed under the direct authority of the prefects.[68] Reforms of the police came fast and furious in the early Second Empire, the centralizing impulse virtually unchecked. One enthusiast of centralized administration gushed, "The administration, assisted by the army . . . has just saved France. . . . Today your task is accomplished and that of the government is about to begin. Its first duty will be to strengthen your power and improve your position." The prefect of the Rhône offered his opinion that "authority is now the sole aristocracy."[69]

In late 1852, Emile de Maupas, the minister of the interior, sent out a circular marked "very confidential" in response to questions that had arisen over relations between the CPs and higher authorities. The circular had added "an important observation: although the commissaires de police are paid from the municipal budgets, it does not follow that they should above all be assigned to municipal service, nor that the mayor can exercise over them the right of investigation or control over all their acts."[70] Tellingly, the CP's oath, previously taken before the mayor, was now sworn before the omnipotent prefect. By the early Second Empire, police manuals "consistently stressed that commissaires, as 'agents of the government' and general police officers, must maintain their 'administrative independence.' They must never forget their preeminent status as 'political functionaries under the direct and immediate authority of the prefect.'"[71] The Second Empire accentuated in some important ways Napoleonic centralization, "the strength of the state [*la puissance publique*]" forming a pyramid, as it did the professionalization of the police.[72] The experience of Lyon confirms the relationship between social conflict, mass politics, and pressure for a more centralized organization of the police.

We turn to a final example, Toulouse, where in 1832 the ministry of the interior had appointed a commissaire central. But here, too, prefects clashed with the claims of independence forcefully put forward by mayors. Two years later, the police in Toulouse seemed "without direction." The commissaire central, Amalry, had little experience dealing with "southern customs," and his relations with the mayor were tense. Reflecting his own view of Toulouse, the prefect tellingly commented that "such obstacles here are aggravated by the vain and envious character of the inhabitants and by their political irritability." The post of commissaire central was eliminated in 1836, reestablished three years later, but then was abolished because of intense opposition from the mayor in 1840.[73]

During the Second Republic, Montagnard influence increased in Haute-Garonne, as in much of the Midi. Reports assessing the performance of CPs sent to the ministry of the interior regularly emphasized services rendered to the government's politics. Toulouse's mayor claimed to "hold all of the strings of the police." Seeing himself as the successor to the *capitouls,* one mayor had even threatened to resign if the ministry appointed another commissaire central. Toulouse's CPs were a lethargic, indecisive lot.[74]

In 1850 the prefect convinced the mayor to request the nomination of a commissaire central. The first choice was sent from Tulle to do some undercover work in Toulouse and provided accurate information on, among other things, Polish refugees and the distribution of Montagnard newspapers. But feeling compromised by such work, he decided that under no circumstances would he serve as commissaire central in "Tolosa," using the Occitan name for the rose city. The prefect first obtained the nomination of one of Toulouse's CPs to assume the post temporarily. Then Philippe-Louis Cazeaux, whom we met in chapter 2 in Tours, was sent from Toulon, where he had done such exemplary service during the cholera epidemic that the prefect recommended he be awarded the legion of honor, to take up the post of commissaire central.[75]

Cazeaux embodied in some important ways the evolution of the police during the first half of the nineteenth century. Cazeaux had been warned by "a hundred" people on coming to Toulouse that the battle against the mayor, who used the corps of surveillants as "his little army," could not be won. Even as he continued to complain about the interference and influence of the mayor, his principal function was political policing, under the close supervision of the prefect. Cazeaux proudly sent the prefect the regulations for policing that he had used in Toulon, modestly describing the "brilliant results" he had obtained in a city "very attached to socialism," and where the most recent elections had brought the election of two "men of order" despite socialist propaganda. Cazeaux recommended more secret agents and better communication between the police and departmental authorities. Yet he had not been long in Toulouse before insisting that the mayor's incessant meddling undermined the system.[76]

After the coup d'état of December 2, 1851, Cazeaux continued to complain about the mayor. Toulouse required police loyal to those who had named them—the ministry of the interior and the prefect, "their hierarchical superiors"—and not to local dignitaries "more interested in being agreeable to their friends."[77] Yet the battle between mayors and prefects had already been won by the central government in Paris. The "police state of Louis Napoleon" only confirmed that triumph.

CONCLUSION

A s French cities and towns expanded in size and complexity, commissaires de police gradually developed a professional identity. The procedures of policing became increasingly routinized and official expectations as to what constituted a good policeman became more standardized and bureaucratized. If all went well, CPs could move up the hierarchy within the police, one that paralleled the urban hierarchy that made cities more important than towns, service in a prefecture more prestigious and lucrative than in a mere sub-prefecture. A policeman in Brive might well receive the good news of a transfer to La Rochelle, with the possibility of Orléans or Nantes perhaps lying in the future. The copies of police dictionaries and instruction manuals; laws, regulations, and ordinances; registers of workers' livrets and of passports; forms for reporting crimes and misdemeanors; and official police stationary took up more space in the small offices of the CPs, reflecting the bureaucratization of policing. At the same time, in their correspondence and petitions, CPs began to refer to their careers. As functionaries, they demanded the right to a pension on retirement, something that came considerably later.

Police professionalization may be seen in the context of the ongoing centralization of state authority, which continued during the Restoration, July Monarchy, and the Second Republic. The state, through the ministry of the interior and the prefects, defeated the claims of municipalities that the first obligation of the CPs should be to the cities and town that paid them. The police were increasingly outsiders in the towns where they worked, something deeply resented by some mayors. Their responsibilities included administrative tasks handed down from the ministry of the interior in Paris, obligations to magistrates because of their own judicial status and functions, and municipal duties overseen by mayors. Many policemen suffered from being caught between aggressively competing authorities. However, CPs were hired, judged, and fired by the ministry of the interior on the recommendation of prefects. Mayors, to be sure, could influence such decisions, but they did not call the shots. We have listened to the complaints of mayors in Lyon and of other towns that CPs had no time to enforce municipal regulations, their time being taken up by orders from prefects or subprefects.

During the early years of the Restoration, men who could reasonably claim to have suffered at the hands of the Revolution while maintaining allegiance to the Bourbons, were hired to serve as CPs, many with the help of powerful political patrons. Those putting forward their candidacy for posts eagerly provided compelling and sometimes even believable accounts of personal dramas of the Revolution. However, during the Restoration, professional performance came to count for much in the systematic assessments of policemen. Many of those who received their posts because they offered convincing accounts of their fidelity to the Bourbons soon found themselves fired for incompetence.

Policing offered men of relatively low social status, many of whom had military experience, the chance to work in a position that provided at least lower-middle-class status (despite chronic complaints by CPs that they were not treated with sufficient respect) and at least a respectable salary. They could proudly (for some, even arrogantly) wear the sash symbolic of their authority. Many of them had gained at least minimal essential reading and writing skills working as clerks (a good many in the army) or as tax officials. A good number knew more than one language, dialect, or patois, essential in policing in Alsace, Brittany, much of Languedoc, Provence, Auvergne, Flanders, and many other parts of France as well. The police were drawn from every region and from very similar social backgrounds. The CPs thus stood between the elites, the protection of whose property occupied much of their attention, and the ordinary people on whom their gaze focused. More often than not, their stays in one post were relatively short—four or five years. Like other functionaries, they were moved around. This in itself was another sign of professionalization. But for all those who fell by the wayside because they were dismissed, victims of the purges that each new regime undertook or of their own incompetence, poor judgment, or dishonesty, many hundreds enjoyed careers in the métier.

We have encountered some CPs, veritable petty bourgeois *urbanistes* who were determined to make the towns in which they served better places to live. They were too savvy to imagine that they could impose perfect order on the cities and towns. The careers of Bertrand Cazeaux and his son suggest essential aspects of evolution of the police in nineteenth-century France. In Tours during the early years of the July Monarchy, the elder Cazeaux reflected systematically on the tasks of municipal policing in Tours, putting forward helpful suggestions to his superiors about the organization of the police. At the same time, he inevitably glanced over his shoulder in the hope of divining what the prefect, who could make or break his career, thought of him. Philippe-Louis Cazeaux followed his father into the profession, which was rare enough. During the Second Republic, the minister of the interior sent the younger Cazeaux to Toulouse to serve as commissaire central in 1850. His most pressing assignment was to coordinate political repression in the *ville rose*. Throughout the period, political policing remained an important part of the duties of CPs. In periods of heightened political contention, haute police could push aside the daily routines of municipal policing, this in itself reflecting the increased centralization of the state. CPs then had to be on the lookout for the arrival of political militants of the opposition—liberals, republicans, socialists, Legitimists, depending on the period—or had to watch closely potential "agitation" by workers meeting to plan strikes or consider political choices. By mid-century, most major cities had commissaires central who were responsible for the coordination of policing, above all, political policing on behalf of the ministry of the interior in Paris and the prefects who represented authority in the provinces. Even if the balance of power between the state and municipality would tilt back and forth in the early Third Republic, the state continued to dominate a fundamentally unbalanced equation.

Policing during the first half of the nineteenth century reveals striking continuities with the Ancien Régime, attitudes toward the wandering, begging poor being just one of them. Beggars remained part of the texture of urban life, many moving from place to place. The police, becoming ever more an instrument of state centralization and following orders from their superiors in the ministry of the interior and prefectures, developed a set of practices intended to regulate geographic mobility. Yet at the same time, the policing of beggars and vagabonds reflected and complemented the strong local sense that indigenous beggars were one thing, outsiders another. The police expelled countless outsiders but were far more apt to tolerate beggars known to be from town. Marketplaces and the octroi, potential *points chauds,* remained focal points for police attention. Although Lyon and arguably Marseille and St. Étienne among provincial cities maintained reputations for crime and occasional turbulence, most towns did not seem overwhelmed by criminality. There was a certain predictability to it all—for example, thefts increased during the hard times that followed cyclical harvest failure.

However, in most towns CPs never encountered a major disturbance, to say nothing of an insurrection. The routines of daily policing went on, even as the growth of cities could make tasks more complex, and workers became a primary focus for surveillance: watching the market; checking the octroi; arresting or chasing away beggars, particularly those not from town; following up occasional thefts; checking the registers of lodgers; verifying passports; watching cafés and cabarets; monitoring prostitutes; anticipating or ending brawls between compagnons; handing out contraventions to those who failed to sweep in front of their houses, apartments, or stores; attempting to provide information requested by superior authorities; giving orders to agents and working with them as best they could; dealing with the unpleasantness of human tragedy; and, when possible, conciliating disputes, domestic and other, while being ready for the unexpected.

The mid-century was a major turning point in modern French history. There were no more grain riots after 1854–55, the last of the classic harvest failures, thanks to the increased production of grain and improved distribution via improved roads and the railroad. *Le grand départ* began—the rural exodus that would accelerate in the 1870s, particularly with the phylloxera epidemic that devastated French vineyards beginning late in the decade. Moreover, if Paris and major cities had been relatively underpoliced during the Ancien Régime and the first half of the nineteenth century, thereafter this was no longer be the case. Military garrisons stood ready to put down movements of social protest, as in the northern town of Fourmies on May Day, 1891, Limoges in 1905, and during the demonstrations by the *viticulteurs* in the Midi in 1907. There had been thousands of riots in eighteenth-century Paris alone, after 1850 there were relatively few.[1]

By mid-century, the preoccupations of the police and indeed policing itself looked quite similar in Lille, Marseille, Nantes, Colmar, and Poitiers, despite the special challenges that each post presented to the CPs who worked there. They developed a sense of professional identity in the context of a defined hierarchy that reflected the strength of the French state as they helped integrate a complex society of many regions and traditions. The CPs continued to play an important part in France's national history during this period and beyond. They increasingly became a symbol of urbanity, part of the urban scene. They took their place on the boulevards and other main thoroughfares in French cities. Required to report on meetings and strikes of workers during the "heroic age of French syndicalism," 1895–1907, they also pointed out new road signs to the first motorists. The CPs stood for something very urban and also very French. They did not break down local traditions—nor did they intend to. But in sharp contrast to the British experience, they helped extend and consolidate the reach, authority, and prestige of the state in what remains one of the most centralized nations in the Western world.

NOTES

Introduction

1. As Howard C. Payne has noted (*The Police State of Louis Napoleon Bonaparte* [Seattle, 1966], p. 18), the English term *commissioner* does not work as a translation of *commissaire*, and I will use the latter throughout. He writes (p. 206) that for ordinary people the policeman's "blue, black, and silver uniform—or more usual, simply his tricolor sash—personified the central authority."

2. Archives Départementales (AD) Vienne, M4 310, subprefect (SP) Châtellerault, July 18, 1815, found also in AD Vienne M4 310, July 18, 1815.

3. AD Dordogne, 1M 66, SP Nontron, September 7, 1831.

4. See Jean Vidalenc, "Armée et police en France 1814–1914," in Jacques Aubert et al., *L'État et sa police en France (1789–1914)* (Geneva, 1979), pp. 135–59; and Clive Emsley, *Gendarmes and the State in Nineteenth-Century Europe* [Oxford, 1999], p. 42. Gendarmes had to be twenty-five years of age and have served at least three years (and later four years) in the army.

5. See John M. Merriman, *The Agony of the Republic: The Repression of the Left in Revolutionary France, 1848–1851* (New Haven, 1978).

6. Clive Emsley, "The French Police: Ubiquitous and Faceless," *French History,* 3, 2 (1989), pp. 226–27. Jean-Marc Berlière has called attention to the fact that "the police has for a long time remained and still remains a black hole in French historiography" (*Le monde des polices en France* [Paris, 1996], p. 12).

7. A definition of *police* from 1759 in Prussia imparts the French sense of the term: "In the widest sense of the word . . . (as) all measures concerned with the internal affairs of the country . . . in a narrower sense 'police' refers to all those things which are necessary for the maintenance of the conditions of civil life" (Clive Emsley, *Policing and its Context 1750–1870* [London, 1983], p. 99). "Police power in France . . . is constitutionally indistinguishable from the authority to govern. *Police Générale* refers to the power of government to make binding regulations in the interests of public order and security" (David H. Bayley, "The Police and Political Development in Europe," in Charles Tilly, ed., *The Formation of National States in Western Europe* [Princeton, 1975], p. 335).

8. Payne, *The Police State of Louis Napoleon Bonaparte*, p. 4.

9. Steven Kaplan, "Note sur les commissaires de police au XVIIIe siècle," *Journal d'histoire moderne et contemporaine*, 28 (October–Décember 1981), p. 678. Because of the

intertwining of the police and the government and its administration, "French theorists found a doctrine of police in the very assumptions underlying administrative centralization itself."

10. AD Indre-et-Loire 4M 2, Cazeaux, 1832.

11. See John M. Merriman, *The Margins of City Life: Explorations on the French Urban Frontier* (New York, 1991).

12. Kaplan, "Note sur les commissaires de police," p. 674.

13. Alan Williams, *The Police of Paris, 1718–1789* (Baton Rouge, 1979), pp. 291–95. David Garrioch, *The Making of Revolutionary Paris* (Berkeley, 2002), pp. 227–28: "The number of employees in the central police offices (increased) . . . and their procedures became more bureaucratic." Williams adds (p. 292): "As the force grew in size and became a more professional unit, it also acquired a relatively stable institutional framework or form." Robert Schwartz argues convincingly that the French became more accustomed to depending on the state in the eighteenth century (*Policing the Poor in Eighteenth-Century France* [Chapel Hill, 1988]).

14. Kaplan, "Note sur les commissaires de police," pp. 679–80.

15. Berlière, *Le monde des polices en France,* pp. 10–11: The Revolution established "the bases of the modern police and notably tried to resolve the contraction between police and liberty"; Payne, *The Police State of Louis Napoleon Bonaparte,* p. 5; Hélène L'Heuillet, *Basse politique, haute police: Une approche historique et philosophique de la police* (Paris, 2001), pp. 190–91. The law distinguished between administrative or preventive and judicial, or "repressive" policing, both of these functions to be combined in the person of the commissaire de police. See also Jean-Marc Berlière, "L'Institution policière sous la Troisième République République, 1875–1914," 3 vols., unpublished doctoral dissertation, Université de Bourgogne, 1991.

16. Howard G. Brown argues that "by paying too much attention to structural changes in policing brought by Joseph Fouché's emphasis on political policing during the Directory and the Empire or Vidocq's appointment to head the *brigade de sûreté,* we distort the evolutionary changes in ordinary police work . . . (relying on) a more extensive police force and the centralized coordination of law enforcement officials" ("Tips, Traps and Tropes: Police Work in Post-Revolutionary Paris," in Clive Emsley and Haia Shpayer Makov, eds., *Police Detectives in History, 1750–1950* [Aldershot, Eng., 2004]), p. 31. In his view, "It was during the last years of the First Republic that a modern image of police detection first emerged" (p. 4), and he notes that when the Prefecture of Police replaced the Bureau Central in 1800, four hundred "large registers" were in use and that "the police system proved remarkably efficient."

17. Alan Spitzer, "The Bureaucrat as Proconsul: The Restoration Prefect and the *police générale,*" *Comparative Studies in Society and History,* 7 (July 1965), p. 376.

18. On professionalism in other professions, see, among others, Guy Thuillier, *Pensions de retraite des fonctionnaires au XIXe siècle* (Paris, 1994) and *Retraites des fonctionnaires: débats et doctrines, 1750–1914* (Paris, 1996); Theodore Zeldin, *France 1848–1945: Ambition and Love* (Oxford, 1979), which offers chapters on doctors, notaries, bankers, and bureaucrats; Daniel Ringrose, "Work and Social Presence: French Public Engineers in Nineteenth-Century Provincial Communities," *History and Technology,* 14 (1998), pp. 293–312; and Geoffrey Cocks and Konrad H. Jarausch, eds., *German Professions, 1800–1850* (New York, 1990). David Troyansky is currently completing a study of magistrates, "Entitlement and Complaint: Ending Careers in Post-Revolutionary France," one in which their requests for pensions provide an essential source.

19. Gabriel Delessert, who served as prefect of police between 1836 and the Revolution of 1848, standardized expectations and regulations for the police, thus improving civilian policing. According to Patricia O'Brien, his term of service "marked the begin-

ning of a concern for the professionalism and neutrality of the police force" ("Urban Growth and Public Order: The Development of a Modern Police in Paris, 1829–1854," unpublished dissertation, Columbia University, 1973, p. 179). For his part, Emsley contends that during the first half of the century, the gradual professionalism of the police could be seen (*Policing and Its Context*, pp. 76, 87, 94). His work on the CPs leads him to conclude in an important article: "A detailed study of the police on the Paris streets in the early nineteenth century provides a rather different image from the traditional pictures of Fouché's men as efficient, menacing and all-powerful, of the Restoration police as hypocritical and sinister concerned with little more than political, moral, and religious surveillance, and of Vidocq's squad of detectives pursuing the thieves with whom they were once confederates. The dossiers and biographies of the *commissaires* and the *officiers de la paix* reveal them as state functionaries competing on the ladder of advancement using family links and patronage to get on" (Clive Emsley, "Policing the Streets of Early Nineteenth-Century Paris," *French History*, 1, 2 [1987], p. 281). William Cohen writes that during the first half of the century the urban police "developed something akin to professional police and fire forces" (*Urban Government and the Rise of the French City: Five Municipalities in the Nineteenth Century* [New York, 1998], p. 79). "Beat" policing—patrols in the district to which a CP was assigned if he did not serve alone in a small town—well preceded the 1854 establishment of the English model, which one historian has taken to mark the existence of a modern police (W. Scott Haine, *The World of the Paris Café* [Baltimore, 1999], p. 23). When the mayor of Toulouse in 1851 assessed the success of policing in his city, he cited foot patrols as a major reason (AD Haute-Garonne, 13M 57).

20. AD Haute-Garonne, 13M 57 ter, mayor of Tulle, November 30, 1849.

21. AD Ardèche 6M 3.

22. Emsley, *Policing and Its Context,* pp. 91–97; O'Brien, "Urban Growth and Public Order," pp. 309–24; Alexandre Nugues-Bourchat concurs, *Représentations et pratiques d'une société urbaine: Lyon, 1800–1880,* 2 vols., unpublished doctoral dissertation, Université-Lumière, Lyon 2, 2004, p. 231; Payne, *The Police State of Louis Napoleon Bonaparte,* pp. 210–11, 283. In 1854, the minister of the interior saluted the civilian police force as superior to dependence on military policing and put into effect higher standards for recruitment and professional discipline, while tripling the number of police in the capital to 3,500 men. G. Metenier's *Guide Pratique de Police* appeared in 1855. Yet by another view the professionalization of the police in the Third Republic brought about the enhanced recruitment, training, and specialization of policemen. Competitive examinations for police posts began only in 1879. See also Marcel Le Clère, "La police politique sous la IIIe République," in Aubert et al., *L'État et sa police en France,* pp. 103–13. Marie Vogel notes the significance of the of 1884, which "permitted the development of a police administration that professionalized progressively, and which acquired a relative autonomy in the definition of its activity" marked by a "real effort to regulate and codify its organization" ("Les Polices des villes entre local et national: L'administration des polices urbaines sous la IIIe République," 2 vols., unpublished dissertation, Université de Grenoble II, 1993, pp. 39, 498). She notes that the articles of the law of 1884 "permitted the control by or direct intervention of the higher administration in the organization of local policing" (pp. 39–40), even if reaffirming the status of the mayor as technically the head of the municipal police. Philippe Vigier concurs, noting the "multiplication and diversification of specialized groups of professional police" (Philippe Vigier, Alain Faure, et al., *Maintien de l'ordre et polices en France et en Europe au XIX siècle* [Paris, 1987], p. 8). See Howard W. Payne, "Theory and Practice of the Political Police During the Second Empire," *Journal of Modern History,* 30 (March 1958), p. 17.

23. As reflected by the municipal law of December 14, 1789: "The limits of political police therefore fluctuated with the executive's strength and sense of expediency. In this fact the elements of a police state existed in nineteenth-century France" (p. 26).

24. Berlière rightly considers police authority as part of a "secular struggle that turned around this fundamental question: was policing to be a municipal prerogative or would it be under the domain of the state?" (*Le monde des polices*, pp. 77–78). He gives one his chapters the title "*la marche vers l'étatisation*." To Vigier, the nomination of a *commissaire central de police* in all large towns in 1854 "became an essential element in the struggle between local authorities and the centralized state, one of the keys to understanding the political history" of the nineteenth century in "Présentation," *Maintien de l'ordre*, p. 9. Cohen is mistaken when he writes that "an organizational chart might show formal authority vested partly in the central government, but until World War II most municipalities controlled their own police forces"; that only in Paris and Lyon was policing centralized; and that each municipality had different requirements for becoming a policeman. Criteria for selection, nomination, and firing were national, as was the hierarchy of salaries. Yet he recognizes that "against the mayors, the central administration was powerful in regards to police affairs" (Cohen, *Urban Government and the Rise of the French City*, pp. 80, 81–84, 90, 102). Jacqueline Gatti assesses, "Already by the middle of the nineteenth century part of liberal doctrine was preoccupied with finding the juridical means to limit local power" ("La notion de police dans l'oeuvre de Maurice Hauriou," in Claude Journès, ed., *Police et politique en France* [Lyon, 1988]). Vogel, "Les Polices des villes entre local et national," pp. 23, 34, 497, writes: "The conflicts over the growth of state authority in one town alter another were skirmishes in a larger battle between local authorities and the central government over the conquest or the conservation of prerogatives concerning the maintenance of order and public peace" (p. 498). Thus Michèle Dagenais and Pierre-Yves Saunier contend that "Municipalities, especially in continental Europe, tended to be seen as extensions of the central state, based in part on the French model stemming from the Revolution and subsequent Napoleonic conquest" (Michèle Dagenais and Pierre-Yves Saunier, "Tales of the Periphery: An Outline Survey of Municipal Employees and Services in the Nineteenth and Twentieth Centuries," in Michèle Dagenais, Irene Mauer, and Pierre-Yves Saunier, eds., *Municipal Services and Employees in the Modern City: New Historical Approaches* [Aldershot, U.K., 2003], p. 17). I follow the reasoning of Clive Emsley and Barbara Weinberger: "Politics' here does not refer in the narrow sense to what the French call *haute police*, that is political surveillance and control by the police—an issue that has tended to dominate much police history, particularly for France and Germany. Rather, the term 'politics' is used here to focus on the interrelationships between police and *government*, both central and local, and also to examine how political events and considerations not immediately related to police and policing have nevertheless considerably affected police development" (Clive Emsley and Barbara Weinberger, eds., *Policing Western Europe: Politics, Professionalism, and Public Order, 1850–1940* [New York, 1991], pp. vii–viii).

25. Vogel, "Les Polices des villes entre local et national," p. 57. She correctly describes the CPs "as traditionally considered come agents of the state" (p. 241). For example, the "Tableaux de renseignements" ordered by the ministerial circular November 19, 1817.

26. Georges Carrot, *Histoire de la police française* (Paris, 1992), pp. 114–16. The law established *commissaires généraux de police* in the three towns with more than 100,000 inhabitants and the decree of September 10, 1805, added twenty-six other towns by virtue of population or strategic position. A decree of March 5, 1811, confirmed the organization of the police and of the CPs in particular.

27. Berlière, *Le monde des polices en France*, pp. 78–79. The Chamber of Deputies on September 16, 1830, had adopted a law giving the mayor the prerogative to present candidates for vacant places, although the ministry of interior still made the appointment. In Paris, in contrast to the provinces, the state contributed to police salaries.

28. AD Jura, CP Lons-le-Saunier, January 7, 1831.

29. Bayley, "The Police and Political Development in Europe," pp. 332, 336, 357,

360–61, 365, 368. Comparing the evolution of national police systems in Great Britain, Italy, Germany, and France, he underscores three factors that linked politics and policing: "1) a transformation in the organization of political power; 2) prolonged violent popular resistance to government; and 3) development of new law and order tasks, as well as the erosion of former bases of community authority, as a result of socioeconomic change." British resistance to even the creation of the bobbies in 1829 may be, for example, placed in the context of an obsession that policing in Britain not be like that in archenemy France. See Clive Emsley, *The English Police: A Political and Social History* (Hemel Hempstead, Hertfordshire, 1991), pp. 234–41; and David Taylor, *The New Police in Nineteenth-Century England: Crime, Conflict and Control* (Manchester, 1997), pp. 1–9, 75–126. On the part played by dislike of French centralization (and Catholicism) and fears that some sort of despotism might trample British liberties in the creation of British identity, see Linda Colley, *Britons* (New Haven, 1992). In Britain, watch committees made up of local elites oversaw policing and of the administration of the Poor Law of 1834 (following elite outcry against what was perceived as largesse of the predecessor law of 1798, the Speenhamland System, in the treatment of the poor), which in itself represented the essence of the administration of local policing. This is what helps make the British case totally different, particularly after the Poor Law of 1834 itself and the Municipal Corporation Act of 1835. Work houses were set up through the payment of local taxes. The London case of the bobbies was exceptional, as opposed to the history of the police in the rest of Britain. The French story is more homogenous.

30. Emsley, *Policing and Its Context*, p. 34. Jacqueline Gatti has described the changing sense of the word *police* from the Ancien Régime and its widest connotation to the nineteenth century, when the police enforced specific laws, with policing part of the structure of administration (*Maintien de l'ordre et polices en France et en Europe au XIXe siècle* [Paris, 1987], esp. p. 225). The stationary of CPs of Lille early in the July Monarchy simply highlighted "the maintenance of order, salubrity, and public security" (AD Nord, M 184/15).

31. Emsley and Weinberger, *Policing Western Europe*, pp. viii–ix: "As the scale of the threat from the 'enemy within' and the 'enemy without' reached beyond local and national boundaries, so the advocates of an increase in central control everywhere gathered strength."

32. Payne, *The Police State of Louis Napoleon Bonaparte*, p. 212.

33. Emsley, *Policing and Its Context*, pp. 53 and 57. See Pierre Riberette, "De la police de Napoléon à la Police de la Congrégation," in Jacques Aubert et al., *L'État et sa police en France*. In 1826, Louis Guyon published a *Biographie des Commissaires de police . . . de Paris*, denouncing 45 of the 48 CPs of the capital.

34. Riberette summarizes: "By the systematic utilization (of methods) that men in power used to retain their position, the Restoration inaugurated a period during which the police, instead of guaranteeing the tranquility of the country, became the private preserve of a faction and an instrument of politics" ("De la police de Napoléon," p. 58). The *sergents de ville* were brought back on September 8, 1830. In January 1828, Louis-Maurice Debelleyme, a forty-one-year-old lawyer who had criticized gendarmes in Paris for breaking up a liberal demonstration, became prefect of police in the capital. Debelleyme undertook a modest purge of the police force. In March 1829, eighty-five sergents-de-ville appeared on the streets of the capital for the first time since the Revolution, in blue uniforms and *bicorne* hats, carrying a white cane during the day and a sword at night. They were part of Debelleyme's plan to restore public confidence in police. Recruited largely from the subordinate *inspecteurs* and sent into the streets to expedite traffic, their new uniform made them seem more civilian than military (Riberette, "De la police de Napoléon," p. 54). A year later, the scathing *Livre noir de MM Franchet et Delavau* was published, at-

tacking the police for being anything but neutral as they carried out their duties. It was perhaps published with Debelleyme's connivance. See O'Brien, "Urban Growth and Public Order," p. 34; Emsley, *Policing and Its Context,* pp. 57–58; and Jean Tulard, *La Préfecture de police sous la monarchie de Juillet* (Paris, 1965), pp. 61, 88. The royal ordinance of August 31–September 17, 1830, established a uniform consisting of a green coat with black trousers and a tricolor sash with a black fringe.

35. Emsley, *Policing and Its Context,* op. cit., p. 87.

36. Ibid., p. 150.

37. Stendhal, *Lucien Leuwen, Oeuvres complètes,* Pléiade, t. 1, 1189.

38. O'Brien, "Urban Growth and Public Order," pp. 67–71, 206; Emsley, *Policing and Its Context,* p. 88; Emsley, "Policing the Streets of Early Nineteenth-Century Paris," p. 281; André-Jean Tudesq, "Police et état sous la monarchie de juillet," in Jacques Aubert, Michel Eudes, et. al., *L'État et la police en France (1789–1914),* p. 75; Vigier, *Maintien de l'ordre et polices,* pp. 64, 75; Berlière, *Le monde des polices en France,* p. 42. In 1831, Vidocq was named head of the *brigade de sûreté,* but it was dissolved the following year.

39. See for example, Pierre Guiral, "Police et sensibilité française," in Aubert et al., *L'État et sa police en France,* pp. 163–75; O'Brien, "Urban Growth and Public Order," pp. 36–38. On Vidocq, see also Louis Canler, *Mémoires de Canler, ancien chef du service de sureté* (Paris, 1986). Thus, the definition of the word *cogne,* which can mean "crime," in the *Larousse: "argot. Gendarme, policier"* (Guiral, "Police et sensibilité française," p. 169).

40. Aubert et al., *L'État et sa police en France,* pp. 166–67; on Lyon, see Nugues-Bourchat, *Représentations et pratiques d'une société urbaine.*

41. Emsley, *Policing and Its Context,* p. 90.

42. Nugues-Bourchat, *Représentations et pratiques d'une société urbaine,* chap. 13; Emsley, "Policing the Streets of Early Nineteenth-Century Paris," pp. 278–80.

43. Alain Faure, noting "this profoundly anchored feeling of hostility . . . an authentic cultural trait . . . a police little loved or detested is a fragile police, demanding, and dangerous in its reactions" ("Nos intentions . . . et quelques resultants," in *Maintien de l'ordre et polices,* p. 19; Guiral, "Police et sensibilité française," p. 171).

44. Emsley, *Policing and Its Context,* p. 92.

45. Payne, *The Police State of Louis Napoleon Bonaparte,* pp. 33, 280.

46. Thus, in principle, a division of duties existed between "administrative" policing within the context of municipality and département, *police judiciaire,* including the repression of crime, and *haute police* in the interest of *sûreté générale.* Payne, *The Police State of Louis Napoleon Bonaparte,* notes that "political police measures were 'acts of government' by qualified executive agents sharing in the immunity of sovereignty itself" (p. 11). Haute police was defined (circular sent to CPs by the prefect of Nievre, July 12, 1841; AD Nièvre, M 1307) as "everything that concerns the security of the king and that of the state and also everything that concerns the public spirit, general expressed opinions, how news that circulate is received, and the conduct of men who are opposed to the governmentt" (article 1), and "political offenses . . . which are committees, such as shouts, words, and seditious writing."

47. Iain Cameron, *Crime and Repression in the Auvergne and the Guyenne 1720–1790* (Cambridge, 1981), p. 5.

48. L'Heuillet, *Basse politique, haute police,* pp. 127, 172, 227, 238, 243. Of the image of the eye, she writes of Louis XIV, "When Louis seized the traditional image of the sun to make clear his authority, he renews a simple commonplace. The sun is an eye that brings lights and makes visible. It was a dynamic principle: he reigned over the visible . . . the eye is a little sun . . . the image of the sun allowed him to bring together authority and proximity" (pp. 228–29, 235–36). She adds "The violence of the state, incarnated in its police, can be compared to a gaze and to an eye" (p. 222). A very successful weekly during

the Belle Époque was called, *L'Oeil de la police*. To Foucault, the "real agents of repression" include the family and doctors, while the police represent "external order." Thus, "the disciplined being is policed" (p. 128). Foucault places the transition between the "police d'ordre" and the "police de sécurité" in the middle of the eighteenth century, "at the moment of the discovery of life as a political object," part of the shift from a territorial administrative stage to "the state of government" (L'Heuillet, *Basse politique, haute police,* p. 131).

49. L'Heuillet, *Basse politique, haute police*, p. 267.

50. Arlette Farge, "Un espace urbain obsédant: le commissaire et la rue à Paris au xviiie siècle," *Les Révoltes logiques*, 6 [1977], pp. 9, 11, and 16; *Vivre dans la rue à Paris au XVI-IIe siècle* (Paris, 1992), pp. 19–21; "L'espace urbaine c'est le lieu de vie privée de ceux qui n'en ont guère, et l'espace obligé de ceux qui n'en possèdent réellement aucun" (p. 9); "le parcours d'une historienne," interviewed by Laurent Vidal, *Genèses*, 48 (September 2002), p. 123; "To prevent crowds, [it] was not enough to make the street legible. [The police] had to go further: to make more hygienic, clean, and enlighten these obscure masses" ("L'espace parisien au XVIIIe siècle d'après les ordonnances de police," *Ethnologie française*, 1982, no. 2, p. 125). To L'Heuillet, *Basse politique, haute police*, p. 143: "The street is the work of the police. Before being able to maintain order there and to regulate traffic and survey hygiene and lighting, first the street must exist, not only to be traced, but also instituted, with a name" (the first street names were affixed in Paris in 1728). Thus prefect of police Louis Lépine in Paris considered himself "le préfet de la rue" in Paris at the end of the nineteenth century.

51. L'Heuillet, *Basse politique, haute police*, pp. 284–85 and 262–63, quoting Foucault, "The power of discipline is exercised by being rendered invisible; on the other hand, on the other hand, it is imposed on those who submit to it the principle of obligatory visibility." Moreover, Bentham insisted on the importance of compiling careful information on those staying in rooming houses and on "an apparatus of files and information." Similarly, Bruno Fortier sees "a progressive implication of the apparatus of the state in the procedures by which space was defined" becoming more constant in Paris after about 1750. By eliminating "every enclave" in the capital, the state could "create in the city a space that could be absolutely appropriated, turned into capital, and open to life," thus anticipating "Haussmann's project." Thus, the role of the police was to "infiltrate urban space in order to separate individuals and to control them"—the "future proletariat"—which could only be accomplished "by the successive rupture of traditional solidarities . . . to break the opacity of space, break down its structures to return the individual to himself" (Bruno Fortier, "La politique de l'espace parisien à la fin de l'Ancien Régime," in Fortier, ed., *La politique de l'espace parisien [à la fin de l'Ancien Régime]* [Paris, 1975], pp. 20, 49, 126, 141–42). Indeed, again reflecting Foucault's influence, Nugues-Bourchat's recent dissertation on the police and policing in Lyon emphasizes the implementation of *quadrillage* (a grid division into districts), in Lyon as a way of watching and controlling ordinary people, reflecting and assisting the "frenzy" for description, detail, and statistics. In theory, "grid policing" (*l'îlotage*) allowed the police to observe "all and everywhere" (*Représentations et pratiques d'une société urbaine*, pp. 170, 204, 206, 256, drawing in particular on chap. 3 of *Surveiller et punir, naissance de la prison* [Paris, 1995]), "*Quadrillage* follows from a triple objective: absolute control, training, and the idea of a protective police" (pp. 171–72) and "Les anormaux," cours au Collège de France, 1974–75 (Paris, 1999), p. 41: "One defines the limits of . . . a certain territory: that of a town, then of a town and its faubourgs, and this territory is constituted as a enclosed territory. . . . The object of a close and detailed analysis, of a meticulous *quadrillage*." To Alain Faure, cutting a city into pieces made it possible to patrol each constantly." Within a few years, "the doctrine of security" would, in his view, extend from "control of the physical body to political and social control" (Faure,

"Nos intentions . . . et quelques résultants," in *Maintien de l'ordre et polices,* p. 17). In a similar vein, Maryvonne Bernard assesses the first stages of the reorganization of the Parisian police during the summer of 1853: "The bourgeoisie succeeded in imposing social order by a process of rationalization of space, in which hygienists, doctors, architects, and, of course, the police participated." Following the coup d'état of December 2, 750 sergents de ville and police patrols day and night divided Paris so that no one could escape surveillance—the axiom being *diviser pour mieux surveiller* ("La reorganisation de la police sous le Second Empire [1851–1858]: 'des bras infatigables,'" in *Maintien de l'ordre et polices,* pp. 123 and 128ff.).

52. Tulard, *La Préfecture de police,* p. 84, from the *Bulletin de Paris,* September 23, 1831.

53. O'Brien, "Urban Growth and Public Order," p. 246. Emsley argues that relatively recent work "has challenged the old certainties about police forces being developed as the successful solution to a rising tide of crime and popular disorder. The origins of policing institutions are now understood, at least in the academic world, as far more problematic, depending on aspirations for new thresholds of public decorum at least as much as on fears of crime and disorder" (*Gendarmes and the State,* pp. 1–2).

54. Andrew Aisenberg, *Contagion: Disease, Government, and the "Social Question" in Nineteenth-Century France* (Stanford, 1999), pp. 41–45. Louis Chevalier, *Dangerous Classes and Laboring Classes in Paris during the First Half of the Nineteenth Century* (London, 1973), the classic restatement of the uprooting hypothesis, "non seulement une ville criminelle et violente, mais une ville malade," and so on. In the words of L'Heuillet, *Basse politique, haute police ,* "La ville, en effet, abrite la foule, qui est elle-même un corps et un masse compacts et turbulents, denses et dangereux" (p. 129, quote from Chevalier, p. 177). Honoré Frégier, *Des classes dangereuses de la population dans les grandes villes et des moyens de les rendre meilleures,* 2 vols. (Paris, 1840).

55. Frégier, *Des classes dangereuses,* vol. 2, p. 257.

56. Clive Emsley, review essay, "The French Police: Ubiquitous and Faceless," *French History,* 3, 2 (1989), pp. 226–27.

57. Ibid. In Foucault's construction, surveillance is everywhere, and therefore nowhere.

58. Thus, like Arlette Farge's *La vie fragile: violence, pouvoirs et solidarités à Paris au xviiie siècle* (Paris, 1986), "this book was born in the archives" (p. 7). I also appreciating her warning (p. 9) that the archives can also *fausser, gauchir,* or simplify the object of the study.

59. On micro-history and its relationship with the bigger picture, see Jacques Revel, ed., *Jeux d'échelles: La micro-analyse à l'expérience* (Paris, 1996), especially Revel's introduction and his chapter 1.

60. Richard Cobb, *The Police and the People* (Oxford, 1970), pp. 18, 26, 72–73. He continues, "that, in short, we have acquired, from over-frequentation of police and judicial sources, the habit of intellectualizing about straightforward matters and of writing our history in the knowing, nudging way." I share in part—but not more than that—Cobb's memorable description of how he organized his books: "Nothing could be further from my intentions than to drill the *petit peuple* into tight formation, march them up the hill, and march them down again. My subject is chaotic, and I may well have written about it chaotically!" (pp. xvii, 49, and 54). Farge warns of the role of the clerk "modifying, selecting, and simplifying" responses of those arrested and interrogated by the police, adding "La réalité glisse à travers les filets de l'interrogation" (Farge, "Un espace urbain obsédant," p. 8).

Chapter 1

1. David H. Bayley emphasizes continuities between the late seventeenth century and the modern period ("The Police and Political Development in Europe," in Charles Tilly,

ed., *The Formation of National States in Western Europe* [Princeton, 1975], pp. 340–41). See also Leon Bernard, *The Emerging City: Paris in the Age of Louis XIV* (Durham, N.C., 1970).

2. Steven Kaplan, "Note sur les commissaires de police au XVIIIe siècle," *Journal d'histoire moderne et contemporaine*, 28 (October–December 1981), pp. 670–71.

3. Richard Cobb, *The Police and the People: French Popular Protest (1789–1820)* (New York, 1972), p. 17.

4. For background, see Clive Emsley, *Policing and Its Context 1750–1870* (London, 1983), pp. 9–33. The *milice bourgeoise* could be called on to police provincial towns, serving as national guard units in the early days of the Revolution, and then placed under military control in 1795 (pp. 39–40). The Ministère de la police générale was created by the law of on 12 nivôse, year 4 (January 2, 1796).

5. René Levy, "Qui détient le pouvoir de police?" in Jean-Marc Berlière and Denis Peschanski, *Pouvoirs et polices au XXe siècle: Europe, États-Unis, Japon* (Paris, 1997), p. 19; Clive Emsley, *Gendarmes and the State in Nineteenth-Century Europe* (Oxford, 1999), p. 19.

6. Emsley, *Policing and Its Context,* pp. 32 and 119.

7. See Alan Williams, *The Police of Paris in the Eighteenth Century* (Baton Rouge, 1979) and Emsley, *Policing and Its Context,* chaps. 2 and 3. See Kaplan, "Note sur les commissaires de police," pp. 669–86.

8. Alain Quéant, *Le Commissaire de police dans la société française* (Paris, 1988), p. 15; Emsley, *Policing and Its Context,* p. 35; Bayley, "The Police and Political Development in Europe," pp. 345, 356–57.

9. The view of Bayley, "The Police and Political Development in Europe," pp. 356 and 372, and that of Cobb, as noted by Alexandre Nugues-Bourchat, *Représentations et pratiques d'une société urbaine: Lyon, 1800–1880* (unpublished doctoral dissertation, Université-Lumière, Lyon 2, 2004), p. 169.

10. See Emsley, *Policing and Its Context,* pp. 9, 36–37. Gendarmes, the successors of the maréchaussée, were excluded from unexceptional tasks of policing in France's urban world unless their assistance was requested under special circumstances. See Emsley, *Gendarmes and the State in Nineteenth-Century Europe.*

11. Emsley, *Policing and Its Context,* pp. 35–36.

12. The most relevant laws were those of 19 vendémiaire, year 4; 9 nivose, year 8; 28 pluvoîse, year 8; 23 fructidor, year 9. See also Circular of March 12, 1817, and May 26, 1820 (AD Nièvre M 1298).

13. Minister of the Interior (Int.). March 12, 1817. In one sample, 60.5 percent of those arrested between 1848 and 1854 in Lyon were immediately freed or were so within forty hours by decision of a CP: Nugues-Bourchat, *Représentations et pratiques d'une société urbaine,* pp. 602, 605. During the Restoration (p. 603), incidents that the CPs could not resolve went before the mayor.

14. Described by Howard G. Brown, "Tips, Traps and Tropes: Police Work in Post-Revolutionary Paris," in Clive Emsley and Haia Shpayer Makov, eds., *Police Detectives in History, 1750–1950* (Aldershot, Eng., 2004). Hélène L'Heuillet suggests that Fouché may have known about Jeremy Bentham's famous Pantopicon (*Basse politique, haute police: Une approche historique et Philosophique de la police* [Paris, 2002], pp. 267–68), noting the Fouché was more interested in the relationship between "the prince" and public opinion, Bentham between society and the individual, although the former arguably created the police in the service of the state, not the prince.

15. Georges Carrot, *Histoire de la police française* (Paris, 1992), p. 143; Emsley, *Policing and Its Context,* p. 38.

16. By the decree of 12 messidor, year 8; Emsley, *Policing and Its Context,* pp. 35–43. The ministry of police lasted until 1818, and then was reestablished in 1852 before being suppressed again the following year.

17. Quéant, *Le Commissaire de police dans la société française,* p. 16.

18. The law itself: III: Municipalities: "In towns, bourgs and other places . . . where the population does not exceed two thousand five hundred inhabitants, there will be a mayor and one deputy mayor; in towns or bourgs with from two thousand five hundred people to five thousand inhabitants, a mayor and two deputy mayors; in towns with between five and ten thousand inhabitants, one mayor, two deputy mayors, and one commissaire de police; in towns in which the population is more than ten thousand inhabitants, beside the mayor, two deputy mayors and a commissaire de police, there will be another deputy mayor for each addition twenty thousand inhabitants, and a commissaire de police for each additional ten thousand people"; text found in J. B. Duvergier, *Collection complète des lois, décrets, ordonnances, réglemens,* vol. 12 (Paris, 1835), pp. 97–98. The law of 18 pluviôse also established a commissaire général under the prefect's authority in all towns with more than 100,000 inhabitants, although this did not last. In Nantes, two commissaires refused to wear the uniform at public ceremonies, citing their lack of resources (AD Loire-Atlantique, 1M 705, prefect, July 25, 1843).

19. See Brian Chapman, *The Prefects and Provincial France* (London, 1955). The hierarchy of salaries for prefects, also established by the law of 28 pluviôse, year 8, followed the population of the *chef-lieu* in which he served, ranging from 8,000 francs annually in a town of less than 15,000 people to 24,000 for a city of more than 100,000 inhabitants and 30,000 francs for Paris.

20. AD Rhône, 4M 1, June 6, 1811, and reply of mayor of Lyon, July 4, 1811, prefect, July 18, 1811. The commissaires généraux were suppressed in 1815.

21. Emsley, *Gendarmes and the State,* pp. 81, 83.

22. See Ted W. Margadant, *Urban Rivalries in the French Revolution* (Princeton, 1992) and Bernard Lepetit, *Villes dans la France moderne: 1740–1840* (Paris, 1988).

23. F7 9855, ministry of interior, note, March 6, 1820, and dossier.

24. As in the case of Dunkerque, AD Nord, M 183/13, SP, July 17, 1822. Within a year or two, a second CP had to be added, as a single policeman could not do all the passport work alone.

25. Exceptions could be made by virtue of article 12.

26. F7 9845, note, November 27, 1820.

27. AD Isère, 56M 28, SP of La Tour du Pin, January 4, 1831.

28. AD F7 9843. Jean-Baptiste Sauce, one of the CPs in the Bouches-du-Rhône, was almost certainly a relative of the man who recognized Louis XVI at Varennes 1791, ending the flight of the royal family (AD Meuse, 88M 1).

29. F7 9859, prefect of the Nièvre, February 9, 1815.

30. F7 9859, prefect of the Nièvre, February 9, 1815.

31. AD Corse, 4M 167, CP, July 3, 1820; mayor of Corte, December 19, 1835; Int., February 18, 1843; prefect, September 16, 1852.

32. F7 9864, note March 29, 1821.

33. F7 9841.

34. F7 9862.

35. AD Allier, (3)M 1032c, Int., January 14, 1841; prefect of the Allier, December 24, 1840, and February 24, 1842.

36. Among them Raon-L'Étape in the Vosges (3,200 residents), Brie-Comte-Robert (2,762), Ham (1,663 inhabitants), Avesnes (3,166), Bar-sur-Seine (2,269), Altkirch (2,819), Marat (2,563), and Aire (1,422) in the Landes (AD Seine-Maritime, 4M 1, n.d., "Etat des villes qui ont obtenu la création d'un commissaire de police").

37. AD Ardèche, 6M 3.

38. MR 1245, 1835.

39. AD Nièvre, M 1308, report to the minister of interior, November 29, 1851.

40. AD Vienne, 4M 312, named January 10, 1851. Three kinds of commissaires spéci-aux included those assigned to the construction of railroads (beginning in 1846), others re-sponsible for the surveillance of printing and the book trade, and some others assigned to frontier posts (see Howard C. Payne, *The Police State of Louis Napoleon Bonaparte* [Seattle, 1966]. p. 19).

41. F7 9855, prefect of the Loire, May 1, 1820; AD Loire, "notes sur les commissaires de police," April 28, 1849.

42. F7 9870, subprefect of Corbeil, February 15, 1817, and prefect of the Seine-et-Oise, October 18, 1816.

43. John M. Merriman, *The Margins of City Life: Explorations on the French Urban Frontier, 1815–1851* (New York, 1991), p. 73.

44. AD Loire-Atlantique, 1M 704, prefect, April 12, 1826. However, the appointment of a CP could mean the elimination of one or two rural guards, since the jurisdiction of a CP extended to the limits of any commune and thus often included some "countryside" as well.

45. AD Loire-Atlantique, 1M 705, prefect, April 25, 1846.

46. AD Haute-Garonne, 13M 57, 57 bis, 57 ter; F7 9843; in addition to Toulon, Antibes, Brignoles, Cuers, Draguignan, Grasse, Hyères, Lorques, and La Seyne.

47. AD Seine-Maritime, 4M 1, n.d. ("État des villes qui ont obtenu la creation d'un commissariat de police").

48. A decree of 23 fructidor, year 9, had established the salaries of CPs for cities with more than 10,000 inhabitants, whereas salaries for CPs in smaller towns set by the min-istry, on the advice of the prefect, and in principle taking into consideration the wishes of the municipal council. The subsequent decree of March 22, 1813, virtually halved the original salaries for large cities. The law of July 18, 1837, made the salary and office of a CP an obligatory municipal expense, which, for all practical purposes, was already the case.

49. The structure of salaries in Paris was complicated by the creation of a *police de 2e classe* in 1828 by Debelleyme, by decree of July 2.

50. AD Loire-Atlantique, 1M 704, prefect, July 16, 1822; AD Nièvre, M 1306, dossier Jules Gourdel.

51. Suzanne, CP in Blois, was lodged in the *mairie*. In Paris during the July Monarchy, the CPs lived in or adjacent to their offices (Jean Tulard, *La Préfecture de police sous la Monarchie de Juillet* [Paris, 1964], pp. 58–59, n. 21).

52. F7 9870, municipal council *extrait*, November 16, 1826.

53. AD Var, 6M 8/1, CP Cartier, July 11, 1834.

54. AD Isère, 56M 7, procureur général, December 18, and mayor, December 23, 1816.

55. F7 9870. Versailles received a fourth CP in 1840.

56. F7 9859; F7 9843; F7 9864; AD Loire-Atlantique, 1M 704, Int., August 11, 1832.

57. AD Indre-et-Loire, 4M 7, undated letter (May 1844).

58. F7 9843; AD Morbihan, M 637; F7 9851.

59. AD Haute-Garonne, 13M 57 ter.

60. AD Vienne, M4 310; AD Haute-Garonne, 13m 57 bis, SP, September 8, 1823; AD Haute-Garonne, 13. M 57 bis; AD Ardèche, 6M 3, municipal council, June 20, 1847.

61. F7 9855

62. In Lyon between 1800 and 1870, 94 percent were married (or were widowed, 6 percent) at the time of their service there; Nugues-Bourchat, *Représentations et pratiques d'une société urbaine,* p. 277.

63. F7 9870, CP of Meaux, Leclerc.

64. AD Vienne, M4 311, Int., December 7, 1843.

65. AD Vienne, M4 310, Int., April 19, 1822. See William M. Reddy, *Invisible*

Code: Honor and Sentiment in Postrevolutionary France, 1814–1848 (Berkeley, 1997), esp. chap. 4.

66. AD Vienne, M4 310, Int., December 6, 1837.

67. AD Corse, 4M 33, letter of SP Calvi, February 23, and Rebora, May 8, 1848.

68. F7 9861[A], prefect of the Oise, August 27, 1829.

69. F7 9855, prefect of the Haute-Loire, September 1, 1826.

70. F7 9845, Ruffin, May 16, 1818, prefect of Corsica, June 10 and August 12, 1818, and CP Meissonnier, August 19, 1829, and October 14, 1830.

71. AD Corse, 4M 168, office of SP, July 23, 1832.

72. F7 9862, letter of CP Gaye, November 29, 1831.

73. Ibid., December 1, 1817, mayor, "Organisation actuelle de la police à Toulouse," and prefect, November 27, 1817.

74. Ibid., mayor, October 21, 1817; *projet de règlement,* n.d.

75. AD Haute-Garonne 13M 57 bis, CP Palisse, August 23, 1819.

76. F7 9866.

77. AD Rhône, 4M 2, lieutenant de police, January 16, 1822.

78. AD Deux-Sèvres, 4M5/5a.

79. AD Seine-Maritime, 4M 1, mayor of Rouen, January 18, 1821.

80. "Manuel de police pour la ville de Lille," par M. Houzé, CP à Lille (1844 and revised and republished in 1857).

81. MR 1166 (1824). Near Caen, soon to be within a couple of hours from Paris by train, when Pierre Rivière, who had recently slit the throats of three family members, was arrested and interrogated during the July Monarchy, a translator had to be summoned, because he did not really understand French. See Michel Foucault, ed., *Moi, Pierre Rivière, ayant égorgé ma mère, ma soeur et mon frère* (Paris, 1973).

82. MR 1169 (1845) and MR 1226 (1822); MR 1266 (1836). The example from the Loire: "D'où revenez vous comme cela? E do vou ramena como co? Je viens du marché de la ville. Vene dou marcho de ve la vilo. Pourquoi êtes-vous venu si tôt? Perque vous sai ano ta vite. Il y a tant de brigands."

83. F7 9864, prefect of Haut-Rhin, October 12, 1822, and Pechetaux, October 7, 1822.

84. F7 9850, mayor of Toulouse, March 8, 1819.

85. F7 9857, prefect of the Lot, April 23, 1816.

86. F7 9846.

87. AD Pyrénées-Orientales, CPs, 1–2, 5 (then in process of being classified into series 4M). See John M. Merriman, *Aux marges de la ville: faubourgs et banlieues en France, 1815–1871* (Paris, 1994), for the plight of one CP during the Second Republic who could not speak Catalan, and yet was expected by the prefect to police the Montagnard-dominated quartier of St. Mathieu.

88. AD Morbihan, M 637, SP Lorient, October 19, 1829. Oddly, the prefect of the Bas-Rhin in 1827 reported that his department had no possibility of conspiracy because ordinary people could not read French and thus were immune to propaganda (F7 6767, "Resumé des rapports . . . sur l'esprit public . . . au commencement de 1827").

89. AD Vienne M4 311, Int., December 11, 1844.

90. AD Loire, 20M 3, April 28, 1849.

91. AD Haute-Garonne, 13M 57, February 1, 1851.

92. F7 9842.

93. F7 9857, prefect of the Manche, May 3, 1827. Their role in the communities they policed stand in sharp contrast with the engineers of the Ponts-et-Chaussées, studied by Daniel Ringrose. The former sought and often succeeded in becoming relatively integrated socially into town through membership in associations and even by marriage (Daniel Ringrose, "Work and Social Presence: French Public Engineers in Nineteenth-Century

Provincial Communities," *History and Technology,* 14 [1998], pp. 293–312). The engineers "produced over time a set of practices and priorities that came to constitute a national style by the early twentieth century," even if their "response to national need is best characterized as decentralized and the product of individual negotiation between the state's agents and regional communities" (Daniel Ringrose, "Organic Origins of a French National Style: Civil Engineers and Watershed Practices in Provincial France," unpublished paper, p. 25).

94. AD Bouches-du-Rhône, 4M 3, commissaire central (CC), March 3, 1849.

95. F7 9841, Andrey, March 7, 1832.

96. AD Haute-Garonne 13M 57 bis, Palisse, August 23, 1819. By 1850–51, in Toulouse, of the six whose place of birth we know, two had been born in the Hérault, one in the Hautes-Pyrénées, one in Le Puy (Haute-Loire), one in Versailles, and one in St. Gaudens.

97. F7 9855, April 20, 1820.

98. F7 9842, prefect of Aveyron, June 10, 1817.

99. AD Loire-Atlantique, 1M 707.

100. AD Vienne M4 311, Bruad, Juy 1, 1835, and Piorry, July 3, 1835.

101. AD Loire, 20M 62, SP January 4, 1831.

102. AD Vienne, M4 310.

103. AD Corse, 4M 2, SP Sartene, June 14, 1836.

104. AD Loire-Atlantique, 1M 704, "réglement conçernant le service actif et sédentaire des gardes-de-ville," mayor Faure, February 26, 1835.

105. AD Nièvre, M 1295, SP, December 13, 1823.

106. A.D Ardèche, 6M 1, mayor of Bourg St. Andéol, January 21, 1829.

107. Alletz referred to "simple agents or *surveillants de la police,* named by the local authority." Agents could not give out or stamp passports.

108. AD Indre-et-Loire, 4M 2, SP Chinon, April 4, 1838.

109. AD Deux-Sèvres, 4M 1.1, March 28, 1823.

110. AD Rhône, 4M 2, "Observations sur le police de Lyon et des communes suburbaines," dated January 1, 1836.

111. F7 9858, prefect of the Meurthe, April 21, 1822.

112. On rare occasions, agents were named to replace CPs who were allowed to be temporarily absent from their duties.

113. AD Nord, M 181/13, mayor, July 29, 1828.

114. AD Vienne, M4 310, August 1830.

115. AD Corse, 4M 168, Santelli's complaints, March 2, and mayor of Ajaccio, March 10, 1832.

116. AD Sarthe, M supp. 396.

117. See AD Vienne M4 310 for responsibilities of the agents of Poitiers.

118. AD Sarthe, M supp. 396 and 400.

119. AD Rhône, 4M 2, mayor, July 2, 1823.

120. Among them, Hippolyte Laviron in Besançon (F7 9846, prefect of the Doubs, March 6 and June 18, 1826).

121. AD Maine-et-Loire, 31M 15, SP, September 7, 16, and 19, 1839.

122. AD Seine-Maritime 4M 3, mayor of Rouen, October 10, 1818 and n.d. (1818).

123. As occurred during a series of strikes in Nantes (AD Loire-Atlantique, 1M 704, mayor of Nantes, September 12, 1836). See also AD Sarthe, M supp. 400, Int., August 6, 1848.

124. AD Doubs, M 819, CP, July 14, 1816.

125. AD Saône-et-Loire, M 105, CP, May 12, 1823; M 111, CP, October 30, 1840.

126. AD Saône-et-Loire, M 109, Int., December 2, prefect, June 4 and December 23, and CP, May 17, 1835; M 111, CP, October 30, 1840; M 112, CP, June 14, 1843.

127. AD Saône-et-Loire, M 110, prefect, August 24, 1836.

128. AD Saône-et-Loire, M 101, Int., December 16, 1817, and February 23, 1818, gendearmerie (gend.), July 9, 1818, prefect of the Rhone, March 2, SP of Chalons, March 13 and September 20, 1818.

129. AD Seine-Maritime, 4M 3, mayor of Rouen, October 10, 1818.

130. AD Bas-Rhin, III M 15, "notes sur la police," 1820.

131. AD Bas-Rhin III M 15, report CC Pungnul, for 1825 and March 18 and 30, September 8, 1825; CP Lille, January 29, 1825; III M 207, decree of March 12, 1823; mayor of Strasbourg, February 9, 1828; F7 9863, mayor, December 6, 1824. On thinking, feeling, and speaking German and French in Alsace, see David G. Troyansky, "Alsatian Knowledge and European Culture," *Francia,* 27/2 (2000), pp. 119–38, esp. pp. 135–36.

132. AD Sarthe, M supp. 400, Int., January 4, 1843.

133. AD Morbihan, M 679.

134. AD Rhône, 4M 2, mayor's decree, December 6, 1833, and CP Bardoz, December 20, 1833.

135. AD Vienne, M4 45, Lachapelle, March 3, 11, 14, 15, April 16, May 22, July 11 and 31, deputy mayor, September 28, 1838; AD Vienne M4 311, letter of Blondeau, January 29, 1838, and mayor of Poitiers, February 8, 1838, mayor of Moulins, June 8, 1838, Int., February 27, 1838.

136. AD Loire-Atlantique M 704, "Réflexions soumises à Monsieur le maire de la ville de Nantes," n.d.; "extrait des régistres des arrêtés de la prefecture de la Loire Infre," June 1820.

137. AD Loire-Atlantique, 1M 704, prefect, February 20 and 27, 1822, CC, February 27, 1839.

138. AD Loire-Atlantique, 1M 704, prefect, n.d. (1831); CC Larralde, July 1, 1838; prefect, June 13, 1840.

Chapter 2

1. CPs named to Lyon over the period 1800–1870 were more likely to be appointed to a post to France's second city while in their forties, although 30.5 percent were under forty years of age, a trend accentuated in the July Monarchy (Alexandre Nugues-Bourchat, *Représentations et pratiques d'une société urbaine: Lyon, 1800–1880* [unpublished doctoral dissertation, Université-Lumière, Lyon 2, 2004], pp. 263–64).

2. Text in APP, D/b 353. The decree of January 13, 1819, suppressing the commissaires généraux placed the "commissaires de police . . . under the immediate authority of the mayors; it is through these officials that they correspond with the prefect, besides specific cases in which the latter asks for direct reports from them." But as we shall see, the authority of mayors over CPs would be increasingly sacrificed to that of prefects. The law of July 18, 1837. made the salary and office of a CP an obligatory municipal expense (which, for all practical purposes, it already was). Article 9 gave the mayor of any commune responsibility for municipal police. But, in fact, the law did not alter the predominant role of central authority (Félix Ponteil, *Les institutions de la France* [Paris, 1970], p. 162). As before, the mayor and the municipal council had to "await the orders of the government," becoming "the arm of executive authority."

3. Clive Emsley, *Policing and its Context: 1750–1870* (London, 1983), pp. 10, 36, 43–33. Richard Cobb places the Parisian CP in the world of the *sans-culottes* during the Revolution. "Rather more may be gathered, both about the assumptions of the repressive authorities, and, especially, about the language and attitudes of the urban *petit peuple,*" he writes, "from the *commissaire de police* of a Paris Section . . . [who was] socially, very close to the *sans-culotte. . . .* His angle of vision was always that of the *sans-culotte*"

(Cobb, *The Police and the People: French Popular Protest [1789–1820]* [New York, 1972]. p. xvii).

4. The backgrounds of commissaires appointed in the Var during the Second Empire points overwhelmingly to a military background (in forty of sixty-seven cases) (Pierre Guiral, "Police et sensibilité française," in Jacques Aubert et al., *L'État et sa police en France [1789–1914]* [Geneva, 1979], p. 167).

5. AD Indre, 4M 21, 3847 bis. In Lyon, the army had provided the previous professional experience for 49 percent of the CPs for whom information was available and who served between 1800 and 1870, followed by municipal administration (34 percent) (Nugues-Bourchat, *Représentations et pratiques d'une société urbaine,* p. 268).

6. On nineteenth-century professions in France, see Jacques Dupaquier and Denis Kessler, eds., *La société française au XIXe siècle: tradition, transition, transformations* (Paris, 1992), esp. pp. 15–16, 19.

7. O'Brien, "Urban Growth and Public Order: The Development of a Modern Police in Paris, 1829–1854," unpublished dissertation, Columbia University, 1973, p. 199.

8. F7 9867, ordinance of October 24, 1815, letter of December 10, 1819.

9. AD Var, 6M 8/2, mayor of Toulon, March 24, 1836.

10. F7 9865, April 15, 1842.

11. AD Nièvre, M 1307, July 12, 1841.

12. F7 9858 prefect of Mayenne, August 18 and 25, 1830.

13. F7 9857, prefect of Maine-et-Loire, July 3, 1824.

14. AD Eure-et-Loire, 63M 3, mayor of Nogent-le-Roi, December 16, 1849.

15. F7 9841, prefect of the Hautes-Alpes, May 21, 1821.

16. F7 9870.

17. F7 9858; he was also accused *vices honteux.*

18. AD Rhône, 4M 27.

19. F7 9847.

20. F7 9868, SP of Sceaux, February 1, 1830. He served the royalists well in the 1827 election November 29, 1815.

21. F7 9845, appointed July 9, 1823; resigned November 21, 1830.

22. Taken from dossiers in Series AN F76693, etc., cited throughout. Terry W. Strieter's study of 607 gendarmes serving during the Second Empire comes up with the following breakdown of social origins: peasants, 47 percent; workers, 27 percent; bourgeois, 14 percent; and military, 12 percent (Strieter, "The Faceless Police of the Second Empire: A Social Profile of the Gendarmes of Mid-Nineteenth-Century France," *French History*, 8, 2 [June 1994], p. 173). He notes that their salaries, though "not exorbitant, they did allow the gendarmes to live better than most peasants or industrial workers." Clive Emsley has studied the dossiers of eighty-four men who served in Paris during the first thirty years of the nineteenth century. He finds that "most of the men who were appointed as *commissaires* had served in some other official capacity before their nomination. Roughly one-half of the sixty or so for whom some biographical details are available had worked for the police before their appointment either in the Prefecture, in the Ministry of Police, in the provinces, or for the Empire. . . . About a quarter were former soldiers, and this was especially noticeable among the *commissaires* of the Restoration, several of whom boasted military careers in the royalist, counter-revolutionary armies. Almost a third appear to have had some form of legal training" ("Policing the Streets of Early Nineteenth-Century Paris," *French History*, 1, 2 [1987], p. 261). See also AD Loire-Atlantique, IM707, list of CPs in service in Nantes, 1834.

23. AD Haute-Garonne, 13M 57 ter.

24. AD Rhône, 4M 27, mayor of Lyon, September 14, 1825. Of the nine CPs, six were married, two were widowers, and no information was provided for the other.

25. AD Jura, M 116.

26. Their counterparts in eighteenth-century Paris "seemed well-off" undoubtedly contributing to contemporary accusations of corruption (Steven Kaplan, "Note sur les commissaires de police au XVIIIe siècle," *Journal d'histoire moderne et contemporaine*, 28 [October–December 1981], pp. 676–77).

27. F7 9857, prefect of the Lot, April 8, 1815.

28. F7 9870.

29. F7 9861 (A).

30. F7 9859.

31. Alan B. Spitzer, "Malicious Memories: Restoration Politics and a Prosopography of Turncoats," *French Historical Studies*, 24, 1 (Winter 2001), p. 37.

32. Including Antoine Martin, whose appointment was confirmed early in 1816, but who subsequently was fired for stealing a watch (F7 9841).

33. F7 9859.

34. F7 9869 (A). See Emsley, "Policing the Streets of Early Nineteenth-Century Paris."

35. F7 9846; he lasted from August 20, 1823, until July 15, 1824, in Saint-Brieuc.

36. F7 9845, Dubreuil, March 19, 1818, and prefect of the Côte d'Or, December 22, 1817, and SP March 6, 1818. Dubreuil may have been selected because of the influence of the mayor, an Ultra, and his own "exaggerated royalist principles" may account for his dismissal in 1822.

37. F7 9846.

38. Emsley, *Policing and Its Context 1750–1870* (London, 1983), p. 93.

39. F7 9866, prefect of police, May 20, 1817.

40. F7 9858.

41. F7 9846; F7 9852, prefect of Hérault, October 10, 1826.

42. AD Rhône, 4M 27, October 19, 1818; at that moment, he seemed to be working as a concierge in the Croix-Rousse.

43. AD Rhône, 4M 27, letter of February 18, 1822. Of Lyon's nine CPs in 1825, a full ten years after the Second Restoration, one had joined forces opposing Bonaparte in 1815 and another had worked for the allies that same year.

44. F7 9864, prefect of the Rhône, note, March 4, 1826.

45. AD Rhône, 4M 27, October 24, 1822.

46. David G. Troyansky, "'I Was Wife and Mother': French Widows Present Themselves to the Ministry of Justice in the Early Nineteenth Century," *Journal of Family History*, 25, 2 (April 2000), p. 203, and "Personal and Institutional Narratives of Aging: a French Historical Case," *Journal of Aging Studies*, 17 (2003), 31–42.

47. Spitzer, "Malicious Memories," p. 37. Spitzer discusses the "weathervanes" (*les girouttes*), "turncoats," as he calls them, who deftly traded their loyalty to the Empire for opportunities under the Restoration. He describes the *Dictionnaire des girouettes* (1815, presumably the work of César de Proisy d'Eppe), which called attention to some obvious examples.

48. David G. Troyansky insists "on the importance of bureaucracy not only for the survival of appropriate historical documents but also for their creation"; see Troyansky's "Aging and Memory in a Bureaucratizing World: A French Historical Experience," in Susannah R. Ottaway, L. A. Botelho, and Katharine Kittredge, *Power and Poverty: Old Age in the Pre-Industrial Path* (Westport, Conn., 2002), p. 16.

49. F7 9866, Boucher, March 22, 1815.

50. F7 9865.

51. F7 9858, de Rochemont April 29, 1823; prefect of Meurthe, May 15, 1819; deputy Vauclisin, April 20, 1823.

52. F7 9848, prefect of the Loire-Inférieure, October 16, 1824; Lelasseux, September 27, 1829.

53. AD Vienne M4 310, prefect of the Vienne, September 28, 1819 and May 21, 1822; SP of Châtellerault, September 5, 1826, and Int., August 16, 1830.

54. AD Vienne, M4 310, prefect of the Vienne, October 18, 1823, August 14 and October 5, 1824.

55. F7 9845.

56. F7 9864.; Schaeffle stood accused of profiting from his position.

57. AD Nièvre, M 1307, prefect of the Saône-et-Loire, April 15, 1841.

58. AD Var 6M 8/2, Henry, January 28, 1833.

59. AD Gard, 6M 30.

60. Quoted by Emsley, *Policing and Its Context,* pp. 143, 149–50.

61. Nugues-Bourchat, *Représentations et pratiques d'une société urbaine:,* p. 294.

62. Louis Canler, *Mémoires,* from Emsley, *Policing and Its Context,* p. 89.

63. APP, D/b 353: "Appréciations générales de la police en France et considérations particulières sur le commissariat, dédié à Monsieur Darcy, sous-secrétaire d'état au ministère de l'intérieur," par M. David, CP de Lyon (February, 1850).

64. AD Loire, 20M 23, SP St. Étienne, May 15, 1838.

65. AD Rhône, 4M 2, including public writers, who had to declare their new address. Nugues-Bourchat, *Représentations et pratiques d'une société urbaine,* p. 603.

66. Hélène L'Heuillot, *Basse politique, haute police: Une approche historique et philosophique de la police* (Paris, 2001), puts a different light on the matter: "La priorité policière est l'exercice complet et illimité du droit de coercion" (p. 108).

67. AD Bouches-du-Rhone 4M 2, mayor of Marseille, July 29, 1817. On rumored plots, see Richard Cobb, *The Police and the People* (New York, 1970).

68. AD Bouches-du-Rhone 4M 3, prefect's assessment of candidate Fassy after the Revolution of 1830, n.d. Yet Arnaud managed to be reappointed after the Revolution of 1830.

69. AD Maine-et-Loire, 31M 15, municipal council report, April 19, 1848.

70. AD Indre-et-Loire, 4M 71, CP report of September 15–30, 1831.

71. MR 1274 (1844).

72. See David G. Troyansky, "Entitlement and Complaint: Ending Careers in Post-Revolutionary France," forthcoming.

73. Guy Thuillier, *Pensions de retraite des fonctionnaires au XIXe siècle* (Paris, 1994) and *Retraites des fonctionnaires: débats et doctrines, 1750–1914* (Paris, 1996); David G. Troyanksy, "'I was Wife and Mother': French Widows Present Themselves to the Ministry of Jutice in the Early Nineteenth Century," *Journal of Family History,* 25, 2 (April 2000), pp. 202–10; "Aging and Memory in a Bureaucratizing World: A French Historical Experience," in Susannah R. Ottaway, L. A. Botelho, and Katharine Kittredge, *Power and Poverty: Old Age in the Pre-Industrial Past* (Westport, Conn., 2000), pp. 15–30 (quote from p. 16); and "Personal and Institutional Narratives of Aging: A French Historical Case," *Journal of Aging Studies,* 17 (2003), pp. 31–42, in which he notes (p. 32) the ambiguity of language over the issue on whether a pension was a favor granted by a generous ruler to reward good work or a right and discusses (pp. 33–34) the 1806 decree. During the eighteenth century, the Fermes générales established a system of *retraites.* In the Consulat, the ministries of war and foreign affairs began a system by which a portion of salaries would be retained for those participating, which Thuillier claims introduced *sans le dire un droit à pension,* at least for fonctionnaires (p. 33). Debates on *caisses de retraites* followed during the Restoration. By 1824, the ministry of finances had seven different caisses (p. 63), which Villèle unified, setting at 5 percent the portion of the salary withheld. The law of June 8, 1853, lasted until 1924. The Falloux Law of March 15, 1850, required that a caisse de retraite be created for the 43,000 *instituteurs* (p. 102), and tax employees also could have one. The new law suppressed all existing caisses de retraites, recognizing that they "have now

only a nominal existence and have a title that lacks exactitude" (p. 103), centralizing those remained within the treasury and imposing the "double rule" of thirty years of service and sixty years of age.

74. F7 9846, prefect of the Doubs, September 18, 1820.

75. F7 9858, SP Reims, April 19, 1821, and Linet, January 16, 1821; AD Loire-Atlantique, 1M 898, letter of mayor, September 25, 1836, responding to the prefect's query as to what kind of pension existed.

76. AD Rhône, 4M 27, *Le Moniteur*, February 16, 1825. The commissaires asked that the decree of 1806 be applied and that sums be withheld from all salaries of CPs by municipal officials.

77. Nugues-Bourchat, *Représentations et pratiques d'une société urbaine,* pp. 277–78, considering CPs from 1800 to 1870: 61 percent less than five years, 17.75 percent five to ten years, 17 percent ten to fifteen years, and just 4.25 percent more than fifteen years. Stays in Lyon were shortest during the July Monarchy and the Second Republic. Most stayed about three years in a specific district.

78. Moreover, Lyon's municipal council, which was virtually at war with the ministry of the interior over control over the police (see chapter 7), added a further condition to the twenty-five years of service in Lyon: henceforth thirty years, or four-fifths of their career had to have been "dans l'enceinte même de cette ville"; 4M 28, mayor, September 14, 1825.

79. AD Rhône, 4M 27, mayor of the Croix-Rousse, August 31, 1823.

80. AD Rhône, 4M 27, mayor, September 14, 1825; AD Bouches-du-Rhône, 4M 3.

81. AD Rhône, 4M 28, mayor, November 14, 1831.

82. F7 9864: letter of the CPs of Orléans, October 10, 1828. They erred in claiming that *commis* and *greffiers* had the automatic right to a pension. The idea of retaining a small part of a salary for a future pension goes back to the Ancien Régime.

83. F7 9869(B), Int., September 15, 1830.

84. AD Loire-Atlantique, mayor of Nantes, September 25, 1836.

85. The decree of October 25, 1806, stated that a CP *could* be awarded a pension after thirty years' service, if his age, infirmities, or illness made it impossible for him to continue, or, in the case of CPs whose post was suppressed, after ten years of service or more (of which five had to be in the police and the rest in other branches of public administration). This paralleled other emerging professions in the public sector. See Thuillier, *Pensions de retraite des fonctionnaires* .

86. AD Loir-et-Cher, 4M 6, Int., June 11, 1845.

87. AD Rhône, 4M 27, prefect, November 28, 1829. Paulin had spent thirty years in the police, but only ten in Lyon; 4M 28, mayor, January 1, 1829. An exception was made, in principle, for a CP injured while in service, but only if he had worked ten years in Lyon. In 1829, the prefect suggested that funds put aside might earn 5 percent interest. The decree of July 4, 1806, specified that a pension could be awarded after twenty-five years of service in the same town. Moreoever, the municipality of Lyon did not consider work undertaken for the prefecture as having been done for the city that paid his salary. F7 9864, letter of Remou, May 16, 1834, who had petitioned the Chamber of Deputies over the issue of the right to a pension for services performed outside of the town which paid a commissaire a pension. One suggestion (besides either the state or the municipality taking charge) was to have a general fund earning interest and require fifteen years' work before its liquidation. The municipal council of Lyon in June 1829 offered to give to the treasury money retained from the salaries of the commissaires so that the state would be responsible with awarding a pension.

88. AD Rhône, 4M 27, mayor, September 14, 1825, prefect, November 28, 1829; 4M 28, mayor January 1, 1829. He first requested his pension from Beaucaire, December 17, 1835; prefect of the Rhone, April 29, 1828; Int. to Comte de St. Aulaire, December 27, 1818.

89. A circular from the minister of the interior dated November 19, 1817, instructed prefects to provide information on the police every six months (AD Haute-Garonne, 13M 57 bis). Thus Nugues-Bourchat writes, "La police faisait partie du quadrillage comme actrice de la surveillance mais aussi comme objet de cette même surveillance"; *Représentations et pratiques d'une société urbaine,* p. 291.

90. Nugues-Bourchat, *Représentations et pratiques d'une société urbaine,* p. 324, based on 103 reports. Clive Emsley has stressed the importance of patronage in the careers of the Parisian police during the Restoration ("Policing the Streets of Early Nineteenth-Century Paris," pp. 257–82).

91. AD Loire-Atlantique, 1M 707, report of March 18, 1837; report of December 1, 1817.

92. AD Loire-Atlantique, 1M 707, mayor, April 6, 1843.

93. AD Loire-Atlantique, 1M 707, report of August 9, 1848.

94. F7 9866.

95. Emsley, "Policing the Streets of Early Nineteenth-Century Paris," p. 263, adding that most who were appointed CP were between thirty and fifty years of age.

96. F7 9841, Int., December 12, 1825, SP, January 20, 1831; F7 9846, prefect, June 18, 1826, and March 6, 1828; AD Haute-Marne, lost *côte,* procureur, December 8, 1849; AD Nièvre, M 1306, mayor of Nevers, July 10, 1820, and December 23, 1840; prefect of the Nièvre, January 16, 1838, and a letter of a tax official (February 15, 1838), complaining that Couderc had been insufficiently punished for having failed in his duties; AD Tarn-et-Garonne, 33M 1.

97. F7 9870.

98. AD Seine-Maritime, 4M 7 and F7 9873. On social networks, see Maurizio Gribaudi, ed., *Espaces, temporalités, stratifications: exercices sur les réseaux sociaux* (Paris, 1998).

99. AD Bas-Rhin 3M 348. Steven Kaplan has suggested that CPs in Paris during the eighteenth century enjoyed remarkable longevity of service in the specific quartiers to which they had been assigned—an average of twelve years ("Note sur les commissaires de police au XVIIIe siècle," p. 682).

100. F7 9866, F7 9852, F7 9848, F7 9842, F7 9858; AD Nièvre, M 1306-07.

101. The St. Gaudens situation was complicated by the fact that Dupuy, who resigned at the beginning of the Second Restoration, still claimed to be the *titulaire,* claiming he had not resigned and had never received official word of his firing, which indeed followed in 1817.

102. F7 9846.

103. AD Aube, M 1184 (1844).

104. AD Seine-Maritime, 4M 7; in Lyon, taking the period 1800–70, 21.5 percent of CPs had been born in the Rhône and 10 percent in Paris (Nugues-Bourchat, *Représentations et pratiques d'une société urbaine,* p. 265).

105. F7 9874, Int. report, December 1827, and AD Loire, 20M 23, subprefect, January 8, 1838, and January 21, 1839; Int., June 4, 1838; prefect of the Loire, June 4, 1838, and September 5, 1839; prefect of the Eure-et-Loire, July 6, 1838.

106. AD Rhône, 4M 28.

107. AD Haute-Garonne, 13M 57 ter, subprefect, January 14, 1850.

108. AD Indre-et-Loire, 4M 7, 1847 report; AD Nièvre, M 1306.

109. See Ronald Aminzade, *Ballots and Barricades: Class Formation and Republican Politics in France, 1830–1871* (Princeton, 1993).

110. F7 9850, prefect of Haute-Garonne, March 19, December 30 and 31, 1816, and January 10, 1817. Pécharmont was replaced in June 1817 despite the mayor's claim of his "pure royalist principles." But with highly placed relatives—his brother was the secretary of the Chambre de Monsieur—he was named to Montpellier in 1822 but did not accept

the post because he did not want to leave his family in Toulouse, and later that year obtained nomination to Toulouse.

111. F7 9850, Rateau, July 20, 1818, mayor of Toulouse, March 8, 1819; Laffite, May 11, 1822; AD Haute-Garonne, 13M 57, "État," January 23, 1818, Int., April 5 and July 28, 1818.

112. F7 9850; AD Haute-Garonne, 13M 57, État des commissaires, March 1, 1815, but comments are from September 12, 1815, thus the Second Restoration; Min. de Police Général, Cte. de Decazes, September 17, 1817, mayor, January 23, 1822, to Laffite, warning him of the coming purge, and "État," March 11, 1822; prefect of Calvados, June 3, 1822.

113. AD Loir-et-Cher, 4M 6, prefect, August 28, 1835, December 24, 1844, and January 6, 1845; CP St. Lary, n.d.; and mayor of Blois, April 2, 1840. On the murder in Blois, see John M. Merriman, *Aux marges de la ville: faubourgs et banlieues en France, 1815–1871* (Paris, 1994), p. 95.

114. For example, CPs were dismissed in 1816, 1822 (when both were fired), 1826, and 1829.

115. AD Indre-et-Loire, 4M 7, CP Chasroy, June 28, 1831.

116. AD Indre-et-Loire, 4M 7, prefect, October 30, 1830; Int., April 22, 1831; February 19, 1832; procureur, March 9, 1832; mayor of Tours, January 1, 1833; Int., July 15, 1833; letter of Chrosciechowki, n.d. (after 1841). Born in 1787, after serving in the army from 1809 to 1823, Painparé had been appointed CP for Amboise after the Revolution of 1830, transferred to Troyes in 1831, and then to Tours in 1833.

117. Tours's population stood at 21,928 in 1828 and reached about 25,000 in 1839, and 33,530 in 1852; MR 1264, reconnaissances militaires, 1828, 1836, 1839, 1840, and 1852.

118. AD Indre-et-Loire, 4M 71, CP reports February and April, 1830.

119. AD Indre-et-Loire, 4M 71, monthly reports, CP Ouest, January–May, June–December 1831.

120. AD Indre-et-Loire, 4M 71.

121. AD Indre-et-Loire, 4M 71, April 4, May 5, and June 5, 1831.

122. AD Indre-et-Loire, 4M 2, CP Cazeaux, April 30, 1832. In 1839, Cazeaux *fils* asked that a permanent military post be established there, arguing that a good number of inhabitants would greet such a move with joy (AD Indre-et-Loire, 4M 7, CP Cazeaux *fils*, November 1, 1839)

123. AD Indre-et-Loire, 4M 7, CP Cazeaux, March 14, 1835.

124. AD Indre-et-Loire, 4M 7, Cazeaux, January 18, 1837.

125. AD Indre-et-Loire, 4M 2, Cazeaux, n.d. (early July Monarchy) .

126. Ibid. Cazeaux noted that no funds were available to hire secret agents to carry out such surveillance. He signed off with, "As for me, I indicated an evil, and am happy to have filled the duty of my conscience, that of a faithful and devoted servant."

127. AD Indre-et-Loire, 4M 7, P.L. Cazeaux, September 2, 1835; AD Haute-Garonne, 13m 57 bis, report in response to circular of December 28, 1850.

128. As with the case of Bruzelin, father and son, in Paris (F7 9866). Not surprisingly, such situations seem to have been far more common in eighteenth-century Paris.

129. AD Indre-et-Loire 4M 7, CP Cazeaux, March 14, 1835, and August 13, 1837. Cazeaux's proposed table of costs gave a total annual cost of 8,100 francs, 100 less than what Tours was then spending, a savings made possible on paper by elminating 400 francs paid to an *inspecteur d'éclairage* and 1,500 francs in *gratifications éventuelles*. Cazeaux père had been suspended for one month in 1835, and survived the minister of the interior's original intention to fire him because of the intervention of the mayor (who resigned over the incident), deputy mayors, and probably the prefect as well; the cause was an affaire involving the escape of the Comte d'Espagne, and Cazeaux stood accused of negligence (Int., May 15, 1835). As he prepared to leave his post, the elder Cazeaux wrote his patron,

the prefect of the Indre-et-Loire, to ask for any kind of recompense, asking the relevant ministers to leave him on the list of "employees who are available to be reassigned, whether in the police or in a prison, or in any other job, and as I have no money at all, you can always count on my great devotion."

130. AD Indre-et-Loire, 4M 7, Int., August 25 and September 25, 1837; resignation of Bertrand Cazeaux, August 13, 1837. It is very natural," he wrote from 23 rue des Blancs manteaux, "that a father think of the future of his son. I would be less affected by the loss of my position if I learned that it would be he who succeeded me. I will not describe his qualities, but I know that you have already demonstrated your confidence in him."

131. AD Indre-et-Loire, 4M 7, prefect, February 15 and December 15, 1840; Int., December 11, 1840; P.-L. Cazeaux, December 8, 1840; prefect of Bouches-du-Rhône, June 20, 1840; CP Painparé, August 28, 1840, claimed that the character of Cazeaux fils was "a mass of dark malice and base perfidy." Bertrand Cazeaux, certainly the cousin of Philippe-Louis Cazeaux and the nephew of Eugène, was appointed CP of St. Gaudens (Haute-Garonne) in 1850. He had spent two years in a seminary before working as an attorney's clerk and then as the secretary to the mayor of Boulogne. He was fired the following year.

132. AD Indre-et-Loire, 4M 7. Delbourg's salary was a whopping 2,400 francs plus 100 francs office expenses.

133. AD Indre-et-Loire, 4M 7, mayor, Febarury 13 and June 6, 1843; Painparé, January 27, 1843, and Legrand, March 7, 1843.

134. AD Indre-et-Loire, 4M 7, municipal council, November 12, 1843; prefect, November 17, 1843, and June 28, 1845, and report on police, 1847. The procureur insisted that the problems of policing in the growing city of 27,000 inhabitants only be ended by putting one of the two CPs in charge as a commissaire-en-chef (AD Indre-et-Loire, 4M 2, procureur, October 30, 1837; he also asked that a *commissaire de police adjoint* be named, thus providing Tours with a third commissaire).

135. AD Indre-et-Loire, 4M 7, Int., March 15, 1848, procureur, October 14, 1848, and prefect, November 22, 1848.

136. AD Indre-et-Loire, 4M 2, mc deliberation, July 8, 1847, and Int., June 20, 1847. In the latter's letter, "l'esprit public et à la police politique" had been crossed out. Despite the mayor's assertion that he called the shots, the commissaire central's authority was spelled out by a letter of the minister of the interior in 1847.

137. AD Indre-et-Loire, 4M 2, "extrait du registre des arrêtés de la mairie de Tours," referring to the decree of July 29, 1850. His salary, thanks to a supplement voted by the municipal council, reached 2,700 francs.

Chapter 3

1. See *La Police et M. Decazes,* a pamphlet just after the assassination, by "Bellemare," a former commissaire général (APP D/b 353); it criticized the police, saying that "avec une police qui, par réputation de vigilance et d'activité" (pp. 16–17). On purges of gendarmes during the same period, see Clive Emsley, *Gendarmes and the State in Nineteenth-Century Europe* (Oxford, 1999), pp. 83ff.

2. Isser Woloch, *The New Regime: Transformations of the French Civic Order, 1789–1820s* (New York, 1994). Alexandre Nugues-Bourchat, *Représentations et pratiques d'une société urbaine: Lyon, 1800–1880,* (unpublished doctoral dissertation, Université-Lumière, Lyon 2, 2004), has looked at 162 assessments of CPs in Lyon, 1800–70: "manque de capacité et d'activité" led the way with 21 percent, followed by "immoralité," 15 percent; "caractère difficile ou faible" and "manque d'instruction," each 13.5 percent; "manque de zèle," 12.5 percent; and "absence de considération publique," 11.5 percent (p. 325).

3. F7 9850; F7 9851, prefect of Gers, January, 1816.

4. Clive Emsley, *Policing and Its Context, 1750–1870* (London, 1983), p. 54; Duc d'Otrante, circular, dated May 24. AD Allier (3)M 433. Of nine CPs serving in the Hérault at the time of Napoleon's return during the 100 Days, the prefects hurriedly named by Bonaparte dismissed three of them (Agde, Béziers, and one in Montpellier). Three others were replaced when the Bourbons returned again. A circular from the minister of the interior dated November 19, 1817, instructed prefects to provide information on the police every six months (AD Haute-Garonne, 13M 57 bis). A circular in 1843 asked for more exactitude in sending information from the prefecture on the CPs (December 7, 1843, AD Marne, 39M 1; AD Allier (3)M 1032c).

5. AD Vienne M4 310, Ginot, July 10, 1815.

6. F7 9845, procureur, March 10, 1819.

7. F7 9867, Leroux, December 10, 1819. The purge followed the ordinance of October 24, 1815.

8. F7 9850. To be sure, politics could be taken as a justification for a firing, when clashes of personality or other factors had intervened, but these cases seem clear.

9. F7 9842, bishop of Carcassonne, September 10, 1823, and Cadas, September 9, 1823.

10. On the White Terror, see Gwyn Lewis, *The Second Vendée: The Continuity of Counter-Revolution in the Department of the Gard, 1789–1815* (Ithaca, 1978), and Brian Fitzpatrick, *Catholic Royalism in the Department of the Gard, 181–1852* (Cambridge, 1983).

11. F7 9843.

12. F7 9852, prefect of Hérault, April 16, 1817.

13. F7 9867, including Gaulthier, January 30, 1819. In Paris, seven of the fourteen CPs appointed in 1816 were still in service six years later (Clive Emsley, "Policing the Streets of Early Nineteenth-Century Paris," *French History*, 1, 2 [1987], p 263).

14. F7 9848, prefect of Finistère, March 1, 1822; David, January 23, February 18, March 14 and 17, April 2, etc., 1817, March 26, 1820.

15. F7 9869(A), procureur général of Rouen, March 8, 1817.

16. F7 9866, "Vincent" and "Bruits publics . . . sur l'inconduite et les prévarications de neuf commissaires de Paris," September 15, 1817.

17. F7 9866, Int., report on CPs, December, 1822; F7 9868, Int., September 11, 1822; F7 9867; and F7 9866, Int., note of November 1823, noting the "bad opinions"of fifteen of the capital's CPs. One who seems, remarkably enough, to have survived the first of these purges was Masson, who had asked rhetorically, "Can France be governed by pigs?" He followed up by boldly announcing, "I am more sure of my position than Louis XVIII of his!"

18. F7 9872, Bellier, April 28, 1818.

19. F7 9852, Arnaud, May 21, and prefect of Hérault, March 26, 1818. Arnaud also stood accused of certain irregularities and arbitrary conduct.

20. F7 9841.

21. F7 9851, Int., August 5, 1822, prefect of the Gironde, August 12, 1822.

22. F7 9858, Retis, February 9, 1822, prefect of the Meurthe-et-Moselle, April 21 and May 6 and 15, 1822.

23. AD Vienne, M4 310, de Gallemont, October 5, 1824, procureur général, October 18, 1823; prefect, September 17 and 22, 1823, and August 14, 1824.

24. F7 9851.

25. For an interesting comparison, see David G. Troyansky, "Personal and Institutional Narratives of Aging: a French Historical Café," *Journal of Aging Studies,* 17 (2003), 31-42 and "'I was Wife and Mother': French Widows Present Themselves to the Ministry of Jutice in the Early Nineteenth Century," *Journal of Family History,* 25, 2 (April 2000), p. 203.

26. F7 9854, December 14, 1817.

27. F7 9843, dossiers Berenguier, Bourguignon, Raymond, Renoux, and Detertre-Desaignement, particularly letter of the prefect of Sarthe, October 20, 1823.

28. F7 9873.

29. David Troyansky, "Entitlement and Complaint: Ending Careers in Post-Revolutionary France," forthcoming.

30. F7 9847, Larivière, April 8, 1822, prefect of the Eure-et-Loire, September 3, 1818, and December 28, 1820.

31. F7 9848, January 1, 1826.

32. F7 9852, note in dossier, April 1822; Prevot, April 26, 1822, and April 29, 1823; mayor of La Rochelle, June 9, 1817.

33. F7 9844; he was dismissed July 23, 1823; May 19, 1823, prefect of Calvados, April 28 and May 30, 1823, subprefect of Falaise, April 18, 1823.l

34. F7 9874, especially mayor, July 15, 1818, note on Arnault, n.d., and Arnault, April 21, 1817.

35. F7 9858, prefect of the Moselle, February 22, 1822.

36. F7 9848, Maistre, December 18, 1824, subprefect, November 30, 1824.

37. F7 9864, prefect of the Rhône, April 3, 1825, and April 16, 1827. To take another example, having served the royalist cause during the Revolution could not keep Pierre Planchenault in his post in 1824; "having good political opinions no longer is sufficient and service suffers because of the incompetence of Planchenault" (F7 9857, prefect of the Maine-et-Loire, July 3, 1824).

38. F7 9872, including prefect of the Tarn-et-Garonne, March 12, 1822, July 26, 1823, and April 27, 1825; David, December 20, 1815, and January 11, 1826, and, particularly, his amazing letter to the Comte d'Artois, December 27, 1821; Pinot de Moira, who was reassigned to Rouen in April 1825, and January 26, 1825.

39. Clive Emsley, *Policing and Its Context, 1750–1870* (London, 1983), p. 34, correctly insists, "Political reliability continued to be important for anyone wishing to be appointed as commissaire throughout the Restoration, while a political *faux pas* could lead to dismissal."

40. F7 9874, report to the king, n.d. (1822), also related by Emsley, *Policing and Its Context,* p. 54.

41. F7 9842. The advent of Debelleyme as prefect of police with the Martignac ministry in 1828 itself led to a minor purge of commissaires considered Ultras, a small echo of the Restoration's first years. Yet the following year, as liberal political opposition to the Polignac government mounted, King Charles X was advised to approve the replacement of six CPs in Paris. In three cases, the report cited suspect political opinions (F7 9867, report to the king, November 1829).

42. F7 9843, prefect of the Bouches-du-Rhône, September 14, 1826, Int., July 26, 1822, and copy of the "alphabet," which was a series of figures made with straight lines and dots.

43. F7 9870, Int., February 19, 1830, and Barral de Baret, June 28, 1828, and March 16, 1830.

44. AD Haute-Garonne, 13M 57 ter.

45. F7 9866, Alletz, October 19, 1820.

46. F7 9844, April 23, 1818.

47. F7 9841, prefect of the Ain, February 27, 1832.

48. F7 9668, prefect of police, January 5 and August 24, 1829.

49. F7 9859, report to the minister of police, April 19, 1815.

50. AD Haute-Garonne, 13M 57, report of May 12, 1810, "Tableau civique," and subprefect, June 26, 1814, May 27, 1815, and mayor, March 15, 1828; Int., October 4 and prefect, October 13, 1820.

51. F7 9668, prefect of police, August 22, 1822.

52. F7 9864, prefect of the Rhône, September 28, 1819, prefect of the Oise, November 29, 1822, and "note" (1826).

53. F7 9856, de Mories, July 30, 1816, and note to prefect of police, March 28, 1819.

54. F7 9847, prefect of the Meuse, January 29, 1816, and procureur, on his behalf, October 14, 1816.

55. F7 9870, petition signed by 102 individuals; Sagot, February 2 and April 17, 1818.

56. F7 9846; he was dismissed July 15, 1824.

57. F7 9846, appointed in year 11 and fired May 30, 1821.

58. F7 9854, Int., March 25, 1830; prefect of the Isère, April 18, 1826; mayor of La Tour de Pin, February 28, 1826.

59. Emsley, *Policing and Its Context,* p. 56.

60. F7 9867, prefect of police, May 20, 1825; Faroux, September 20, 1828.

61. F7 9862, Int., n.d., and mayor of Tarbes, June 7, 1819.

62. AD Var 6M 8/3, Int., March 9, 1830. The pun is that of David Troyanksy.

63. F7 9858.

64. F7 9871, Int., report of June 1824, and prefect of the Deux-Sèvres, June 11, 1824; AD Deux-Sèvres, 4M 5/5a, mayor, May, and Int., May 21, 1824. See Louis Canler's discussion of male prostitution, *Mémoires de Canler, ancien chef du service de sûreté* (Paris, 1986), pp. 316ff.

65. F7 9869(B); Alexis Manuel was dismissed August 14, 1822, Simeon-Mongy appointed the same day and replaced August 20, 1823.

66. F7 9845, including report of May 10, 1816.

67. F7 9867, prefect of police, July 2, 1828.

68. F7 9873, especially prefect of the Var, August 28, 1823.

69. F7 9854, (former) prefect of the Isère, December 24, 1824.

70. AD Indre, M 2551, May 3, 1832.

71. AD Vienne M4 311, Lachapelle, November 26, 1837.

72. F7 9867, Gombeau, August 24, 1829, and August 14, 1830.

73. Ibid., Int., September 21, 1830, and De la Tour, November 9, 1830; mayor, August 5, 1830; Turies, August 9, 12, and 30, 1830.

74. Ibid., État de signalement de MM. Les commissaires de police de la ville de Toulouse, mayor, January 8, 1831.

75. Jean Tulard, *La Préfecture de police sous la Monarchie de Juillet* (Paris, 1964), pp. 56–57.

76. F7 9843; AD Bouches-du-Rhône, 4M 3 contains the relevant correspondence and lists. In Nantes, five of the eight CPs in service in 1834 had been appointed since the July Revolution four years earlier (AD Loire-Atlantique, 1M 707).

77. AD Loir-et-Cher, 1M 90, municipal council, August 14, 1830.

78. The text of circular of October 12, 1830, which can be found in a number of other departmental archives, including Yvelines (4M2 127) and Nièvre (M 1298).

79. F7 9843, prefect of the Bouches-du-Rhône, April 26, 1817.

80. AD Haute-Garonne 13M 57 bis, Palisse, August 23, 1819, "Organisation de la police de Turin."

81. Palis had once been sentenced to hard labor for theft, unfairly in his view.

82. AD Haute-Garonne, 13M 57 ter, Palis, August 11 and 22, September 4, mayor, September 25, 1830; Palis, September 28, 1830; prefect of Doubs, September 6, 1830.

83. F7 9864.

84. F7 9866, Baille, May 18, 1825, and April 29, 1831, written from 4 rue Montmorency; mayor of Rouen, September 18, 1825; Baron Hyde de Neuveile, September 27, 1825, and so on.

85. F7 9870, Leclerc, June 9, 1818, and August 9 and 14, 1830.

86. F7 9845, especially Int., report of July 1823, and prefect of the Corrèze, June 12, 1823; procureur général of Limoges, April 11, 1823.

87. Emsley, *Policing and Its Context,* p. 88.

88. AD Vienne, M4 310, prefect of Vienne, September 9, 1830, and subprefect of Châtellerault, September 14, 1830.

89. AD Vienne, M4 311, prefect of Vienne, January 22, 1831.

90. F7 9842, Murat, June 26, 1832; prefect of the Aude, April 18, 1828.

91. AD Saône-et-Loire, M 111, mayor of Mâcon, January 7, 1840, CP Bouillay, January 3, and prefect January 30, 1840. On the small war between Mâcon and St. Laurent, see John M. Merriman, *The Margins of City Life: Explorations on the French Urban Frontier, 1815–1851* (New York, 1991), pp. 207–9.

92. AD Vienne, M4 308, circulars; AD Allier, (3)M 1032c, Int., May 31, 1848. In May, his successor complained that some commissaires of the new republican government had immediately taken it on themselves to replace CPs. At the same time, none of those replacements effected since April 15 were assumed to be legitimate, unless their fate had been determined at the ministry in Paris, and explanations had to be justified in each case.

93. AD Ardèche 6M 1, SP of Tournon, January 8, 1831.

94. Following the comings and goings of CPs is considerably more difficult during the July Monarchy than in the Restoration, largely because of less systematic information in F7 and in many departmental archives as well.

95. AD Nièvre, M 1307.

Chapter 4

1. Cited at the beginning of Philippe Vigier et al., *Maintien de l'ordre et polices en France et en Europe au XIXe siècle* (Paris, 1987).

2. BB18 1199, procureur général, September 1831. A similar incident occurred in Grenoble on February 11, 1807. A certain Perret had been condemned to death, a convicted murderer and arsonist. The blade stopped just inches above the condemned man's neck, which the executioner then tried to break. The crowd succeeded in freeing the prisoner, at least temporarily; Clifford Harmon, "'Ordinary Passions': Crime in the Isère, 1800–1815," *Consortium on Revolutionary Europe: Selected Papers,* 2002, pp. 330–31.

3. Alexandre Nugues-Bourchat, *Représentations et pratiques d'une société urbaine: Lyon, 1800–1880,* unpublished doctoral dissertation, Université-Lumière, Lyon 2, 2004, p. 68. See Daniel Arasse, *Guillotine and the Terror* (London, 1989). The distinction in English between a "crowd" and a "mob" does not really exist in French, although an adjective can provide such a distinction "une foule furieuse," for example. The concept of and word *crowd* are themselves extremely political.

4. Clive Emsley, *Gendarmes and the State in Nineteenth-Century Europe* (Oxford, 1999), pp. 90–91, 108.

5. See Louise Charles and Richard Tilly, *The Rebellious Century, 1830–1930* (Cambridge, Mass., 1975).

6. Richard Cobb, *The Police and the People: French Popular Protest (1789–1820)* (New York, 1972), pp. 18–20, 37. Thus, Steven Kaplan writes of eighteenth-century Paris, "The commissaires de police subscribed to a politics of social control based on a conception of the social order that at its base was apocalyptic" ("Note sur les commissaires de police au XVIIIe siècle," *Journal d'histoire moderne et contemporaine,* 28 [October–December 1981], p. 679).

7. See David Garrioch, *The Making of Revolutionary Paris* (Berkeley, 2002), p. 119.

8. See Charles Tilly and James Rule, "Political Process in Revolutionary France, 1830–1832," in John M. Merriman, ed., *1830 in France* (New York, 1975).

9. AD Haute-Loire, 6M 81, prefect, May 8, 1832. See Richard Bessel and Clive Emsley, eds., *Patterns of Provocation: Police and Public Disorder* (New York, 2000).

10. AD Rhône, 4M 2, prefect of the Rhône, January 28, 1822. Nugues-Bourchat, *Représentations et pratiques d'une société urbaine,* p. 599: "Along with a basic confrontation between the police and the population corresponded a link that was equally strong which united the Lyonnais to their commissaries de police, a link marked by mutual respect and understanding."

11. AD Rhône, 4M 155, CP Vaché, November 5 and 7, 1822.

12. AD Rhône, 4M 155, mayor of Lyon, January 25, 1828.

13. AD Rhône, mayor, June 2 and 3, 1823, CP June 2, 1823, and chef de poste de pont de la Guillotière, June 2, 1823.

14. AD Rhône, 4M 155, commander of Military Division, March 10, 1837, and mayor, January 26, 1838; mayor, April 12, 1842.

15. Clive Emsley, *Policing and Its Context, 1750–1870* (London, 1983), p. 142.

16. AD Var, 6M 813, prosecutor. March 27. and gend.. March 3, 1839.

17. AD Moselle, 74M 1 bis, police report, August 23 and 24, 1833.

18. See F7 6770, gend., December 31,1829.

19. For example, AD Deux-Sèvres, 4M 11/1, gend., July 27, 1840, relating a banquet in Parthenay. See Pamela Pilbeam, *Republicanism in Nineteenth-Century France, 1814–1871* (Houndsmills, Basingstoke, 1995).

20. Steven Laurence Kaplan, *Provisioning Paris: Merchants and Millers in the Grain and Flour Trade During the Eighteenth Century* (Ithaca, 1984), pp. 23, 27, 29.

21. Emsley, *Policing and Its Context,* p. 10.

22. See Charles Tilly, "Food Supply and Public Order in Modern Europe," in Charles Tilly, ed., *The Formation of National States in Western Europe* (Princeton, 1975). At the market of Alençon after the Revolution of 1830, only consumers and bakers could enter during the first hour. Then, when the bell rang, "outside purchasers" were free to enter, a (temporary) strategy intended to keep the price of grain down (AD Orne, deputy mayor, September 18, 1830).

23. AD Nièvre, M 1307, n.d.

24. See Garrioch, *The Making of Revolutionary Paris,* p. 120; Cynthia A. Bouton, *The Flour War: Gender, Class, and Community in Late Ancien Régime French Society* (University Park, Pa., 1993); Nicolas Bourquinat, *Les grains du désordre: l'état face aux violences frumentaires dans la première moitié du XIXe siècle* (Paris, 2002).

25. AD Sarthe, 78M bis 3, CC March 22, April 25, and May 22, 1847; prosecutor, April 8, 1847.

26. AD Morbihan, M 638, n.d.

27. AD Puy de Dôme, carton number misplaced, June 2–3, 1816; prefect, June 5, 1817, justice of the peace, June 5.

28. Charles Tilly, "How Protest Modernized in France," in William O. Aydelotte, Allan G. Bogue, and Robert William Fogel, eds., *The Dimensions of Quantitative Research in History* (Princeton, 1973) and "The Changing Place of Collective Violence" in Melvin Richter, ed., *Essays in Theory and History* (Cambridge, Mass., 1970).

29. AD Loire-Atlantique, 1M 705, November 2, 1847.

30. AD Somme Mfd 80896, prefect, October 16, 1837, and Int., October 22, 1837.

31. On the butchers of Limoges, see John M. Merriman, *The Red City: Limoges and the French Nineteenth Century* (New York, 1985), chap. 1.

32. AD Calvados, M 2849, CP, November 25, 1815.

33. AD Alpes-de-Haute-Provence, 1M 3, prefect, September 14 and October 4 and 11, 1830.

34. AD Orne, M 1298, prefect of the Orne, February 17, 1836. See Jack Thomas, *Le*

temps des foires: foires et marches dans le Midi toulousain de la fin de l'Ancien Régime à 1914 (Toulouse, 1993).

35. F7 9662, mayor of Bordeaux, October 20 and November 5, 1823.

36. For example, AD Dordogne, 1M 65, Int. October 10, 1829, also in AD Aveyron, 1M 306. In the Third Republic, too, even official festivity had to be authorized. See David G. Troyansky, "Monumental Politics: National History and Local Memory in French *Monuments aux morts* in the department of the Aisne since 1870," *French Historical Studies,* 15, 1 (1987), pp. 121–41 and "Memorializing Saint-Quentin: Monuments, Inaugurations and History in the Third Republic," *French History,* 13, 1 (1999), pp. 48–76.

37. AD Haute-Marne, 69M 4, SP Langres, August 28, 1849.

38. AD Haute-Loire, 5M 72, SP Brioude, October 10, 1849; gend., March 13 and director of tax collection, March 14, 1848; Int., January 17, 1851, and prefect of the Haute-Loire, April 29, 1851.

39. Noted by Pierre-Yves Saunier, "Logiques de l'agrégation: l'agglomération lyonnaise au XIXe siècle," paper presented to seminar "Sociologie des découpages," Institut d'Etudes Politiques de Lyon, 1990, p. 2.

40. F7 9854; F7 9852; AD Vienne M4 311, mayor of Châtellerault, September 5, 1839, SP, January 11 and 30, 1840; Int., February 26, 1840.

41. AD Rhône, 4M 27, prefect, November 28, 1829.

42. AD Cantal, 36M 1, mayor of Aurillac, August 16, 1830.

43. AG E5 2, report of tenth military division, September 20, 1830, and E5 3, prefect of the Yonne, October 16, 1830; D3 131, report of eleventh military division, July 31, 1830.

44. AD Lot, 1M 100, mayor, October 23–29, juge d'instruction, November 3, PG of Agen, March 8, 1832.

45. AD Hérault, 58M 17, SP of Béziers, March 13, 1843. See Maurice Agulhon, *Le Cercle dans la France bourgeoise: 1810–1848, étude d'une mutation de sociabilité* (Paris, 1977).

46. AD Orne, M 1298, CP, November 26, and prefect, December 12, 1833.

47. See AD Hérault, 39M 116.

48. AD Indre-et-Loire, 4M 71, CP Jaume, September 19, 1822.

49. On rumors see François Ploux, *De la bouche à l'oreille* (Paris, 2003), and John Merriman, "On the Loose: The Impact of Rumors and *Mouchards* in the Ardèche during the Second Republic," in Jonathan Sperber, ed., *Europe 1848: Revolution and Reform* (London, 2000).

50. F7 6770, gendarmerie report, December 31, 1829.

51. AD Gironde, 1M 351, CC, May 20, 1835.

52. D Nord, M 184/23, September 24, 1841.

53. See John M. Merriman, *The Agony of the Republic: The Repression of the Left in Revolutionary France, 1848–1851* (New Haven, 1978), pp. 97–101. One could be arrested for wearing red hats and belts.

54. AD Indre-et-Loire, 4M 342, Int., November 21, 1851, and January 2, 1852.

55. AD Isère, 56M 7. See Arlette Farge, *La vie fragile: Violence, pouvoirs et solidarités à Paris au XVIIIe siècle* (Paris, 1986), chap. 2, 1, "À l'atelier."

56. AD Rhône, 4M 2, September 7, 1826, and responses from each arrondissement within Lyon, and the "villes" of Vaise, La Guillotière, and Croix-Rousse.

57. AD Seine-et-Marne, M 10193, prefect of the Seine-et-Marne, September 6, 1830.

58. AD Nord, M 184/17, CC, March 16 and May 7, 1832.

59. See Cobb, *The Police and the People,* pp. 43–44.

60. William H. Sewell, *Work and Revolution in France: The Language of Labor from the Old Regime to 1848* (New York, 1980). For a respectful but blistering critique of Sewell's conclusions, see Lynn A. Hunt and George Sheridan, "Corporatism, Association, and the Language of Labor in France, 1750–1850," *Journal of Modern History,* 58, 4 (1986), pp. 813–44.

61. AD Seine-Maritime, 4M 117, SP Havre, June 7, 1831.

62. AD Vienne, M4 43, Int., April 23, 1835.

63. See AD Loire-Atlantique, 1M 2308, CP Nantes, December 5, 1831; prefect of Loire-Inférieure, September 19, October 27–29, 1833, etc.

64. AD Saône-et-Loire, M 109, n.d. (1834, following the passage of a law on associations).

65. For the repression of voluntary associations during the Second Republic, see Merriman, *The Agony of the Republic,* chap. 10.

66. AD Hérault, 39M 125, prefect, December 5 and 25, 1833.

67. AD Puy-de-Dôme, 10M 137, SP Thiers, April 11, 1818.

68. John M. Merriman, *Aux marges de la ville: faubourgs et banlieues en France, 1815–1871* (Paris, 1994).

69. AD Côte-d'or, 20 M 189, prefect, June 26 and 28, 1848, and CP, June 28, 1848. See W. Scott Haine, *The World of the Paris Café* (Baltimore, 1999), pp. 61–62, and p. 155.

70. AD Côte d'or, 20 M 189, CP June 28, 1848, and AD Ain, 8M 10 2 bis, CP June 29, 1848.

71. AD Indre-et-Loire, 4M 71, deputy mayor of La Riche, August 29, 1822.

72. AD Loire-Atlantique, 1M 704, mayor, January 27, 1837; 1M 705, prefect, November 30, 1846, and commissaire en chef, November 20, 1846; commissaire central Larralde, January 15, 1847, and April 21, 1849; prefect, January 25, 1847; Int., July 2, 1850.

73. MR 1208 (1834 and 1841). See also AD Rhône 4M 155, mayor of Vaise, July 10, 1833, and prefect, July 12, 1833.

74. Bertrand Barère, quoted by William B. Cohen, *Urban Government and the Rise of the French City: Five Municipalities in the Nineteenth Century* (New York, 1998), p. 130.

75. F7 9662, prefect, August 31, 1820.

76. F7 6693, SP Bayonne, March 15, 1823.

77. F7 6693, prefect, April 21, 22, 23, 30, May 2, 7, June 19, 1825; CP Ballay, April 20 and 22; gend., May 5; Int., May 5, 1825; Sheryl Kroen, *Politics and Theater: The Crisis of Legitimacy in Restoration France, 1815–1830* (Berkeley, Calif., 2000). See also Paul Friedland, *Political Actors: Representative Bodies and Theatricality in the Age of the French Revolution* (Ithaca, 2002).

78. F7 6693, prefect, November 1, 1826. See Jeffrey S. Ravel, *The Contested Parterre: Public Theater and French Political Culture, 1680–1791* (Ithaca, 1999).

79. F7 6993, for example, in the Théâtre des Celestins in Lyon, 1828, leading to the arrest of a number of canuts.

80. F7 6993, prefect of the Pyrénées-Orientales, May 21, 1824.

81. F7 6993, SP Boulogne-sur-Mer, March 14, 1825.

82. AD Marne, 51M 11, CP, March 11, 1818. The CP indicated that the actor, Barbaut, had not raped the girl but "permitted himself a certain fondling that was unworthy of a gallant man."

83. F7 6693, gend., June 5 and esp. June 12, 1830, and prefect, June 10, 12, and 21. In Bruxelles, the insurrection that led to Belgian independence began when the audience in the theater poured into the streets, transformed into a revolutionary crowd.

84. AD Seine-et-Marne M 10221, gend., December 16, 1819, and April 6, 1820. SP Fontainebleau, May 24, mayor of Nemours, April 10, gend., April 25, and mayor Fontainebleau, December 21, 1820; SP Meaux, April 9, 1825.

85. AD Seine-et-Marne, M 10221, prefect, December 22 and 29, 1820, and report for January 1823, bishop, January 9, 1824.

86. AD Puy-de-Dôme, M 093, mayor of Clermont, April 2 and 23, 1818, prefect, April 22.

87. For example, AD Seine-et-Marne M 10221, SP Coulommiers, April 26, 1821, and SP Fontainebleau, December 17 and 20, 1820. Yet de Rauzan himself had urged "that the

past be forgotten" during the mission at Fontainebleau in December 1820 (AD Seine-et-Marne, M 10221, mayor of Fontainebleau, December 21, 1820).

88. AD Seine-et-Marne M 10221, prefect, December 17, 1819, and SP Meaux, January 22, 1822, and royal ordinance of April 25, 1821; Int., n.d.; prefect, January 21, 1822; bishop, December 29, 1820.

89. AD Seine-et-Marne, M 10221, SP Coulommiers, March 27; SP Fontainebleau, December 20, 1820.

90. AD Seine-et-Marne, M 10221, expression of the mayor of Fontainebleau, December 21, 1820.

91. AD Marne 47M 21, list of crimes committed in February 1821.

92. AD Saône-et-Loire, M 101, report of M. Bellocq, April 24, 1819; F7 9698, prefect, August 3, 1819.

93. AD Seine-et-Marne, M 10221, December 22 and 29, 1820.

94. See Paul d'Hollander, *Bannière et la rue: les processions dans le centre-ouest au XIXe siècle, 1830–1914* (Limoges, 2003).

95. This brief history is provided by a plaque at the base of the cross.

96. AD Dordogne, 1M 66, SP Sarlat, September 10–12, 14, 18, Vielmont, September 15, 1830, mayor, January 25, 1831, SP, September 26, 1830, prefect, January 28, 1831, mayor, February 11, 1831, Int., February 2, 1831.

97. Nugues-Bourchat, *Représentations et pratiques d'une société urbaine,* pp. 183, 192, emphasizes that official festivals had in part the goal of "educating and disciplining" the people (p. 205). Lyon "posed a difficult task: discipline, civilize, and moralize. It was to be an ordered space, that is to say, a space where ordinary people—considered by elites to be naturally disponed to disorder—could be firmly channeled. The repression of popular games was part of this . . . [if] the smallest group of people on the public way was thus formally prohibited; the police watched for and dispersed any tentative to form a crowd."

98. AG D3 126, mayor of Longwy, July 24, 1829; F7 6779, gend. report of April 17, 1835.

99. Farge, *La vie fragile*, pp. 22–23.

100. AD Creuse 1M 153.

101. AD Hérault 39M 86, prefect, February 2 and 15, 1819, and 39M 90, prefectoral decree of February 11, 1819, and letter of Miquel's brother, February 1.

102. F7 6781, gend. report, July 25, 1837.

103. Charles Tilly, "Charivaris, Repertoires and Urban Politics," in John M. Merriman, ed., *French Cities in the Nineteenth Century* (London, 1981), pp. 73–91.

104. AD Vosges, 10M 1, prefect, August 20, 24, and September 12, 1831.

105. AD Loir-et-Cher, 1M 80, CP Blois, January 20 and 23, 1834; gend., January 23.

106. AD Seine-Maritime, 1M 174, prefect, August 12, and municipal decree, August 15, 1820.

107. AD Corse, 4M 33, CP Sartène, August 8, and SP Sartène, August 21, 1851.

108. AD Hautes-Pyrénées 1M 207, prefect, March 28, 1822.

109. For example, proclamation of the prefect of police, January 25, 1826 (BB18 1134).

110. AD Rhône, 4M 155, mayor Rambaud of Lyon, January 17, 1825.

111. BB18 1135, prosecutor, February 26 and May 9, and procureur général of Aix, May 22, 1826.

112. BB30 362, PG Montpellier, February 27, 1849.

113. See John M. Merriman, *The Margins of City Life: Explorations on the French Urban Frontier, 1848–1851* (New York, 1991), chap. 5.

114. AD Nièvre, M 1307, prefect of the Nièvre, July 12, 1841. See Clive Emsley, "Policing the Streets of Early Nineteenth-Century Paris," *French History*, 1, 2 (1987), pp. 257–82.

115. AD Landes, 1M 98, CP, September 27, 1833, and mayor, September 28, 1833.

116. AD Drôme, M 1297, prefect of the Drôme, June 13, 1829.

117. AD Meuse, 71M 10, p.v. June 22, 1823.

118. AD Dordogne, 1M 66, SP Sarlat, April 6, 1831.

119. See, for example, AD Vienne, M4 43, CP, September 21, 1836.

120. AD Orne, M 1298, CP Alençon, September 29, 1833.

121. AD Meuse, 71M 11, Int., February 6, 1836.

122. AD Loiret, 4M 113, minister of police général, November 24, 1815, and report of May 1816.

123. AD Rhône, 4M 2, prefect of the Rhône, January 28, 1822.

124. AD Rhône, 4M 2, September 7, 1826, and responses from each arrondissement within Lyon, and the "villes" of Vaise, La Guillotière, and Croix-Rousse, dated September 11, 16, 18, 19, and so on.

125. AD Hautes-Pyrénées, 1M 208, Int., n.d. (December 1822).

126. AD Deux-Sèvres, 4M 6, 6, Int., November 13, 1828, recalling ordinance of October 29, 1820.

127. AD Maine-et-Loire, 1M 6/32, mayor, March 25, 1833.

128. AD Maine-et-Loire, 1M 6/32, interrogation of Biard, April 20, 1833; prefect, April 20 and 24 and May 9, 1833; mayor of Angers, April 15, 1833.

129. AD Isère 53M 13, prefect of Isère, November 16, 1830; CP Vienne, November 17, 1830.

130. For example, F7 9662, prefect of Gironde, March 24, 1821.

131. AD Vienne, M4 43, letter, perhaps anonymous, n.d. (1835); CP, September 21, 1839; AD Aude, 1258, report of October 20, 1835.

132. AD Indre, M 2550, prefect, November 26, 1832.

133. AD Landes, 1M 98, prefect of the Landes, December 24, 1839.

134. AD Indre-et-Loire, 4M 71, CP Delisle, August 6, 9, and 23, 1823.

135. AD Sarthe, 78bis 1, Int., November 25, and gend., December 31, 1833; CP, January 2, 1834, gend. report, April 21, 1834, and Int., February 27, 1835.

136. AD Indre, M 2545, prefect of police, n.d. (1826); extract of the civil tribunal of Le Blanc; deputy mayor of St. Gilles, February 24, 1826.

137. AD Haute-Garonne, 4M 046, Delmas, July 20, 22, 1822, prefect, July 23 and 27, and Int., August 6, 1822.

Chapter 5

1. AD Bas Rhin 3M 378, CP canton Nord, July 18, 1847. The law of June 13, 1790, specified that people begging in communes not their own were to be returned home.

2. Article 270 of the Penal Code applied to "dishonorable people [gens sans aveu], who have neither a home nor means of subsistence and who habitually exercise no trade nor profession."

3. See Robert M. Schwartz, *Policing the Poor in Eighteenth-Century France* (Chapel Hill, 1988). See also Charlotte Catherine Wells, *Law and Citizenship in Early Modern France* (Baltimore, 1995); John C. Torpey, *Invention of the Passport: Surveillance, Citizenship, and the State* (New York, 2000); Thomas McStay Adams, *Bureaucrats and Beggars: French Social Policy in the Age of Enlightenment* (New York, 1990); and Olwen Hufton, *The Poor of Eighteenth-Century France, 1750–1789* (Oxford, 1974). David Garrioch has described the tasks of the police of eighteenth-century Paris as "twofold: to keep the city orderly and to keep the social body healthy by removing elements that might harm it, physically or morally: the undeserving poor, able-bodied beggars, vagabonds, thieves and criminals, prostitutes" (*The Making of Revolutionary Paris* [Berkeley, 2002], p. 132).

4. Eugen Weber, *France, Fin-de-Siècle* (Cambridge, Mass., 1986), pp. 176–77: and "Only one category of urban (or semi-urban) centers provided the exception to the almost general rule that condemned locals to dreariness and outsiders to isolation: the spas and holiday resorts which developed at an incredible state throughout the century" (p. 178).

5. By royal ordinance of October 29, 1820.

6. Alexandre Nugues-Bourchat writes, "Each individual had the right to move to a city, on the express condition that the authorities [*le pouvoir*] could observe him" (*Représentations et pratiques d'une société urbaine: Lyon, 1800–1880* [unpublished doctoral dissertation, Université-Lumière, Lyon 2, 2004], p. 185).

7. AD Charente, M 1186, mayor, July 23, 1832.

8. F7 9662, mayor of Bordeaux, May 20, 1823.

9. AD Moselle, 71M 1bis, Int., December 11, 1826.

10. AD Haute-Loire, 5M 62, SP St. Etienne, August 6, 1831.

11. AD Saône-et-Loire, M 117, CP Chalon, March 29, 1851.

12. AD Deux-Sèvres, 4M 6, 6, ct. gend., August 2, 1825.

13. Clive Emsley, *Policing and Its Context, 1750–1870* (London, 1983), p. 86.

14. On the policing of *garnis,* see Daniel Roche, ed., *La ville promise: mobilité et acceuil à Paris (fin xviie–début xixe siècle)* (Paris, 2000), especially chap. 1 (by Vincent Milliot) and chaps. 6 and 7 (by Daniel Roche).

15. AD Isère 53M 13, CP Voiron, May 10, 1818; AD Rhône 4M 455, mayor, October 13, 1818. The civil code stated that an innkeeper or hôtelier, or who ran a garni who lodged for more than twenty-four hours someone who committed a crime and whose presence had not been entered on the register could be responsible for damages he or she committed. Nugues-Bourchat, *Représentations et pratiques d'une société urbaine,* p. 297, notes that police were more tolerant on Sundays and Mondays, perhaps trying to avoid what residents might consider "abusive" arrests.

16. AD Saône-et-Loire M 99, Int., October 28, 1819, and mayor of Mâcon, November 8, 1817.

17. AD Indre-et-Loire 4M 71, CP, August 17, 1822.

18. AD Orne, côte misplaced, Int., October 6, 1826.

19. AD Rhône, 4M 2, mayor of Lyon, July 18, 1833.

20. AD Vosges 10 M 1, "États des voyageurs." On nights later in the same month, five, six, and twenty visitors were counted by the police in Epinal.

21. AD Morbihan, M 643, "État nominatif des voyageurs qui ont circulé dans Vannes dans la journée de . . ."

22. AD Allier, (3)M 567, CP Moulins, February 7 and June 16, 1839, and (3)M 570; AD Haut-Rhine, 4M 267, SP, n.d., for August 24/25, 1833.

23. AD Indre-et-Loire, 4M 71.

24. See, for example, Hufton, *The Poor in Eighteenth-Century France,* and Richard Cobb, "La Montée à Paris" in Richard Cobb, *Paris and its Provinces 1792–1802* (Oxford, 1975).

25. AD Vienne, M4 43.

26. AD Haut-Rhin, 10M 8, CP Mulhouse, May 22, 1826.

27. AD Rhône, 4M 455, CP reports, February 7 and 8, 1823.

28. AD Rhône 4M 455, mayor of Lyon, June 17, 1831. Moreover, anyone who entered a false name for a client could receive a jail sentence ranging between three months and a year.

29. F7 6767, "Resumé des rapports . . . sur l'esprit public . . . au commencement de 1827."

30. MR 1202 (1835).

31. MR 1304 (1844).

32. AD Puy-de-Dôme M 092, SP, February 10, 1821; MR 1282 (1842). See Abel Poitrineau, *Remues d'hommes: essai sur les migrations montagnardes en France au XVIIᵉ et XVIIIᵉ siècles* (Paris, 1983) and Abel Châtelain, *Migrations temporaines des campagnes françaises au XIXᵉ siècle et au début du XXᵉ siècle* (Villeneuve d'Asaq, 1976).

33. Richard Cobb, *The Police and the People* (Oxford, 1970), p. 241.

34. AD Meuse, 71M 10, May 29, 1830. During 1826–30, about 25,000 emigrants passed through (MR 1245, 1832).

35. AD Vosges, 8M 17, prefect July 1, 1817.

36. AD Deux-Sèvres, 4M 15/3.

37. AD Meuse, 71M 10, prefect of the Meuse, February 22, 1823; gend., February 25, 1823; SP Verdun, February 20, 23, 1822, and February 20, 1823, and mayor of Verdun, February 22, 1822.

38. The obligation for workers to carry a livret was reinforced by the laws of April 1, 1831, and December 30, 1834.

39. AD Haut-Rhin, 4M 266, prefect of the Haut-Rhin, August 22, 1825.

40. AD Rhône, 4M 455, Int., March 29, 1822, prefect of the Rhône to prefect Loire-Inférieure, March 24, 1822, interrogation, March 3, 1822, prefect of the Rhône, June 24, 1822.

41. AD Pyrénées-Orientales, 3M1 59, n.d., interrogation of Jacques Marcou; Nugues-Bourchat, *Représentations et pratiques d'une société urbaine*, p. 535.

42. AD Isère, 53M 14, CP Voiron, February 9, and prefect of the Isère, February 14, 1851.

43. AD Aube M 1255, copy of letter of the prefect of Cantal, December 31, 1817, and prefect of the Yonne, December 16, 1817; Int., December 20, 1817.

44. AD Rhône, 4M 455, mayor, February 14, 1822, p.v. of arrest, and prefect, February 16, 1822.

45. AD Meuse, 71M 10, prefect of the Meuse, October 16, and mayor of Bar-le-Duc, November 21, 1822.

46. AD Ardèche 6M 38, mayor of Aubenas, January 19, 1827, and mayor of Villeneuve-de-Berg, December 6, 1820.

47. AD Maine-et-Loire, 34M 1, attestation, March 9, signalement, and gend., July 9, 1831.

48. AD Loire, 2M 19, interrogations of April 17, 18, and 23, 1829.

49. AD Ardèche, 6M 41, prefect Pyrenées-Orientales, March 1830, and SP Largentière, April 3, 1830.

50. AD Puy-de-Dôme, M 0141, prefect, December 6, 1837.

51. AD Deux-Sèvres, 4M6.6, Int., March 4, 1823.

52. AD Marne 30M 14, prefect Meuse, August 11, 1822.

53. AD Rhône, 4M 2, SP Villefranche-sur-Saône, August 14, 1819.

54. See, among others, Hufton, *The Poor of Eighteenth-Century France,* Richard Cobb, "*La bande juive*," in Cobb, *Paris and its Provinces*, pp. 142–93; Michel Vovelle, *Ville et campagne au 18e siècle: Chartres et la Beauce* (Paris, 1980); and Howard Brown, "Tips, Traps and Tropes: Police Work in Post-Revolutionary Paris," p. 10. Brown suggests that the success of stopping such bands during the Directory reflected improvements in policing.

55. AD Maine-et-Loire, 34M 1, attestation March 9, signalement, and gend., July 9, 1831.

56. AD Haute-Loire, 5M 62, prefect, October 3, 1833.

57. AD Rhône, 4M 155, prefect, May 9, 1834.

58. AD Puy-de-Dôme, M 095, "liste et signalement," 1820, and mayor of Clermont, August 13, 1820.

59. AD Moselle, 69M 1bis, Int., September 22, 1843.

60. F7 9640, prefect of Charente, December 31, 1817.

61. On the eighteenth century, see David Garrioch, *The Making of Revolutionary Paris* (Berkeley, 2002), pp. 43, 55.

62. By this law, indigents carrying passports could receive fifteen centimes per day and were permitted to beg if they had a certificat d'indigence, providing they did so within their canton of residence and could not work.

63. Law of March 28, 1792, and article 6 of the law of 10 vendémiaire, year 4.

64. AD Isère 53M 13, CP Voiron, February 26, 1818.

65. See, for example, AD Isère, 53M 13, PG Grenoble, February 5, 1818.

66. AD Vienne, M4 42. Whoever added up the figures in 1848 somehow came up with 1,931; part of the mistake came from counting 430 for 1847 (a figure that, given the distress of the year, is not impossible).

67. F7 6767, "Relève des rapports des préfets dont les départements paraissent être dans une situation fâcheuse, par suite de l'élévation du prix des subsistances pendant la saison rigoreuse."

68. AD Morbihan, M 679, mayor of Palais, November 27, 1831.

69. AD Bas-Rhin, 3M 380, report of May 4, 1843; 3M 378 and 10M 33, "état des mendiants, indigents, aliénés, sourds-muets, aveugles, et enfants trouvés," 1847.

70. AD Lot, 4M 43, prefect of the Lot, April 17, 1840; 6M 30, 1850 national survey.

71. AD Eure-et-Loire, 1M 18, mayor, July 16 and 17, 1830.

72. AD Côtes-d'Armor, SP Guingamp, November 20,1849.

73. For example, AD Morbihan, M 638, prefectoral decree, January 20, 1831 (articles 270, 274, 275, and 276 of the *Code pénal*), and AD Haut-Rhin, 4M 249, prefect, September 21, 1848, using the same definition of a vagabond; see AD Gard, 6M 30, 1850 survey.

74. AD Nord M 199/5, prefect of the Nord, February 24, 1817.

75. AD Hérault, 39M 87, decree of mayor, July 7, 1818, and prefect, July 18, 1817.

76. AD Saone-et-Loire M 102, prefect, July 19, 1820.

77. AD Saône-et-Loire, M 1791, prefect, August 7, 1840, SP of Autun, July 13, and SP of Charolles, July 8, mayor of Chalon, July 7, mayor of Cluny, July 3, SP Louhans, June 29, mayor of Mâcon, July 30, and mayor of Tournus, April 9. The prefect of the Saône-et-Loire claimed that in Autun (population 10,435) there were 1,500 impoverished people and 500 to 600 beggars. The departmental report of August 13, 1840, divided beggars between "habitual" beggars and those who "beg on some days" in Autun (40/150), Chalon (60/200), Charolles (20/70), Louhans (25/60), Tournus (30/70), Mâcon (80/120), and Cluny (20/50); the numbers helped were 1,600, 1,800, 360, 90, 560, 680, and 120 respectively.

78. National survey, 1850, results found in AD Gard 6M 309.

79. AD Morbihan, M 638, n.d. (1831).

80. Emilie Carles, *A Life of Her Own: The Transformation of a Countrywoman in Twentieth-Century France* (New York, 1992), translation of *Une soupe aux herbes sauvages* (Paris, 1977).

81. AD Hautes-Alpes, 1M 21, prefect reporting on his tour of the département, 1823.

82. AD Aube M 1257, mayor of Troyes, May 4, 1821.

83. AD Rhône, 4M 1, mayor, 14, 1822.

84. AD Nièvre, M 1295, prefect, June 11, 1818.

85. AD Marne, 72M 2, petition dated September 15, 1816. An accompanying note said that six children should between them be able to take care of their parents, and the old man and his wife were left on their own.

86. 6M 30, survey of 1850; MR 1177 (1826). Only seventeen départements had taken active local measures, and another nine had at least formally studied the problem.

87. AD Saône-et-Loire, M 1791.

88. AD Indre-et-Loire, 4M 71, October 8, 1822.

89. AD Loir-et-Cher, 4M 150, prefect, October 31, 1829. AD Gard, 6M 30.

90. AD Isère, 53M 14, CP Grenoble, March 30, 1848.

91. AD Rhône, 4M 455, mayor, February 12 and 19, 1822.

92. AD Eure, 1M 230, prefect May 2, 1828, citing the laws of August 8, 1790; July 22, August 3, and November 29, 1791; and of 10 vendémiaire and 27 germinal, year 4.

93. AD Aube, M 1286, n.d.

94. AD Loire-Atlantique, 1M 2308.

95. AD Haute-Marne, 61M 14, prefect of the Aude, October 10, 1811; SP of Langres, April 6, 1812, April 20, 1820, and March 21, 1829; prefect of the Haute-Marne, March 20 and May 25, 1812, May 5, 1815, September 12, 1817, August 18, 1818, and March 7, 1822; procureur of Chaumont, May 23 and September 9, 1817, and July 24, 1819; Léonard, June 20, 1817; mayor of St. Dizier, January 1 and May 13, 1823.

96. AD Indre-et-Loire, 4M 71, interrogation, February 20, 1823. See Hufton, *The Poor of Eighteenth-Century France.*

97. AD Allier, M 293, including May 3, 1821.

98. AD Eure, 1M 228, Int., August 24, 1826.

99. AD Indre-et-Loire, 4M 136, procureur, September 28, 1849.

100. AD Indre-et-Loire, 4M 136, prefect of the Loir-et-Cher, November 15, 1841, and March 21, 1842.

101. AD Vienne, M4 43, prefect of Vienne, April 24, 1835; prefect Charente, September 5, 1835.

102. AD Rhône 4M 455, mayor of Lyon, December 27, 1822, prefect of the Rhône, January 30, 1823, CP report, January 23, 1823.

103. AD Corse, 4M 165, prefect, June 5, 1827; prefect, n.d. [1827].

104. AD Indre-et-Loire, 4M 71, CP report of February 8, 1830.

105. AD Nord, M 184/25, CC Lille, July 19 and August 3, 1843.

106. AD Vosges, 8M 18, SP, October 17, 1848.

Chapter 6

1. AD Indre-et-Loire, 4M 7, Roussin's report, October 12, and prosecutor, October 14, 1848. To be sure, the story of the Lescalverts relates closely to questions of family patriarchy, leading one to ask if the state enforces the "male gaze" and policing of women, including that by the husband, who was not controlling his wife. Issues of gender here are important and complicated. I will leave it to others to investigate the Foucauldian policing of family.

2. David Garrioch, *Neighbourhood and Community in Paris, 1740–1790* (New York, 1986), p. x. See the excellent discussion of attitudes toward vagrants in Alexandre Nugues-Bourchat, *Représentations et pratiques d'une société urbaine: Lyon, 1800–1880,* unpublished doctoral dissertation, Université-Lumière, Lyon 2, 2004.

3. W. Scott Haine, *The World of the Paris Café* (Baltimore, 1999), p. 154. See Arlette Farge, *Vivre dans la rue à Paris au XVIIIe siècle* (Paris, 1979).

4. Nugues-Bourchat, *Représentations et pratiques d'une société urbaine,* p. 168. He goes on, "Les chiens, les ambulants, les vagabonds et les mendiants furent désignés comme des anomalies à supprimer" (p. 217).

5. Jennifer Davis, "Urban Policy and Its Objects: Compative Themes in England and France in the Second Half of the Nineteenth Century," in Clive Emsley and Barbara Weinberger, eds., *Policing Western Europe: Politics, Professionalism, and Public Order, 1850–1940* (New York, 1991), p. 2. Nugues-Bourchat, *Représentations et pratiques d'une société urbaine,* p. 102: "In the eyes of the authorities, *les mauvais sujets* had no legitimacy."

6. Nugues-Bourchat, *Représentations et pratiques d'une société urbaine,* p. 184.

7. Quoted by Clive Emsley, *Policing and Its Context 1750–1870* (London, 1983), p. 87. Louis Chevalier's *Laboring Classes and Dangerous Classes in Paris during the First Half of the Nineteenth Century* (London, 1973, first published in 1959) is now generally recognized as brilliantly presenting elite views of ordinary people. However, decades of work by social historians have cast great doubt on the "uprooting" hypothesis that views popular protest and indeed revolution as extensions of criminality.

8. Louis Canler, *Mémoires de Canler, ancien chef du service de sûreté* (with an introduction by Jacques Brenner) (Paris, 1986), pp. 117ff.

9. Claude Châtelard, *Crime et criminalité dans l'arrondissement de St. Étienne au XIXème siècle* (St. Étienne, 1981). Châtelard's takes the years 1841–43, 1859–61, 1882, and 1905. He concludes that the former period marked the beginning of a marked "progression of criminality" that reflected the development of "a criminal mentality in the great industrial valley, particularly in its most populated town, St. Étienne." During the July Monarchy, he argues (pp. 14–15, 25, 31, 37, 42, 45, 273–86), crimes were not often violent (in contrast to the end of the century), and murder was rare (the single murder in 1842 was in Firminy, though he seems to have missed the one in Rochetaille mentioned in the text) and invariably associated with drinking. Most crimes were against property, particularly the theft of food during the first part of the century. By his view, immigration pushed the level of criminality even higher.

10. MR 1233 (1843).

11. AD Indre-et-Loire, 4M 71, CP Cazeaux, January 11, 1831.

12. Such as a special Mass for the army held in Lyon in 1824 (AD Rhône, 4M 2, mayor of Lyon, May 13, 1824).

13. AD Aube, M 1286, mayor of Troyes, December 12, 1819.

14. AD Moselle 71M 1bis, prefect, January 20, 1843.

15. AD Bouches-du-Rhône, 4M 1, CC, November 4, 1848.

16. AD Gers, 1M 42, prefect, April 30, 1819; 1M 38, prefect, February 13, and mayor, March 8, police report, April 25, 1832, etc.

17. AD Isère, 53M 13.

18. AD Seine-et-Marne, M10139, December 8, 1821.

19. AD Seine-et-Marne, M 10139, November 30, July 29, and June 13, 1821.

20. AD Vosges, 8M 17, SP Mirecourt, June 9, SP Neufchâteau, June 23, and prefect, July 1, 1819; police reports, 1821–22.

21. AD Isère, 53M 13.

22. AD Nord, 184M/28.

23. AD Seine-Maritime, 4M 116, SP, August 18, 1824.

24. AD Indre-et-Loire, 4M 71, reports, 1824.

25. AD Indre-et-Loire, 4M 71, January 11, 1831: 34 *billets d'hôpital,* 21 various complaints, 20 requests for information, 14 miscellaneous requests, 11 procès-verbaux, 7 various petitions or opinions offered, 7 certificates to join the army as a replacement, 5 complaints about prostitution, 4 certificates to join the army, 4 excessive nighttime noise, 4 cases of breach of trust or swindling, 4 thefts, 3 fires, 3 verification of weights and measures, 2 inspections of the residences of paroled convict, 2 gatherings of compagnons, 2 missing children, 2 inspections of bakers' shops, 2 indigents' certificates, 2 missing objects located, 1 sudden death, 1 complaint against a usurer, 1 attempted rape, 1 drowning, 1 burial of a Jew, 1 kidnapping of a girl, and 1 dog bite.

26. William Sewell Jr. demonstrates that immigrants were more likely to commit crimes in Marseille than those born there: See "Social Mobility in a Nineteenth-Century European City: Some Findings and Implications," *Journal of Interdisciplinary History,* 7, 2 (1976), pp. 217–33 and *Structure and Mobility: The Men and Women of Marseille, 1820–1870*

(Paris, 1985). See also William H. Cohen, *Urban Government and the Rise of the French City: Five Municipalities in the Nineteenth Century* (New York, 1998), p. 83.

27. AD Ardèche, 6M 38, CP Madier, February 1, 1827.

28. Richard Cobb, *The Police and the People* (Oxford, 1970), p. 38.

29. AD Indre-et-Loire, 4M 7, CP p.v., September 39 and October 11, 1831; AD Vosges, 10M 1, mayor April 4, 1832.

30. AD Hautes-Alpes, 4M 19, CP Briann, February 11, 1818.

31. AD Doubs, M 3091; M 989, police report, August 17/18, 1824.

32. AD Vienne, M4 299, anonymous letter of December 31, 1850, signed "votre dévoué serviteur" and n.n., n.d.

33. F7 9662.

34. F7 9662, prefect of Gironde, February 21, 1822. At the end of 1833, Bordeaux's three jails held 230 people (AD Gironde, 1M 351, 1833).

35. F7 9662, prefect of Gironde, January 30, 1827 and April 3, 1830.

36. AD Isère, 53M 12, "Journal des opérations du commissaire de police de Vienne pendant le mois d'avril 1818."

37. AD Vaucluse, 1M 746, "crimes, délits et événemens," 1823, and bulletin des evenemens, 1826 and 1827.

38. AD Rhône, 4M 155, lieutenant of police, December 10, 1817; commander of gendarmerie, December 12, and mayor of Lyon, December 11, 1817.

39. AD Rhône, 4M 2, CP Rousset, February 20, 1822.

40. AD Rhône, 4M 78.

41. MR 1220 (1825).

42. AD Deux-Sèvres, 4M 15/2B, gend., September 17, 1824.

43. AD Indre-et-Loire, 4M 72, CP, January 24, 1843.

44. AD Sarthe, 4M 48, CP, December 14, 1837, and April 6, 1845.

45. AD Haute-Loire, 5M 62, prefect, August 14, 1832, and November 17, 1831.

46. AD Vienne, M4 42, gend., September 1, 1832.

47. AD Loire, 20M 10, mayor of St. Étienne, November 6, 1828.

48. AD Loire, 21M 11, prefect, August 1 and 28, 1833, and mayor, August 19, 1833.

49. AD Loire, 2M 19, interrogation, May 25, and letter of mayor of St. Chamond, May 27, 1829.

50. AD Loire, 2M 19, police, May 18/19, 1834.

51. AD Loire, 10M 30, CC, April 7/8 and November 13 and 19, 1849.

52. AD Loire, 21M 20, CP, April 29/30 and August 2, 1840.

53. AD Loire, 21M 13, CC, February 19, 1841.

54. Châtelard, *Crime et criminalité dans l'arrondissement de St. Étienne,* p. 283.

55. F7 9868, for example CP J. M. Tirel, a former avocat.

56. Alain Corbin, *Women for Hire: Prostitution and Sexuality in France after 1850* (Cambridge, Mass., 1990) and Jill Harsin, *Policing Prostitution in Nineteenth-Century Paris* (Princeton, 1985). See Canler, *Mémoires,* pp. 340–68.

57. AD Haute-Saône, 35M 2, CP, January 6, 1829.

58. AD Ardèche, 6M 38, February 20 and September 8, 1827.

59. See John M. Merriman, *Aux marges de la ville: faubourgs et banlieues en France, 1815–1871* (Paris, 1994), chap. 3.

60. AD Nord , M 184/11, petition, May 7, and mayor, May, 18, 1827.

61. AD Vienne, M4 299, n.n., n.d.

62. AD Rhône, 4M 2; in 1825, 180 and in 1827 483 prostitutes were bound over to the hospice of Antiquaille.

63. AD Rhône, 4M 2, "Projet de réformes dans la police," by Prat, commissaire central.

64. AD Puy-de-Dôme, M 091; F7 9689, CP, June 20, 1818.

65. AD Loir-et-Cher, 4M 214, mayor, n.d., 4M 6, prefect, August 28, 1835.

66. AD Lot 1M 2+, prefect, December 18, 1819, and 4M 38, mayor of Gourdon, May 20, 1820.

67. AD Puy-de-Dôme, M 090, prefect, September 11, 1840.

68. AD Doubs, M 3092, mayor of Besançon, July 26, 1823.

69. AD Hautes-Alpes, 1M 21, prefect of Hautes-Alpes, March 24, 1821.

70. AD Meuse, 71M 9, prefect of Meuse, June 30, July 7, and April 21, 1817.

71. AD Rhône, 4M 455, mayor Rambaud, November 5, 1821, and January 26, August 13, 1822, and prefect of Isère, May 25, 1822.

72. AD Vienne, M4 50, mayor, December 16, 1846.

73. AD Rhône, 4M 2, procureur, September 27, SP Villefranche, December 17, and CP Vaché, September 30, 1822. In fact, mayors and deputy mayors had the right to arrest people and, in doing so, served as auxiliaries of the judicial authorities, but a procès-verbal would be required, but the subprefect argued that in this case that the mayor's authority over prostitution extended only to the regulations of "administrative police," not to crimes and misdemeanors.

74. AD Calvados, M 2849, CP third arrondissement, October 26, 1815.

75. Patricia O'Brien, "Urban Growth and Public Order: The Development of a Modern Police in Paris, 1829–1854," unpublished dissertation, Columbia University, 1973, p. 196.

76. AD Nord, M 184/27, mayor, June 11, 1845; CP, May 25, 1845, and procureur, June 10, 1845.

77. AD Nièvre, M 1307, Int., August 31, 1843, and prefect of the Nièvre, October 7, 1843.

78. AD Charente M 784, SP, September 9, 1843; AD Aube, M 1286, prefect's decree, July 2, 1818, banning games such as "à la blanche, tourniquet, chevilles, passe-dix, biribi, routelle, petits-paquets, loterie" among others. The decree also banned those "who make their living by predictions or prognostications, or by interpreting dreams."

79. AD Tarn-et-Garonne, 33M 1, prefect, September 3, 1838, and February 7, 1850; urban letter, September 3, 1830

80. AD Tarn-et-Garonne, 33M 1, Mairel, August 15, 1834, and May 29, 1836; mayor, May 30, 1835; prefect, July 24, 1834, January 17, April 8, 1837; Int., March 17, 1834.

81. AD Gironde, 1M 347, mayor of Bordeaux, March 25, 1818.

82. AD Gironde, IM 347, prefect of Gironde, November 14, 1817, and August 1, 1818.

83. AD Indre-et-Loire, 4M 71, CP, August 8 and 14, 1825. The list of masters to be boycotted included one in Nantes, demonstrating the links between compagnons in the two towns. On the compagnonnage, see Cynthia M. Truant, *The Rites of Labor: Brotherhoods of Compagnonnage in Old and New Regime France* (Ithaca, 1994).

84. AD Indre-et-Loire, 4M 71, CP, March 10 and May 19, 1826.

85. AD Loire-Atlantique, 1M 2307, "Rivière," December 24, 1824, mayor, May 6 and July 17, 1824, January 11, 1825, January 19, 1824, prefect, July 18, 1824.

86. AD Loire-Atlantique, 1M 705, November 2, 1847.

87. AD Loire-Atlantique, 1M 514, prefect, September 20, CP, September 1–10, 15/16, etc., 1836; 1M 2308, July 16, 1833, September 20, 1834, September 10, 14–16, 1836, etc., including January 4 and February 8, 1847.

88. AD Vaucluse, 1M 755, CP, July 5 and 29, 1819; municipal ordinance of June 3, 1820.

89. AD Vaucluse, 1M 755, CP, September 27, November 24, 182,3 and January 27, 1824; mayor, August 4, 1837; gend., May 22, Int., May, and CP, June 3, 1846.

90. See William Sewell, *Work and Revolution in France: The Language of Labor from*

the Old Regime to 1848 (New York, 1980). Brawls among compagnons undercuts some of Sewell's argument that the language of labor led to working-class consciousness in the early years of the 1830s. For a critique of Sewell's important book, see Lynn A. Hunt and George Sheridan, "Corporatism, Association, and the Language of Labor in France, 1750–1850," *Journal of Modern History*, 58, 4 (1986), pp. 813–44.

91. See AD Haute-Saône, 14M 8, SP Gray, May 28, 1848, and Merriman, *Aux marges de la ville*.

92. BB18 1107, procureur général of Paris, June 12, 1824.

93. AD Seine-Maritime, 4M 116, SP, July 1 and 3, 1823, and 4M 117; 4M 116, SPH, date obliterated, (1824 or 1827).

94. AD Oise, nonclassfied, 1817; AD Aube, M 1257, mayor, May 2, and prefect, February 2 and June 3, 1835; AD Indre-et-Loire, 4M 136, report of August 1, 1842.

95. John M. Merriman, *The Agony of the Republic: The Repression of the Left in Revolutionary France, 1848–1851* (New Haven, 1978), esp. pp. 96–101.

96. Haine, *The World of the Paris Café*, p. 155.

97. AD Loire-Atlantique, 1M 898, prefect, March 20, 1851. See Haine, *The World of the Paris Café*, esp. pp. 10–17, 28. Haine, whose study is principally concerned with the second half of the century, argues that during the earlier period the police were taken to be lax in the policing of Parisian cafés (p. 5).

98. "A vital part of the policeman's job was to try to establish a good relationship with the café owners on his beat. This relationship became both possible and necessary after the 1820s, with the rise of the modern counter as a site of sociability, an innovation that made the nineteenth-century café owner a much more integral part of the neighborhood than his or her eighteenth-century predecessor" (Haine, *The World of the Paris Café*, p. 27).

99. AD Drôme, M 1558, petition, March 1828, and mayor, March 29, 1828.

100. AD Rhône, 4M 455, mayor of Croix-Rousse, March 19, 1850.

101. AD Deux-Sèvres, 4M 6.6, prefect of Deux-Sèvres, February 5, 1823; AD Rhône, 4M 455, n.d. That this was no small task emerges from the thirty-one contraventions written up in Lyon on February 5, 1824, eleven on March 8, and six on Pentecost, June 6 (AD Rhône 4M 155, "États des contraventions à l'observation des dimanches et fêtes" and 4M 455, CP Halle aux blés, January 31, 1822. Comestibles could be sold inside shops, with the shutters open, but without any external signs).

102. Quoted by Howard C. Payne, *The Police State of Louis Napoleon Bonaparte* (Seattle, 1966), p. 211.

103. AD Ardèche, 5M 10, CP, November 23, 1849.

104. AD Tarn-et-Garonne, 33 M 1, n.d..

105. AD Hautes-Alpes, 4M 19, prefect, June 13, 1837.

106. For example, AD Loire-Atlantique, 1M 704, mayor of Nantes, December 31, 1832.

107. MR 1233 (1842); for example, AD Puy-de-Dôme, M 088; AD Haute-Saône, 21M 1, March 6, 1819.

108. MR 1168, 1820.

109. MR 1201, 1827.

110. F7 9870, prefect of the Seine-et-Oise, August 23, 1821; Int., October 22, 1826 and October 20, 1826.

111. AD Vienne, M4 39, prefect, January 8, 1825.

112. AD Haute-Garaonne, 4M 046, mayor of Toulouse, January 15, 1817, and Int., December 5 and 8, 1817.

113. F7 9689, CP Abel, July 6, 1820.

114. MR 1234 bis (1837).

115. AD Var, 6M 8/2, dated June 11, 1836; accused of weakness, despite having drawn up 197 procès-verbaux during his eight months of service.

116. AD Corse, 4M 168, CP Martinelli, n.d. (early July Monarchy).

117. AD Corse, 4M 167, CP Bastia, report of February 22, 1821.

118. *Michelin, Corse*, (Clermont-Ferrand, 1981), p. 141.

119. AD Corse, 4M 74, dir. général, August 18, 1820.

120. AD Corse, 4M 165, CP, April 5, 1824.

121. F7 9873, prefect of Corse, August 1, 1834, and November 14, 1835.

122. AD Oise, M, nonclassified (at least in 1987), reports of February 2 and May 27, 1835.

123. AD Indre-et-Loire, 4M 72, CP Chaumont, October 7, 1843.

124. AD Indre-et-Loire, 4M 72, CP, January 9, 1844.

125. AD Haute-Garonne, 4M 046, mayor, April 13, 1829.

126. AD Hautes-Pyrénées, IM 208, SP Bagnères, May 19, 1827.

127. AD Eure, 1M 168, gend., December 29, 1834.

128. AD Eure-et-Loire, 4M 189, CP report of April 17, 1850; MR 1176 (1822); MR 1168 (1829); MR 1273 (1845); MR 1245 (1835); AD Lot, 1M 153, report of the Commission d'administration, October 8, 1815.

129. AD Landes, 1M 99, police reports, April 23–30, 1850.

130. AD Deux-Sèvres, 4M 6.6, mayor of Niort with CP report, December 14, 1829.

131. AD Vienne, M4 39, CP, October 4, 1826.

132. AD Doubs, M 3092, CP, November 13/14, 1823.

133. AD Rhône, 4M 455, CP, January 3, 1822, and February 24, 1822.

134. AD Indre-et-Loire, 4M 71, n.d. (1826).

135. AD Nord, M 184/13, Int., October 7, 1828.

136. AD Nord, M 183/14, prefect of the Basses-Alpes, April 24, 1829; AD Charente, mayor of Angoulême, June 8, 1845.

137. AD Nord, M 184/14, SP Cambrai, March 31, 1829.

138. AD Ain, 10M 4, CP, October 20, 1843.

139. AD Rhône, 4M 455, mayor, February 13, 1822. Other requests that came to police offices sought information not on people but stolen goods. For example, in 1822 the office of the procureur général in Grenoble sent around a printed letter specifying the size, color, and complete description of pieces of cloth, "vulgarly known as Limoges," that had been stolen with the help of "false keys" (AD Rhône, 4M 455, October 18, 1822).

Chapter 7

1. AD Eure-et-Loire, 1M 18, subprefect of Nogent-et-Rotrou, July 19, 1830; MR 1176 (1822).

2. Félix Ponteil, *Les institutions de la France, 1814–1871* (Paris, 1970), pp. 30–33.

3. Isser Woloch, *The New Regime: Transformations of the French Civic Order, 1789–1820s* (New York, 1994), p. 144. Woloch makes the transformation seem more complete than the case of the police suggests. The law of December 14, 1789, article fifty, recognized functions of municipal authority, but under the surveillance of administrative authorities. The law of 28 pluviôse, year 8, expressly in article one, declared that prefects were alone charged with administration. The original law proposed to give to the mayor the right to name CPs, but the government had refused to accept this proposition. A decree in year 8 formally removed the power of appointing commissaires from the municipalities.

4. AD Eure-et-Loire, 1M 18, Int., May 31, 1830; mayor of Chartres, July 17, 1830; mayor of Châteaudun, n.d., January 1830.

5. See, for example, John M. Merriman, *The Red City: Limoges and the French Nineteenth Century* (New York, 1985), chap. 2.

6. Le Mans was thus typical of French towns: "the situation was hardly modified during the period of 1815 and 1848: centralization was definitively established and the action of the prefects was very preponderant" (François Dornic, ed., *Histoire du Mans* [Toulouse, 1975], p. 249).

7. Indeed in 1837, the minister of the interior wrote to remind all prefects to read the deliberations of municipal councils with particular attention in case they had to be annulled. The law of 28 pluviôse (year 8) had set out the attributions of the municipal councils.

8. AD Dordogne, 1M 67, SP, August 16, 1832.

9. The municipal council had done its homework, basing its case on the laws of December 22, 1789, and March 27, 1791, neither of which forbade public session, and the decrees of January 1 and September 2, 1792, which permitted publicization of proceedings, and the constitution of year 3, which did not forbid either public sessions or their publicization.

10. AD Dordogne, 1M 67, Int., July 23, September 3, and October 8, 1832; mayor of Sarlat, June 29 and July 10 and 28; municipal council deliberations, June 26 and August 13; SP, July 7 and 27, October 6 and 10; prefect, September 14 and 15, 1832; prefect of the Isère, November 9, 1832.

11. A law proposed to the Chamber of Deputies on February 25, 1834, sought to "conciliate the rights of communes with the rights of government" to achieve "a true municipal system" ("Loi sur les attributions municipales," nonclassified document, AD Oise) that would leave communes "all rights that are not indispensable to the prosperity of the grand commune." The "great commune," was of course France. The commission reaffirmed that mayors, under the "supervision and the immediate surveillance of the prefect," appoint only employees whose functions were "purely communal." Such appointments did not include CPs, even if their salaries remained in the category of "obligatory expenses." Reporting on March 19, 1835, the commission emphasized the importance of conserving "with care the healthy centralization of power" and of avoiding a type of federalism, "in which the mayors would escape the surveillance of the representatives of the government and would find themselves independent in most of their acts."

12. AD Marne 39M 1 and AD Haute-Garonne, 13M 57 bis, Int., May 26, 1820; AD Meuse, 88M 1, prefect, May 31, 1820. In 1842, the procureur général of Douai admitted that it was difficult to determine with exactitude the attributions of the commissaires and their obligation to the mayors. The commissaires were magistrates of the judicial order, charged with enforcing the laws, as well as officials of the administrative order responsible for "preventive policing." In his view, commissaires should send procès-verbaux of *délits* and *contraventions* to the *tribunal de simple police,* by virtue of serving as an extension of the local chief magistrate himself (AD Nord, M 181/3, procureur, August 5, 1842).

13. F7 9689, CP Abel, July 6, 1820. Cazeaux, in his report on Tours in 1832, insisted that the mayor should be the source of municipal police authority (AD Indre-et-Loire, 4M 2, Cazeaux, n.d. [1832]).

14. F7 9855.

15. Pierre-Yves Saunier, *L'esprit lyonnais XIXe–XXe siècle* (Paris, 1995), pp. 169–87, quote from p. 171. Such contention indicates "that the power of the state was still seeking the uniform imposition of its sovereignty on urban collectivites" (p. 169). Thus he describes this specific mentality: "Tout ce qui touche à la question municipale fait partie d'une culture politique appuyée sur les souvenirs du passé (maintenu vivant par un fort travail symbolique), arc-boutée sur l'affirmation de la spécificité lyonnaise et que maintien vivace la continuité de l'effort d'uniformisation nationale en matière politique et administrative" (p. 178).

16. AD Rhône, 4M 1, Int. January 27, 1816. On struggles during the Empire, see Saunier, *L'esprit lyonnais,* p. 173.

17. AD Rhône, 4M 1, lieutenant général de police, January 20, 1817.

18. AD Rhône, 4M 1, prefect of the Rhône, August 22, 1818. The prefect of the Rhône, Albert de Lezay-Marnesia, understood perfectly well that "the police of the state and the municipal police will always be in a state of rivalry and conflict." Yet at a time when the government feared liberal plots, the CPs had to be interested in every local event (F7 9864, Int., April 26, 1817; prefect of the Rhone, May 1, 1817; mayor of Lyon, April 10, 1817). When the mayor complained that the CPs had sent a report directly to the ministry of the interior, the prefect asked that the minister of the interior remind the Lyon police that their primary responsiblity was to the mayor.

19. AD Rhône, 4M 1, mayor of Lyon, July 7, 1819; AD Rhône, 4M 1, municipal council, June 11, 1819, and prefect to Int., February 1, 1820; lieutenant de police, June 10, 1820, telling the CPs that they were to report only to him.

20. The laws of 23 fructidor, year 8, and 21 frimaire, year 14, as well as the decree of 5 brumaire, year 9.

21. AD Rhône, 4M 1, mayor, June 8 and 16, 1820; lt. de police, November 27, 1820.

22. AD Rhône, 4M 1, mayor of Lyon, June 26, 1821, and mayor, April 23, 1823; other municipal council deliberations included June 11, 1819, and July 4 and December 1820.

23. AD Rhône, 4M 1, prefect of the Rhône, June 15, 1820, and prefect, May 6, 1821. Once again, the prefect contemptuously rejected the municipal council's request that the CPs be divided into two groups, one of which would be under the supervision of the mairie; Delphin, one of the deputy mayors, was specifically charged with overseeing the police in Lyon.

24. This despite the fact that a royal ordinance of January 16, 1822, returned to the mayor many of the rights he had held under the Empire (Alexandre Nugues-Bourchat, *Représentations et pratiques d'une société urbaine: Lyon, 1800–1880,* unpublished doctoral dissertation, Université-Lumière, Lyon 2, 2004, p. 235). When the suppression of that post occurred in Marseille in 1820, the prefect announced almost triumphantly that "the suppression of this post leaves in my hands without any divergence this part of public responsibilities that had belonged to that functionary," reminding the police and other authorities to "be sure to correspond with me in all such matters" (AD Rhône 4M 1, prefect of Bouches-du-Rhône, March 14, 1820).

25. AD Rhône, 4M 2, conseiller d'état, January 24, mayor's reply, January 26, and prefect of the Rhône to the CPs, January 28, and to mayor, January 29 and February 3, 1822. The prefect wrote the mayors of La Guillotière, Croix-Rousse, and Vaise, informing them that they should correspond with him, and him alone, on matters concerning the police (February 6, 1822). Nugues-Bourchat, *Représentations et pratiques d'une société urbaine: Lyon,* p. 235.

26. AD Rhône, 4M 2, prefect, April 8, and mayor, April 21, 1823.

27. AD Rhône 4M 2, prefect, September 30, 1823.

28. AD Rhône, 4M 2, prefect, April 16 and 29 and n.d., and mayor, April 21, May 2, and July 31, 1823. Baron Rambaud responded with yet another plan to reorganize Lyon's police, which would leave five CPs responsible to him alone.

29. AD Rhône, 4M 2, prefect, July 31, October 13, 1823, and n.d, mayor, July 11 and November 14, 1823; mayor, July 11, 1823, and May 29, 1824.

30. AD Rhône, 4M 2, Int., August 11, 1823, rejecting the municipal council's deliberation, and mayor, July 11, 1823, and May 29, 1824; n.d. signed Richard, and prefect, April 17, May 6, July 12, August 17, and October 20, 1824; Nugues-Bourchat, *Représentations et pratiques d'une société urbaine: Lyon,* p. 243. They were 120 strong in 1840. Saunier, *L'esprit lyonnais,* p. 174, quotes de Brosses in 1825, assessing a "permanent rivalry encouraged by memory and local pretensions that have become a kind of political opinion."

31. AD Rhône, 4M 2, prefect, September 19, 1825, and September 7, 1826.

32. AD Rhône, 4M 2, prefect, March 28, and Int., September 19, 1826; prefect, n.d. (1826). In 1825, the municipal council again infuriated Prefect de Brosses for again asking the ministry to violate the law by requesting a reduction in the number of CPs assigned to Lyon. Now Lyon had ten CPs, twelve agents, three inspecteurs, and sixty nighttime surveillants, as well as one chef de division overseeing five *chefs de bureau,* who were responsible for passports, sûreté, politics, *logements militaires,* and *voierie,* as well as nine employees, two *concierges de bureau,* and two concierges "du violon."

33. AD Rhône, 4M 28, prefect, May 1, 1826, noting the mayor's complaint about the CPs' judicial responsibilities, and mayor, July 29, 1828.

34. 4M 2, deliberation of November 27, 1826: Ainay, Louis le Grand, Hôtel Dieu, Halle aux blés, Palais des arts, Hôtel de ville, Jardin des plantes, Chartreux, Métropole, Pierre Seize, and Fourvière.

35. A.D. Rhône, 4M 2, *mémoire,* prefect March 3, 1828, repeating in some places word for word the angry denunciation of the municipal council made by his predecessor February 1, 1820, and July 16, 1828.

36. P. Clerjon, *Histoire de Lyon, depuis sa foundation jusqu'à nos jours* (Lyon, 1829), p. 42, quoted by Saunier, *L'Esprit lyonnais,* pp. 177–78, the latter quoted on pp. 178 and 182, citing Joseph Bard and discussing the role of the *Revue du Lyonnais.*

37. AD Rhône, 4M 2, July 31, 1818, June 11, 1819, July 4 and December 19, 1820, June 18, 1824, September 9, 1825, and November 27, 1826.

38. AD Rhône, 4M 2, January 22, 1829.

39. AD Rhône, 4M 2, extract from *Précurseur,* May 5, 1829.

40. AD Rhône, 4M 2, mayor of Lyon, December 30, 1828, and January 1 and 12, 1829, prefect, May 1 and procureur, June 10, 1829, Int., January 2 and September 30, 1829.

41. AD Rhône, 4M 2, statistics, and CP Berthout, January 5, 1829; mayor of Lyon, January 15, 1829, and prefect, February 17, 1829.

42. AD Rhône 4M 28, "État des renseignements," January 22, 1829. See David Troyansky, Entitlement and Complaint: Ending Careers in Post-revolutioanry France," forthcoming, and "Aging and Memory in a Bureaucratizing World: A French Historical Experience," in Susannah R. Ottaway, L. A. Botelho, and Katharine Kittredge, eds., *Power and Poverty: Old Age in the Pre-Industrial Past* (Westport, Conn., 2002).

43. AD Rhône, 4M 2, municipal council, January 9, 1829, and prefect, n.d. The municipality also demanded that surveillants and the various inspectors be allowed to hand out procès-verbaux.

44. AD Rhône, 4M 27, prefect, April 13, 1830.

45. AD Rhône, 4M 2, mayor of Lyon, January 18 and March 11, 1831. The municipality thus reduced the number of surveillants from 100 to 60.

46. AD Rhône, 4M 2, AD Rhône, 4M 28; mayor, December 28, 1831, mayor, December 26, 1833; Pierre-Yves Saunier, "Logiques de l'agrégation: l'agglomération lyonnaise au XIXe siècle," *Bulletin du Centre Pierre Léon,* 1 (1992), p. 8 and *L'esprit lyonnais.* p. 174, noting that whereas during the Restoration, Lyon's political elite imagined a return to the Ancien Régime, "the liberals of the July Monarchy wanted more simply the simple exercise of the right of citizenship and of property by means of the election of the municipal council and the mayor. The 'prerogatives' demanded by the mayor in 1814 had been transformed into 'rights.'"

47. AD Rhône, 4M 2, mayor of Lyon, June 13, 1831.

48. AD Rhône, 4M 2, mayor of Lyon, December 6, and municipal council deliberation of December 6, 1831.

49. Nugues-Bourchat, *Représentations et pratiques d'une société urbaine,* p. 238.

50. Saunier, "Logiques de l'agrégation," pp. 4–5. Saunier notes that such expansionism also generated resistance, for example, from wealthy landowners who did not want Brot-

teaux joined to Lyon, because such annexations would add expenses to the municipal budget, or from fears of generating popular disturbances. He writes, "Under regimes as diverse as the Directory, the Restoration, the July Monarchy, the Second Republic and the Second Empire, the division of Lyon into arrondissements always served as a destructive arm aimed to break the opposition, or simply as a source of municipal authority" (in "La ville en quartiers: découpages de la ville en histoire urbaine," *Genèses*, 15 [March 1994], p. 107). See also Philippe Paillard, "L'organisation de la police lyonnaise. Divergences entre le Préfet du Rhône et le Maire de Lyon, 1800–1852," *Annales de l'Université Jean Moulin*, tome 2, février 1979, as well as Saunier, "Lyon au XIXe siècle: les espaces d'une cité," unpublished doctoral dissertation, l'Université Lumière-Lyon II, 1992.

51. Saunier, "Logiques de l'agrégation," p. 8. In 1833, on his own Mayor Prunelle divided the police into "police de sûreté" and "police municipal." He established the post of commissaire central, which he considered to be transitional in the wake of the revolution. His role would be to assist the mayor with the daily audiences with the CPs at the mairie, along with the delivery and monitoring of livrets, the surveillance of maisons publiques, the arrest of beggars, and assisting the procureur. He named a certain Rousset, an able CP of his liking, to serve, but the minister of the interior had appointed Prat to the post. In December, the mayor requested the suppression of the post itself, complaining about Prat's work and his refusal to realize that he "was my direct subordinate" (AD Rhône, 4M 2, mayor, December 26 and 29, 1833). Prunelle also criticized the CPs for not sending reports directly to him. The post of commissaire central in Lyon lasted only until 1839.

52. Nugues-Bourchat, *Représentations et pratiques d'une société urbaine: Lyon,* , pp. 236, 309; he argues (p. 308) that the system of quadrillage in itself "aboutissait à la dévalorisation des pouvoirs municipaux en matière de police au profit d'une centralization étatique." From 1830 to 1839, a commissaire central de police municipal and a commissaire de police de sûreté existed in Lyon, in the latter year the former was replaced by a commissaire spécial de police at the prefecture.

53. Jacques Aubert in Jacques Aubert et al., *L'État et sa police en France (1789–1914)* (Geneva, 1979). Yet the very next year, Mayor Prunelle complained that the CPs were subject to "demands coming from three different directions," missing meetings with him because they were carrying out other duties. Some CPs seemed to profit from this administrative confusion by doing as little as possible, claiming to the mayor that they had been following orders given by the prefecture. Prunelle insisted once again on behalf of the municipality that no CP be named without the nomination of the mayor (AD Rhône, 4M 2, CP reports January 4 and September 16, 1834; mayor, March 10, 1835). The Chamber of Deputies on September 16, 1830, adopted a law giving the mayor the prerogative to present candidate for vacant places, although the ministry of the interior still made the appointment, through the king.

54. AD Nord, M 181/3, SP Douai, October 4, 1830.

55. AD Marne, 40M 7, prefect report of March 17, 1843.

56. AD Nord, M 181/5, CP, July 21 and 23, mayor, July 23, and procureur, August 5, 1842.

57. A circular of the minister of the interior in March 1848 had asked that CPs send political reports directly to him, but the normal hierarchy was back in place by January 1849, if not before (AD Nièvre, M 1307, circular of March 20, 1848).

58. John M. Merriman, *The Agony of the Republic: The Repression of the Left in Revolutionary France, 1848–51* (New Haven, 1978); Ted W. Margadant, *French Peasants in Revolt: The Insurrection of 1851* (Princeton, 1979).

59. AD Deux-Sèvres, 4M 4.1, AD Jura, M 121, AD Loire 20M 1, Int., November 13, 1848. Immediately following the Revolution, the provisional government had asked CPs

to send reports directly to the minister of the interior, but this changed. The centralized police repression was accentuated by the ministry appointed in November 1849.

60. AD Bas-Rhin 3M 208, Int., June 20, 1849, prefect, June 11, 1849.

61. AD Bas-Rhin, 3M 74, prefect, September 3, 1851, etc.; prefects' reports in 3M 76; BB30 360, PG Colmar, July 26, 1849, and prefect, August 26, 1849; 3M 348, CC Comte, August 25, 27, 29–30, September 3–4, September 8–9, September 26–27, October 22–23, November 2–3, 18–19, December 23, January 30–31, February 17–18, April 2–3, July 22, 1850, etc.; 3M 208, Int., March 23, 1850, and November 8, 1851, CC, August 10, and prefect, August 18 and 22, 1849, municipal council, August 17, 1849.

62. AD Marne, 4M 6, municipal council of April 11, 1850; decree of April 26, 1850; John M. Merriman, *The Margins of City Life: Explorations on the French Urban Frontier* (New York, 1991), chap. 7.

63. Saunier, "Logiques de l'agrégation," p. 9.

64. AD Rhône, 4M 3, Int., July 30, 1851.

65. AD Rhône, 4M 3, mayor of Lyon, October 1, 1851 and "règlement portant organisation du service de police de l'agglomération lyonnaise," as specified by the law of June 19, 1851. Lyon's mayor wanted to conserve seven CPs (and one commissaire-en-chef) for the mairie, and demanded the appointment of even more agents.

66. AD Rhône, 4M 3, October 1, 1851; Int. to prefect, December 11, 1851; commissaire spécial, "observations" on mayor's letter of October 3, 1851.

67. Saunier, "Logiques de l'agrégation," pp. 10–12; MR 1209 (1851). Paris did not have a mayor until the late 1970s. Saunier summarizes: "In 1849–51, and even more during the Second Empire, a large part of the social and economic elite of Lyon accepted the authoritarian measures of the government . . . the maintenance of public and social order and the promise of economic prosperity made them forget the defense of their old rights" (Saunier, *L'esprit lyonnais,* p. 175).

68. Clive Emsley, *Policing and Its Context, 1750–1870* (London, 1983), p. 92; Howard C. Payne, *The Police State of Louis Napoleon Bonaparte* (Seattle, 1966), p. 105; AD Maine-et-Loire, 31M 15. The prefects escaped the decentralization brought by the decree of March 25, 1852, which "sharpened the actuality of *centralized* administration in the prefects' favor" (Payne, *The Police State of Louis Napoleon Bonaparte,* p. 107). The number of CPs increased from about 1,000 to 1,700 three years later. The law also set yet again salaries for the various classes of CP, beginning at 300 francs. Citing the supposed needs of country people to feel reassured of public order (with the insurrection against the coup d'état in mind), CPs were added so that there would be one in each cantonal chef-lieu, no matter how small. That November, the ministry of the interior asked the commander of the gendarmerie to draw up a list of retired or retiring junior officers and gendarmes who had recently left their services, who could be considered for appointment as CPs because of their sense of "discipline and hierarchy."

69. Payne, *The Police State of Louis Napoleon Bonaparte,* pp. 73–74.

70. AD Ardèche 6M 3, circular of November 25, 1852. The decrees in question were those of March 25 and 28, 1852.

71. See Emsley, *Policing and Its Context,* p. 92; Payne, *The Police State of Louis Napoleon Bonaparte,* p. 208. The ministry of police générale, created in 1853, was abolished the following year, in part because of pressure from prefects.

72. Félix Ponteil, *Les institutions de la France,* pp. 371, 379. Payne refers to this period as "the police state of Louis Napoleon Bonaparte," emphasizing the role, anticipated by the "mixed commissions" that dealt with those accused of political crimes following the insurrection of December 1851, of executive authority by decree, the arbitrary power of prefects, and the primacy of political policing (*The Police State of Louis Napoleon Bonaparte*). Two years later commissaires spéciaux were named to large cities, and a year later assigned to the

railways (in fact, they had already been assigned to them in some places during the Second Republic). By the law of June 10, 1853, the prefect of police took over all police functions that remained with the mayors of the suburbs. The law of May 5, 1855, took back from the mayors of the largest cities (chefs-lieux with more than 40,000 inhabitants) their powers of police générale, with the exception of "the very secondary agents of central power, leaving to them responsibility for 'muncipal' policing" (J.-F. Tanguy in Philippe Vigier et al., eds., *Le Maintien de l'ordre en France et en Europe au XIXe siècle* [Paris, 1987], pp. 167–68). During the liberal empire, the law of July 24, 1867, partially restored some of the mayors' rights, but until 1884 the mayors of large towns were still named by the central government). See Maryvonne Bernard, "La Réorganisation de la police sous le Second Empire (1851–1858)," in Vigier et al., eds., *Maintien de l'ordre en France*, pp. 119–35. The law of 1884 (articles ninety-four and ninety-seven) recognized the prefect as "the master of the municipal police" with the right to annul any decree by any mayor. Thus, Jean-Marc Berlière (*Le monde des polices en France* [Paris, 1996], pp. 80–86) concludes that the law can be seen as making mayors responsible for municipal policing, but that the law can also be read as "a law of centralization which, under the cover of liberalism, gave the the basic essentials of power to the state." The battle between Lyon and the state continued, with reference to the contest here related. See Saunier, *L'esprit lyonnais,* p. 171.

73. AD Haute-Garonne, 13M 57 ter, prefect, June 6, 1834, August 20 and November 24, 1836, and Int., November 15, 1836, and September 9, 1837; municipal council procès-verbal, August 12, 1837; Int., December 6, 1839, and March 2, 1840.

74. AD Haute-Garonne, 13M 57 bis, prefect, September 23 and December 4, 1850, such as the description of Blache in the small town of Montréjean: "He succeeds in his functions with zeal and courage. He has rendered services to the cause of order."

75. AD Haute-Garonne, 13M 57, mayor of Tulle, November 30, 1849, and Caubet, September 6, 1850; Int., July 31, 1851; prefect, March 22, 1850, and prefect of the Var, April 27, 1850.

76. AD Haute-Garonne, 13M 57, Cazeaux, May 5, July 11, 20, and 24, 1851, and mayor, April 4 and July 28, 1851. For his part, the mayor in April 1851 recommended that four of the six CPs of Toulouse be replaced, including one who had been appointed right after the February Revolution of 1848. Only two of Toulouse's seven CPs seemed above reproach (Cazeaux, September 22, 1850, and June 4, 1851, and Int., May 7, 1851).

77. AD Haute-Garonne, 13M 57, Cazeaux, May 1, 4, and 29, 1852. Cazeaux even claimed that the mayor had appointed as agents some men who seemed to be enemies of the government, who he suspected (without any proof) had even tipped off "demagogues" they were supposed to be following.

Conclusion

1. The Paris Commune of 1871 was obviously considerably more than a riot; it and insurrections in major provincial towns, leading to the massacre perpetuated by the so-called forces of order during Bloody Week, were at least in part reactions against the increasingly centralized state (Lewis Greenberg, *Sisters of Liberty: Marseille, Lyon, Paris and the Reaction to a Centralized State, 1868–1871* [Cambridge, Mass., 1971]). The changing social geography of Paris and its suburbs was making the capital itself an increasingly elite space and, at the same time, the "forces of order" were imposing in number and readiness.

BIBLIOGRAPHY

Primary Sources

Archives Nationales (Paris)

BB18 1086, 1104, 1107, 1134–35, 1181, 1185–88, 1199, 1241, 1355
BB30 359, 360, 362
F7 6693, 6767, 6770, 6779–81, 6792, 9662, 9689, 9840–48, 9850–52, 9854–59, 9861 (A), 9862, 9864–74

Archives of the Ministry of War (Vincennes)

MR 1145, 1166, 1168, 1169, 1201–2, 1208–9, 1220, 1226, 1233, 1239, 1245, 1266, 1273, 1304
D3 125–27, 131, E5 1–4, D3 126, 131

Archives of the Prefecture of Police (Paris)

D/b 353

Departmental Archives

Ain (Bourg-en-Bresse), 8M 2, 5, 10M 4, 18M 1 (2 bis)
Allier (Moulins) M 293, 570, (3)M 433, 438, 567, 570, 1032c
Alpes-de-Haute-Provence (Digne), 1M 3–4
Hautes-Alpes (Gap), 1M 21, 4M 19, 4M 157–59
Ardèche (Privas), 5M, 10, 6M 1, 3, 38–39, 41
Aube (Troyes), M 1164 A, 1184–85, 1255, 1257–59, 1286
Aude (Carcassonne), 5M 24
Aveyron (Rodez), 1M 306
Bouches-du-Rhône (Marseille), 4M 1–3
Calvados (Caen), M 2849, 2852
Cantal (Aurillac), 4M 2–3, 36M 1, 174M 1
Charente (Angoulême), (old series) M 643, 784, 1180, 1186

Charente-Maritime, 4M 2/20

Corse (Ajaccio), 4M 2, 33, 165–68, 4M 74

Côte-d'or (Dijon), 20 M 189, 358, 360, 1025

Côtes du Nord/Côtes d'Armor (St. Brieuc), 1M 325–26

Creuse (Guéret), 1M 151, 153, 4M 3

Dordogne (Périgueux), 1M 65–67

Doubs (Besançon), M 819, 1198, 3091–92

Drôme (Valence), M 1297, 1340, 1558

Eure (Evreux), 1M 168, 228–30

Eure-et-Loire (Chartres), 1M 18, 35, 4M 189, 204–5

Gard (Nîmes), 6M 30, 227, 309

Haute-Garonne (Toulouse), 4M 046, 13M 57, 57 bis, 57 ter

Gers (Auch), 1M 38, 42

Gironde (Bordeaux), 1M 347, 351

Hérault (Montpellier), 39M 80, 86–87, 90, 107–8, 112–13, 116, 120, 122, 125;
    58M 17, 4R 220, 242

Ille-et-Vilaine (Rennes), 1M 98, 101, 106

Indre (Châteauroux), M 2545, 2550–51, 2559, 4M 21/3874 bis

Indre-et-Loire (Tours), 4M 2, 4, 6–7, 71–72, 136, 342

Isère (Grenoble), 53M 12–14, 56M 7, 28, 96M2

Jura (Lons-le-Saunier), M 11, 13, 121

Landes (Mont-de-Marsan), 1M 98–99, 4M 154

Loir-et-Cher (Blois), 1M 79–80, 90–91, 4M 6, 66, 150, 214, 464, 466

Loire (St. Étienne), 2M 19, 10M 30, 20M 1, 3, 10, 20, 23, 62, 21M 11, 13, 19–20,
    27

Haute-Loire (Le Puy), 5M 61–62, 64, 72, 81

Loire-Atlantique (Nantes), 1M 504, 508, 513–15, 704–5, 707, 898, 890, 2307–8

Loiret (Orléans), 4M 113

Lot (Cahors), 1M 2+, 7+, 100, 146, 153, 202, 4M 15, 38, 43

Lot-et-Garonne (Agen), M 1243 bis, 4M 18

Maine-et-Loire (Angers), 1M 6/25, 6/32, 31M 15, 34M 1

Marne (Châlons-sur-Marne), 30M 14, 39 M 1, 40M 6–7, 47M 21–22, 51M 11,
    72M 2

Haute-Marne (Chaumont), 61M 14, 16, 68M 3, 69M 4, 102 M3

Mayenne (Laval), 4M 39

Meurthe-et-Moselle, 4M 253

Meuse (Bar-le-Duc), 71M 9–11, 88M 1, 248 M1

Morbihan (Vannes), M 517, 637–38, 643, 679, 694, 3021

Moselle (Metz), 69M 1 bis, 71M 1 bis

Nièvre (Nevers), M 1295, 1298, 1306–8, 1503

Nord (Lille), M 181/3, 181/13, 183/13–14, 184/9, 184/11, 184/13–14, 184/16,
    184/23, 185/15, 184/17, 184 /25, 184/27, 184/29, 201/2

Oise (Beauvais), M nonclassified at the time consulted

Orne (Alençon), M 907, 1030, 1298, 1300

Puy-de-Dôme (Clermont-Ferrand), M 0121, 0333, 0888, 086, 090–95, 0141,
    10M, 39, 137

Hautes-Pyrénées (Tarbes), M 1243 bis, 1M 207–9, 212, 4M 61

Pyrénées-Orientales (Perpignan), commissaires de police, 1–2, 5 (then in
    process of being classified into series 4M), 3M1 59

Bas-Rhin (Strasbourg), 3 M 15, 28–30, 48, 50, 74, 76, 207–8, 348, 378, 380–81

Haut-Rhin (Colmar), 10M 8, 4M 77, 249, 266–67

Rhône (Lyon), 4M 1–3, 27–28, 155, 455, 508

Haute-Saône (Vesoul), 14M 7–8, 21M 1, 35M 2

Saône-et-Loire (Mâcon), M 99–102, 105, 109–12, 117, 1791, 1796

Sarthe (Le Mans), M supp. 389, 396, 398, and 400, M 78 bis 1–4, 4M 48

Seine-Maritime (Rouen), 1M 174, 4M 1, 3, 7, 116–17

Seine-et-Marne (Melun), M10139, 10193, 10221

Yvelines (Versailles), 4M1 46, 4M2 127

Deux-Sèvres (Niort), 4M 1/1, 4M 11/1, 12.1A, 15/3, 5/5a, 6/6, 15/3

Somme (Amiens), Mfd 80896, 80924

Tarn-et-Garonne (Montauban), 33 M 1

Var (Draguignan), 6M 8/1, 8/2, 8/3, 8/13

Vaucluse (Avignon), 1M 694, 746, 755, 4M 121

Vienne (Poitiers), M4 39, 42–43, 45, 50, 291–92, 299, 308, 310–12

Vosges (Epinal), 8M 17–18, 8 bis M 58, 10M 1

P. J. Alletz. *Dictionnaire de la police moderne pour toute la France.* 4 vols. Paris, 1820 (second edition, 1823).

Houzé, commissaire de police à Lille. *Manuel de police pour la ville de Lille.* Lille, 1844.

Secondary Sources

Aisenberg, Andrew. *Contagion: Disease, Government, and the "Social Question" in Nineteenth-Century France.* Stanford, 1999.

Aminzade, Ronald. *Ballots and Barricades: Class Formation and Republican Politics in France, 1830–1871.* Princeton, 1993.

Arnold, Eric A. *Fouché, Napoleon and the General Police.* Washington, DC, 1979.

Aubert, Jacques, et al. *L'État et sa police en France (1789–1914).* Geneva, 1979.

Bayley, David H. *Patterns of Policing.* New Brunswick, 1985.

Bayley, David. "The police and political development in Europe," in Charles Tilly, ed., *The Formation of National States in Western Europe.* Princeton, 1975, pp. 328–79.

Bellemaire. *La police et M. Decazes.* Paris, 1820.

Bergès, Michel. "Michel Foucault et la police," in Jean-Louis Loubet del Bayle, ed., *Police et société.* Toulouse, 1989, pp. 315-352.

Bergès, Michel, and Jean-Claude Thoenig. *Gérer la police, gérer le pouvoir. L'étatisation des polices municipales.* Fontainebleau, 1980.

Berlière, Jean-Marc. *Le monde des polices en France.* Paris, 1996.

Berlière, Jean-Marc. "The Professionalization of the Police under the Third Republic in France, 1875–1914," in Clive Emsley and Barbara Weinberger, eds. *Policing Western Europe: Politics, Professionalism and Public Order, 1850–1940.* New York, 1991.

Berlière, Jean-Marc, and Denis Peschanski. *Pouvoirs et Polices au XX siècle.* Paris, 1997.

Bernard, Leon. *The Emerging City: Paris in the Age of Louis XIV.* Durham, NC, 1970.

Bernard, Maryvonne. "La réorganisation de la police sous le Second Empire (1851–1858): 'des bras infatigables,'" in *Maintien de l'ordre et polices en France et en Europe au XIXe siècle.* Paris, 1987.

Bollenot, Gilles. "La police secrète à Lyon sous la monarchie de juillet," *Procès (Cahiers d'analyse politique et juridique)* (1984), 25–39.

Brennan, Thomas. *Public Drinking and Popular Culture in Eighteenth-Century Paris.* Princeton, 1988.

Brown, Howard G. "Tips, Traps and Tropes: Police Work in Post-Revolutionary Paris," in Clive Emsley and Haia Shpayer Makov, eds., *Police Detectives in History, 1750–1950*. Adlershot, 2004.

Brown, Howard G. "From Organic Society to Security State: The War on Brigandage in France, 1797–1802," *Journal of Modern History,* 69 (1997), 661–95.

Calhoun, Arthur Fryar. "The Politics of Internal Order: French Government and Revolutionary Labor 1898–1914." Unpublished dissertation. Princeton University, 1973.

Cameron, Iain A. *Crime and Repression in the Auvergne and the Guyenne 1720–1790*. Cambridge, 1981.

Canler, Louis. *Mémoires de Canler, ancien chef du service de sûreté*. With an introduction by Jacques Brenner. Paris, 1986.

Carrot, Georges. *Histoire de la police française*. Paris: Tallandier, 1992.

Carrot, Georges. *Histoire des forces civiles de maintien de l'ordre*. Paris, 1986.

Carrot, Georges. *Le Maintien de l'ordre en France*. 2 vols. Toulouse, 1984.

Castan, Yves, and Nicole Castan. *Vive ensemble. Ordre et désordre en Languedoc, XVIIe–XVIIIe siècles*. Paris, 1981.

Chapman, Brian. *The Prefects and Provincial France*. London, 1955.

Châtelard, Claude. *Crime et criminalité dans l'arrondissement de St. Etienne au XIXème siècle*. St. Etienne, 1981.

Cobb, Richard. *The Police and the People: French Popular Protest (1789–1820)*. New York, 1972.

Cobb, Richard. *Les Armées révolutionnaires, instrument de la terreur dans les départements*. 2 vols. Paris, 1961–63.

Cohen, William B. *Urban Government and the Rise of the French City: Five Municipalities in the Nineteenth Century*. New York, 1998.

Corbin, Alain. *Les filles de noce, misère sexuelle et prostitution au XIXe siècle*. Paris, 1979.

Dagenais, Michèle, Irene Maver, and Pierre-Yves Saunier, eds. *Municipal Services and Employees in the Modern City: New Historical Approaches*. Aldershot, Eng., 2003.

Emsley, Clive. "A Typology of Nineteenth-Century Police," *Crimes, histoire et Sociétés/Crime, History and Societies,* 3 (1999), 29–44.

Emsley, Clive. *The English Police: A Political and Social History*. London, 1996.

Emsley, Clive. "The French Police: Ubiquitous and Faceless," *French History,* 3, 2 (1989), 222–27.

Emsley, Clive. *Gendarmes and the State in Nineteenth-Century Europe*. Oxford, 1999.

Emsley, Clive. "Policing the Streets of Early Nineteenth-Century Paris," *French History,* 1, 2 (1987), 257–82.

Emsley, Clive. *Policing and Its Context: 1750–1870*. London, 1983.

Emsley, Clive, and Barbara Weinberger, eds. *Policing Western Europe: Politics, Professionalism and Public Order, 1850–1940*. New York, 1991.

Farge, Arlette. *La vie fragile: Violence, pouvoirs et solidarités à Paris au XVIIIe siècle*. Paris, 1986.

Farge, Arlette. "L'espace parisien au XVIIIe siècle d'après les ordonnances de police," *Ethnologie française,* 2 (1982), 119–26.

Farge, Arlette. "Le Mendiant, un marginal? Les Résistance aux Archers de l'Hôpital dans le Paris du XVIIIe siècle," in Bernard Vincent, ed., *Les marginaux et les exclus dans l'histoire*, Paris, 1979, 312–29.

Farge, Arlette. *Vivre dans la rue à Paris au XVIIIe siècle*. Paris, 1979.

Farge, Arlette. "Un espace urbain obsédant: le commissaire et la rue à Paris au XVIIIe siècle," *Les Révoltes logiques,* 6 (1977), 7–21.

Farge, Arlette, and Michel Foucault. *Le désordre des famillas. Lettres de cachet des Archives de la Bastille.* Paris, 1982.

Faure, Alain. "Nos intentions . . . et quelques résultats," in *Maintien de l'ordre et polices en France et en Europe au XIXe siècle.* Paris, 1987.

Fortier, Bruno, ed. *La politique de l'espace parisien (à la fin de l'Ancien Régime).* Paris, 1975.

Foucault, Michel. *Dits et écrits,* IV. Paris, 1999.

Foucault, Michel. *Les anormaux, cours au Collège de France, 1974–1975.* Paris, 1999.

Foucault, Michel. *Les mots et les choses: Une archéologie des sciences humaines.* Paris, 1998.

Foucault, Michel. *Surveiller et punir, naissance de la prison.* Paris, 1975.

Garrioch, David. *The Making of Revolutionary Paris.* Berkeley, 2002.

Garrioch, David. *Neighbourhood and Community in Paris, 1740–1790.* New York, 1986.

Haine, W. Scott. *The World of the Paris Café: Sociability among the French Working Class, 1789–1914.* Baltimore, 1996.

House, Jonathan M. "Civil-Military Relations in Paris, 1848," in Roger Price, ed., *Revolution and Reaction: 1848 and the French Second Republic.* London, 1975.

Hufton, Olwen. *The Poor of Eighteenth-Century France, 1750–1789.* Oxford, 1974.

Journès, Claude, ed. *Police et Politique.* Lyon, 1988.

Kalifa, Dominique. *Crime et culture au XIXᵉ siècle.* Paris, 2005.

Kaplan, Steven Laurence. "Guilds, 'False Workers,' and the Faubourg Saint-Antoine," in James L. McClain, John M. Merriman, and Ugawa Kaoru, eds., *Edo and Paris: Urban Life and the State in the Early Modern Era.* Ithaca, 1994.

Kaplan, Steven Laurence. *Provisioning Paris: Merchants and Millers in the Grain and Flour Trade during the Eighteenth Century.* Ithaca, 1984.

Kaplan, Steven. "Note sur les commissaires de police au XVIIIe siècle," *Journal d'histoire moderne et contemporaine,* 28 (October–December 1981), 669–86.

Kaplan, Steven. "Réflextions sur la police du monde du travail, 1700–1815," *Revue historique,* 261 (1979).

Kroen, Sheryl. *Politics and Theater: The Crises of Legitimacy in Restoration France, 1815–1830.* Berkeley, 2000.

Le Clère, Marcel. *Histoire de la police.* Paris, 1947.

Lepetit, Bernard. *Villes dans la France moderne: 1740–1840.* Paris, 1988.

L'Heuillet, Hélène. *Basse politique, haute police: Une approche historique et Philosophique de la police.* Paris, 2001.

Ludtke, Alf. *Police and State in Prusia, 1815–1850.* Cambridge, 1989.

Margadant, Ted W. *Urban Rivalries in the French Revolution.* Princeton, 1992.

Mercier, Louis-Sébastien. *Tableau de Paris.* Amsterdam, 1782–1788.

Merriman, John M. *Aux marges de la ville: faubourgs et banlieues en France, 1815–1871.* Paris, 1994.

Merriman, John M. *The Red City: Limoges and the French Nineteenth Century.* New York, 1985.

Merriman, John M. *The Agony of the Republic: The Repression of the Left in Revolutionary France, 1848–1851.* New Haven, 1978.

Nugues-Bourchat, Alexandre. "Représentations et pratiques d'une société urbaine: Lyon, 1800–1880." 2 vols. Unpublished doctoral dissertation, Université-Lumière, Lyon 2, 2004.

O'Brien, Patricia. "The Revolutionary Police of 1848," in R. D. Price, ed., *Revolution and Reaction: 1848 and the Second French Republic.* London, 1975.

O'Brien, Patricia. "Urban Growth and Public Order: The Development of a Modern Police in Paris, 1829–1854." Unpublished dissertation, Columbia University, 1973.

Paillard, Philippe. "L'organisation de la police lyonnaise. Divergences entre Le Préfet du Rhône et le Maire de Lyon, 1800–1852," *Annales de l'Université Jean Moulin*, tome 2. February 1979.

Payne, Howard. *The Police State of Louis Napoleon Bonaparte*. Seattle, 1966.

Pinol, Jean-Luc. *Le monde des villes au XIXe siècle*. Paris, 1991.

Ponteil, Félix. *Les institutions de la France de 1814 à 1870*. Paris, 1970.

Quéant, Alain. *Le Commissaire de police dans la société française*. Paris, 1998.

Raeff, Marc. *The Well-Ordered Police State: Social and Institucional Change through Law in the Germanies and Russia 1600–1800*. New Haven, 1983.

Rey, Alfred, and Féron Louis. *Histoire du corps des gardiens de la paix*. Paris, 1894.

Riberette, Pierre. "De la police de Napoléon à la Police de la Congrégation," in Jacques Aubert et al., *L'État et sa police en France (1789–1914)*. Geneva, 1979.

Ringrose, Daniel, "Work and Social Presence: French Public Engineers in Nineteenth-Century Provincial Communities," *History and Technology*, 14 (1998), 293–312.

Roche, Daniel. *Le peuple de Paris*. Paris, 1981.

Roche, Daniel, ed. *La ville promise: mobilité et acceuil à Paris (fin xviie-début xixe siècle)*. Paris, 2000.

Saunier, Pierre-Yves. *L'esprit lyonnais XIXe–XXe siècle*. Paris, 1995.

Saunier, Pierre-Yves. "La ville en quartiers: découpages de la ville en Histoire urbaine," in *Genèses*, 15 (March 1994), 103–14.

Saunier, Pierre-Yves. "La ville et ses découpages," in Philippe Boutry, Heinz-Gerhardt Haupt, and Yves Lequin, eds., *Le quartier urbain en Europe (XVIIIe–XIXe siècle): Mélanges de l'École Française de Rome, Italie et Méditerranée*, 2 (1993).

Saunier, Pierre-Yves. "Logiques de l'agrégation, la formation de l'agglomération lyonnaise au XIXe siècle," *Bulletin du Centre Pierre Léon*, 1 (1992).

Schwartz, Robert M. *Policing the Poor in Eighteenth-Century France*. Chapel Hill, 1988.

Sewell, William H. *Work and Revolution in France: The Language of Labor from the Old Regime to 1848*. New York, 1980.

Spitzer, Alan B. "Malicious Memories: Restoration Politics and a Prosopography of Turncoats," *French Historical Studies*, 24, 1 (Winter 2001), 37–61.

Spitzer, Alan B. *The French Generation of 1820*. Princeton, 1987.

Spitzer, Alan B. "The Bureaucrat as Proconsul: The Restoration Prefect and the *police générale*," *Comparative Studies in Society and History*, 7 (July 1965).

Storch, Robert D. "The Policeman as Domestic Missionary: Urban Discipline and Popular Culture in Northern England, 1850–1880," *Journal of Social History*, 9, 4 (June 1976), pp. 481–507.

Strieter, Terry W. "The Faceless Police of the Second Empire: A Social Profile of the Gendarmes of Mid-Nineteenth-Century France, *French History* 8, 2 (1994), 167–95.

Tanguy, Jean-François. "Autorité de l'État et libertés locales: le Commissaire central face au maire et au préfet 1870–1914," in *Maintien de l'ordre et polices en France et en Europe au XIXe siècle*. Paris, 1987.

Taylor, David. *The New Police in Nineteenth-Century England: Crime, Conflict and Control*. Manchester: Manchester University Press, 1997.

Thuillier, Guy. *Retraites des fonctionnaires: débats et doctrines, 1750–1914*. Paris, 1996.

Thuillier, Guy. *Pensions de retraite des fonctionnaires au XIXe siècle*. Paris, 1994.

Tilly, Charles. "Charivaris, Repertoires and Urban Politics," in John M. Merriman, ed., *French Cities in the Nineteenth Century*. New York, 1981.

Tilly, Charles. "Food Supply and Public Order in Modern Europe," in Charles Tilly, ed., *The Formation of National States in Western Europe*. Princeton, 1975.

Tilly, Charles. "How Protest Modernized in France, 1845–1855," in William O. Aydelotte, Allan G. Bogue, and Robert William Fogel, eds., *The Dimensions of Quantitative Research in History*. Princeton, 1972.

Tilly, Charles. "The Changing Place of Collective Violence," in Melvin Richter, ed., *Essays in Theory and History*. Cambridge, Mass., 1970.

Tilly, Charles, and James Rule. "Political Process in Revolutionary France, 1830–1832," in John M. Merriman, ed., *1830 in France*. New York, 1975.

Tombs, Robert. "Crime and the Security of the State: The 'Dangerous Classes' and Insurrection in Nineteenth-Century Paris," in V. A. C. Gatrell, Bruce Lenman, and Geoffrey Parker, eds., *Crime and the Law: A Social History of Crime in Western Europe since 1500*. London, 1980.

Troyansky, David G. "Aging and Memory in a Bureaucratizing World: A French Historical Experience," in Susannah R. Ottaway, L. A. Botelho, and Katharine Kittredge, eds., *Power and Poverty: Old Age in the Pre-Industrial Past*. Westport, Conn., 2000. 15–30.

Troyansky, David G. "'I Was Wife and Mother': French Widows Present Themselves to the Ministry of Justice in the Early Nineteenth Century," *Journal of Family History*, 25, 2 (April 2000), 203.

Troyansky, David. G. "Personal and Institutional Narratives of Aging: A French Historical Case," *Journal of Aging Studies*, 17 (2003), 31–42.

Tulard, Jean. *La Préfecture de police sous la monarchie de Juillet*. Paris, 1965.

Vigier, Philippe, Alain Faure, Alain Dalotel, et al. *Maintien de l'ordre en France et en Europe au XIXe siècle*. Paris, 1987.

Vogel, Marie. "Les Polices des villes entre local et national: L'administration des polices urbaines sous la IIIe République." 2 vols. Unpublished dissertation, Université de Grenoble II, 1993.

Williams, Alan. *The Police of Eighteenth-Century Paris*. Baton Rouge, 1979.

Woloch, Isser. The New Regime: *Transformations of the French Civic Order, 1789–1820s*. New York, 1994.

INDEX

commissaire de police
  career ladder, 37
  purges and dismissals, 66, 68, 76–77, 78, 80, 83
  salaries, 20
  tenures, 54
demonstrations and insurrections, 3, 11–12, 14, 92, 93, 97
as industrial center, 6
patronage, 42
political refugees, 114
prefecture of police establishment, 16
prostitution, 151
parlements, 14
  passports, 127, 185, 187
  agents, 32
  beggars and, 130–31, 133, 135
  travelers and, 119–20, 122, 131
  workers with, 123, 124
patois, 6, 27, 186
patronage. *See* political patronage
Paulin (commissaire de police), 53, 97, 100, 112
peddlers, 118
pensions
  commissaire de polices, 37, 50–53, 80, 185
  gendarmes, 51
  magistrates, 51
  military officers, 38
Périgueux, 28
Perpignan, 96–97, 103
Pétiton, Raymond, 67–68
Philipon, Charles, 111
phylloxera epidemic, 187
Pianno, Pierre, 146–47
pickpockets, 144, 145
Piedmont, political refugees from, 114
placards, "seditious," 111
Poitiers, 166, 188
  agents, 30, 31
  beggars, 135
  child abandonment, 164
  commissaire de police
    appointments, 29, 35–36, 46
    purges and dismissals, 66, 70–71
  passports issued, 131
  political policing, 19, 100
  political refugees, 114
  prostitution, 152, 153–54
  special policing challenges, 160, 161
Poland, 114
police
  antecedents and history of, 3, 6–8, 14
  areas of authority of, 5–6
  bureaucratization and, 7, 15, 54, 65, 185
  centralized state control and, 7, 8, 9, 12, 14–17, 36, 65, 169–84, 185, 187

civilian establishment of, 7
hostility toward, 6, 10
institutional structures of, 12, 14–36
legislative mandates and, 7, 8
national culture development and, 6
surveillance by. *See* surveillance, police
See also commissaires de police; political policing
police administrative, 38
police générale, 16
police judiciaire, 8, 38, 173
police offices, 24–25
political dissent. *See* social protest and political dissent
political loyalty, 37, 41–42, 65
political patronage, 37, 41–47, 74–76, 87, 186
political policing, 7, 8–10, 15, 16, 36, 151, 166, 186–87
  commissaires spéciaux and, 19
  haute police and, 90, 110–17, 187
  during July Monarchy, 9, 10, 90–91, 93, 100, 108, 110–12, 159
  in Lyon, 91–92, 100, 102, 104, 111–12, 166, 171–74
  ministry of the interior and, 8, 10, 91, 99, 103, 110, 111
  mouchards and, 9, 33–34
  prefects and, 91, 99–101, 103, 105, 107, 110, 111–12
  in public spaces, 102–10
  report filing and, 39
  during Restoration, 9, 90, 102, 104–5, 110, 111, 171–74
  during Second Republic, 10, 19, 91, 99, 101, 109–10, 159, 180–82
  social protest and, 89–117, 188
  surveillance and, 90–91, 98, 99–102, 110–17, 158–59, 171–74
  of travelers, 112–13
political refugees, 113–14
political symbols, 111
Ponteil, Félix, 168
poor people
  begging by, 130–35, 138
  charitable efforts for, 132
  mobility of, 123, 124
  official information on, 131
  Second Republic focus on, 140
popular justice, 106–10
population growth, 162, 166
Portal, Baron, 75
poverty. *See* poor people
prefects, 36
  begging and, 133, 140
  centralized government and, 167–69